GOD'S CRAZY QUILT

God's Crazy Quilt

Patricia Cox

2017

All Scripture is NKJ, unless otherwise noted.
Some names have been changed or abbreviated.
All information is as accurate as possible.
If your memory of an incident is different than mine,
I will be happy to hear it.

DEDICATION

This book is dedicated to my Creator, Redeemer, and Guide.
I pray it honors and glorifies Him.
Without Him it would be a heap of scraps.

It has been pieced together for my grandchildren:
Rebecca Coetta Cox
Hannah Lynn Cox Cooper
Morgan Louise Rice
Megan Elizabeth Cox
Kensey Jane Rice
Lydia Nichole Cox
Emily Grace Cox
Jonathan William Cox

It introduces them to some who have gone before,
and tells of my journey.
I trust it illustrates the importance
of a personal relationship with God.

Like a cloth crazy quilt, this book has no recognizable pattern
and is only somewhat chronological.
To elaborate or make a point, I move about in time.

Golden threads of imagination
will always be found
woven into the fabric of a human life,
And it affords
one of the sweetest pastimes to old age
To sit down and slowly unravel them,
Recalling the hours
when first they were spun.

(James Lendall Basford - 1845-1915)

ACKNOWLEDGEMENTS

A book isn't produced alone. My team came together over many years, and without them it wouldn't have happened. My mother loved words and books, my dad insisted I do my best, and my husband encouraged me to spread my wings.

Three people specifically motivated me to write: Kay Whitley, Dr. Dale Linebaugh and Barbara, an email friend I never met face-to-face. I was also encouraged by those who responded to my weekly newspaper columns, those who were challenged and entertained by my puppet scripts, and those who respond to my Adventure prayer letters.

The seed to write this book was planted by Kent Rice and he did the final proof reading. Marcia Carlstrom found and joined me in a class on writing memoirs. Gerri Cooper read it before it was condensed. Morgan Louise Rice edited and kept me focused. Kensey Jane Rice created the cover design. Ardeen Zearfaus, who lived through much of it with me, critiqued the story line.

I am thankful to those who fine-tuned my memories: my kids and grandkids, Connie Peck, Paula and Skip Dobis, Elly Childress, Sharon Gale, Norris Bunn, Thomas Eliason and others.

As the apostle Paul said in Philippians 1:3,
"I thank my God upon every remembrance of you…"

CONTENTS

WHAT'S A CRAZY QUILT?
FUN FABRICS

In the late 1800s crazy quilts were all the rage. Early quilts were of fine fabrics such as velvet and satin. Odd-shaped pieces were hand appliqued onto a backing fabric with silk embroidery stitches covering the seams. These quilts often featured fancy buttons and decorative embroidery. The idea trickled down to housewives who began using scraps of fabric left from everyday sewing projects and putting them together the same way. Without the elaborate embellishments, they were more serviceable. We have one like this from my Nana.

Most crazy quilts were created without a plan, though sometimes the quilter incorporated patterns within the montage of pieces. It has occurred to me my life is like a crazy quilt made up of seemingly unrelated pieces. However, the Master Designer, my Creator, had a plan for me even when I was in my mother's womb.

It would be impossible for me to write about my life without bringing God into the telling. He preserved me from the beginning and never gave up on me, even when my choices were foolish. I can never be grateful enough for His forgiveness and long-suffering love. I marvel at how all the pieces of my life have been part of a wondrous design by my Heavenly Father. He is the designer, the foundation, the adhesive holding all the pieces together; He is also the filler.

For You formed my inward parts;
You covered me in my mother's womb.
(Psalm 139:13)

GATHERING THE QUILT PIECES
CUTTING AND SHAPING

Louise snuggled under a bear skin robe as Bill drove home. It was December 31, 1932. She would have been content to see the New Year in at home with her Mother and Dad, but Bill convinced her to join their friends. He was the more gregarious of the two.

"Delicious food—too much food," Louise thought as she rubbed her belly.

Bill turned into the driveway at 344 Meeting House Lane and helped Louise into the house. Her parents were leaning close to the radio listening to the music of Guy Lombardo, broadcasting on CBS from the Roosevelt Hotel in New York City.

Ella rose quickly when she saw Louise enter the room. "What's wrong?" she asked.

"Nothing's wrong," Louise answered. "I must have eaten too much. You know how I love all those fancy sandwiches. We even had plum pudding with hard sauce. It was delicious, though maybe not as good as Mother Rainey's."

Ella examined Louise more closely. "Bill, call Dr. Lafferty, I believe this baby is on the way!"

In moments, all four of us were on our way to Hahnemann Hospital in Philadelphia. Bill, Ella, Louise ... and me! Obviously, I was not simply too much to eat!

Bill and Louise were living with Louise's parents, so they could save money to buy a house. They hoped to wait a while before starting a family, but God had a different plan.

Much earlier, when a concerned aunt heard Louise was pregnant sooner than hoped, she said her doctor could give Louise something to take care of the problem. *Problem huh, apparently that's how some people saw me!* Louise said, "No thanks."

My mother shared this with me only a few years before she left us for her heavenly home. She told me she was glad she hadn't taken *something* to get rid of me.

I thanked her. I was glad too.

RAINEY AND WEBSTER
IRISH LINEN AND ENGLISH BROADCLOTH

Our story begins in the First Presbyterian Church of Ballymena, County Antrim, Ireland where Margaret McDowell and Robert Rainey were married on April 24, 1857. Robert was a weaver, as was his father. Margaret's father was also a weaver.

Margaret and Robert bore four children in Ireland: James, Sarah, Mary Ann and Jane. They immigrated to Pennsylvania in the mid-1860s. Sarah died before they left Ireland and James died after they arrived in the states. In Pennsylvania they had Susie, Alexander, Robert, Margaret, Charters, Sarah, William and Elizabeth.

The 1870 United States census lists Robert as a laborer and Margaret kept house. His brother William was a weaver but later owned a potato chip company in the Philadelphia area and did very well. Family history says he developed a process used throughout the potato chip industry. He and his wife, Sally, never had children but they were fond of my dad who was Uncle Bill's namesake.

Uncle Bill died when I was a wee lass so I have no personal memories of him, but I do remember Aunt Sally. She always welcomed us warmly when we visited. Their home was elegant but not ostentatious. I know my mother was often on edge, fearing my brother or I might damage a fragile treasure. I did love to look with my fingers.

I remember a grandfather clock in the hall that not only chimed the hours but also the half and quarter hours. I'm laughing right now as I think how my son-in-love, Kent, would be frightfully annoyed with its chiming!

When I was a little girl, Aunt Sally said she would leave me her diamond-covered wristwatch. I fear I may have asked for it. When she didn't, I was a little disappointed. Now I'm glad! I wouldn't have worn it and selling it would have seemed disrespectful!

While my grandfather Charters was growing up in America, William Pardoe Webster and Arabella Sarah Webster had a little girl named Charlotte in Sheffield, South Yorkshire, England. William was a plumber. Charlotte was nine years old when she immigrated to the states. In later years when people asked if she would like to visit her homeland she said, "Not until they build a bridge."

I don't know how Charters and Charlotte (Lottie) met, but meet they did. The census shows they lived in Philadelphia in 1900, and in Bala Cynwood in 1910.

Charters was the town barber. My favorite photo of him is in a small silver frame on my brother's bedroom dresser. By his side is an Irish setter named Gypsy. Uncle Cliff told me Gyp was his buddy when he was a lad. I have no personal memories of Grandfather Rainey. He died before I was born.

Lottie's days were filled with being the mother of eight youngsters: Charters Junior, William, Hilda, Arabella, Wyatt, Evelyn, Sheldon and Clifford. Occasionally she wet-nursed an infant whose mother needed help.

Their eldest son, my Uncle Charters, was prone to drinking excessively. This led to brawls at the local pub where my father was dispatched to retrieve him. Uncle Charters married Madeleine Plet who died giving birth to their baby girl, Madeleine. I remember visiting Aunt Madeleine's parents because they had a pet monkey who attacked females. I'm still not fond of monkeys.

Uncle Charters served in the Navy during World War II. I didn't see him often, but I liked him. After the war he married Amy who owned and operated a resort hotel in the Poconos.

Aunt Hilda married Paul Kohler, a hairdresser. They loved children but weren't blessed with them. I remember Uncle Paul cutting my hair while I sat on a kitchen stool with a cape around my shoulders. He was fun and gentle. I missed him when he died of cancer, too young.

Grandmom Rainey lived with Uncle Paul and Aunt Hilda after Grandfather Rainey died. I remember Grandmom being easy-going, with a splendid sense of humor and a twinkle in her eye. It was Grandmom who showed me how to layer potato chips in a sandwich to give it a tasty crunch.

I enjoyed visiting Grandmom and Aunt Hilda in their third-floor apartment in Ardmore. The Rainey clan often gathered there. We sometimes sat on the porch overlooking Lancaster Avenue, watching the people and cars go by. Those were happy times.

Grandmom and Aunt Hilda raised Madeleine from infancy, though she had a good relationship with her dad and later with her stepmother. She was the oldest of our generation. I was next in line and looked up to her for two reasons: I admired her, and she was six feet two. She was a beautiful young woman. She married Bob Hayes, who was six feet four and they had two tall children, a boy and a girl. Madeleine was only in her fifties when she died.

Aunt Hilda worked for Bell Telephone until she retired. She doted on all her nieces and nephews. In my pre-teen years she gave me a lovely dress every Christmas. My favorite was teal taffeta with a twirly skirt. I believe all little girls love twirly skirts. I know I did.

She purchased government bonds each month, naming each of us nieces and nephews as co-owners. When she died, we received the bonds. I used mine to make a down payment on my first car, a 1940 Pontiac coupe. My brother did the same.

Our bonds were the most popular savings bonds, costing $18.75 and maturing at $25.00 in ten years. After the Japanese attacked Pearl Harbor on December 7, 1941, the name was changed from Savings Bonds to War Bonds. To help the war effort we were encouraged to purchase ten cent savings stamps at school. These were collected in stamp albums until there were enough stamps to purchase a bond. We also collected tin cans at school for the war effort. They had to be cleaned, labels and both ends removed, and then squashed flat.

Uncle Wyatt was the sibling I believe was most like my dad, in looks and temperament. He married Virginia Barley, aka Ginny, and had two children, Ken and Judy. I was the flower girl at their wedding. In the past few years I was blessed to visit her several times. She left us this year at ninety-eight, though she liked to say she was in her ninety-ninth year.

Aunt Arry (Arabella) married William Price and had two daughters, Barbara and Nancy. For many summers, they rented a beach house in Avalon, New Jersey. The Raineys sometimes gathered there for a day at the beach. It was there I learned to love steamed clams with drawn butter!

Aunt Evelyn married Harry Deeds and they also had two daughters, Harriet and Carol. Some years after Uncle Harry died, Aunt Evelyn married Owen Thomas Foreman.

The Raineys had two children per family with two exceptions, George and Harriet, and Bill and I. Harriet laughed when she said, "It looks like we're either good Catholics or passionate Protestants!"

Along with raising Madeleine, Grandmom and Aunt Hilda raised the two youngest boys, Sheldon and Clifford. Both men served our country during World War II. Uncle Cliff was in the Army stationed in Alaska. Uncle Shel was a yeoman in the Pacific fleet. He gave me two pins, one was an anchor with USN on it and the other was made from a sea creature's tooth. Both these treasures have gone missing-in-action, but they still live in my memory.

Uncle Shel and Uncle Cliff were the only two siblings who graduated from college. Uncle Shel worked for the Philadelphia Evening Bulletin and was their Sunday Magazine editor. Sadly, he was addicted to alcohol and forfeited his job and his marriage. My parents lost touch with him, Aunt Dotty and their two daughters, Joanne and Nancy. Later, Uncle Shel gave his life to Christ and ministered to other alcoholics.

Uncle Cliff married Judy (Julia) and had two sons, Michael and David. He worked for the Chester Times and wrote extensively even after retirement. Uncle Cliff and I shared family stories on the telephone. He died in February 2011, the last Rainey of their generation. Aunt Judy is alive and well, the last of an era.

When Aunt Hilda died, she willed her engagement ring to Madeleine and she, in turn, gave it to me. Matthew presented it to our daughter-in-love Jenni as her engagement ring. She now wears it with our love. Aunt Hilda would be pleased.

I've saved the best 'til last. William John Rainey was the most important of the Rainey siblings to me, he was my dad. When he was a young lad he helped in his father's barbershop. One of his chores was sweeping the floor. He sometimes slept on the pool table in the back until time to go home.

He was twelve years old when he began his first job as a delivery boy for a grocery store. When school was in session he began delivering bread and buns at six a.m., then after school until six. Deliveries were made by horse and wagon unless it snowed, then by horse drawn sleigh. On Saturdays he worked all day. His pay was $2.50 a week.

Summertime, he made deliveries from six a.m. to six p.m. except Saturdays, when he worked until eight or nine. His summer wages were $7.50 a week

My dad didn't complete the ninth grade. I've wondered what he might have done if he'd continued his schooling. He always did well with math and could figure problems more quickly in his head than most people with pencil and paper. He wasn't much of a reader, other than the newspaper and his Bible.

For a time, he was apprenticed to a carpenter. This was not his choice but his father's. Though he didn't go far beyond apprenticeship, his knowledge of the trade was helpful with his own homes and in helping us build our homes. His expertise was also useful in the churches he attended and the schools where he worked. You will find him scattered throughout my book. He was an admirable father and a godly man. I miss him.

GODEFROY & BILLINGS
BATISTE AND GOLD CHAIN

Bordeaux, France is known for its fine wine. It also produced my maternal great-great-grandfather, Emile LaTour. He was the second son of Emile LaTour Sr. and Ella Louise Godreau. His older brother was Louis Frances LaTour. We know from family history that Emile and Ella divorced when Emile Jr. was eight. Ella brought Emile to the states and Louis stayed with his father in France.

When Ella arrived in America, she opened a French dressmaking shop in Jersey City, New Jersey. There she met and married Adolph Ambrose Godefroy, a local watchmaker. Emile took his stepfather's name, as well as the English version of Emile. He became Edward Godefroy.

Ella was strict and known for her volatile temper. Perhaps opposites do attract because Ambrose was a gentle soul. He studied for the priesthood in France but didn't agree with the church's stance on confession, so he left before he took his vows. Ella preceded Ambrose in death leaving him to raise Edward.

Meanwhile, back in France, Emile Sr. died. Family history says Louis convinced everyone Emile (Edward) had gone to the United States and died, making him the sole beneficiary of an inheritance. Did he really believe Edward was dead? Whatever happened, Louis immigrated to the states, bringing his inheritance with him.

When Louis arrived, he invested in a saloon in New York City. It was in an area with a promising future so it appeared to be a good investment. Unfortunately, his partner swindled him and he lost everything. From New York, he went to Chicago. Since he was well-educated and spoke seven languages, he became an interpreter in the court system.

There are conflicting tales about Edward and Louis'

relationship. A cousin told me Edward felt cheated out of his inheritance and had no time for Louis. However, my Aunt Clara remembers Uncle Lou (Louis) visiting Edward. The brothers spoke to each other in French. My Nana remembered this also and said they got along well.

<O><

My maternal great-great-grandmother, Eleanor Louise Delatache, was born in Wales about 1844. She was of Holland-Dutch descent. When she came to the states she married William Warren Billings of Boston, Massachusetts. He had a printing or publishing business and left her well-off when he died.

Their daughter Ida Louise Billings was born near Boston, Massachusetts in 1864. She had two brothers, Everett and Harry. Harry died when he was five years old.

<O><

Edward Godefroy and Ida Billings were married around 1880. They had six children: Ella Louise (my grandmother), Esther Emma, Clara, Irene, Harry Ambrose Louis Edward and Grace Frances. Harry was named for two grandfathers and two uncles. He later went by Harry Ambrose Godefroy.

The older children helped with the younger ones and everyone completed twelve grades of school. All but Clara worked to help with family expenses. She helped Mom at home.

When Grandma Billings arrived for visits, Nana said she pinned layers of garments and underclothes under her skirts. I have no idea how it worked, or how it looked, but she should be admired for creative packing.

Edward didn't care much for his mother-in-law but always treated her with respect. He called her Mother-Mother and warned the children they had better be careful how they talked to her.

On later visits, Grandma Billings brought along a young man named Warren who may have been an adopted son or even a traveling companion. After Grandma died, he went out west and was never seen again; a mysterious offshoot on our tree.

"Families are like fudge – mostly sweet with a few nuts."
(Anonymous)

Edward and Ida Godefroy, my maternal great-grandparents, lived in a three-story brick row house in West Philadelphia. We called them Pop and Mom.

Their income was small and their family large, allowing for few extravagances, but contentment prevailed. Pop worked in the New York division of the Pennsylvania Railroad: first as a brakeman, then a fireman, then as an engineer. He first drove coal-burning steam trains, then diesel/electric. He drove the first electric engine from Omaha, Nebraska to Philadelphia, Pennsylvania.

Pop was also a semi-professional vaudeville performer best known for his Dutch comedian act. Nana said when she and her sisters were at the theater to watch the show Pop would have them come onstage and sing. He died when I was two years old.

I remember Mom well. When I was a little girl she let me fix her hair and paint her fingernails. She crocheted, hummed a lot, and liked to hear or tell a story. My mother said, "She always took time to stop what she was doing and play with the children." I never heard her raise her voice or get upset.

Mom read tea leaves and playing cards. I pestered her to read my tea leaves and later learned she pretended to read them for me. She stopped reading them after predicting her daughter Irene's death. Yes, we all die, but Irene died tragically in childbirth. I'm glad Mom stopped her involvement in things best left alone.

While we're on the subject, my Nana removed warts by a method called powwowing. She moistened her thumb with saliva and rubbed it over the wart while whispering. When I asked what she whispered, she said it was Scripture. I know some whose warts she removed but such things can be questionable.

A traditional powwower never asks for payment. He believes he is a mediator between the patient and God. It was prevalent in rural communities and embraced by Pennsylvania Germans, as well as some groups of Amish, Dunkers and Mennonites. There is still a following among some who claim to be Christians.

I started to write there is a fine line between black and white magic, but there really is no line! God's Word is emphatic; anything to do with witchcraft is sin. It's right in the middle of a list of sins we should avoid in Galatians 5.

Sad to say there is another blight on our branches. Mom was concerned about having more children after Grace was born so she did the only thing she knew to do, she and Pop no longer slept in the same room. This led Pop to have an inamorata. Nana and Aunt Esther followed him and discovered his secret. Did they tell him? I doubt they did. Nor do I believe they told Mom.

Our tree isn't a perfect specimen, but it's real!

<O><

Before she married, Ella was a bookkeeper in Philadelphia. She commuted to work by walking or riding the trolley. She kept meticulous records and her handwriting was excellent. I've not inherited her efficiency or her handwriting.

One day after work Ella was walking home past a construction site where safety boards were put up along the sidewalk. The boards were rough cut, with knot holes. Some holes were at eye-level allowing people to view the project and others were lower. She saw something poking through one of the lower holes. Curious, she looked more closely. Without a second thought, she whacked the offending appendage with her purse and went on her way. I suspect he never did it again!

Esther married a butcher, Al Hiller. Uncle Al was a jolly fellow who wore a big white apron showing evidence of his occupation. We seldom saw the Hillers, Aunt Esther and Nana didn't get along.

Their hostility came from two lamentable events. When Grace was thirteen, she complained of abdominal cramps. The doctor said to put ice on her until he could get to their home. Aunt Esther thought Grace had menstrual cramps and used a hot water bottle. Grace died with peritonitis from a ruptured appendix. Ella blamed Esther for her death.

The second was when Nana disagreed with Esther's interfering in their sister Irene's love life. Esther encouraged Irene to marry an affluent young man rather than the nice young man she was seeing. Nana said Irene's death was from a sexually transmitted disease from her ne'er-do-well husband. Irene's death certificate says she died from chronic interstitial nephritis, two days after delivering her still born son. At this point it doesn't matter.

Nana had photographs of both Irene and Grace in her bedroom until she died. My concern is she didn't forgive, nor give up the bitterness she felt toward Esther. Yes, the circumstances surrounding both their deaths were unfortunate. Maybe they could have been avoided. However, there are things over which we have no control. If we hold onto those grievances, we only harm ourselves. Ephesians 4:31-32 says:

"... be ye kind to one another,
tenderhearted, forgiving one another,
even as God for Christ's sake hath forgiven you."

<O><

After Grace died, Clara was the youngest of the Godefroy girls. She was as easy going as Ella and Esther were determined. She married Charles V. Rice, an insurance salesman who made rounds to his clients on foot or by trolley. They had one son, Charles Edward, who became a Presbyterian minister.

When Bill and I were dating we liked visiting them. Bill and Uncle Charlie sat and talked while smoking their pipes. Both men were good at fixing things and enjoyed working with wood.

Harry Ambrose, Uncle Buzzy, married Anne Coryell. He also was an engineer with the Pennsylvania Railroad but, unlike his father, he went to work in a sport shirt. There were no coal-burning engines. Aunt Anne worked for Strawbridge & Clothier's mainline store in Ardmore. They had two daughters, Harriet (Mickey) and Eileen.

Mickey was always close to us. She often stayed with Nana on the Reichner farm when she was a wee lass and was like a little sister to my mother. She married William McAllister and they had five boys: William, Harry (Skippy), Steven, George and John. I saw their family as what I hoped to have someday. However, things aren't always as they seem. Bill had a wandering eye and he and Mickey eventually separated. She continued working hard to keep her family together. Years later she remarried. My Bill and I enjoyed visiting Mickey and Bill Thompson. They were our kind of folks and Mickey was one of my heroes.

"... the Lord does not see as man sees; for man looks at
the outward appearance, but the Lord looks at the heart."
(1 Samuel 16:7)

REICHNER AND WILHELM
ROBUST COTTON AND LEATHER

Lewis Reichner, Sr. born South Philadelphia
"A good old man everybody's friend."
Anna Eliza Wilhelm born Baltimore, Maryland
"She was patience itself."

"On September 27, 1917
Grandmother and Grandfather Reichner
celebrated their Golden Wedding
and they surely had a glorious good time.
They had a family of four sons, one daughter, four
granddaughters, one grandson,
and one great-granddaughter (living).
Grandmother only lived six weeks after her anniversary."

"On June 24, 1953, Mr. & Mrs. S. V. Reichner celebrated
their 50th wedding anniversary."

My Nana carefully scripted these comments into the old family Bible.

The Reichners never owned the property they farmed, they rented. At the turn of the century, they farmed in Bala-Cynwood at the junction of Meeting House Lane and Levering Mill Road, where my mother grew up. They had five children: Lew, Harry, Carrie, Walter and Samuel.

Lew, the oldest, married Fannie but had no children. He was the farm foreman. When they no longer farmed, he managed their retail grocery store.

Harry married Annie Eliza Elliott who was born in Ireland. He was a trucker. They had one daughter, Mary. Harry joined the Ardmore police department and became a sergeant but had to resign his post because of Annie's affiliation with the Ku Klux Klan. That certainly doesn't elicit family pride.

Carrie, the only Reichner daughter, married Ephraim Jackson, a Philadelphia mounted policeman. They had no children. I'm not sure if Nana was keen on Carrie. She didn't mention specifics but I knew when she told me, "You're just like Carrie Reichner," it was not a compliment. I don't know why, but it's too late to be concerned now!

Walter married Ethel Melvine and had four children. Caroline, Anna, Grace and Walter Jr.

Samuel Vautier Reichner was the youngest child and my Poppop. Ella Louise Godefroy, my Nana and my maternal grandmother, met him when his family huckstered farm produce in Philadelphia. Sam worked on the family farm with his father and brothers. After Ella and Sam married they lived on the family farm. I wonder if Nana realized they would be living with her in-laws. Let's hear it for premarital counseling! Another thing Ella didn't know was Sam used "Red Man" chewing tobacco.

Moving from the city where they had running water and indoor plumbing, the old farmhouse was certainly a challenge. Water came from a hand pump in the kitchen, and toilet facilities were down a path. There was no central heat and transoms over the inside doors helped the heat to circulate freely.

One night, Ella and Sam were in bed and heard a sound at their bedroom door. There was Grandmother Reichner peering at them through the transom. She was a very short woman. I've heard she was nearly as wide as she was tall. She'd pulled a dresser over to the door so she could climb up and look through the transom. They covered the transom.

Since the rest of the Reichner sons and their families lived off the property, they ate their noon meal together, along with any hired hands. Grandmother Reichner and Ella prepared the meals and served them.

The entourage also showed up for Sunday dinner with their families, even guests. My Nana became very protective of Grandmother Reichner and gradually took on most of the kitchen responsibilities. The rest didn't help much with serving or cleanup.

The sons didn't receive a salary. If they needed anything they asked their brother Lew for money. Sam was the baby of the family and a docile fellow. Ella was not docile. Their marriage was unsettled at times.

Both Sam and Ella wanted children. One of Ella's ovaries had been removed, as well as part of the second one. The doctor told her she would never conceive. After eight years of hoping, along came Gertrude Louise. The doctor referred to her as a miracle baby.

Their marriage sometimes prickled with differences. Their Golden Wedding Anniversary was one of those times. My mother planned a surprise celebration. When Nana got wind of it she adamantly refused to be involved. It was too late to reverse the plans so the celebration went on with a grim Nana and a smiling Poppop. Most of us had a great time! She did note the event in the family Bible, though briefly.

In 1925 Sam, Ella and Louise moved into a new home they built at 344 Meeting House Lane, Narberth. About this time the Reichner family stopped farming and opened a grocery store in Bala-Cynwood.

I was close to Nana, she was like a second mother. I loved her and enjoyed being with her. I was not close to Poppop. I wish I'd gotten to know him better. Early in our marriage my Bill broke his ankle and had to stay off it. He and Poppop sat on upturned 5/8 baskets and sorted potatoes in the backyard. He developed a great appreciation for Poppop.

I'm glad.

MY PARENTS
HOMESPUN AND FLANNEL

My parents first met when Lottie Rainey brought seven-year-old Bill Rainey to visit newborn Gertrude Louise Reichner. I'm sure he had no idea they would marry!

Louise wrote in her wedding album on June 10, 1931:

> *"We have known one another all through life, Bill having come to see me with his mother when I was but six days old. However, it was not until September of 1927 that we met on terms of friendship between girl and boy; and it was not until the Sunday before Christmas of that very year that we went anywhere together; and it was to church that we went—even as it was in church that we met. We began to be friends, Bill going with no other girls and (me) going with no other boys. This true friendship culminated in our marriage."*

Gertrude is of German origin, meaning strong spear. Louise means warrior maiden. When you put them together, it makes quite a statement. Though it's difficult to imagine my mother as a warrior maiden with a strong spear, she was no pushover!

When some referred to her as Gertie, Nana used her middle name. Louise has been a family name for generations, starting with my mother's great-grandmothers, and continuing to my granddaughter, Morgan. My mother was the only one called by Louise. Even that changed when little cousin Mickey couldn't pronounce Louise and called her Weezie, which stayed throughout her life.

Louise grew up on the Reichner farm as an only child, playing by herself except when cousins visited. She liked pretending, playing with dolls, and reading.

Like many farm girls, Louise felt she wasn't up to the town

girls' standards. Her clothes were homemade and few. She had friends but was shy around people she didn't know well. She walked a mile to and from school, and walked home and back within an hour for lunch. School was seldom called off because of the weather.

Bala Cynwood had a grocery store, a drugstore, Grandfather Rainey's barber shop, a shoe repair shop, a novelty store, a carriage shop and a blacksmith. When they went to town, Philadelphia, they walked two miles to the trolley car at City Line, then two miles back home.

Louise wrote, *"It was a pleasant walk in good weather, but in inclement weather it was muddy and miserable."*

Ella was a loving mother, though not always warm and fuzzy. She was protective and kept Louise under close supervision. She was the main caregiver for everyone in the household as well as advocate for her husband.

Bill Rainey came from a different background. They, like the Reichners, were working class folks. However, unlike the Reichners' somewhat isolated farm environment, the Rainey family lived on the edge of town and were constantly involved with people.

I don't know how often their paths crossed during their early years but when Louise was in her teens, and Bill in his early twenties, they were involved in the Bala-Cynwood Methodist Protestant Church youth group. The group met for church events but also enjoyed other activities. Louise found Bill interesting but he always seemed to be with Roxie, a girl closer to his age. When Louise found out Roxie had a boyfriend, and it wasn't Bill, she asked Roxie if she could sit in the front seat of the car with him. From then on, they were paired up within the group. During a campfire outing they both accepted Christ as their Savior.

Louise was an academic student at Lower Merion High School. She studied French for four years and enjoyed using a French word or phrase. She loved words and was a stickler for proper usage and spelling. She was also an avid reader and read the dictionary for fun. I tried and never got past aardwolf. She enjoyed both reading and writing poetry. I have a little book of poetry she wrote and illustrated with colored pencil drawings for her senior English class.

Louise took piano lessons for nine years from Mrs. Griest, who rented the upstairs apartment of their home. She played piano well and in later years played the organ. She loved music, both popular and classics. George Gershwin was probably her favorite composer. She especially liked his Rhapsody in Blue.

After high school she graduated from business school and was secretary to the manager of Strawbridge and Clothier's Main Line department store in Ardmore.

When Louise and Bill married on June 10, 1931, she was twenty and Bill was twenty-six. Nana made and sold mint jelly to pay for the wedding, a lot of mint jelly. Louise wore a form-fitting lace gown with an heirloom lace veil. Their reception was held in the Bala Cynwood Women's Club.

After a honeymoon in Ocean City they moved in with Ella and Sam to save money to purchase a home. Bill was working for the Springfield Water Company as a meter reader. Louise continued working at Strawbridge & Clothier until she realized she was pregnant. Back then women didn't work when a pregnancy became apparent. Plans for their own home were shelved. This was fine with Sam because he didn't want them to leave.

They enjoyed having tropical fish and had a variety over the years. One tank of guppies lived up to their reputation and were prolific. For a while they moved them to washtubs in the basement, but lack of space determined their end. They were fed to the alligators in the showroom of Albrecht's Greenhouse and Nursery. Hey, they need to eat too!

Before and after they were married, they rode horseback. There were many riding stables in the area. They rode English and wore jodhpurs and riding boots. I liked to play dress-up in my mother's jodhpurs. They were gabardine and classy, more modest than some of the skin-tight riding pants worn today.

Though she enjoyed riding Louise would have been quick to tell you she was not an accomplished horsewoman. One time they were riding on a trail along the Wissahickon Creek when her mount spooked, jumped a fence, and raced back to the stable. She hung on with Bill in pursuit. "Hold on, Squeezer!" That was one of his pet names for her. And yes, she rode again.

They also played tennis. They had their own racquets and played on private and public courts. I sometimes went with them and watched them play. They even bought a child-sized racquet for me but my brief foray into the world of tennis came years later.

I'd like to share a special story about Weezie. She served on a jury in Montgomery County, Pennsylvania. I don't remember what the trial was about but it was a difficult case. When they took a straw vote early in the process she stood alone. During their deliberations the jurors, a few at a time, changed their vote to her way of thinking. When they made their final decision, they were called back to the courtroom. The judge congratulated them on their findings. He told them he had come to the same conclusion. They had been called in to corroborate a decision he had already made. I am proud of her being willing to stand alone!

My father and mother grew up during a period of cultural change. In 1901 Connecticut instituted the first speed limits for motor vehicles—12 mph in cities and 15 mph on country roads. The PBJ sandwich was first referred to in print in 1901 and Oreos went on the market in 1912. In 1903 the Binneys developed colored wax crayons and sold them eight colors to the box as Crayola Crayons. In 1903 baseball held its first World Series. In 1932 a bleacher seat for the series in Wrigley Field was $1.00 plus 10 cents tax.

On a more serious note World War I, also known as The Great War, began in 1914. The United States remained neutral until threatened personally in 1917. Some called this The War to End All Wars, an unfulfilled prophecy.

In 1925 Radio-Vision paved the way for Television's arrival in 1927. Most homes had radios and families sat around them to listen, as they did later to watch TV. Now they sit around cell phones, tablets and computers.

There was unrest in the land when Bill and Louise married in 1931. The previous two decades and the great depression formed the backdrop for the beginning of my parents' life together. Though the specifics are different, those years weren't dissimilar from my growing up years, or even yours. We weathered the storms and so will you.

...there is nothing new under the sun."
(Ecclesiastes 1:9)

MY ARRIVAL
BIRDSEYE COTTON

On New Year's Eve 1932, Bill and Louise attended a party at a friend's home. Food was plentiful and good so when Louise felt cramping she thought she'd eaten too much. Shortly after midnight, cramping became contractions. Though I tried my best, it took a while to make my grand entrance. I arrived at 8:30 am, too late to be the first baby born in 1933.

My mother had a private room which cost $5.50 a day. The charge for the delivery room was $5.00 and anesthesia was $10.00. We were in the hospital for a full week and the total bill was $92.00.

There was another charge, not from the hospital but from the Philadelphia Bureau of Police. My dad was cited for parking illegally at the hospital and had to pay $6.00 because his car was impounded. The ticket cost more than the delivery room!

When my dad brought us home from the hospital it was to 344 Meeting House Lane. We lived with my maternal grandparents. The Great Depression was still felt throughout the land and it might be quite a while before they would be able to strike out on their own.

I was Patsy Bill until I was born. Some thought they could tell the baby's gender by the way the mother carried the baby but there was still only a fifty-fifty chance they were correct.

My birth certificate reads: Patricia Louise Rainey. Patricia, from the Latin, means *of noble birth* and you may remember Louise means *warrior*. I guess that makes me a noble warrior.

When I was a little girl I climbed up into our flowering cherry tree and pretended I was a princess. When I accepted Christ as my Savior, I became royalty—a child of THE KING OF KINGS.

GLADWYNE
RUFFLES AND BOWS

It was 1936 and I sat in the back seat of our Chevy sedan with Nana's caged canary on one side and house plants on the other. We drove up an inclined driveway and stopped in front of a big gray stone house, like many homes in the area. The house was a duplex, we lived in one side and the poultryman's family lived in the other side.

We all moved from Meeting House Lane when my grandfather left the family grocery business and began working at Shipley School Farm in Gladwyne. He managed the fields producing food for Shipley School, a preparatory school for Bryn Mawr College. There was also a poultry man, a dairyman who managed a herd of registered Guernsey cows, and a gardener who tended the lovely flower gardens surrounding the house where the headmistress lived.

Nana rented their home in Narberth to her brother Buzzy and his family. Poppop was happy because we were all together.

The poultryman and his wife had a granddaughter who visited. One day we were playing in the side yard when she suggested we play doctor. That seemed like fun until she, the doctor, decided I needed an enema. I knew about enemas and didn't want any part of having one, especially when I saw the stick she was brandishing. I headed for the house and never played with her again.

My parents enjoyed landscaping. They developed a lovely rock garden along the driveway. There was a huge horse chestnut tree in the center of the backyard with a wooden bench around its base. A thick rope swing with a heavy wooden seat hung from a high branch. I spent many happy hours on the swing.

One of my favorite things to do was go out and meet my grandfather and the field hands at the end of the day. They let me ride the work horses in from the field. I sat up behind the big old horse collar, holding onto the hames.

Sometimes I sat along the edge of the field with the men when we took water out to them. They were always nice to me and seemed to enjoy my chatter. One of them wove grasses into miniature street lamps with a little red berry for a light. I loved watching him make them. He spoke with a heavy accent. I had no idea how talented he was until years later.

On Sunday afternoons we took walks on the property and around the neighboring area. On one walk we discovered the pigs had gotten out of their pen. I remember running back to the house because my mother and grandmother were sure they were going to attack us. I doubt they would have, but it was an exciting experience! They presented a formidable display running en masse.

In the summer it was a treat to visit the rose garden at the main residence that we referred to as the big house. There were rows of fragrant roses and other flowers in season. The full-time gardener was an Italian fellow who spoke broken English. He took pride in his work and loved having visitors.

We sometimes visited the pen where they kept Oscar, the herd's resident sire. It was next to the main road and just below road level. It had stone and cement walls topped with metal rails. The big ring in his nose made him seem especially fierce. He worried and tossed a large rusty barrel to the delight of passers-by. Cars would stop just to watch his antics. I was admonished to stay back from the edge. I didn't need to be told!

The dairyman named one of the registered calves Patsy. I was delighted. Our family doctor wasn't pleased I was being raised on raw milk but the cows were well kept and it obviously didn't hurt me. I still prefer raw milk when it's available.

There was a stone wall along the main road on the lower edge of the front lawn. I liked to walk along the top of it. It was high enough to be exciting but low enough to enjoy. When I was younger my mom or dad would hold my hand. Later, I bravely walked alone.

On July Fourth we sat on the wall and watched several area fireworks displays in the distance. Sometimes we even saw the Aurora Borealis, also known as the Northern Lights. Later in the summer we saw shooting stars, probably the meteor showers we look for in mid-August.

At the back of the farm there was a hockey field with benches along the surrounding embankment. I liked to watch the students play. They arrived in the parking lot of the main house and walked along our back fence on their way to the field. Sometimes the girls smiled or waved as they passed by.

We often had family and friends visit us. One Sunday afternoon after dinner we walked back to the hockey field. We had fun rolling down the embankment. An older cousin, sister-in-law to my grandfather, somehow removed her corset from under her dress and waved it at a bi-plane flying overhead. She was a rather large woman so it was quite a spectacle. We laughed until our sides hurt.

The hockey field was one of the areas where my grandfather searched for mushrooms. He knew which ones were edible and which were poisonous. There were plenty to be found there and in the cow pasture. I love mushrooms but have no idea which ones are edible, another thing I should have learned from my grandfather. He also brought home fresh watercress from nearby streams.

I had my first dog on the farm. Tippy was my constant companion. One day he got into a skirmish with a stray dog on our property. He was kept in the pantry and I was told not to go in there. I didn't obey and he nipped my finger. Rabies was suspected and later confirmed.

I don't remember my rabies shots. I've been told there were 40 of them given in my abdomen. I remember going up the stone walkway to the doctor's office holding my mother's hand. Years later I asked my doctor if I would be immune to rabies if bitten again. Evidently another bite means 40 more shots. I guess I won't be a heroine and intervene.

I started school in first grade at Gladwyne Public School, there was no kindergarten. I vividly recall going into the school that first day. The other students were in place when I arrived. The class was singing *Oats, Peas, Beans and Barley Grow* and everyone seemed to know the song. I'd never heard it before. I guess I didn't begin on the first day of school.

I don't remember much about first grade but I do have a

couple of unpleasant memories. We were outside at recess and were to go down the sliding board. I fearfully reached the top of the ladder but could not bring myself to go down the slide. There was a line of children waiting behind me so the teacher helped me climb back down the ladder. I wonder if my tears made the steps slippery? I didn't go down a sliding board until years later when I showed my little brother how to do it. I was bigger, or was the sliding board smaller?

Another time, in the lunchroom a boy tossed a partly eaten sandwich and it landed in my bowl of Scotch broth. I have not eaten Scotch broth since. I doubt I even liked it before it was polluted by the sandwich. This may be a factor in my dislike of school lunchrooms and their associated odors. Even when I taught school, lunchroom duty was never something I enjoyed.

My brother, William John Rainey Jr., was born while we lived on the Gladwyne farm. Those were the days when pregnancy wasn't discussed. I know my mother and I stayed in the car while other family members attended a viewing for Uncle Paul Kohler, or was it Uncle Bill Rainey? Some folks believed a pregnant woman shouldn't view a dead body because it might mark the unborn child. My mother didn't believe the fable but felt it best not to make waves. It was then I knew I was going to have a sibling, so I decided I would have a sister, or maybe a pony.

Grandmom Rainey stayed with me when my dad drove my mother and Nana to the hospital. When Grandmom said I had a little brother I was evidently not impressed. This resulted in my cutting holes in the slipcover on the living room couch. Was I punished? I can't imagine I got away with such behavior. Whatever happened is tucked away in brain files currently inaccessible.

NARBERTH
TAFFETA AND TWEED

We moved back to Narberth after my brother was born. It seems odd I remember the move from Narberth to Gladwyne, but recall nothing about the move back, though I was three years older.

Poppop resigned his job at the farm due to administrative problems and easily found work as a gardener for an estate. Mrs. Neff was an elderly lady, aristocratic in appearance but gracious. She had a housekeeper/cook and a chauffeur. It was a lovely property with a spring house, a fish pond, and beautiful landscaping. I enjoyed exploring the paths, statuary, and water features. Sadly, the hilly grounds were difficult on Poppop's arthritic knees so he reluctantly sought other employment.

He next worked for the Slater family. The terrain was not as physically challenging. They also employed a housekeeper and a cook. Nana occasionally stayed with their children when they were away. I was intrigued by their baby grand piano with its unusual keyboard. The naturals were black and the accidentals were white.

World War II was heating up and my dad left the Suburban Water Company. He wanted to join the Seabees but learned he was too old. Still wanting to serve, he applied at Cramps Shipyard in Philadelphia. They built cruisers, submarines, and work vessels. He was put in charge of the slipways, commonly called ways. They are the structures on which ships are built. When the ships were seaworthy they were launched from the ways. One time my mother took me to see a submarine launched. We rose before daylight and traveled by elevated train and subway to the shipyard. What an adventure!

When we first moved back to Narberth, the upstairs apartment was being rented to an artist and her family. I sometimes posed for her art students. When they moved out, my grandparents moved upstairs. There are advantages in having two families living together but there can be problems. I never heard quarrels but I remember some tense times. Being in the same house but having our own space was good for all of us. I was blessed with a wonderful childhood and the years in Narberth were among the happiest.

Across the front of the house was a large glassed-in sunporch with crank-out windows. Nana had plants on the windowsills and in jardinières on the floor. The sunporch was great for playing on a rainy day. It was also the location for one of two recurring childhood nightmares.

In the first one I was on the sunporch looking at the plants when I saw a tiny red spider. As I watched, it began to grow. I woke up! I never did like spiders. My second nightmare had nothing to do with spiders. My parents and I were on a train going to the seashore. Suddenly I was standing on the tracks watching the train go away! I woke up. Was I afraid of being left alone? When I was a child, I remember praying we would all die together.

When Nana and Poppop moved upstairs I had the first-floor front bedroom. French doors with sheer curtains covering the glass panes led to the living room. During the holidays our Christmas tree was right on the other side. The colored lights diffusing through the sheer curtains created the perfect background for flights of imagination. It was magical.

On my eleventh birthday, I received a solid maple twin bed and a dresser with a built-in desk. Billy had the other twin bed in his room. The faux pegs on the Early American style furniture intrigued me. I decided to scratch my initials into the pegs on the dresser top, which was not accepted well by my parents. I never personalized my furniture again.

One place in the living room does not bring pleasant memories; the green wingback chair. That's where I spent time when I'd been naughty. It wasn't called time out but served the same purpose. Being sent to the chair wasn't my only punishment. I was sometimes spanked, though it was more being swatted. Weezie was quick on the swat when necessary. My dad never swatted or spanked me. Just a look or a word from him was the toughest discipline I ever experienced.

When I was sick I stayed in bed. Weezie always made it fun. She read to me or brought books for me to read when I was old enough. We played games, colored, and sometimes folded and cut out paper snowflakes. I enjoyed *The Book of Knowledge,* an encyclopedia with illustrated fairy tales. It also had a section called *Things to Make and Things to Do* which was full of fun ideas.

Sometimes she brought in our big tin of marbles and we pretended they were people. White ones were nurses and brown ones were soldiers. To get a better idea of how it worked you might like to read Robert Louis Stevenson's *The Land of Counterpane.* A bed can provide all manner of mountains and valleys for pretending.

Our living room had a small chandelier in the center of the ceiling. Weezie kicked so high she could touch the chandelier with the toe of her shoe. I believed she could have been a Radio City Rockette. We would sometimes dance around the living room; Weezie and me, and sometimes Big Bill. I loved watching them dance together.

Big Bill could do the Charleston. Weezie was adept at doing something called *falling off a log*, a Lindy dance step. With practice, I also learned. Should I try it now? Not a chance!

My brother had the bedroom at the back of the house. When he took a nap, my mother would bundle him up in his crib and open the windows, even in winter. In milder weather, he would nap outside in his baby buggy. My parents were believers in the need for fresh air. My dad used to say, "You need to go outside and get the stink blown off."

There were two trees in the front yard. One was an old Kwanzan flowering cherry with low branches. It was the only tree I ever climbed and I spent a lot of pretending time in it. When it was in bloom I was surrounded by fluffy pink blossoms, fit for a princess. The other tree was a stately maple. When I was a toddler, there was a wooden tub sunk in the ground against its trunk. Goldfish lived in it year-round.

Weezie wrote on my 1985 birthday card: *"I remember how you loved to go out in the front yard in Narberth and look into the wooden tub where the goldfish cavorted amidst a garden of water plants. You weren't allowed to play out there alone so I would sit on the front steps enjoying your joy as you rocked back and forth, striving to follow their movements through the green leaves."*

We had lots of flowers and Poppop raised vegetables in a garden along the driveway. We played on the swing-set or in the sandbox in the back yard.

The outside of the house was stucco embedded with tiny stones. Do you know how difficult it was not to pick off those little stones? I was told not to, but I did. I was scolded which reminds me of a song we sang in Sunday School.

> *"O be careful little hands what you do*
> *O be careful little hands what you do*
> *There's a Father up above*
> *And He's looking down in love*
> *So, be careful little hands what you do"*

NARBERTH PUBLIC SCHOOL

I transferred to Narberth School in second grade. My teacher had a daughter about my age and we sometimes played together.

In third grade we learned cursive writing. We used a pen holder with a nib. When the nib was new we touched it to our tongue before dipping it into the inkwell. I think it allowed the ink to better adhere to the nib. Cursive was not my best subject but I believe it should still be taught.

In fourth grade, I remember writing and illustrating a poem about fall leaves floating to the ground like little fairies. I like writing an occasional poem but seldom enjoy reading poetry. My mother loved doing both. My Bill liked poetry as does Matthew, who especially appreciates cowboy poetry.

We had music and art classes in all grades. They combined art and music appreciation with hands-on instruction. We learned about artists and musicians, and were exposed to great works of art and classical music. One Halloween our teacher played a recording of Danse Macabre and we drew our impression of it. I drew dancing skeletons.

We had several years of Home Economics with a half-year each of cooking and sewing. We cooked everything from scratch. I don't think mixes even existed. We also learned to set a proper table, but I'd already learned that at home.

I didn't like sewing class. I didn't like to sew. We first learned to sew by hand, then we used a sewing machine. At least the sewing machine stitches were straighter than mine. Our first projects were a pincushion, a needle-book, and a drawstring bag to hold our equipment. I still use the needle-book, though it's falling apart.

Nana helped me survive those classes. I learned from watching her. Later, when I wanted to sew, she encouraged me. I doubt I would have been as interested in making clothes were it not for her example. I made some of Billy and Matthew's clothes as well as many of Karen's and mine. I never made men's trousers but I did make a sport coat for Bill, as well as vests for him and Billy. At Christmas I did a lot of sewing for gifts. Since my sewing machine was in our bedroom, Bill made a sign and put it on the door: *Elf at Work.*

Janice and I once made over thirty stuffed pillows for a school for kids with disabilities. The pillows had happy faces, as well as ears, hands and feet. One young fellow called his pillow, George. From then on, they were all called George.

Nana made my clothes when I was younger. When we moved to New Jersey some were made with printed feed sacks. Nana went to the feed store and picked out pretty ones. Later on I received hand-me-downs from my cousins. I still enjoy hand-me-downs. There's no shopping involved and the price is right!

I also remember being thrilled to receive store-bought clothes, like the dresses Aunt Hilda gave me at Christmas. One Easter, Weezie bought me a new dress for Palm Sunday, and a new tweed suit for Easter. That was special!

Back in Narberth I joined the Brownies and then became a Girl Scout. Our meetings were held in the public library. After school, I walked there along a path next to a stream. I loved moving from rock to rock but wasn't always on target. I wonder if my mother noticed my shoes were wet when I got home.

One time my Brownie leader took her daughter and I to lunch at an upscale restaurant. I don't remember the name of the restaurant, nor do I remember what we ate, but I do remember it was the first time I had a finger bowl served with my meal.

In Girl Scouts we sometimes went to the YWCA in Philadelphia to swim. We traveled into the city by train, on the Paoli Local. I earned badges and enjoyed my years in Scouts. When we moved to New Jersey there wasn't a scout troop nearby. I worked on badges for a while but lost interest when I couldn't turn them in for credit.

OUR NEIGHBORHOOD

We often took Sunday afternoon walks. We sometimes meandered through Albrecht's Greenhouses. Near the showroom entrance there was a stone wall around a shallow well. It was surrounded by tropical plants and little alligators thrived just out of reach at the bottom. We called them alligators but I now believe they were caimans. I enjoyed watching them. In case you're wondering, this is where my parents brought their excess guppies.

Near the junction of Meeting House Lane and Montgomery Avenue was Danenhauer's Pharmacy. There was a soda fountain where a soda jerk concocted the usual ice cream treats, as well as the popular phosphates.

Along a side road, there were Victory Gardens during World War II. We had a garden in our side yard but I wanted to have my own Victory Garden. I remember planting the garden but I don't remember harvesting anything. Knowing my dislike for weeding, I doubt I was much help in the war effort.

Our closest neighbors were Edna and Harky. When I had a loose tooth I always asked Harky to pull it. He put a thread around it and yanked it out. They never hurt when he pulled them.

We lived around the corner from the Italian section of town. Ethnic groups tended to live in the same area. Nana used to buy meat at Mariani's Meat Market. She knew her meat and told Mr. Mariani exactly what she wanted. Mr. Mariani said, "Mother, you just come around here and cut it yourself." She did.

Ice cream was purchased from a little shop near Mariani's. We brought a glass bowl from home. It was five cents a dip, whether in the bowl or in a cone.

About this time, I decided I no longer wanted to be called Patsy and preferred Patty. There was a young man named Patsy who lived nearby and I didn't want a boy's name! For a while I was Patty, then I decided Patti was better. I started signing all my artwork with my own creative signature, *PattiR*. I have relatives who remember me best as Patty and I enjoy them calling me that.

I also like Patsy since I read an account of George and Martha Washington's relationship; he called her Patsy.

Fourth of July fireworks displays were held on the baseball field, near the Public Library. I loved sitting on the bleachers and watching the rockets bursting overhead and we could see the fiery pinwheels, blazing American flag, and sparkling waterfall at the finale.

In the 1940s hucksters came along our street. Some sold freshly grated horseradish. We never purchased it because Nana grated what Poppop grew. Another huckster called in a sing-song voice, "Any knives or scissors to grind?" He wore a heavy apron and carried a stone grinding wheel, worked with a foot treadle. Nana sharpened her knives with her own steel.

My Bill remembered a man selling clothes props where he lived. "Clothes props, get your clothes props here!" Nowadays, few folks hang clothes outside. In my day, clothes props kept the clothes from dragging on the ground. Modern clothes dryers are great but can't replace the scent of windblown bed sheets.

Street vendors are just a quaint memory. Now they'd need a license to ply their trade and couldn't go door-to-door. I guess it's progress.

Because of the war we were all encouraged to take first aid training. A friend and I attended evening classes in first aid at the elementary school. One of the classes fell on the night before Halloween, known as mischief night. Having never done so before, we decided we would do some mischief. We wrote with chalk on the front sidewalk of a house across the street from the school. We didn't realize the homeowner was standing behind a tree watching us. Imagine our surprise when she stepped out and ordered us to clean off what we had written! Thus ended my first and only mischief night escapade!

As I write this I marvel at two young girls out by themselves at night. It was a different world, even in wartime.

SCHOOL CHUMS

I remember many friends from my Narberth school years but these are the ones who seem relevant to my story.

Carol Lee had curly brown hair and big brown eyes. She was an accomplished dancer, tap and ballet. I doubt she realized she was the reason for my first, and only, permanent wave. My hair had a natural wave but I wanted my hair to do something different. My mother gave in and made an appointment for me to have a permanent wave. Lest you think this was anything like today's permanents, let me set you straight! (pun not intended) Strands of hair were wrapped around metal rods and clamped to a machine. Electrical current provided the heat to set the curls.

I believe I may have had the first Caucasian Afro. I sported a "wide frizzy bush" which is the dictionary definition of a fro. I never had another perm.

Patsy Ann was a good friend and we were together through several grades. She was blonde, popular, and athletic. Several of us used to play Lone Ranger and Tonto during recess on the school playground. We reenacted the radio program from the prior evening. Patsy was always the Lone Ranger. I was a member of her posse. I don't think we were ever bad guys.

In fifth grade Patsy stopped coming to school. We were told she was very sick. Her mother asked if I could come to visit. I did and we played together while she was in bed. Several of us also visited as a group. Not long after our visit we heard Patsy had died from leukemia. It had never occurred to me that children could die. I still think of her and wonder if I will see her again.

Most of the families on our street were older. However, when I was ten or eleven a new family moved in across the street. There were two children. The girl was a little younger than me. She had a sharp tongue and a sassy attitude, much like her mother. Her younger brother was about my brother's age. We never played together. In fact, a cold war developed, occasionally breaking out in harsh word exchanges from opposite sides of the street.

Though normally passive, I got riled up when she and her brother taunted my brother! I remember lying in bed at night thinking of ways to retaliate, none of them kind. To be truthful, they were hateful.

I am appalled at the depravity of a mind so young, but should I be? As the old radio show said, "Who knows what evil lurks in the hearts of men? The Shadow knows!" I doubt the Shadow always knew, but God does know, which is why Jesus came.

I never carried out my devious plans for the little blonde vixen and they finally moved away. This brought a blessing into my life and certainly improved the character of our neighborhood. The Blum family moved into the house across the street.

Kathryn Blum and I were friends in sixth and seventh grades. We played with paper dolls and took violin lessons together. I applaud my parents for their willingness to tolerate my screeching and scratching. I also appreciate Mr. Barone's patience with my feeble attempts to play pieces I had obviously not practiced.

Kathryn was a fine violinist. She practiced diligently. Though we took our lessons together, we weren't of the same caliber. She played first violin and was Concert Mistress of our school orchestra. I sat first chair in the second violin section, probably due to age, there were two younger fellows better than I.

Kathryn not only played the violin but also sang beautifully. Miss Fricke, our music teacher, sent me a newspaper photograph of her with Mr. Barone when she made her operatic debut with the Philadelphia Civic Grand Opera at the Academy of Music in Philadelphia in 1951. She sang in America and Europe before she married and was a member of the New York City Opera. She was perhaps my closest childhood friend. For years I kept the leather change purse she gave me when we moved away. We corresponded a few times but eventually lost track of each other.

Recently, while researching the correct spelling of Mr. Barone's name, I found Kathryn. I knew Mr. Barone was associated with the Bryn Mawr Conservatory of Music but didn't realize he had been the director since its founding in 1934. The current director and head of the Voice Department is Kathryna Blum Barone. I wrote to her letting her know I have not forgotten our friendship from all those years ago. She wrote a lovely letter in return.

<O><

I had another neighbor I wouldn't call a friend but she produced a memory. June lived two houses away and was a few years my senior. June and I got along well enough but she occasionally enticed me to do things I knew I shouldn't do. I was rather naïve and a people pleaser, not a good combination.

Sometimes June used words I knew not to use. One day she said a word I'd never heard before. It was the abomination of all words, though I didn't know it at the time. I asked her what it meant. She laughed, "Ask your mother."

One day my mother was taking June and I somewhere in our car. We were sitting in the back seat. She nudged me and whispered, "Did you ask your mother?" I evidently knew what she meant because I asked my mother right then and there.

My mother was an admirable woman. She quietly told me what it meant and it was a word which should never be used by me or anyone else. I wish now I'd looked at June's face because I'm sure she realized my mother knew who had told me that word! I also commend my mother for taking it all in stride and not being flustered. She was a very special lady.

I don't remember Weezie telling me about *the birds and the bees* but she always answered my questions. When I didn't understand something, she explained what I needed to know.

I believe one reason Weezie was so open with me was because she had a rather difficult introduction to puberty. Nana had not yet talked with her about what to expect. Since she was only ten I'm sure her becoming pubescent was not anticipated. Aunt Ann Godefroy was with Louise when this took place and provided the necessary equipment.

Isn't it wonderful how God provides for our needs?

SPECIAL FAMILY FRIENDS

The McCrackens weren't related to us but were long time family friends. Uncle Bill was a boarder in my grandparents' home, when my mother was a teenager. He was a merchant marine seaman and brought unique gifts to them from his trips overseas.

On his last trip home, he brought a bride from England, Aunt Madge. We knew little else about her but she was very much a part of our lives. Their home was full of exotic treasures.

I visited them for a week when I was nine or ten years old and planned to go back for a second week but a sudden attack of homesickness changed the plan.

One night I gave them a shock when I walked in my sleep. Aunt Madge awoke with me standing beside her bed. She said I looked like an apparition in my white nightie. She led me back to bed and I didn't remember it.

I enjoyed fishing in a nearby canal with paper clip fishhooks. I never caught anything but liked watching the fish nibble the bread ball bait. We also went to Riverview Beach on the Wilson Line. The Park had a great carousel but the cruise on the steamship was the best part of the adventure.

When traveling between Pennsylvania and New Jersey we usually rode the ferry. I loved standing on the deck pretending I was on the high seas. Of course, riding the ferry with Uncle Bill was the best! He knew all the black gang (engine room workers) below decks and I saw places I'd never have seen without him.

The McCrackens didn't have children so they applied for a foster child. Olivia was twelve when she came to live with them. They brought her to our home in Narberth and invited me to come for a visit so we could spend time together. I'd enjoyed my first visit so I was happy to go.

Olivia and Aunt Madge taught me to ride my two-wheel bicycle. Olivia ran along behind while steadying my rear fender. I saw her shadow and knew when she let go but kept on peddling. We rode our bikes a lot, went on day trips, played board games in the evenings and had a great time.

Every afternoon we had tea with Aunt Madge. We even did some baking and cooking together. I assured Aunt Madge I knew how to make icing with 10x sugar and water. I obviously hadn't watched very carefully when Weezie made frosting. Though the frosting was a disaster, Aunt Madge chuckled over it.

We had a snack before bedtime which I called *our nightly food*. Aunt Madge got a kick out of my expressions, like catty-corner. We Americans do use different colloquialisms than the Brits.

We sometimes played with a couple of neighbor boys. Maybe I should have detected a red flag when one of them kissed me behind the McCracken's garage. I was eleven and not impressed.

One afternoon we went to the canal to fish. Instead of staying with me she told me she was going to meet somebody up behind a billboard. She was gone a long time and I finally went back to the house without her. When Aunt Madge asked where she was, I told her Olivia was meeting someone.

When Uncle Bill came home, he confronted Olivia. She had been involved in clandestine activity for quite a while. They had hoped to adopt her. They decided against adoption but allowed her to stay under closer supervision. She came from a home with deplorable conditions. My week-long visits ceased.

During World War II, blackouts were often observed in residential areas and always in sensitive areas. The electric facility in Deepwater was one of those areas. The skylights were painted black in case of an enemy air attack. One dark night, Uncle Bill was up on the roof to repair damage and inadvertently stepped on one of the skylights. He fell 30 feet to his death.

I don't remember whether Olivia left their home before or after Uncle Bill died. I know she joined a carnival, riding a motorcycle in a motordrome called the Wall of Death. She married another performer and had a child.

After Uncle Bill died, Aunt Madge came to the farm every weekend. It was nice having her around and we looked forward to her visits. She stayed in Nana's guest room and was good company.

She worked for a while in a dress shop doing alterations. When I was sixteen she asked me to model for a fashion show. It was a fundraiser for the Eastern Star. I was to model teen fashions and two professional models would do the rest. The two pros were very nice and it was great fun!

Madgie, as we called her, sometimes invited me to visit her friends who happened to have sons my age. One family rented part of their farm to a traveling circus. We watched the circus arrive and set up and were allowed access to areas not open to the public.

I was invited to an Eastern Star ball at an elegant hotel. It was a blind date with one of her friend's sons. He was very nice and it was a pleasant evening. We wrote to each other a time or two.

Aunt Madge died unexpectedly at home. I saw Olivia at her funeral. She tried to assert herself as Aunt Madge's heir but her attempt failed. Though friends had cautioned Aunt Madge to be sure her will was in order, her beneficiary was still Uncle Bill. Her home, with all its lovely treasures, sat vacant for several years until the state found distant cousins in England. Her home was then auctioned off with all its contents.

These were folks I loved but I don't know if I'll ever see them again. I know they heard the gospel when they went to our church but sadly it wasn't something we talked about. We should talk about what's important. Knowing where we will spend eternity is undoubtedly the most important decision we'll ever make!

"But as many as received Him,
to them He gave the right
to become children of God,
to those who believe in His name"
(John 1:12)

WHAT WE DID FOR FUN

I was an only child for seven years, so I learned to amuse myself. I also liked to watch my parents and grandparents while they worked, even help when I was allowed. Nana had the pleasure of my company more than most. I not only asked questions but liked to touch things like chicken entrails or fresh dough. Sometimes she gave me chunks of pie dough to make my own little pie, and I always licked the beaters!

I played with dolls but didn't take good care of them. Doctor's and nurse's kits helped diagnose family and doll illnesses. My chemistry set wasn't as exciting as I hoped, but my microscope provided hours of interest. I also liked coloring books, and paint-less paint books. I made hot pads on a little hand loom, crocheted, and crafted American Indian designs on a bead loom.

Doing laundry with Nana was interesting and offered many opportunities for involvement, and getting wet. I watching the clothes twisting and turning in the washing machine. An article of clothing surfaced, then was gone into the depths, only to rise again.

Most children like to play in water and I was no exception. When white clothes went through the washing machine wringer into a tub of blue water, I swished them around. The bluing helped to whiten the clothes but also tinted my hands a lovely color. I wasn't allowed to put clothes through the wringer but I caught them and dropped them into the water or basket. I was never enlisted to do these jobs, I volunteered. I'm sure my help was necessary, though Nana sometimes seemed a little tense.

My little brother, Billy, was an interesting addition to our household. After he arrived I was no longer the only child. When he was in his playpen or high chair I remember playing, "I throw it, you pick it up." He tossed a toy and I gave it back to him. I can't say I always enjoyed that but I did enjoy reading to him. Many of the books were ones previously read to me. We also colored together after he could be trusted not to eat the crayons.

One day we were in the little hall at the bottom of the stairs to the second floor. Billy was just tall enough that his mouth was level with my ample tummy and he bit me! I can't imagine I did anything to warrant it, but sometimes memories can be elusive.

He was more fun when he was older and we did things together. Outside we played in the sandbox making roads for trucks and cars. When we played inside we constructed buildings, walls, and fences with blocks, an erector set or TinkerToys. We sometimes played police and fire department. Since I was the oldest I was chief of police. Sometimes another boy came to play with us making a bigger department. We even had equipment, Billy's pedal fire truck and red express wagon.

Our house was one of three properties scooped out of Albrecht's Nursery. It was an older section of the nursery with large craters left from digging out trees, great places to play! Some of the older holes were grass covered and they were carpeted with violets in the spring. We lived in town but it felt like living in the country.

Playing in the snow was always popular. One winter Big Bill cut blocks of snow and we built a fort in the side yard. Snow days from school were a rarity. We bundled up in snowsuits and boots to walk to school. Unless it was bitter cold we played outside at recess. Can you imagine how long it took teachers in the lower grades to get us ready?

There was a gentle slope from Iona Avenue down Meeting House Lane, leveling out in front of our house. I used to ride my blue Schwinn bicycle in the street and roller skate on the sidewalk. The skates clipped onto my shoes and were tightened with a skate key.

One Christmas I received a magic set. I practiced and felt I could work the tricks enough to put on a magic show. I put a sign in front of our house and set up a card table in the backyard, along with several chairs for my audience. I don't know if I charged a fee. I have an idea I thought only my family would come. Two older boys arrived for the show. I didn't know them, had never seen them before. I was surprised but the show must go on and it did. The only trick I remember doing was water changing to wine and back to water. It worked. The fellows were polite and left quietly when it was over. I never did it again!

I felt very comfortable with our older neighbors. On warm summer evenings, I sang and danced for them on their porches. They evidently liked my performances, or maybe just liked having a child around. If I didn't remember those private shows and someone told me I did it, I'd probably deny it!

We went to Ringling Brothers, Barnum and Bailey circus. Back then you could buy chameleons as souvenirs at the circus. They weren't true chameleons but they changed color depending on their surroundings. They had little collars and leashes so you could pin the leash to your clothing and wear them, a living brooch. They cost about a dollar and were doomed to short lives.

When I brought mine home, I wore it when we went to the supermarket. It was fun watching the expressions when my brooch moved! For a while it lived on a plant on our sunporch windowsill. I fed it flies. I don't remember how long it lived but it eventually disappeared. I'm glad they can't sell them anymore but it was fun while it lasted; for me, probably not the chameleon.

We occasionally went to Woodside Park near Philadelphia. I loved the merry-go-round and a few of the tamer rides.

One summer our family rented a cottage in Stone Harbor. It was several blocks from the beach. Weezie, Billy and I stayed for three weeks and Big Bill came for long weekends. We went to the beach every day, pushing Billy in his stroller and carrying our blue and yellow beach umbrella, along with sand toys and other stuff.

We fished off a little bridge near our cottage and ate the sea bass we caught. We even caught an eel but didn't know they were good eating until several years later. We also caught blow-fish and threw them back after they destroyed our fish hooks. Years later we learned they were a delicacy. Blow-fish in New Jersey waters aren't poisonous like the southern varieties.

We watched excitedly for my dad's arrival each weekend and then wished he didn't have to leave for work so soon. It was probably our best family vacation. Family memories are a blessing!

By now you've noticed I called my parents by their first names. When my brother Billy was born, he did the same. As Billy grew older my dad became Big Bill and Billy was Little Bill. Louise became Weezie early on because it was easier for her little cousin. I didn't know it was unusual.

When I asked Weezie why we did it she said it was because we lived with our grandparents. Nana and Poppop referred to our parents by their first names and we followed suit. When a relative told them it was disrespectful, it apparently fueled a latent ember and first names continued.

Calling my parents by their first names didn't bother me until I started calling Bill's mother Mom. Then I began to feel I was being disrespectful, so I began referring to her as Mother, jokingly at first. Later I noticed my brother doing the same thing. We also didn't call our father Dad or Daddy. Now I wish I could give him a big hug and say, "I love you Daddy."

<O>

Did we watch television? I never even saw a television until I was seventeen. Instead of TV being the centerpiece, we read books, newspapers, and magazines, and listened to the radio. We also played games, sang around the piano and talked with each other. Weezie did cross stitch or knitted. Nana crocheted or embroidered, sometimes stitching silk floss on velvet, the lustrous flowers contrasting with the black background.

If we'd had television I'd have missed out on pretending. In fact, my favorite weekly radio show was Let's Pretend, broadcast on Saturday morning. The shows were productions of fairy tales, adding fuel to my pretending fires. My favorite was *Cinderella*.

The Lone Ranger not only provided school recess play but was a close second on my list of favorites. *The William Tell Overture* was a stirring intro at 7:30 pm as the announcer proclaimed:

"Return with us now to those thrilling days of yesteryear. From out of the past come the thundering hoof-beats of the great horse Silver. The Lone Ranger rides again!"

The show was over at 8 pm and I was off to bed to dream about silver bullets that never killed and the mystique of the old west. I wonder what Rossini might think about a masked cowboy enhancing the popularity of his overture.

On the radio we heard everything from the Metropolitan Opera to the Grand Ole Opry, as well as big bands like Glenn

Miller and Tommy Dorsey. Many comedians became famous on radio; Red Skelton, Jack Benny, and Victor Borge, to name a few. I so hoped Victor Borge would play just one piano selection through to the end without a pratfall from his piano bench.

I loved all kinds of books, including comic books like Wonder Woman, Sheena Queen of the Jungle and Captain America. You know, they haven't aged at all!

All my family loved Tarzan movies. Johnny Weissmuller, the *ONLY* Tarzan, made twelve films and we saw them all. The most memorable for me was when Jane made an omelet for a group of visitors with one egg—an ostrich egg. Weissmuller invented the famous Tarzan yell and at his request a recording of it was played three times as he was lowered into his grave.

My mother drove me to the Narberth movie theater on Saturday afternoons where I attended the matinee. I always went to the front row and sat with older ladies. In 1940 matinee seats were ten cents for children and seventeen cents for adults. It was thirty-five cents for evenings. Prices may have differed by area but we didn't foresee today's outrageous prices.

Aunt Hilda took me to see The Wizard of Oz when I was six. The transition from black and white to color still takes my breath away and the songs are delightful. However, I am still traumatized by Miss Gulch becoming the Wicked Witch as she rides by the window on her bicycle. And I still cringe at the flying monkeys.

I loved Shirley Temple and Sonja Henie movies. You probably recognize Shirley Temple but Sonja Henie was an Olympic champion ice skater. Esther Williams, a national champion swimmer, also made movies. She would have competed in the Olympics but they were cancelled in 1940 due to World War II.

We had many positive role models. Was it because the media didn't delve as voraciously into their personal lives? Perhaps we don't need to know every tidbit regurgitated before us. We should be thankful we still have God-fearing heroes to emulate and be careful to sift out the chaff of the world.

Sometimes my parents went to Philadelphia with friends. Both the Earle and Faye's Theaters showed movies along with stage shows. Faye's had Follies type shows which were sometimes risqué.

The Earle was family-oriented. That came into question when

my parents took me there when I was ten or eleven. A show girl started stripping onstage. My parents were flustered but before they could scoot me into the aisle and out of the theater the gal stepped out from behind a mannequin shell, fully clothed. Big Bill found the situation more amusing than Weezie did.

On a kids' radio show they gave away free tickets to the Philadelphia Zoo for correctly answering questions at the end of the program. I took notes, so we often had free tickets.

A RANDOM MUSIC AND DANCE PATCH

Weezie seated herself at her piano. Morning sun streamed in the window as she paged through the hymnal.

Big Bill scratched his head, picked up another hymnal and asked, "What number is *In the Garden*?"

It was Sunday morning and they were scheduled to do special music in our little country church. Weezie's fingers ran through the introduction. Then she and Big Bill began to sing.

Some of my favorite memories are of all of us singing around the piano, often songs from the '20s and '30s like *Pennies from Heaven* and *When It's Springtime in the Rockies.* One song often gave Weezie and I the giggles. It was *The Road to Mandalay*, with lyrics from Kipling's poem; the original, not the later Sinatra version.

Weezie played a variety of genres but I loved hearing her play more challenging works like *Rachmaninoff's Prelude in C sharp minor* and *Gershwin's Rhapsody in Blue.* Sometimes we sang *On the Good Ship Lollipop* or *Animal Crackers in My Soup.*

Both my parents sang with the Bala-Cynwood church choir. When I was a little girl I told Eleanor Thompson, the contralto soloist, I wanted her to sing at my wedding. Years of planning went out the window when I instead retained a coworker who'd won a TV talent contest. Choices have consequences. Jimmy sang well but I've regretted not having Eleanor sing.

I enjoyed being around the choir members. Each year during the Christmas season they sang from the mezzanine of the Strawbridge and Clothier store in Ardmore. When I was eleven Howard Tussey, the choir director, invited me to sing with them. My junior choir robe with its white surplice and big red bow stood out in contrast to their black robes. It was exciting!

In early December the choir sang *Handel's Messiah* in the church, beginning my Christmas season. I usually sat with the choir director's wife and fell asleep before it was over. One time I began to hiccup and holding my breath wasn't helping. Mrs. Tussey took me to where communion was prepared and gave me a little glass of grape juice. I drank it and my hiccups stopped. I was concerned we had broken some rule about drinking communion juice but she assured me it was all right.

Years later, when we worked at Owens-Illinois, my parents and I sang with The Choralaires, a chorus made up of employees from all areas of the plant. We sang at company functions, community events, and even sang in a prison. Though I sang in New Jersey, I never sang a solo until I joined the First Baptist Church choir in Commerce, Georgia. I don't know if the choir director liked my voice or my pronunciation. He often asked me to pronounce words so the rest of the choir could hear my *proper* English.

My first solo was *Nearer Still Nearer*. When we returned to New Jersey and Hardingville Church I again sang with the choir. I also directed the children's choir and even sang an occasional solo. A special memory is of a trio Mary Gant, Barbara DuBois and I sang in an Easter Cantata. My most difficult solo was singing for the funeral of a friend, only possible with God's help!

In third grade I began piano lessons. My piano teacher was Mrs. Griest, my mother's instructor. I must have been a disappointment. My mother took lessons for nine years and was an accomplished pianist. I took lessons for three years and accomplished little. I trudged to my weekly lessons from school. The walk seemed to take forever. After my lesson I happily skipped home. Mrs. Griest tried to make learning fun, like using the letters of the notes on the music staff to make up stories. I used the same tactic when I later taught piano.

Remember my violin lessons? The instrument was on loan from the school so it stayed behind when we moved. I wasn't devastated when my lessons ceased.

Playing the piano became a major outlet for my teen emotions. When things weren't going well I played *Be Still My Soul*, ad infinitum. Even now, it is one of my favorite hymns. During stormy times in my courtship with Bill I nearly wore out the piano keys! I'm surprised someone didn't say, "Get over it!"

When Bill told me his favorite classic was Debussy's *Clair de Lune*, I bought the sheet music and practiced, a lot! I played it for him when he was home on leave. We also shared a love for musicals, Gershwin, and some of the popular classics.

I wish I had practiced more when I took piano lessons but I'm thankful God has used my limited ability. I played either part time or full time in every church we attended.

In Bumpville I taught piano for a while. It was to help financially but turned out to be a blessing. Most of my students were children. Some did well, my own children not so well.

One young girl was already playing the violin. Her grandfather, an accomplished violinist, was her teacher. At the end of a year I suggested they find a more experienced teacher. She was a joy to teach but I knew it was the right thing to do.

Judy Yager wanted to learn and teaching her was just guiding her. Adult students often do well because they really want to learn. She soon began playing the organ in church.

My mother bought her baby grand when she worked at Strawbridge and Clothier. Even though I didn't enjoy practicing, I liked the piano and was disappointed when she traded it in for a home organ. Bill later bought me a nice spinet which took up less space. Karen and Matt began lessons on it in New Jersey. Their teacher lived just down the road. Unfortunately, their practice habits were like my own.

We moved the piano with us to Skeetrock and then to Bumpville. In Bumpville I played the piano in church and never played at home so I sold it. Later I had a keyboard purchased by my Bible Study ladies in Pound. It was a nice keyboard but not a piano. I still think about having a piano but maybe I'm just in love with the idea of having a piano.

Nana sang while rocking my brother and I, and later when she rocked our children. There were the traditional songs like *Rock-a-bye Baby*, but my favorite is *All Aboard for Blanket Bay*. Both Nana and Weezie sang it to us and I later sang it to my babes. I also sang it to Weezie during her last hours on earth.

A non-traditional song Nana sang was *Three Men Went A' Hunting*. It's a silly song but it makes me smile.

"Three men went a'hunting and nothing could they find.
They came upon a hedgehog and they left it far behind.
Oh, the Englishman said, 'Tis a hedgehog,
And Scotty he swore, Nay. But the Irishman said,
It's a pin cushion with the pins stuck in the wrong way."
<OX<

When I was a wee lass I took tap dance lessons. I don't recall my first recital but I've heard enough to share the event. I was three years old and did a solo number with a teddy bear nearly as big as me. I evidently liked the spotlight because once onstage I was reluctant to leave. Maybe I thought I was the next Shirley Temple.

I began ballet and had learned the five basic positions when my dance lessons were discontinued because my teacher married and moved out west. I was six or seven years old.

A few years ago, I decided to show my grand-girl Lydia the fifth ballet position. It entails positioning the feet next to each other with the toes pointing outward. It was not a good idea and I will not try it again. Some things are best explained, not demonstrated

In seventh grade my mother enrolled me in ballroom dance classes. One dance I learned was the waltz and it's still my favorite dance.

Dancing was on hold for a few years but became more significant when I was in high school. When we finished eating lunch in the cafeteria we went to the gym where they played popular records and we danced. When Bill was home on leave, he visited the school and danced with me! He was an excellent dancer and I loved dancing with him.

NEW JERSEY
FEEDSACK FABRIC

Life was good in Narberth but Poppop had crippling arthritis in his knees and was unable to continue working as a gardener. At the same time, World War II was nearly over and my father's job at Cramps Shipyard was winding down. This brought about the decision to move to New Jersey.

We looked at several properties. The only drawback to the farm in Hardingville was there was one house with just two bedrooms. Nana agreed to the purchase with the stipulation a house be built for her and Poppop. I remember her saying, "I want it to be 24 ft. by 28 ft." My dad was the builder and knew what she wanted wouldn't fit into those dimensions.

We moved on May 1, 1944, a cold, wet, blustery day. It was late evening before the moving van was unloaded and nearly 10 pm when we finally ate dinner. Fresh spinach and asparagus from the garden never tasted better.

With two bedrooms for six of us, my brother slept in our parents' room and I slept in our grandparents' room. The only bathroom was on the first floor so Poppop needed to tote a chamber pot upstairs at night.

Nana's house took longer to construct than planned. To save money and get started she agreed to have it built onto the main house. It was a great day when Nana and Poppop moved into their own home, and Billy and I had our own bedrooms. We even had a bathroom on the second floor. The large downstairs bathroom became the dining room which it still is today. When I sit at Jeff and Linda's dining table I smile to myself. I remember what used to be.

There were three large chicken houses full of leghorn chickens producing eggs. There was also a round brooder house, a barn with a hayloft, a corn crib, a cow shed, and a paint house at the end of a path. "What's a paint house?" This one was a remodeled outhouse with storage shelves.

The cow shed held one cow, a small one. Shortly after we were settled, Bonnie was purchased. She was a nice little Guernsey, fit the barn well and was an easy keeper. We had her for several years but old age caught up with her and she left us.

After Bonnie, we had two more cows, both Holsteins and larger than Bonnie. One had a nasty habit of kicking over the milk bucket. The other one barely fit through the door and didn't fit in the stanchion. No more cows. We bought milk from our pastor, who delivered it directly to our refrigerator if we weren't home.

Most of our acreage was dedicated to truck crops, often auctioned through the local co-op. One major crop was tomatoes. Sometimes we were under contract to a cannery and delivered truckloads of tomatoes to their loading station. The inspectors picked one basket, examined the contents, and decided on the quality of the load. That sounds fair, right? It should be, but subjective assessment was sometimes pro-company and anti-farmer. Even if a basket was judged to have a high percentage of rot, it was put back into the general population. Was the bad stuff removed at the cannery? I didn't eat store-bought catsup for a long time!

Hay was put up loose the first couple of years. Getting it into the barn with a storm brewing was exciting. I remember it now when I see the Amish bringing in hay.

Whether hay was loose or baled the hayloft was a great place to play, especially when new kittens were to be found. I climbed a wooden ladder on the inside wall and maneuvered through the opening. Did I have flashbacks to my first-grade sliding board incident? Had it not been for my desire to find those kittens I couldn't have done it!

When Big Bill's job at Cramps Shipyard came to an end he worked full time on the farm. Poppop and Nana had a very small social security check and a twenty-five-acre farm couldn't support two families so when he heard a school bus driver was needed he applied and was hired. Weezie was his substitute. She and Nana also began working in the Aura School lunchroom.

Each driver had to provide a garage for his bus so he built a garage on the side of the barn. Billy and I no longer needed to watch for the bus in the morning because we boarded in our backyard.

Driving a school bus was different back then. The driver had absolute authority. An unruly student was corrected quickly. If he continued to disobey he could be suspended from riding the bus. If a student was disrespectful or didn't pay attention to the driver, the driver could put him off the bus immediately and he had to walk home. I only remember one being put off. Wade was angry but apologized and rode the bus for the rest of the school year. Later, when he came home on leave from the Army, he came to see my dad and told him he appreciated his discipline.

<O><

We were now farm kids with chores. We were not overworked, though I'm sure I sometimes thought so. Is it possible the lack of work ethic prevalent today might be overcome if kids had more responsibilities at home?

One of my jobs was mowing the lawns and they were huge, though now they seem smaller. I pushed a reel mower. As soon as I finished mowing it was time to begin again. It was not my favorite task. When I graduated high-school and had a full-time job I no longer had to mow lawns. It was then my dad purchased a gas-powered mower. I jokingly question the timing, but I know it was purchased because our parents began working to supplement farm income. Our first television arrived about the same time.

Each spring I looked forward to helping plant tomatoes. That brought on my first suntan of the season. One time comes to mind. Big Bill asked me to bring Harry, our work horse, to the barn so he could harness him to the wagon. I obviously didn't know you don't push a horse, you lead it. With my less than competent guidance, Harry stepped on my canvas-shod foot. He moved away but not before I was sure every metatarsus was broken and my shoe filled with blood. I moved Harry into position and went into the house to bring out the kitchen wastebasket, its contents destined for our burning barrel. Just before I reached the barrel I passed out, flattening the metal wastebasket.

On close inspection, I had a significant bruise but nary a broken bone, nor any shed blood. I also learned how to lead a horse which came in handy during future horse-related activities.

Weeding was not a job I enjoyed. Though my dad used Harry

to cultivate crops, some weeds were hoed or pulled by hand. Another job was more play than work. Billy and I hunted tomato worms, precisely hornworms. They feed on the leaves and stems of tomato plants. We were to seek and destroy the invaders with scissors! We looked for plants with leafless stems, then searched out the little devils and cut them in half with scissors.

Other search and destroy missions were for potato and bean beetles. It was full-fledged war! Beetles required a different technique. We gathered them by hand and popped them into a can of kerosene which made a fine blaze at the end of the day!

Bean beetles laid clusters of yellow eggs on the underside of leaves and finding them wasn't easy. I usually folded the leaf over the eggs and squished them, effective but messy.

The first tomatoes were picked as *blush* tomatoes; green, with tinges of pink on the blossom end. Big Bill was a man of integrity. He made sure the produce packed in the baskets was good throughout. Some growers put inferior tomatoes on the bottom. Buyers at auction didn't buy from them again or paid less.

Packing tomatoes was like putting together a jigsaw puzzle. That skill was helpful when I worked in a peach packing shed between my junior and senior years in high school. The packing was similar but working in a peach packing shed was an itchy business. The fuzz from the peaches permeated the area and a shower after work was a necessity!

Marketing produce has changed since the middle of the twentieth-century—some good changes and some not so good. That makes me wonder what changes will come about in the twenty-first century. Seems we were better off when we produced our own food and farming hadn't gone big business. It's nice to get many fruits and vegetable year 'round but I wonder how they are produced? It is what it is but ...

"When we all get to heaven
What a day of rejoicing that will be ..."
(Brad Paisley)

AURA SCHOOL
I enrolled in Aura School during the last month of seventh grade. My class had less than twenty students so it was hard to go

unnoticed. I was always among the youngest in my class but these students seemed older. Later I learned several had been retained. There was also more interest in the opposite sex and some were dating.

Seventh grade English was my nemesis. The class was diagramming sentences, something I'd not done before. My new teacher no doubt felt they'd gained nothing from the arrival of this dullard from Pennsylvania.

Not only was I thrust into a world where we did terrible things to sentences, but I missed eighth grade in Narberth where I would have studied a half year each of Latin and French. I didn't look forward to learning the languages as much as I did Christmas caroling through the school halls singing *Adeste Fidelis* in Latin.

I survived those last few weeks of school and it was summer vacation! Vacation? Maybe not like it was in Narberth where:

"Summertime, and the livin' is easy
Fish are jumpin' and the cotton is high
Oh, your daddy's rich and your mamma's good lookin'
So hush little baby, don't you cry."
(*Porgy & Bess*, George Gershwin)

Okay, I'm exaggerating but summers did change! We now lived on an honest-to-goodness farm where people worked, and those people included me. On the farm in Gladwyne I was too young to be part of the work force and summer in Narberth was vacation time.

My brother was in Kindergarten in Narberth School. They went half-days, learned some basics and had lots of play time. Aura Kindergarten was full-days and they learned to read! This is not to cast a shadow on either school system but it does show schools in different areas often have different approaches. One isn't better than the other but changing schools mid-stream can be difficult.

Weezie worked on reading with Billy so he could enter first grade. Though he started out at a disadvantage, he had a great teacher and made it through the school year.

We survived our first summer as farm kids and were ready for school in the fall. We no longer walked to school, the bus stopped right in front of our house! I still felt like the new kid on the block but now I was on a level playing field.

Bill Fenton served double-duty as eighth-grade teacher and school principal. We didn't have specific art or music classes but they were incorporated into regular classes. I didn't realize it then but Mr. Fenton was pivotal in shaping my future, planned by God before I was born. Being unnoticed didn't work in Mr. Fenton's classes. He didn't pay attention to whether my hand was up or not, he called on me.

In music class Mr. Fenton played several recordings for us to identify. Most of the class knew Anchors Aweigh, The Army Caisson Song, and The Marine Hymn. Then he played one and no one seemed to know it. I did, but didn't raise my hand.

Sure enough, he asked me, "Patty, do you know what it is?"

I nodded, "It's the Coast Guard Song, Semper Paratus."

I knew because my dad enjoyed the music of Waring's Pennsylvanians and had several of their recordings. One was of all the Armed Forces' songs. I knew the tunes and most of the lyrics.

I didn't always make A's, but I did well academically. When I brought home a grade lower than an A, my dad asked, "Why didn't you get an A?" Education was important to him.

One day a classmate brought me a note from her brother. I had no idea how he knew me because I didn't know him. In the note he said he had seen me and asked me to go out with him. He was eighteen and I doubt he knew I was twelve. I took the note home and showed it to my mother. I told her I didn't know what to say to him.

She read it and said, "This is your first mash note."

"Mash note? What's that?"

"Sort of a love note," she smiled.

"So, what should I do about it?"

"Answer it."

"How?"

"Well, you might mention you're too young to date."

I answered the note, telling him I was twelve and not allowed to date. I never heard from him again.

Toward the end of the school year our class voted on which of us would receive the American Legion Award. Those who receive the medal and certificate must exemplify six qualities defining character: courage, honor, leadership, patriotism, scholarship and service. We discussed these attributes before we voted.

I considered all my classmates and decided to vote for Mary. She was a quiet girl and worked hard in school and at home. There were mornings when she smelled of the cow barn where she worked before she came to school. She had a shy smile and was friendly. Imagine my surprise when Mary got one vote and the rest were for me! I never thought that would happen. I'm glad I voted for Mary. She became a schoolteacher and I'm sure she blessed her students.

My big party was another story. I wanted to have a party with girls and boys. We sent out invitations and Weezie and Nana prepared lots of food. The big night arrived and the girls showed up but not one boy! I was disappointed. My dad had us all pile into his car and he drove us around country roads to find the boys. Several came back with us. Even the boys said the party was fun and they were glad they came.

Now I cannot imagine going out looking for boys. What were we thinking? But it worked!

<O><

Eighth-grade was a major turning point. I began to speak up more in class and felt more at ease with peers. Though praise still made me uncomfortable, I enjoyed recognition. God was redirecting and changing me, and I was beginning to like what was happening.

I turned thirteen during the school year. I remember looking in the mirror on my birthday morning and I looked the same as when I was twelve. Maybe I'd hoped the ugly duckling had turned into a graceful swan. I was a chunky little girl yearning to be a willowy young woman.

Toward the end of the year our class spent a day at Glassboro High School. We each went to classes with a current Freshman student. When we met the students from the other sending schools, I felt like we were country cousins visiting Glassboro's turf. The attitude of a few of the Glassboro students encouraged those feelings and, with some, continued beyond high school.

With my parents' encouragement, I enrolled in Commercial Secretarial courses. My goal was to be a secretary like my mother. I had no desire to go to college, partly because I knew we couldn't afford it but even more so, I wasn't interested.

Any graduation is important, whether it be from kindergarten or high school. Eighth-grade graduation was no different. We sang, heard encouraging words, and received awards and diplomas. I knew I'd miss Mr. Fenton but his soon-to-be wife, Miss Angeline Maruca, was going to be my Spanish teacher. He told me she was looking forward to having me in her class. I felt the same. We became acquainted when Mr. Fenton hired me to help her with some housecleaning projects.

Becoming a teenager was positive but my family relationships were changing. Prior to this, my life revolved around my family and my peer relationships were few. This changed in eighth grade though I'm not sure how it began. I do know my twin friends were part of it. They were fellow classmates and I sometimes visited their home. Our home was rather quiet and conventional, theirs seemed more exciting.

My family consisted of my maternal grandparents and parents, my brother, and me. We laughed, teased, and enjoyed a good time but my friends' family took it to another level. It was a large family. They were into Country Western music and it seemed like everyone sang and played guitar. I'd not paid attention to that music genre so it intrigued me. When we moved on to high school we weren't in the same classes and didn't see each other.

It was then Annie and I became friends. She was a year ahead of me in school but we saw each other on the bus and our families attended weekly meetings of the Aura Grange. The Grange is a national farmers' organization—locally it was a social club. When we joined, it was a secret organization. I don't believe it is now.

Every Wednesday evening, we went to the Grange Hall. After the meetings, there were informative programs or entertainment followed by refreshments. Many of our neighbors were members. Some of us sang around the piano: Annie played guitar, I played piano, and John Turk played the fiddle. It was a fun time.

We all held various offices in the local Grange. I held an office in Pomona (county) Grange but the higher the level, the less I was interested. One activity I enjoyed was the drill team. Six to eight couples marched to music, like military drills. I enjoyed choreographing as well as participating. When appearing in Pomona or State Grange we wore evening clothes. Locally it was more casual.

During the summer between eighth grade and high school we continued to work on the farm, visited family and friends, went swimming at Lake Gilman or Lake Garrison, and went to the seashore.

Toward the end of summer, I was extremely sick and unable to eat for days. Dr. Harris came to the house. Yes, doctors made house calls. After learning I'd been helping Nana can sausage, and I'd tasted a lot of it, he concluded the excess fat had clogged my bile ducts, thereby causing jaundice. I had to eat egg whites and I don't think they were cooked. They certainly weren't palatable.

Jaundice can also be caused by viral hepatitis so I've never been able to donate blood. I was willing and repeated what our doctor said, but they were right to be cautious.

Being sick was the bad news. The good news was I lost weight, enough so I went into my Freshman year of high school considerably slimmer. I don't recommend illness to lose weight but I was ecstatic it happened, when it was over.

I have many good memories of being a teenager but I wanted to stretch my wings and wasn't ready to jump off the edge of the nest. I was laying the groundwork which led me into questionable arenas. My choices weren't always wise.

"The righteous should choose his friends carefully..."
(Proverbs 12:26)

GLASSBORO HIGH SCHOOL

Adjusting to high school wasn't difficult. I was on a secretarial track so my classes were business oriented. Commercial English was grammar basics and writing business letters. We did a little creative writing but not as much as I desired. I wrote an essay on *Turning the Heel*. For non-knitters, turning the heel on a sock is a challenge. It was a humorous piece and my teacher had it published in our school newspaper, *The Hub*.

Mrs. Isenberg taught Shorthand and Office Practice. In Office Practice we studied office procedures. In our Senior year we worked in the high school office with the secretaries. We dressed appropriately for a business office in a dress or skirt and blouse, nylons and dress shoes. We answered phones, delivered messages, filed, typed letters and whatever they felt we could handle. It was good hands-on experience.

Mrs. Fenton was my Spanish teacher and the adviser for *The Hub*. She suggested I choose the newspaper as my club activity in my sophomore year. I did and enjoyed writing news as well as editorials and features. I also liked setting the paper up for printing. We didn't have computers. We typed the articles on manual typewriters, then cut and pasted (scissors and paste) onto the setup pages, along with photographs. The pages were delivered to a printer in town. He set them in moveable type and printed a proof copy which he sent back to us. After proofing, the copy was sent back to the printer. We had gone to press.

In my Junior year I was assistant editor, then editor-in-chief in my Senior year. We won several honors through the Columbia Scholastic Press Association. At the end of my Junior year I attended the Columbia Scholastic Press Association Conference in New York City, along with several other students and our adviser. Just being in The Big Apple was thrilling. We stayed in a hotel, walked on Broadway, ate at The Brass Rail and had a wonderful time, until the last day of the conference. I don't know if it was something I ate or a bug but I missed the last morning of meetings because I was sick.

I had planned to spend the weekend with Aunt Min and Uncle Fred who lived in the Bronx. Aunt Madge drove from New Jersey and was to drive me home on Sunday. After spending the morning in bed I felt better. Aunt Min and Aunt Madge picked me up at the hotel and took me to Radio City Music Hall to see the Rockettes. We finished the day at their home. We had a great time.

Miss Helen Elliott taught us English in our Junior year which was a treat since she normally taught Academic English. We read Shakespeare's Romeo and Juliet, and Julius Caesar aloud in class. We also did more creative writing. Her classes made me wish I had taken Academic English.

In my senior year I was on the yearbook art staff. All graphics were hand drawn. I liked working with Norma Griffin, Curtis Singleton, and two other young men. Curtis and I were in art classes together. Though our skin color was different we were friends. I hoped to see him at our class's Fiftieth reunion but he had died.

When I was a Freshman I knew who Bill Cox was but, even though we were both in art classes, our paths never crossed. The first time I noticed him was when he was walking down the stairs with another Freshman girl. They made a striking couple. I never dreamed someday I would date him, let alone marry him!

I went out for girls' basketball in my Sophomore year but soon realized I wasn't an asset to the team. I confess, I was relieved when I strained my sacroiliac and couldn't play. Being scorekeeper was more to my liking!

I learned how to knit in high school. My friend, Alberta Lichtman, taught me. She knit differently than I learned when I was younger and it worked better for me. Bertie helped me knit socks for Bill. When I asked him what color he'd like, he said anything but black or navy blue. He wanted a break from Navy issue. He suggested green. I chose Kelly green wool. The socks fit but Bill's feet turned bright green.

Rising to the challenge I tried patterned argyle socks. This time a nice warm brown with vibrant fall colors. The first sock was fun and turned out well. The second did also but I had lost interest when the first one was completed. Later I heard it's good to do both at the same time but I have no desire to knit more socks.

Bertie was my first Jewish friend and she was the first of our group to marry after graduation. Her fiancé was Methodist so they were married in the living room of their new home by a rabbi and a Methodist minister.

Our crowd was a varied lot. One was Quaker, one was Jewish, the rest attended Christian churches. I remember a sleepover at Sydney's home when we sat around on the floor and talked about our beliefs. It was interesting and we remained friends even though our beliefs differed. Too bad it doesn't happen more often.

I attended a Quaker meeting with Scotty. We sat on wooden benches with each row slightly higher than the one in front. We sat quietly and every so often someone stood and spoke. When we lived in Narberth, there was a very old Friends Meeting House at the end of our street. Their cemetery had wonderful old grave stones. I loved to read the inscriptions. I was never in the meeting house but I did peek in the windows.

A friend left school in our Junior year because she was

pregnant. She and her husband had a marriage beyond the fifty-year mark and produced a fine batch of kids.

"He who is without sin among you,
let him throw a stone at her first."
(Jesus in John 8:7)

The only time I set out to break the rules was in my Senior year. I was scheduled for art class and wanted to work on the yearbook in the library. One of my friends was in Office Practice so she called me out of art class to go to the library. Soon after I arrived in the library the librarian and the art teacher figured out what we had done. A trust had been broken. They didn't mete out punishment except that which we heaped on ourselves. Years later I realized all sins, even those which seem insignificant to us, are ultimately against God.

"...you have sinned against the LORD;
and be sure your sin will find you out."
(Numbers 32:23)

The Class of 1950 was unique since we were at the halfway point of the 20th century. We participated in a time capsule placed behind a wall in the high school auditorium. It was opened in 2000 at our 50th class reunion. A variety of items were included, among them a copy of *The Hub* and a cassette recording of student messages.

Bill was overseas so I chose not to attend my Junior and Senior proms. I helped decorate the gymnasium but had no desire to go. He kept insisting I date so I gave in and accepted an invitation to the Senior dance.

GHS Senior classes traditionally went to Washington D.C. When Bill's class went in 1947, white students were housed in one hotel and colored students in another. None of the students thought it was right but that's how it was in Washington. When our class went in 1950 we didn't stay in a hotel. We did all the usual tours during the day but spent nights on a Chesapeake Bay cruise ship, together.

We left by train from Glassboro dressed in our Sunday best. Girls wore dresses or skirts, and guys wore suits and ties.

We were on the cruise ship overnight and I loved the motion of the ship, feeling the salt spray and smelling the sea breeze. I wakened early to go on deck and watch the sunrise, knowing Bill was on the other side of the ocean. Some were unable to enjoy breakfast because they were seasick. I found it delicious.

We visited Jamestown and Williamsburg, Virginia as well as D.C. We climbed the Washington Monument, visited the Lincoln Memorial, the Capitol, and the U. S. Mint. We toured the Smithsonian Institute, saw The Spirit of Saint Louis, and lots of natural history exhibits. A highlight for me was the changing of the guard at the Tomb of the Unknown in Arlington Cemetery.

The Sunday before graduation was Baccalaureate, a non-denominational religious service held in the school auditorium. These services were still held when our kids graduated, in fact Bill spoke at Matthew's. Some schools still have them but they have become less popular and are usually in churches.

The night before Graduation was Class Night. We wore gowns and the young men wore suits and ties. We sat on the stage in view of invited family and friends. My parents, grandparents and brother were in the audience, as were Bill's parents and sister. The program was extensive but my predominant memory is Anthony playing Clair de Lune. I don't know if we didn't have a printed schedule of events or whether I just hadn't seen one, but when he started to play it completely overwhelmed me. I missed Bill and this was our special song. I didn't just weep, I sobbed. I have no idea what my family or others thought and was too embarrassed to ask. No one mentioned it so maybe they didn't notice. There were class night parties but I didn't participate.

I graduated with honors, sixth or seventh in my class of one hundred thirty-seven. Bill sent flowers with a note congratulating me. I suspect his mother sent them for him.

Bill and I attended one of my early reunions. When we lived in southwest Virginia it wasn't possible to make the trip. The 50th was well planned but we missed some of the festivities, including the opening of the time capsule. We hadn't seen the schedule so the former editor of The Hub wasn't on hand when they called her name. I know where she was. She was buying a pair of shoes!

We attended several of Bill's reunions. One was held at The White Sparrow Inn. Rich and Margaret Iles, Earl and Myrtle Gant, and Bill and I sat together. We didn't need alcohol to loosen up. We laughed more than any other table. Another was in Cape May where we took a walk on the boardwalk with Earl and Myrtle.

There are a handful of my former classmates who get together now and then. It's been several years since I've lunched with them. Our numbers are dwindling.

"The afternoon knows what the morning never suspected."
(Robert Frost)

COX AND ZIEGLER
ENGLISH, GERMAN AND UNKNOWN MATERIALS

So far I've talked *about* my Bill, but it's time to introduce his section of our family tree. A tree is an interesting structure with a complex root system. The roots may cover a vast amount of territory or they may stay contained in a limited area. This is also true of a family tree.

Let's first look at the Cox roots. There's not a lot of information on them but I hope to unearth more as we dig into the past.

Cheyney Cox is the earliest Cox ancestor I've found. He was born about 1820 in Chester, Pennsylvania and was a ship joiner. He married a young lady from England named Anna Speakman. They had two children, William Franklin and Albert. William was my Bill's great-grandfather.

William married Clara Elmira Parker, whose father, John, was born in England. William and Clara lived in Delaware and brought Harry Parker Cox Sr. into the world. He was my Bill's grandfather.

Harry married Ella May Morrow who was born in Philadelphia to James Edward Morrow and Annie F. Long. James was a machinist and his father was a shuttle maker from Ireland. His mother and her parents were Pennsylvanians.

Dad and Mom Cox agreed Harry Parker Cox Sr., Granddaddy Cox, was a rigid man. Ella, Grandmother Cox, possessed a sweet temperament. They produced Harry Parker Cox Jr. and my father-in-law William Franklin Cox II.

Harry Jr. married Marie. They had two daughters, terminating the continuation of the Cox name on that branch of the tree. William married Frances Georgianna Duval, producing William Franklin Cox III (my Bill) and Barbara Kay Cox.

When Clara died, leaving Harry Sr. to his own devices, he remarried quickly. The second Mrs. Cox, another Marie, was unlike Clara. While Clara was willing to do without for herself and careful with finances, Marie was eager to use whatever was available. This produced strained relations within the family since Uncle Harry and Aunt Marie condoned the marriage and Mom and Dad Cox did not.

Harry Sr. died of a heart attack. The story goes that he thought he had indigestion and drank a 7up. He belched once and was gone. Marie's nephew helped her dispose of everything of value, including handmade carpentry tools left from Cheyney Cox's ship joiner days.

Are you wondering what a ship joiner is? The terms ship fitter and ship joiner refer to someone who joins together two pieces of wood or metal. These craftsmen ran the gamut from heavy construction to fine finishing. My Bill said ship joiners took great pride in their decorative woodworking in the cabin of the captain's launch.

Back to Cheyney's woodworking tools. They had been stored in the tool chest he kept on the job site. Evidently Harry's widow, Marie, didn't realize the value of the chest, or maybe it was too difficult to move. The wooden mosaic interior is beautifully crafted with drawers for hardware and racks for small tools. If Dad Cox hadn't left it to Bill in his will, we wouldn't have it today. Another heirloom is a secretary desk crafted by Cheyney. His craftsmanship can be seen in his attention to detail. The back of the desk is finished as carefully as the front.

My husband's maternal great-grandparents were George Ziegler born in Germany, and Franziska Sitter born in Bavaria. They immigrated in 1882 and were married in 1883. They had two children, Catherine and John. John married Pearl Hendricks McNeill and their union produced two children: Dorothy and Charles. Mom Cox was very fond of her Uncle John.

Great-grandmother Franziska was known as Frances here in the states. She was a loving woman and had a significant impact on my Bill's early life since she cared for him while his mother worked. Her primary language was German so Bill spoke and understood German as well as English when he was very young.

Frances Georgianna, Mom Cox, was born out-of-wedlock and Catherine refused to tell Mom her father's name. Mom remembered a man watching her when she played in the front yard of their Germantown home. When Catherine saw him, she rushed Frances into the house. Mom later tried to find out about her father but was told her birth records were destroyed in a fire in the Catholic Church near her home.

Wanting to find out who this mystery man was brought about my original interest in genealogy.

We do know that Catherine's disposition was unlike her brother's and she did not possess her mother's sweet nature. Her flights of temper were legendary. She was contrary and headstrong, priding herself on being a modern thinker and embracing radical ideas.

On December 5, 1911 she married Claude Ormond Duval and he gave his name to Frances. Claude was born in France. Bill said he heard that Claude was a civil engineer involved in building the Philadelphia subway system. However, U. S. Census reports don't corroborate that information and bring more questions.

The 1910 Census shows Claude, Catherine, and four-year-old Frances living in Philadelphia. It indicates Claude was born in France in 1873 to parents born in France and they emigrated to the states in 1874. Catherine's parents were born in Germany and married after they emigrated to the United States which fits nicely with what we know. But the Census also states Claude and Catherine were married for seven years, meaning they were married for three years before Frances was born. Claude's occupation is listed as a sailor in the U. S. Navy. My sister-in-law, Barbara, remembers hearing years ago that he was a sailor.

The 1920 Census shows Claude's birthplace as Massachusetts. It states his father was born in Massachusetts and his mother in Pennsylvania. Later his death certificate lists him and his parents all being born in Massachusetts. Could Catherine have been hiding from Frances' biological father? There are many puzzle pieces to be found and fitted into place.

In later years Claude and Catherine lived in Germantown. They had a little tobacco and ice cream store across the street from their apartment. The store did well, probably due to Catherine's business sense and Claude's cronies who hung out in the backroom, smoking cigars and playing cards.

Claude's calm acceptance of Catherine's tirades often triggered negative reactions. One time she hit Claude on the head with a cast iron frying pan. He laughed it off, making the situation worse.

<O><

I don't know where or how Bill and Frances met. However, on May 12, 1928 William Franklin Cox II and Frances Georgianna Duval went against her mother's wishes and eloped. They tied the knot at the Little Church around the Corner in New York City. After the ceremony they took up housekeeping two doors down the street from Bill's parents in Pitman, New Jersey.

On January 31, 1929 William Franklin Cox III was born. Frances was hit with a garage door during a wind storm causing Baby Cox to arrive early. He began life as Binky but soon became known as Billy. Later that year the Coxes lost their savings when the banks closed.

In 1930 they still lived in Pitman and Dad Cox worked as a clerk in the Philadelphia offices of the Pennsylvania Railroad. There are two stories about Dad's job with the railroad and both are possible. One is he lost his job due to downsizing. The other is he left the railroad of his own volition and Grandfather Cox never forgave him. Harry Sr. and Harry Jr. stayed with the railroad.

They lived with Catherine and Claude for a while, then in 1934 they moved to Torresdale. Bill started first grade in 1935 when they lived on Rockland Street and continued his schooling at William Levering Elementary when they moved to DuPont Street in Roxboro in 1937.

After DuPont Street, the Coxes moved to Mitchell Street in Roxboro. Bill fondly remembered an old stone house with deep windowsills but there was also an unhappy memory. He was playing outside with Bunny his English setter. She ran across the street and he called her. She obeyed and was hit by a car. He was devastated and blamed himself for her death.

The family then moved a few blocks to Peachin Street. That property had a rock garden and Bill enjoyed playing with little cars all around the rocks and plants. One of his favorite pastimes was making little figures and animals out of clay and then acting out different scenarios. He didn't need action figures or Legos, though I'm sure he would have enjoyed them. He also remembered pretending, sometimes with a cape like Superman.

The Coxes always had animals. Mom said Bill sometimes

arrived home with a dog, saying, "It followed me." He not only liked being with animals, but had an affinity for taking care of them. This no doubt led to his dream of becoming a veterinarian. Though the dream never came to fruition, he was actively involved with the lives of family and friends' pets and farm animals.

The Cox's second child, Barbara Kay, arrived on September 24, 1938. Bill was no longer an only child. He was intrigued with this new little sister and most of the time was happy to help entertain and care for her. When they were both in school Mom went back to work and Bill was in charge until their parents got home.

Bill remembered a time when Barbara made some comments to several boys on her way home from school. Her parting remarks were made as she skedaddled for home with the boys gaining on her.

She yelled to them as she ran to the house, "My big brother will beat you up!"

Fortunately for her, they saw he was bigger than they were when he met them at the front door.

Bill and Barbara had their skirmishes! He related a tale involving kitchen knives. Is that a common sibling occurrence? It also happened between Karen and Matthew. No siblings were cut on either occasion. We heard our story years later, too late to punish the offender(s). I'm sure no one was without fault.

One of Bill's favorite memories was living near a riding academy. He worked mucking stalls, as well as grooming and exercising the horses boarded there. One owner specifically asked for Bill to exercise his horse, Prince. Even hay fever didn't keep him away from the stables. A four-year stint in the Navy seemed to ease that problem.

In 1940 Dad drove a Freihofer's bread wagon in Philadelphia. His regular horse knew the bread route well. She waited while he went to a house, then started on to the next stop as soon as he stepped on the wagon. One wintery day he had a substitute horse that wasn't as well trained. It was pie day and the wagon was full. The horse spooked and took off down the street heading for the stable. Road conditions were icy and the wagon wheels caught in the trolley tracks. Unable to make a turn, the wagon turned over in a busy intersection. Pies were scattered everywhere.

When he was a lad, Bill pulled a wagon making deliveries for an A&P grocery store. He also used his wagon to deliver lemon meringue pies when the Methodist Church had their annual pie sale. Mom made the very best lemon meringue pies. I used her recipe for years.

One of Bill's passions was art. He was talented in drawing, sculpting and modeling, pastels, painting and wood carving. He took art classes in school and attended classes at the Philadelphia Museum of Art.

When he was an older teen he worked in a drug store. He was a soda jerk but also delivered orders and helped with other pharmacy tasks. The pharmacist liked him, and his work ethic, and offered to send him to college, then on to pharmacy school. He declined the offer because he wasn't interested in becoming a pharmacist. He also didn't want to stay with the pharmacist and his wife when his family moved to New Jersey, which was already in the planning stage. He never regretted the decision.

<O><

When the Coxes moved to Williamstown, New Jersey in the summer of 1945 they purchased a home on the Black Horse Pike and settled into rural life. Dad and Mom commuted daily to The Evening Bulletin in Philadelphia. Dad worked in accounting and Mom on the switchboard.

Claude had passed on and they tried to get Catherine, Nanny, to come and visit, especially at holidays. Even when Mom convinced her, she immediately made excuses to go back home. Mom was devastated and Dad was frustrated.

Nanny could be quite charming. Her neighbors thought she was great and wondered why her family didn't pay her more attention. They didn't realize how she acted with her family.

When Bill was home on leave, we all visited her ice cream shop. She gave us huge hand-dipped ice cream cones. She carried Breyers ice cream and, because of her excellent sales, she had all the latest flavors. She was gracious to me on the few occasions I was around her. I've wondered if Nanny treated me well because she knew Mom wasn't sold on this intruder who was stealing her son's heart.

Mom Cox had a strong personality, at least on the surface. She had been hurt by her mother so it's hard for me to put myself in her shoes. Also, I was rather passive which may have irritated her.

Bill was president of his Freshman and Sophomore classes at Roxboro and was elected to the same position for his Junior and Senior years at Glassboro. He was an Academic student and took all the art courses he could fit into his schedule. He also enjoyed history and that broadened to include Bible history after his conversion.

Mrs. Lutz was his senior English teacher. She was the principal's wife and a tough instructor. She had an aristocratic carriage but students in her classes say she was approachable and understanding.

Bill unintentionally put this to the test. He delayed writing a book report because he hadn't finished reading the book. To expedite the project, he wrote his report from the back flap of the book jacket.

"Mr. Cox," she said. "Your book report was quite interesting. However, I suggest in the future you read the entire book and not just the book jacket." After that he read the book.

He excelled at football and was a first-string varsity lineman at both high schools. He played right guard in his senior year and made all-state. He completely committed himself to football and everything he did. His coach told him, "The player who hits first and hardest is hurt least." He followed his coach's advice but still sustained injuries. Being kicked in the coccyx led to back problems that plagued him the rest of his life.

Because she didn't want to see him injured, Mom Cox didn't attend his games. When she finally relented and attended a home game he took a hard hit. The doctor encouraged him to lie still for a few minutes. Blood from his broken nose pooled in his eyes so when he stood up blood poured over his face. She never attended another game.

The 1947 yearbook shows how Bill was viewed by his classmates. They voted him most handsome, most versatile, best personality, most ambitious, as well as most popular. He was president of the hall patrol and judge of the student court.

During the summer of 1946, Bill worked with his dad at the Philadelphia Navy Yard. He joined the Navy Reserves while in school. World War II was over but the Korean War, called a conflict by some, was in full force. Wanting to serve his country, he looked forward to active duty after graduation. While waiting to be called up, he worked for Kimble Glass Company as a quality control inspector.

Bill was also chosen by his classmates as most likely to succeed. I believe they chose well. He may not have met the world's standards of fame and fortune but he was a good husband and father, an exceptional school teacher, a caring pastor/teacher, an inciteful pastor to missionaries, a mentor for men ... and the list goes on.

Well done, good and faithful servant."
(Matthew 25:2)

BILL MEETS PAT
THREADS BEGIN TO TWINE

Bill Cox and his dad were active in Boy Scouts of America when they lived in Philadelphia and continued that involvement with the Williamstown troop in New Jersey. My dad served Gloucester County as the Boys Scout's neighborhood commissioner. This brought our families together.

I wasn't a social butterfly so when my dad asked if I was going to the Sophomore Hop I told him I hadn't been asked, and didn't know anyone I could ask. He said he knew someone.

"Who?" I asked.

"Bill Cox," he replied.

"Bill Cox! He'd never go with me. He doesn't even know me!" I could hardly contain my laughter.

It seems on a recent camping trip my dad had shown Bill my photo and he had admired it. What else could he do!

My dad was sure he would go, so I told him to go ahead and ask. It turned out he already had plans. So much for that. I wasn't surprised.

Several weeks later, on a Sunday afternoon, we all piled into the family car for a ride. We sometimes went for rides so that wasn't unusual. What was unusual was that we were stopping by the Coxes' to drop off Boy Scout materials.

We pulled into their driveway, my dad got out of the car, and Bill and his dad came out to meet him. They talked for a while by the right front fender of the car. The windows were open so we could enjoy the warm spring breeze.

The scene is imprinted in my memory. Bill's left hand rested against the right front window frame. I was fascinated by his hands. They looked masculine and strong but somehow gentle. Of course, I also liked the way his hair sort of fell over the side of his forehead, and how his eyes crinkled up when he smiled, and ... well, you get the picture! His good looks did not escape me! Nor did his voice and considerate manners. He had my attention, though I doubt he was looking for it.

We were all introduced but there was absolutely nothing in our first meeting that foretold what was ahead for us. I admit I thought of him a few times but figured he was out of my league.

Our next meeting was quite a shock to me, and maybe even to him. We received a call or note from his parents. He was going on active duty in the U. S. Navy. His parents were giving him a surprise going-away party at their home and wanted me to come. I wanted to attend but my social life up to this point was just about non-existent and I was nervous. I hesitantly accepted, wondering if I'd know anyone.

On the evening of the party my dad drove me to their house and went in with me. He chatted with Mr. & Mrs. Cox for a few minutes before leaving. The Coxes said Billy would drive me home. Really?

Just as I feared, the living room was filled with guys and gals from the classes of '47 & '48. Then I saw Rosemarie, we were in the same gym class, and she took me under her wing. Bill's sister, Barbara, also put me at ease.

I don't know what I expected as I hadn't been to a party with boys since eighth grade. They talked, I listened. We played post office. I felt overwhelmed. I'd never kissed a boy, other than family, except for that ten-year-old that kissed me behind the McCrackens' garage. This was different!

I was included in the game, though my inexperience must have been obvious. Now that I think of it, that was our first kiss. I didn't hear bells ringing or see rockets blasting but it was very nice.

Even though I felt out of place, I had a good time. Bill's buddies were friendly, and his parents and Barbara were great. We got to know each other as he drove me home. Much to my surprise he asked if I'd like to go to the movies with him. I wonder if I sounded as excited as I felt.

The next week went by slowly as my anticipation grew. This was my first real date and I had no experience with dating. What should I wear? What should I say? Would he hold my hand? Would he kiss me good night? This dating business was scary!

Until Bill drove into our driveway I wasn't sure he would show up. After chatting with my dad and mom we were off to Pitman to the movies. He parked on a street where there was a little hill, making it easier to push/start the car if necessary. That wasn't uncommon back in the day.

I don't remember what movie we saw but I remember how he laughed at the cartoons. He laughed so hard that people turned around to see who was laughing. He always enjoyed cartoons!

After the movie we went to a diner in Williamstown. Again, I didn't know what to order nor did I know what he could afford. When he asked what I wanted, I asked him to suggest something. He said he was going to have a hamburger and a large strawberry milkshake. That sounded good, so I said, "I'll have the same thing." The hamburger was great. The milkshake was delicious but more than I could handle. I should have ordered a smaller shake and asked for chocolate.

On the way home he said he'd like to go out again before he left for boot camp. I was thrilled. He got me home within the time frame set by my dad, walked me to the door, and said good night.

Are you wondering if he kissed me goodnight? No, he did not. Did he put his arm around me in the movie? No. Did he hold my hand? No. Was I disappointed? Yes, I probably was. However, now I know he was the best kind of date and the one I want for my grandchildren. Hopefully, they still exist.

One week went by, then two. He didn't call. I heard he was still home and figured he'd changed his mind about wanting to see me.

Finally, I received a letter from him from boot camp. He wrote that he was sorry he hadn't been able to take me out again but he didn't have money for a date and had been too embarrassed to tell me. He wanted me to write to him and send him a picture, of me! His request set in motion a correspondence that lasted for four years and led to a marriage lasting nearly 55 years.

More immediately it set in motion a quest for the right picture. I armed my brother with my Brownie camera and had him take photos of me with Rusty, my Irish setter. I knew Bill liked dogs.

No professional camera shoot could have been better planned. Since cameras weren't digital we had to wait until the photos were developed before we could pick the best one. Bill carried it in his wallet for a long time. Then he replaced it with his all-time favorite shot of me in jeans, a white shirt, and a peaked cap. It was taken out along Cape Cod. He even carried it after we were married so it was about worn out.

We soon wrote to each other every day. When he was out to sea the letters arrived in bunches, both at home and on shipboard. We both felt we got to know each other better through letters than if we'd dated. Those letters contained four years of our lives which included personal problems and our dreams for the future.

When he was discharged we burned our letters. The ones I had written to him had been stored in the attic at his home and he found them spilled on the attic floor. I wish we hadn't destroyed them. It would bless me to reread the ones he wrote to me, even share some of them. I did save the first and last letters he wrote. A word of wisdom, don't be too quick to clear away the things of the past. Today's clutter could be tomorrow's treasure.

I thought it would be exciting to be married to my sailor, live on base, get to see him off on voyages, and greet him when he came home. Bill didn't agree. He had seen too many marriages break up because of long separations. He could have enjoyed staying in the Navy for a career but he wanted us to marry so it wasn't an option.

When I think of those long separations, I know Bill made a wise decision. As for his being unfaithful, that was never a concern. He was honorable and trustworthy. Even before he chose to become a follower of Christ, he was a man of high moral character.

When we first met, Bill was living in a way he believed to be right. When he later learned the truth of the Word, he aligned himself with it.

> *"But as many as received him,*
> *to them he gave power to become the sons of God,*
> *even to them that believe on his name."*
> (John 1:12)

NAVY BLUES AND DRESS WHITES

After serving a year in the reserves, Bill was inducted into the Navy in 1948. He and other recruits traveled from Philadelphia to the Great Lakes Naval Station by train. They arrived at two in the morning, were directed to a barracks and told to get some sleep. They climbed into their bunks fully clothed.

At five-thirty a sailor ran a nightstick around the inside of a metal GI can, turned on the lights, and shouted, "Rise and shine!" Bill jumped out of the top bunk and landed on his feet. In Bill's words, "They fed us, took our clothes, and shot us with needles." They spent hours naked, being examined by medical personnel, some fully dressed WAVES.

During a routine exam they found Bill had an enlarged heart, so he was put into a holding group. He received his Navy-issue clothing but wasn't told why he was pulled from his original group. While waiting for further instructions, he was assigned to work in the butcher shop. He soon realized butchering was not going to be his life work since the smell of fresh meat made him nauseous.

The powers-that-be finally decided Bill's heart was enlarged due to playing football. He got his first military haircut and had a tooth pulled. When they took his photo in uniform he didn't smile because of the missing tooth.

His original Company was well on its way through training, so he was transferred to a different one. Due to time in the Navy Reserves, and his leadership ability, he was made RPOC (Recruit Petty Officer Chief). Their Company regularly received the rooster flag for excellent performance. He was beginning to enjoy Navy life. He excelled when tested for swimming and did well in classes on military law, Navy history, and standards of conduct.

He wrote me about cleaning the barracks for inspection. They holystoned the decks, scraped dirt from between the floorboards, and had a white glove inspection. My mother was nervous about his visiting on leave. He assured her he wouldn't wear white gloves.

> *Holystone: A pumice stone for cleaning a wooden deck. The name derives from a sailor stating that "anything that would cause a seasoned sailor to bend his knees, and curse the name of his maker must surely be holy."*

After two months of boot camp he was assigned to a Class-A Radar School.

His first ship was the USS J. C. Owens, DD 776, out of Norfolk. Norfolk is the home of the legendary sign, "Dogs and sailors keep off the grass."

The Combat Information Center (CIC) was Bill's work station. He sat at a radar scope watching for vessels, planes, and landforms. Sonar equipment was also located in CIC. You've probably seen the scope and heard the sonar ping in movies.

The Radarman operated and maintained radar and electronic warfare equipment. They were also specially trained in emergency repair procedures. The Radarman rate was RD during Bill's time in the Navy but was later changed to Operations Specialist (OS). These men play an important role with search and rescue teams involving man overboard and directing helicopters to downed pilots at sea.

The Owens operated along the Atlantic coast when Bill was onboard. In 1949 they were in Panama where Bill saw an abundance of tropical vegetation and mosquitoes. They also put into Guantanamo Bay Naval Base (GITMO) in Cuba.

Not only did the Owens visit the tropics, she also operated in the North Atlantic where storms provided frightening and memorable experiences.

He served on the Owens until she was de-commissioned, April 1950, and was transferred to the USS Myles C. Fox DDR 829. He was underway to the Mediterranean in May.

The Owens was re-commissioned within five months and moved to the Pacific fleet. She ran blockade patrols along the Korean coast, engaging enemy shore batteries. She silenced several but sustained six direct hits. She then patrolled those coastal waters on peacekeeping duty until May 1954.

Bill served during the Korean War but didn't see action because he was on the Fox. If he had been on the Owens it might have been different. Am I reading too much into this by seeing God's hand at work again?

The Fox's operations with the 6th Fleet included simulated attack problems with submarines as well as other fleet exercises. Her first port-of-call was Lisbon, Portugal where Bill had breakfast at a local restaurant. The waiter assumed they all wanted steak and eggs. Bill had never eaten steak and eggs for breakfast but decided he'd try it. He was not impressed.

They passed through the Straits of Gibraltar and stopped at Palmas Bay, Sardinia, off the west coast of Italy. They made port in Sicily, the largest island in the Mediterranean. In Naples he visited Pompeii. I've read the smell of volcanic Sulphur is pronounced but the only odor Bill mentioned was the pleasant scent of fennel when they approached Italian ports.

One of my favorite gifts is a hand-carved cameo from Italy. I've always wanted to have it set in a ring. Bill watched them carve the cameos and was impressed by the workmanship. It was a family shop where even the children had jobs.

After Naples, they made their way to Golfe Juan, France, near the principality of Monaco, as well as Cannes, Nice, and Grasse. In Cannes he visited a perfume shop where he bought gifts. He sent me a scented advertising card from the perfume shop and a photo of the salesgirl with what appeared to be her name and phone number on the back. A tease on his part? It worked.

He also shopped for shipmates. In every port there were men who stayed on board to play poker. They gave Bill their wives' or girlfriends' sizes, along with money to purchase gifts. Did the recipients know who bought their gifts?

Another port-of-call was Istanbul, Turkey, at the entrance to the Black Sea. Bill was impressed with The Blue Mosque. It was built in the early 1600s and named for the blue tiles adorning the interior walls. While in Istanbul he went to an open-air bazaar. He enjoyed the handcrafts but was not impressed with the music and had no desire to spend more time there.

When they were underway from Istanbul they noticed a foul odor in the sleeping compartments. The source was leather goods purchased at the bazaar. Turks in the region often used dung to cure leather. A lot of treasures were pitched overboard.

Putting into port on the Greek coast they met a group of Eastern Orthodox monks traveling over the mountains to their monastery on the Mount Athos peninsula. The weather was inclement, so the Fox took them by sea. An interesting note is that the entire peninsula is considered a monastery and all females, human or animal, are banned; except for cats.

They made port in Salonika, Greece, on the Aegean Sea. Salonika was formerly known as Thessalonica, one of the cities the apostle Paul visited during his second missionary journey. After several more stops in Greece and Turkey it was time to head back to Newport, Rhode Island. They cleared Gibraltar October 1, 1950.

On Bill's final Med cruise they anchored in Nice, Marseilles, and Cannes in France; Trieste, Venice, Leghorn, and La Spezia in Italy. They docked at Soudha Bay, Crete and cleared Gibraltar on October 4, 1951. After landing in Newport, Rhode Island they went to the Boston Navy yard where the ship remained until February 1952. Bill put in for discharge before another cruise.

Bill enjoyed his work. On several occasions he directed the ship into harbor, even to dock. The ship's captain placed his faith in Bill and turned the con (control) over to him. Bill gave orders from the CIC where he could not physically see where he was going and relied completely on the radar screen. One captain officially commended him for bringing the ship "snug up" to a buoy in a New England bay.

During one cruise, when the cold war was heating up, they were operating in the eastern Mediterranean near the Suez Canal. When low flying Russian MIGs checked them out they could see the pilots' faces clearly. No shots were fired but they were on high alert.

A scary incident took place in Turkey or Greece. Bill and a shipmate were assigned to pick up and deliver U.S. Mail, including guard mail handcuffed to his wrist. He was given a gun but it wasn't loaded because of international law. The communist line wasn't well marked and the directions difficult to follow so they ended up in communist territory. They didn't realize this until they came to a checkpoint going the wrong way. It turned out alright but they experienced quite an adrenaline rush!

If Bill had liberty stateside and was unable to come home he sometimes spent the night at the YMCA because it was safe and inexpensive. A fellow shipmate, John, shared a room with him. They didn't work in the same area aboard ship. John was in the black gang, or engine room, and Bill was in CIC. Their tastes in entertainment were also different. Bill enjoyed sightseeing in the daytime and slept in the room at night. John slept all day and went out drinking at night. When John drank too much, he sometimes ran into trouble. He had a temper and occasionally was involved in fights. When he was picked up by the shore patrol he always asked for Bill to get him back to the ship. When the

Myles C. Fox website was formed several years ago, John called Bill from California. It was an odd friendship but long lasting.

Bill liked being a Radarman but a couple of years into his enlistment he considered transferring to UDT (Underwater Demolition Team). He was a superb underwater swimmer. He knew it was dangerous duty and was excited about the possibility until he realized he had to ship over for another four years. By then our relationship was becoming serious so he decided against the change.

When it came time for discharge, he had a month of accumulated leave. He had been at sea more than in port. When the ship was stateside he was sometimes able to get home for a weekend. Money was tight so he hitchhiked or caught a ride with someone. When he met Ray Pental, who had a car and lived in Trenton, he came home more often.

Over his service time, Bill's Navy pay averaged about $100 a month, after taxes. He had a portion of his check sent home to put into savings, leaving him with little spending money. He counted on his savings as a nest egg for the future but it wasn't there when he came home.

When we realized we had a future together he suggested we save dimes. We put them into a big glass jug and when we married we had over $200 in dimes. They helped with our first car purchase, along with trading in both our vehicles.

In his letters from overseas he often said he hoped to revisit his ports-of-call with me. That was never financially feasible and as the years went by he lost interest in travel, preferring to stay at home.

Bill was a 2nd Class Petty Officer when he was discharged. The only thing keeping him from 1st Class was the waiting time between ranks. I gained a good husband—the Navy lost a fine man.

Though Bill had been discharged for over fifty years when he died, this saying still held true: "Once a tin can sailor, always a tin can sailor." The camaraderie among shipmates is evident even when they served at different times.

There used to be a saying, *Join the Navy and see the world.* Bill saw parts of the world he wouldn't have seen if not for the Navy. He enjoyed seeing places of interest in foreign ports. Along with other attractions, he visited the leaning tower of Pisa, the Parthenon, every zoo he could find, and as many natural wonders as he could afford.

After he became a Christian he regretted being so close to Ephesus and Thessalonica without seeing them and pointed this out in his teaching.

"God is able to take your life with all of the heartache,
all of the pain, all of the regret, all of the missed opportunities,
and use you for His glory."
(Chuck Swindoll)

MY TESTIMONY
WASHED WHITER THAN SNOW

From birth to twelve I attended Bala Cynwyd Methodist Church with my family. Both my mom and dad were saved as young people under the ministry of Pastor Grey. They were active in the church until Rev. D replaced Pastor Grey. Then my dad backed off from serving in official capacities. He didn't agree with Rev. D's focus on money. The church had some very wealthy members and he apparently tended them well but he paid little or no attention to the rest of us.

We didn't go to church in the summer because the choir didn't sing then. We didn't read the Bible regularly at home nor did we pray together except when we said grace before meals. Weezie repeated memorized prayers with us at bedtime. Their walk with the Lord became more important after we moved to New Jersey.

When I was eleven, I attended membership classes taught by Rev. D and accepted into membership. I never heard about salvation. Could I have missed that?

When we moved to Hardingville, I was accepted into membership in Siloam Bible Protestant Church via a letter transferring my membership. In retrospect, it seems they let a goat slip into the sheep fold. After hearing our new pastor talk about salvation in his messages, this goat began wondering, "What's salvation?"

One evening, Pastor Miller was sitting in our living room and I asked, "How does someone get saved?" He said, "Just believe."

Believe what? I believed in God. I believed Jesus is God's Son and He died on the cross and was resurrected from the dead. I even believed there was a Holy Spirit but had no idea how He figured into the equation. Was that all there was to it? There had to be more. I wrestled with these questions for the next three years.

When I was fifteen I attended a Bible Protestant Youth Conference at Tri-State, our denomination's conference center and camp near Port Jervis in the mountains of northern New Jersey.

There were three teens in our little church and I was the only one who went to the conference. Since I was alone, a youth group from our sister church in Glassboro took me under its wing. They were all older than me but we attended the same high school. They included me in group activities and we ate meals together. A nice young man from another group joined me on our walks along the river. We wrote to each other for a time. However, this was the same summer I met Bill so my letters to Doug dwindled as the ones to Bill became more numerous.

One message I heard caught my attention. It concerned Lazarus being raised from the dead. I don't remember the point of the message being salvation but God used it to that purpose for me, proving we don't always know how God will use what we say.

One night after returning home, I was lying in bed mulling over salvation. I realized I had an intellectual knowledge of Jesus Christ but not a relationship with Him. I knew who God was, knew Jesus was His Son and He died on the cross. However, I'd never received the gift of salvation He offered me. How was I to receive it?

That night, right in my bed, I accepted His wonderful gift! I confessed I was a sinner, repented of my sins and asked Him to cleanse me. I asked Him to save me! There were no fireworks, no tears, just relief. I finally understood the answer to the question, "How can I be saved?"

When I visit my nephew and his family, who now live in our old family home, I enjoy visiting their upstairs bathroom. Linda sometimes cuts my hair there. It used to be my bedroom and that's where I made the most important decision of my life.

I'd like to say I was always the young woman God wanted me to be but that would be a lie. I kicked over the traces a few years later. I even wondered for a time whether I was really saved that summer when I was fifteen. I struggled with the answer more times than you might imagine. I now believe I was truly saved and belonged to Christ. I was, however, a wayward sheep who often caused Him grief. Most people saw me as a good little church girl.

For a while that was true but there were several years when my life didn't line up with anyone's interpretation of what a Christian's life should look like. I'd also missed an important point. I'd not made Him Lord of my life. That came years later.

When I wondered if I was saved, a pastor friend told me he believed I was saved at fifteen because God never stopped convicting me of my sin. I knew what I was doing was wrong. He kept me safe through situations that could have been devastating. He never gave up on me.

One of God's attributes is long-suffering. That is evidenced in my life. The pieces of my crazy quilt range from beautiful to ugly. I don't want to ignore the offensive pieces because they serve as a reminder of what might have been if not for God's intervention.

Though God forgave me for what I did during those times of disobedience and rebellion, it took a while for me to forgive myself.

STAINED-GLASS WINDOWS

Bala Cynwyd Methodist Church was a beautiful edifice. It was built of gray stone in a Gothic style with gorgeous stained-glass windows. The interior featured a high vaulted ceiling with pointed arched windows, and wood and stone details. The acoustics were excellent.

I remember the Sunday school room had big colorful pictures on the walls: Jesus the shepherd, Jesus with children, and Jesus carrying the lost sheep. I learned that God and Jesus loved me. I heard Jesus was born in Bethlehem. I was taught about His miracles. I learned He died on the cross, came alive again, and went back to Heaven to be with God. I believed that from when I was very young. Did I miss the part about Him wanting to be my Savior?

We heard stories from the Bible and sang *Jesus Loves Me*, *Jesus Loves the Little Children* and *Savior Like a Shepherd Lead Us*. One Easter we sang *Jesus Wants Me for a Sunbeam* while sitting on the stone steps at the front of the church. I felt very special with a gold lamé cloth atop my head.

Mrs. Fricke taught us little ones. Her daughter, my music teacher in school, was my Sunday School teacher when I was older. I never got to know the other girls in my Sunday school class. We lived in different towns and went to different schools.

I looked forward to Lent. When we attended church services we received a little gift and if we attended every Sunday, we chose either a Bible or a hard-backed book. I still have my illustrated book of hymns and stories.

We didn't have junior church services so we sat with our parents. I believe it's good for children to learn to sit quietly in church but they may also benefit from services directed to their level of understanding. Our children sat with us in church. We usually sat in the front row because there were fewer distractions.

Just a thought:

The church is not a beautiful edifice made of stone and wood. Nor is it a cozy clapboard building with a bell tower. We can certainly be blessed by our surroundings, be they stained glass windows, or hand-hewn benches. But remember, the true church is made up of people who belong to God through Jesus' death and resurrection, indwelt by the Spirit. It is, we are, the Bride of Christ. If you are a believer, you take the church with you wherever you go.

INTO THE WORKFORCE
RAYON AND GABARDINE

Graduating from high school meant finding a job. I planned to work near home and pay board to help with expenses. Most of my peers stayed close to home.

Becoming a secretary was my plan, but I considered other options. I thought about the art field. Uncle Sheldon was an editor at The Evening Bulletin in Philadelphia and arranged for me to meet with their art director. I took along a portfolio of my artwork. I'm embarrassed now when I think of the quality of my work, but he was kind and suggested I go to art school.

I also investigated becoming an airline stewardess. Though I was two pounds below the weight limit of 135, I was an inch and a half over the 5 ft. 6 in. height limit.

Back to my original choice, secretary. Some of us were offered positions through the school. My first interview was for an insurance office in Glassboro. The interview went well and I was offered the position. I declined when I learned the salary was $18 a week and the hours stretched over six days instead of five.

The second offer was working for the President of the Board of Education who managed the White House Vinegar plant. That was a five-day workweek and the pay was better so I accepted. The women I worked with were helpful and friendly, and Mr. Z was very nice. I didn't have a car, or a license, so my mother drove me to and from work.

I'd only been on the job for two weeks when I learned of a job opening with better pay and benefits, as well as a ride to work. I was hesitant to change jobs but talked with my parents. They said if I was going to make a change I should do it right away.

I applied for a position at Owens-Illinois Glass Company. The local factory produced metal and plastic bottle caps and closures.

I was interviewed and offered the job but there was a snag. I was only seventeen. I'd be working in an office but the office was in a factory building so I had to be eighteen. I don't know how they worked it out but I was hired. The pay was good, $.925 an hour for a 37 ½ hour work week plus excellent benefits. I also had a ride to work until I could afford a car.

I was required to give a blood sample. I'd never had blood drawn and was apprehensive. The plant nurse, Miss Z, was sympathetic and tried to relieve my anxiety. Dr. P was the plant doctor and did the honors, though not particularly well. If someone is going to stick you, opt for a nurse or good phlebotomist. Dr. P didn't find a vein so he fished around with the needle without withdrawing it. I stoically looked away from the carnage.

I thought I was doing well but Miss Z said, "Dr. P, she's had enough for today. Why don't we just get it later."

After the doctor left the office, Miss Z said, "You were getting so pale I thought you were going to pass out." I had an impressive bruise on the bend of my arm as a souvenir. They never tried for another blood sample and I worked there for nearly five years.

Now that I had a regular income, we looked for a car. My dad checked with the service station where we took our automotive work and they suggested a black 1941 Pontiac coupe. My dad test drove it and decided it was the right car for me. It was in good condition with a manual transmission, standard back then, and its white wall tires made it look a little sporty. I used the bonds I inherited from Aunt Hilda to make the down payment and the bank loaned me the rest.

Bill's encouraging me to date others wasn't setting well so I named my car Pagliacci. Our relationship sometimes reminded me of the aria *Laugh Clown Laugh*, sung by Pagliacci. Later vehicle names weren't nearly as melodramatic.

Next was learning to drive. Weezie took me on back roads and before long I was speeding along at 20 mph. I was sure I'd never go faster. We may forget people over the years but I still remember the officer at the DMV who checked out my driving skills. He was a man of few words but a formidable appearance and a big cigar. What relief I felt when I passed the test.

There was a dress code for women at Owens. We wore dresses, or skirts and blouses. Blouses were not to be sheer or otherwise revealing. We also wore nylons and closed shoes. On the factory floor, women could wear slacks. I don't know if there was a dress code for men, but most wore sport shirts with slacks, and managers wore suits with dress shirts and ties.

Six desks were grouped and Kas Ale's desk faced mine. She was a great mentor. Her husband had been in the Navy and he was in a local business with his dad.

I'd worked there a short time when Kas found she was pregnant. After little Charles was born she was a stay-at-home mom. I babysat for them a few times. He was the first baby I ever diapered. I don't think he noticed I was a novice. Kas and I remained friends over the years. We didn't talk about spiritual things when we first met but we did later. Bill and I visited her and her daughter, Kim, several times after Charles passed away. She went on to Heaven in June 2012.

Our Service Manager's personal stenographer was Josie, who was friends with another girl Bill was dating, Grace. We weren't going steady (the term back then for dating exclusively) but I didn't know the other girls in his life.

<O><

Many in the office smoked so it didn't take long for me to try. Kas told me it wasn't a good idea and the men in my department said the same thing. However, my best friend smoked, as did Bill and his family. I should have listened to Kas.

In my teens my dad said, "I'll make you a deal. If you don't smoke until you're twenty-one, I'll give you a $25 savings bond." I didn't earn the bond. When my mother worked at Owens, I smoked in her presence, but I never smoked in front of my dad, though he knew I smoked. Was my choice out of fear, or respect? The answer is respect. My only fear was fear of disappointing him, and I'd already done that.

I never inhaled well and my cigarettes spent a lot of time smoldering in the ashtray. That may be why it was easy to stop a few years later when I was pregnant. Little was said about the dangers of smoking back then but I didn't like seeing a pregnant woman with a cigarette dangling from her mouth.

Not only was the office a smoke-filled workplace, it was also a setting replete with profanity and coarse jokes. I'd heard swearing but rarely at home and never blasphemies. Though some of the men in our department swore, most were guarded around me. That changed when I began to swear and get involved in suggestive conversations. I lost their respect, and didn't deserve it.

There were several women in the office who didn't get involved in that kind of behavior. I respected them then and still do. I wish I had been more like them.

"Let the words of my mouth and the meditation of my heart
Be acceptable in Your sight,
O Lord, my strength and my Redeemer."
(Psalm 19:14)

<O><

My job as a clerk/stenographer included typing letters, taking shorthand dictation, typing from Dictaphone recordings, filing and other general office duties.

When Josie left to be married, I was promoted to her position. Mr. N expected competency and efficiency and I did my best to comply. He was fatherly toward me and often shielded me from inappropriate comments.

I worked for him for two years when he left for another position in the company. Then I had a new boss, Mr. G. He was different from Mr. N and more approachable. I only worked for him a short time before I left to be married.

You may have noticed I referred to my bosses as mister. My parents taught me I shouldn't call my elders by their first names. That's why we had so many aunts and uncles. When I began working I wasn't comfortable calling my bosses by their first names. It was even a while before I used first names with my coworkers. When I later went to college, students sometimes called professors by their first names. I didn't. It isn't just elders that are due respect, but others because of their position.

I learned to operate the Teletype machine and filled in for the regular operator. The Teletype was used extensively for intracompany communications. What we typed was transposed to a tape in coded form. When the tape was ready to be sent, it went through the transmitter making a ticking sound. I only read the code well enough to be efficient at sending. I liked working the teletype. It could get hectic but I liked working alone.

An area I enjoyed more than the teletype was the telephone

switchboard. I was backup for the regular operator. When I sat at the switchboard in Strawbridge and Clothier as a little girl I never expected to work on one! It was also a loner job but an interesting one. This tells something about me doesn't it!

Since our switchboard operator wasn't known for her pleasant disposition, my friendliness was an asset. I enjoyed contact with people, and the challenges presented. I searched for people and information. The job was part receptionist and part detective. It was also encouraging when people I'd never met thanked me for being helpful. Another perk was that I could read if the switchboard was quiet! It didn't happen often but it was nice when it did.

After being at Owens for a couple of years, I began filling in for the Plant Manager's secretary. By now Mr. W was retired and the new manager seemed more approachable. I was uncertain about working for the top man but he soon put me at ease. If his secretary had moved on I would have enjoyed being considered for the position. That wasn't going to happen though, wedding bells were tuning up.

<O><

Shortly after I began work at Owens, both Weezie and Big Bill were hired. My mother worked quality control in the Laboratory. The folks in the Lab were a close-knit group. Sadly, Weezie's feet felt the results of walking on metal and concrete floors, which led to her retiring from Owens. A big positive was that her hospitalization insurance was with her until she died many years later. Her next job was in a car dealership and she enjoyed getting first chance at good used cars. After several years, changes in management there precipitated her final retirement.

Big Bill worked in the Shipping Department at Owens, and that recalls an amusing story. When I was a little girl my dad whistled to get my attention, a distinct whistle. My job often took me out to the factory floors, laboratory, and shipping departments to deliver papers and get signatures. I went about my business and ignored the occasional comments and wolf whistles.

One day when Big Bill was working on the shipping dock he saw me walking to the shipping office and said to his coworkers, "See that girl over there? I bet she'll look over here if I whistle at her."

"Nah," they said, "She never looks when we whistle."

"Just watch," he said, and he whistled. I looked his way, smiled and waved. He pulled this off several times before they were on to him.

It was great working in the same facility with my parents, though we worked in different departments and didn't always work the same hours. I worked days and they worked rotating shifts. Sometimes Weezie and I even ate lunch together.

<O><

When my dad left Owens, he was hired as the Aura School custodian, responsible for cleaning and maintenance. When I saw how some teachers took better care of their rooms than others I was impressed. When I taught, we straightened up the room at the end of the day.

A new principal, Jack K, was hired and he and Big Bill became friends. One time Jack needed a substitute teacher and no one on the sub list was available so he asked Big Bill to substitute. He did so well he was asked to fill in several more times. His substituting ceased when someone realized he hadn't graduated from high school. The school board even agreed he had done well but he could no longer substitute.

When plans were being made to build a regional high school. Jack was to be the Principal. He asked Big Bill to go with him as custodian of the new school. My dad represented the administration in overseeing the building project. When the school was completed he knew all the details about the plumbing, the electrical wiring, and the heating system. He even knew what was in each wall making him a great trouble-shooter.

<O><

Owens-Illinois was known for having a company union. The factory workers belonged to the union but office workers did not. I felt the workers were treated fairly, both in the office and the factory. I'm sure there were instances when they weren't but that can happen anywhere, even with a union in place.

Some office workers decided we should belong to a union. I didn't want to belong to a union. I knew my dad had belonged to a union when he worked at the shipyard and even held an office, though he was not always pro-union. A vote was scheduled. It looked like the union was going to be defeated so a walkout was called and we were told not to come to work.

I wasn't keen on having someone tell me I couldn't go to work and decided I was going to cross the picket line and go to work anyway. When I mentioned that at home I was quickly told I was not to go. My dad had seen situations when things got out of control and people were hurt. Though I wanted to brave the picket line, I yielded to my father's wisdom. When we voted, the vote was against having a union.

Unions were often necessary to change the way workers were treated years ago, and that may sometimes be true today. However, too often the union officials care not a whit for the workers. The problems and solutions have little to do with what's best for them. It has more to do with greed, power, and money on both sides of the issues.

> *"Whatever you do, do your work heartily,*
> *as for the Lord rather than for men, ...*
> *It is the Lord Christ whom you serve."*
> (Galatians 3:23-24)

OUR QUILT TAKES SHAPE
FABRIC BLENDS

Bill came home on leave the first Christmas he was in the Navy. We had been writing for a while so I wanted to buy him a gift, but what? I asked my mother for help. She said the gift should be impersonal. I decided on quality handkerchiefs, two because the price reflected their quality. He gave me a red wool head scarf.

I believe it was the second Christmas that he gave me a pearl necklace. I still have it. It hasn't aged well because the pearls weren't produced by oysters. The last gift he purchased for me was a cultured pearl necklace. I treasure them both.

Bill loved giving and receiving gifts. I've never known anyone who enjoyed his birthday as much as he did. He started celebrating weeks before the big day arrived! He reveled in the anticipation of celebration, especially with kids and grandkids.

Karen and Matt seem to have Bill's ability to find the perfect gift. They are observant, paying attention to what people enjoy. Jenni is also adept at connecting gifts with individuals. I fall short.

Bill also chose flowers carefully. For a Christmas dance he gave me a corsage of bright red anthurium. It was unique and lasted a long time. He knew I liked talisman roses so that's what he purchased. When he realized I preferred living plants to cut flowers, he gave me plants. For years at Christmas time, Bill bought me a poinsettia; usually from Lowe's, where we spent a lot of time.

Here is a memory of flowers that Bill did not give me. It happened before he was discharged from the Navy. Nana and Poppop wanted to go to my cousin Eileen's wedding but didn't feel comfortable driving in the city. I didn't feel comfortable doing that either and asked Bill to drive us in my Poppop's '37 Chevy.

The wedding was in a Catholic church. I didn't understand most of it since it was in Latin, but the vows were in English. As

Bill and I stood side by side I repeated the vows in my head and I meant every word. I even thought about how a vow before God was not to be said lightly.

When Eileen tossed her bridal bouquet, I caught it! Since it came straight to me I suspect that may have been planned. Bill took it in stride. This may sound melodramatic but I took the incident very seriously. I came away feeling I had tied the knot even if it was one-sided. Catching the bouquet was icing on the wedding cake. What if we never married? I was convinced, then and now, I'd never be interested in another man.

MY FOOLISH YEARS

Bill was four years my senior and concerned he might be too old for me. During his early years in the Navy, he realized I wasn't dating anyone else and said I should. I wasn't interested in dating anyone else but I also didn't have suitors storming my door. Why did he suggest I date others? He told me he wanted me to be sure of my feelings. Did he also want to test his feelings? For a while I ignored his urging but I finally decided to date and keep him fully informed.

I rarely dated anyone more than once. Would you suggest a second date when conversations always seemed to get around to Bill? The only one I dated several times was ten years my senior, knew about Bill, and didn't care.

Some of my dates resulted from bar-hopping with Annie. This part of my life disturbs me even now. I knew my activities would grieve my parents and they certainly grieved the Lord.

I was living a double standard. I went along with others, but they were still my choices. I later wondered if I was really saved when I was carousing. (Webster says carousing means "making merry with liquor.") It seemed like fun at the time, but fun loses its luster when you know what you're doing is wrong.

I may have fooled others but God knew. He heard me play the piano and sing *You Are My Sunshine* in a resort tavern in Lake Hopatcong. Did He prompt the bartender to suggest I go back to my room? He saw me trying to find Annie and watched over me as I picked my way down an unlit path. He knew I felt the room spin when I sprawled fully clothed on the bed. He saw me pass out.

God was there one Saturday night when I sat on a bar stool in Camden, New Jersey and brashly quipped, "I may be three sheets to the wind tonight but I'll be teaching my Sunday school class tomorrow morning."

When I eventually asked God to forgive me, I know He did because He says He will!

"If we confess our sins,
He is faithful and just to forgive us our sins
and to cleanse us from all unrighteousness."
(I John 1:9)

However, I remarked to a friend, "I know God has forgiven me, but I can't forgive myself!"

He replied, "When you don't forgive yourself for something God has forgiven, you're claiming your standards are higher than God's standards."

Ouch! I knew my standards weren't higher than God's. Though it took a while, I forgave myself.

Coming through that period of my life unscathed was only because of God's mercy and grace! There were many situations that could have ended far differently than they did. I know God protected me from my foolishness. I can never be grateful enough for how He cared for me!

I haven't written these words to shock anyone. Instead, it's to show how God had His hand on me through that wayward time of my life. He protected me from harm. He kept me from dangers beyond my imagination. These sordid memories help me realize just how much God loves me! I no longer dwell on them and only recall them now so you can see how God worked in my life.

He wants to care for you the same way. We've all sinned. God knows every detail and stands ready with outstretched arms waiting for us to run to Him. I'm elated that He didn't give up on me! He won't give up on you either! I like the well-known John 3:16 but I especially like verse 17:

"For God sent not his Son into the world to condemn the world;
but that the world through him might be saved."

When Bill was honorably discharged from the Navy he wasn't

sure what he wanted to do. Mom Cox no longer worked at The Evening Bulletin and was working the switchboard for a Philadelphia employment agency. He met with one of the agents and was referred to Federal Electric Products. They were looking for an office manager. He applied and was hired to work in their office on Cherry Street. He also enrolled in evening business classes at Temple University.

It wasn't a large office but he oversaw two young unmarried women who provided drama, and several salesmen who supplied rivalry. He fielded telephone sales, oversaw the stockroom, and learned more than he wanted to know about interaction in the workplace. He didn't like sales, or working in an office, but he did his best.

Bill and I enjoyed being together and were drawing closer both emotionally and physically. Is it any wonder that I believe courting and short engagements are the best plan? The beginning of our relationship was like courting in that our fathers were involved. The latter part was not.

Sometimes I went to Philadelphia after work and met Bill for dinner. We liked eating at the Turin Grotto, an Italian restaurant, and the Cathay Tea Garden, a Chinese restaurant. One time he took me to a restaurant in a lovely old home in the city. It was fine dining and my second encounter with a finger bowl!

Getting to know one another through letters and infrequent visits was one thing. When Bill was home it was different. We spent more time together and the dynamic of our relationship was changing. We went to movie theaters, drive-in movies, dinners, dances, picnics, hikes and to the shore. We spent time with our families and a few times we went on double dates, but most of the time it was just the two of us.

When Owens-Illinois sponsored a costume dance, Bill suggested we go as French adagio dancers, probably influenced by watching Gene Kelly in *An American in Paris*. I came home from work the day of the dance and asked my dad to cut my hair in a poodle cut. That hair style was a fashion that went well with a dance scene from the movie. My dad didn't enjoy cutting hair but he did a great job!

Bill wore black pants, a black pullover jersey with a bandana at the neck and a beret. I wore a black skirt with a deep side slit and an off-shoulder white peasant blouse. We not only looked the part but danced the part. Exceptionally close dancing coupled with several drinks laid the groundwork for what we later regretted.

Virginity is a priceless gift that should be held gently and given only to your partner in marriage. Once it is given, there is no way to retrieve it. We had the original gift to give to each other but it was tarnished in the giving. The circumstances were not the sanctity of the marriage bed. When we realized what we had done Bill wanted to go to my dad and ask forgiveness. I was afraid and asked him not to. He wanted to do what was honorable, the right thing. I shouldn't have stopped him.

There is a paradox here. I was a professing believer, though a carnal and worldly one. Bill had head knowledge but no personal relationship with Christ. I won't even ask who was the better person. It's obvious, is it not?

I would like to say we never indulged again. Once the line is crossed it is difficult not to cross it again. Some think I am obsessed in my stand on unmarried couples refraining from snuggling and touching. That's because I know how it is. I believe our situation has been repeated far more often than most admit.

Today's world standards have loosened and it's socially acceptable to be free with each other's bodies. Society approves pre-marital sex and living together but that doesn't make it right. The world may change, but the Word of God does not change.

Years ago, Bill agreed I should share our story when I taught a teenaged girls' class on personal purity. I know we stand together though we are presently worlds apart.

I am forever grateful that Bill later accepted Jesus as his Lord and Savior, even though I was not a good example of a godly young woman. God had His hand on both of us!

"Don't sacrifice the permanent on the altar of the immediate."
(Dr. Bob Jones, Sr.)
No, that isn't Scripture but it sure is wisdom!

BILL MOVES TO CONNECTICUT

When Federal Electric sent Bill to Hartford, Connecticut for further training, he hunted a flat for us to rent. He found one near a park and not far from the business district. He rented it, moved in, and suggested I visit to see it. I stayed with friends.

I went by bus from Philadelphia and had a brief layover in New York City's Penn Station before boarding the train to Hartford. I'd never traveled alone before but suppressed my fear and focused on seeing Bill. I dressed carefully because I wanted to look good.

While waiting in Penn Station I noticed a stain on my skirt. My concern was noticed by a fellow traveler. He walked to a newspaper stand and came back with a small bottle of Renuzit. I removed the stain. When I offered to pay him for the Renuzit he said, "Just do something for someone else." Unexpected gifts of kindness have been around for a while.

The couple I stayed with were nice folks. Bill showed me our apartment and I was delighted. That probably had more to do with our impending marriage than it did with the accommodations. I would have been happy anywhere. My host and hostess had a family picnic for us before I left for home. It was a lovely weekend.

TYING THE KNOT
SATIN AND LACE

You've probably heard people say, "We should have eloped!" We were planning a quiet wedding and reception in our little country church. What could go wrong?

First, we had not planned to find termites in the timbers under the church floor. When Big Bill saw the riddled supports, he insisted we limit the guest list. We originally planned to invite more family and friends and open the invitation to all who attended our church. It was humbling to see neighbors standing outside to catch a glimpse of the wedding party. Though disappointing, it was a necessary precaution and my dad was relieved when our guests left the building.

Not much could have been done to change that situation. However, there were some things I could have done differently. I could have asked my mother to go with me to choose my wedding dress. We missed a special time together.

Instead, one afternoon Annie and I drove by a bridal shop and, on a whim, went in to look at dresses. I found one I really liked, ordered it and paid for it. I had planned to pay for my gown since my parents were taking care of all the other expenses.

The gown was strapless with a fitted bodice and a full multi-layered skirt of lace and tulle over satin. It had a fitted lace jacket with a peter pan collar and long fitted sleeves, pointed at the wrist. The lace was sprinkled with pearls and rhinestones. I wore a lace cap with a waist length tulle veil. I felt like a princess and pictured wearing the dress on future formal occasions. I wonder where I thought I'd be going!

When the gown arrived, it was too short. There was time to make the changes and they replaced the satin underskirt with heavier satin than the original. Though lovely, I never wore it again.

Shopping for bridesmaids' gowns was a challenge. The bride is theoretically supposed to plan her wedding but I sometimes felt the process was out of control. My mother was great. She stood by me and encouraged me when I was discouraged. At times both Bill and I wondered if the whole wedding thing was worth the effort. Eloping was an easier option, with our parents' knowledge of course. We were typical first-borns!

Annie was my maid-of-honor and Bill's sister, Barbara, was my bridesmaid. Because Barbs was a teen, Mom and Dad Cox went with us to shop for dresses. Cost was an issue. Color became a problem. What I hoped for wasn't going to happen. I wanted crimson for Ann and forest green for Barbara. We ended up with dark shrimp and turquoise. After seemingly endless shopping the girls looked beautiful! My desired colors were only available for a winter wedding.

Ray was Bill's best man. His ushers were his high school buddy Bob Ormsby, my brother Bill, and a coworker Robert Kane.

The attendants' bouquets were red roses and white daisies. Daisies have always been my favorite flower and red roses set them off beautifully.

We ordered a square tiered wedding cake. The topper was an open Bible with our names on it. To match the bouquets, we asked to have red roses and white daisies around the base.

The evening before the wedding, Bill unexpectedly stopped by to see me. He was on his way home after meeting with Pastor Adams. Premarital counseling wasn't the norm back then and I wasn't aware of their meeting.

Pastor Adams thought I was born again but wasn't sure about Bill. I didn't realize the Bible teaches a believer shouldn't be unequally yoked with an unbeliever. At first, I was in awe of Bill, and then head over heels in love with him so I doubt it would have made a difference if I had known. Now, I understand the reasoning behind the teaching and agree.

When Pastor Adams talked with Bill in his parsonage bedroom, he found Bill knew about Jesus Christ but didn't have a personal relationship with Him. Does that sound familiar? It was my condition just a few years before. On the eve of our wedding, Bill accepted Christ as his Savior.

Though Bill stopped to see me after meeting with Pastor

Adams, he didn't share his decision. He was with me only a few minutes when his mother called. She was upset because he wasn't home. I don't know what was said but Bill was concerned and left.

Our relationship itself wasn't stormy. The turbulence wasn't *between* us but *around* us. Before we were engaged he told me he didn't want to marry me for the wrong reason, to spite his mother. I didn't want that either. We were not engaged until he was confident marriage was right for both of us. Knowing there was some tension on our wedding eve, I didn't know what might happen on our wedding day and decided not to go to the church until I knew Bill was there.

I awakened on my wedding morning to sunbeams filtering through the plants on my window sill. I stretched and surveyed my room. This was my last time to wake up as Patricia Louise Rainey. I would be Patricia Louise Cox in less than six hours.

I could hear the bustle of activity in the kitchen below and went downstairs. Weezie, Nana and Aunt Ann were preparing food, chatting and laughing. Big Bill was outside getting the backyard ready to park vehicles. Poppop and Uncle Buzzy were visiting in Nana's living room.

Our wedding gifts were on display in our dining room. Weezie had arranged them on the table and sideboards. There were silver serving dishes, Russell Wright dinnerware from Bill's parents, crystal goblets, linen and damask tablecloths with matching napkins, kitchen appliances. It was an impressive array.

Big Bill and Weezie gave us a Bible inscribed to both of us with a dedication and Scripture verse. They also gave us a vacuum cleaner. Help for us to be clean both inside and outside!

I drove to Glassboro to have my hair and nails done. That was my first professional manicure. I stopped at the church on my way home and went into the fellowship hall to see the wedding cake. Oh no! The red roses were missing. I told my mom and dad and they agreed we should just ignore it. Obviously not having red roses on my wedding cake didn't affect our marriage.

The wedding was scheduled for 1:30 because Nana said it was good luck to be married when the minute hand was on the upward turn. It was an old superstition we didn't believe, nor did we believe in luck. As it turned out, we couldn't have been legally married until 1:30 because Bill's blood test broke in the mail and had to be resubmitted. The waiting period wasn't over until 1:30. Nothing like cutting it close!

I knew I needed to get dressed but was putting it off until the last minute. When I walked out into the church parking lot the photographer had just arrived.

"Is this where the Rainey/Cox wedding is?" he asked.

"Yes, it is," I answered.

"Can you give me directions to the Rainey home?"

"Sure, follow me."

"Are you part of the wedding party?"

"Yep, I'm the bride."

"You're not getting ready?"

"I will be as soon as I get home!"

Back at the house the photographer prepared to go into action. Aunt Ann and Scotty did also. Scotty, a friend from high school, arrived while I was at the church. They quickly had me into my gown.

I wore a necklace of crystals that were my great grandmother's. I'd purchased earrings to match. I also wore the traditional blue garter but we never considered the groom removing it. Did they even do that back then?

Aunt Ann asked me to carry a little charm of the Virgin Mary. She explained that 1954 was a Marion year in the Catholic Church and being married during that time had special significance. Though our beliefs differed I was pleased Aunt Ann wanted to bless us. I tucked the symbol into my wedding flowers, a white Bible adorned with a going-away corsage of white roses and baby's breath.

Scotty was a good friend through high school. She was there when you needed her and lent laughs to every situation. With the undercurrent of my insecurity about Bill's showing up at the church she was a welcome presence.

When it was time to put on my veil I was struck with its symbolism. It stood for purity and I had no right to wear it.

"I don't want to wear the veil!" If we lived in the south my attitude might have been just short of a hissy fit! Aunt Ann and Scotty calmed me and persuaded me to wear the veil.

Fortunately, the photographer was downstairs during this

outburst. I don't know if others in the house knew what was going on. They certainly must have heard me. I'm just thankful for Aunt Ann and Scotty being patient. By this time, Annie and Barbara had arrived looking beautiful in shrimp and turquoise.

The photographer did an excellent job with posed and candid photos. The owner of the business was a different story. When we picked up our photo albums after our honeymoon there was a 10x17 photograph of us in an elaborate white and gold frame. We said we hadn't ordered it and he told us friends had purchased it for us. What he didn't tell us was he told our friends we wanted the framed photo but weren't able to afford it so they bought it for us. So much for integrity!

I wasn't the only one having a stressful morning. Bill passed out a half mile from the church. He was slowing for an intersection, drifted into a shallow ditch, and bumped into a telephone pole. Ray was following in his car and got him to the church. When he arrived, Jean Adams, our pastor's wife, used smelling salts to bring him around. Some may wonder if he passed out because of a bachelor party the night before? No, he went to dinner with his dad and Ray.

My dad drove me to the church after I was assured Bill had arrived. As I stepped out of the car the garters on my new garter belt released and dropped to my shoes pulling down my nylons. The photographer snapped a photo just as I felt them fall. My facial expression showed my surprise. When we later chose the photographs, we wanted in our album, it was the photographer who was surprised.

"I guess you won't want this one."

"Oh yes, I do!" I replied. That was part of the day and needed to be in there. It was a touch of comic relief.

Jean Adams again came to the rescue, this time mine. She got up under all those layers of satin, tulle and lace and re-attached the garters.

From the church vestibule, we could hear our family friend Betty Shober at the organ. As we entered the church I saw Bill standing up front with Pastor Adams and Ray. I had no idea what had happened to him though I noticed his hands were cold when we exchanged wedding rings.

After the wedding, Ray drove us around the neighborhood in

his car, complete with rattling cans, horn blowing, and just married written on the back window. Then it was back to the reception where we greeted relatives and friends.

Since our wedding was at 1:30 we were past the lunch hour and well before the supper hour. At the reception we had homemade cakes, cookies, wedding bell shaped ice cream, punch, candies and nuts.

We had sandwich fixings back at our house for a late supper for folks from out of town. Mom Cox was disturbed because we weren't having more food at the reception. We considered it but frankly couldn't afford it. Mom Cox planned something similar at their home so it all worked out.

Back at my parents' we changed into our travel clothes and the photographer took photos of us looking at our wedding gifts. Bill wore a white shirt and tie, dress pants and a sport coat. I had sewn my going away outfit: a print cotton sheath with a beige linen coat lined with the same material as the dress. I wore a hat with a tiny veil, gloves, high heels, and carried a basket purse. My corsage and Bill's boutonnière shouted *honeymooners*!

When Uncle Buzzy and Aunt Ann arrived early in the morning we knew Uncle Buzzy brought his portable bar. He set it up in a corner of the kitchen and offered mixed drinks to any who wanted them. He handed us drinks when we came downstairs from changing clothes. We carried them around, then dumped them. Though we drank socially, we didn't drink on our wedding day.

We said our good-byes, then took a detour to Bill's parents' home. We were sent off with well wishes in both places.

The road to marriage was sometimes rocky, but we now breathed a sigh of relief. The tough times brought us closer than we might have been if the way had been smooth.

HONEYMOON
QUILTING PARTY OF TWO

When we were finally across the Delaware River Bridge it was getting dark and we were tired and hungry. We hadn't eaten much at either reception. We saw a little road house and stopped for dinner. We had spaghetti, Bill's favorite meal. That began our first family tradition. We had spaghetti for dinner on our wedding anniversaries.

Bill arranged for our honeymoon through a travel agent in Hartford. She suggested a hotel for our first night so we stayed at The Harrisburger in center city Harrisburg. We took our marriage certificate with us to prove we were married. No one asked, even when Bill signed in as William Cox and Patricia Rainey.

Sometime during the night, I was awakened by a man's voice! It was Bill. I had no idea he talked in his sleep! He was sitting up in bed muttering something I couldn't understand. Then he lay down and went right back to sleep. I wasn't awake for long, it had been a long day. We called room service for breakfast the next morning. Our room cost $11.00; room service was extra.

Our next stop was a little cabin. It was rustic and more to our liking. Then we were on our way to Le Chantecler, a ski resort near Montreal. The travel agent booked us there because off-season rates were reasonable. We were looking forward to seeing the local sights, hiking, and going fishing.

The scenic drive through New York state and Canada was lovely. Now we could relax and enjoy being together. As we drove through Montreal we admired the beauty of the city as well as the French atmosphere. Drawing on high school French and several trips to France Bill understood some of the signage. Fortunately, most were also in English or had graphics.

We wound our way through the foothills north of Montreal into the Laurentian Mountains. Right after a sign signifying Le Chantecler was ahead, we rounded a bend in the road and saw...a castle? It wasn't a castle but it looked like one.

Our car was in stark contrast to the other cars in the parking area but the attendant didn't appear to notice. He took our luggage to the front desk where we were told dinner would be served shortly and then shown to our room.

After freshening up, we headed for the dining room. There were white linen tablecloths with cloth napkins folded neatly next to fine china and crystal. A candle glowed softly in an attractive centerpiece.

"Nice," we agreed as we were seated. Our waiter, with a delightful French accent, introduced himself and asked if we would like something to drink. He presented us with the menu which was in French, but it wasn't the French words that were a problem. It was the prices! If we ate dinner we couldn't afford gasoline to get home!

Bill quietly got up from the table and went to see the gentleman at the front desk. He explained our situation. We thought meals were included but was that possible? That lovely gentleman immediately put Bill at ease. He explained our meals were indeed included and we could have anything on the menu with no additional charge!

Bill returned to our table smiling—we could eat. And eat we did! We started off the meal with snapper soup, with a generous dash of sherry. We also had shrimp cocktail. The main course was beef au jus which also had a generous dash of sherry. I don't remember the sides or dessert, but we ate our fill. Following dinner, we walked hand in hand to the edge of Lake Roun and took in the beauty of the evening.

In the morning, we decided to visit a fish hatchery. We had a multi-course breakfast, skipping the finnan haddie, and set out with directions from our friend at the front desk. We had not yet arrived at the fish hatchery when I told Bill I needed a bathroom, soon. It was a holiday in Canada and many places were closed. My need was becoming urgent, so Bill stopped at a service station where several men were working on a vehicle. They were closed but said I could use their bathroom if I didn't mind it was used by men. At that point I didn't care if it was used by chimpanzees!

I barely made it to the bathroom and it was fortunate I wore a skirt! I returned to the car ready to go back to our room.

By the time we arrived at Le Chantecler Bill also was in urgent need of a bathroom. We hurried to our room and spent the rest of the day taking turns in the bathroom and reading magazines. How romantic is that!

We gave our maid something to smile about. Every time we left our room she came in and straightened it up. That afternoon we didn't leave the room. We saw her whispering to another maid later in the day. I'm sure she didn't realize we were reading magazines and vowing to never again indulge in so many rich sauces and splashes of sherry!

The next day we were provided with a rowboat for fishing, and the kitchen staff supplied us with a picnic lunch. They said they would cook our catch for us. We enjoyed our day on the lake but had nary a strike. Our front desk friend told us people did occasionally catch fish but there was an abundance of natural food in the lake. In fact, the fish hatchery harvested it to feed their fish. It was good we enjoyed the process of fishing as much as the catching.

We saw our first curling rink near the edge of the lake. Neither of us knew what curling was so our friend at the desk explained it to us. It was spring and curling is a winter sport so it was years before we saw the sport in action, on television.

The next day we took a walk along the edge of the lake and into the neighboring woods. We were enjoying the natural beauty when we heard something thrashing in the brush ahead of us. Was it a bear? We began to backtrack quietly when the thrasher came into view. It was a skunk! He was busy searching for food in the dry leaves and apparently unaware of our presence. That ended our walk. We returned to the inn!

Our stay at Le Chantecler was only $21.00 a day, for a total of $82.00. We arrived on Tuesday afternoon and left for home after breakfast on Saturday morning. We enjoyed our time there and hoped to return one day.

We again traveled through Montreal on our way home to Hartford. This time we heard a strange noise in the engine. Not only did we have no extra cash but we were in another country! We joked that it was all downhill and we could coast. The car kept on going and no parts fell off. We were relieved when we pulled into our backyard parking space on Collins Street.

HARTFORD, CONNECTICUT
ADJUSTING THE PIECES

I know I saw our little flat through rose-colored glasses. Allow me to show you around. We'll enter through the back door, the only door except the one to the adjoining cellar. Stepping through the door we enter the screened-in porch, my favorite place. The houseplants we moved from my bedroom in New Jersey were our garden. They flourished.

The first room is our living/bedroom. We had a sofa-bed, my hope chest and a chair. The hope chest was our dresser. We had a table lamp and telephone on the dresser and had to move them every time we put away or removed clothes. It wasn't convenient but it worked.

The second room was the kitchen. There were two sinks: a deep sink and a large shallow sink. We didn't have a washing machine so I used a washboard in the deep sink. There was a laundromat across town but I'd never been to a laundromat and was afraid to try it. I washed our clothes and bedding and hung them out on the clothesline in the back yard. That was fine unless a breeze from the train yard blew soot on them.

I washed everything satisfactorily, except handkerchiefs. Tissues were available but some still used handkerchiefs, and Bill was one of them. At home handkerchiefs went into the washing machine and we didn't have personal contact with them. I didn't really want to wash soiled handkerchiefs by hand so I put them into a big kettle with water and soap and boiled them. This made a slimy mess that I lifted out of the pot with a wooden spoon and rinsed in the deep sink with a lot of water. I only did it once. It was many years before I convinced Bill to use paper tissues. It was a hard sell.

Nana taught me to darn socks, so I darned. It was practical then but doesn't work with socks today. I don't miss doing it.

Back to our tour. There was a gas stove and it was a monster. I'd never cooked with gas before. Of course, I'd not cooked much with electric either. This gas stove had an attachment, a glass jug of kerosene upside down on a rack next to the stove with a tube leading to the gas stove. I don't know what it was for but we believed we would shoot into space if it ever caught fire! Weren't there regulations for that?

Next to the gas stove, lurking in the corner, was our gas-fired water heater. It didn't have a thermostat. If you wanted hot water you lit the water heater. When you were finished with hot water you turned it off. The trick was to turn on the gas and poke a lit match into a little hole on the front of the water heater. When this worked properly you had hot water in a few minutes. Sometimes the gas built up behind the little hole and when you tendered the lit match a flame shot out! I only tried to light it once. Even with his expertise, Bill's eyebrows were singed several times.

Next was the bathroom. Bill liked dark, solid color walls so we painted it a beautiful forest green. The room was small and had no window so dark walls might not have been a good idea. However, the white fixtures stood out nicely!

Speaking of windows, we had two windows in the kitchen and two in the living/bedroom. They were high up along the outside wall and we could see the trash collectors' feet as they walked by.

We had a problem with electricity. We received several electrical appliances for wedding gifts: a blender, waffle iron, mixer, toaster, vacuum cleaner, and iron. We soon learned we couldn't use more than one at a time or we blew a fuse. This didn't just affect our apartment but the entire house. Was there an electrical code?

The inside wall of our apartment separated us from the cellar. The first time we blew a fuse Mrs. Franceour hurried from the first floor and replaced the fuse. She wasn't happy that we caused the fuse to blow. From then on, I overcame my fear of electrical connections, got to the fuse box, and replaced the fuse before she arrived.

There were pleasant things about living in Hartford. We sometimes walked into the city at night after the stores were closed. We couldn't afford anything but it didn't cost to look in the department store windows. Hartford was the cleanest city I'd ever seen. Cars parked off the streets at night and the streets were washed using equipment with huge circular brushes.

We were a short distance from the park in town so we often walked there. Sometimes we took a picnic and drove to a park outside town where we could look out over a little lake. Occasionally we went to a drive-in movie.

Mrs. Franceour and most of our neighbors were Catholic. We went to church only once in Hartford. It was a Congregationalist Church. The people weren't friendly and we weren't sure about their doctrine. Truthfully, we weren't in Hartford many weekends because we went home to New Jersey most of them. We stayed with Bill's folks one weekend and my folks the next.

Bill started his woodworking endeavors in our apartment. He built our first dining table in the living room. The top was of pressed plywood with a thick beveled edge. He did it all with hand tools. It was good he didn't have power tools with our fuse situation. The top of the table was clear finished and the edges were painted black to match the wrought iron legs. We used the table for thirty years.

<O><

When we arrived in Hartford after our honeymoon we went to the grocery store. Though I'd often gone shopping with my mother, I'd only shopped for one meal and I'd had help with that. We moved through the grocery store together, going by the meat counter several times. This was before prepackaged meats so purchasing meat meant bellying up to the meat counter and telling the butcher what you wanted.

Bill asked, "Are we going to buy meat?"

I confessed, "I don't know what to ask for!"

My knight in shining armor, the man who braved the Navy butcher shop, came to my rescue. We bought meat, and then he showed me how to cook it.

There were times my inexperience was obvious. One time I prepared what my Nana called hash. She made it from leftover roast beef ground with carrots, potatoes and onions. Back home we ate it served on bread and it was delicious. Since we had leftover roast beef, we'd have hash for dinner. I ground everything and put it in a pan to cook. Well, I didn't grind everything! I didn't remember the onions. It smelled and looked okay when I placed it on the table. We thanked God for the food and began to eat. We both looked up at the same time, shaking our heads.

Bill hesitantly announced, "Honey, it tastes like dog food."

He was right! It did taste like dog food. I didn't know whether to laugh or cry. Why didn't I add onion and try again? Maybe we didn't have onions? Why didn't we add Bill's all-time favorite condiment, catsup? He must have tried that!

There was another blooper. I decided to bake Bill an applesauce cake, his favorite. It was from scratch; no cake mixes back then. Our food prep area was on a board covering the deep sink. The pantry shelves were overhead. I had just measured a teaspoon of vanilla into my batter and was mixing it in when I smelled, pine? Oh no! I had used pine cleaner instead of vanilla!

No, I didn't bake the cake and was happy I found my error before the cake went into the oven. I also moved the cleaning products from the food storage area.

My cooking skills improved and we ate well, thanks to Bill and my Betty Crocker cookbook.

<O><

One weekend we brought Barbara home with us for a visit. We enjoyed having her. While Bill was at work we had an interesting time with electrical appliances. It seemed natural for one of us to make grilled cheese sandwiches while the other ironed a shirt. Not so! We blew a lot of fuses that week but made record time getting to the fuse box.

When Barbs went home I looked for a job. We weren't sure how long we had before Bill was transferred so I applied to a temp agency. My first job was working in the office of a metal plating company. The work was fine but the girls in the office weren't friendly. It was a two-week stint and I was glad to see it end.

One temp job was one of the best jobs I've ever had. I worked for Bidwell Hardware answering phones and doing clerical work. I worked for and with several salesmen. Normally I don't care for salesmen but these men were considerate and fun.

When you work as a temp you sign an agreement that you will not hire on with any of the companies where you are a temporary worker. In turn, they agree they will not try to hire you. The girl I was replacing was not pleasant to callers or her coworkers. Mr. Bidwell tried to figure out how to replace her with me. I knew it wasn't possible but it was nice to know they appreciated me.

On my last day they surprised me by decorating the office and providing a cake, a gift, and a Dictaphone recording of them singing a song they wrote. If we stayed in Hartford it would have been a pleasure to work there.

Our new vacuum cleaner made it easy to clean our little abode. Finding the right time to clean was another story. Mrs. Franceour had a boarder who worked night shift and slept in the daytime. I always seemed to run the vacuum at the wrong time. If I ran it in the daytime, I woke the boarder. If I ran it at night, I woke Mrs. Franceour. We never saw the boarder.

The vacuum cleaner wasn't the only problem. My cooking was another. I purchased meat that required tenderizing. I looked forward to using my new aluminum meat mallet. It was mid-afternoon when I set up my wooden cutting board, dusted it with flour, and proceeded to attack the meat. Within a few minutes my telephone rang.

"Hello," I said expectantly.

"This is Mrs. Franceour, dear," was the reply.

Oh no!

"What are you doing, dear?"

"Tenderizing meat, Mrs. Franceour."

"You know, you can have the butcher do that for you."

"I didn't know that, but I can add seasoning this way."

"Well, I thought you'd want to know. It's very loud up here."

Sigh!

When we married, we both had coupes. We took his on our honeymoon and then traded both in on a Ford Victoria. It was a nice-looking car, just a couple of years old. When we had the old coupe Mrs. Franceour seemed happy to have us park in the backyard. When we parked the Victoria in the same place, she said she thought our car might make the ground sink so we needed to park it in a lot down the street.

That lot had room for six cars and an assortment of vagrants. We never saw the people who hung out there, but did see the empty bottles in the morning. We were relieved our car was still there in the morning.

<O><

One evening we were invited to the plant manager's home for a cookout with several other salesmen and their wives. The get-together started out fine. The manager and his wife were attentive to us which didn't go over well with some of the others, mainly the wives. We were the new kids on the block! The manager was quick to point out how well Bill was doing and how he expected great things from him when he moved on to Newark, New Jersey.

The subtle infighting came to a head when the manager gave Bill a lighter sporting a Federal Electric logo. It was evidently a coveted item and none of the rest had one. This brought on some cheap shots between some of the men. Even their wives made snide remarks. We were flabbergasted. All this over a lighter that may have cost a couple of dollars?

We left before the rest and on the way home we examined our situation.

"You know, Pat, this life isn't for us."

"I agree. I can't imagine having to deal with this craziness."

"I've seen some of it at work but here it was much worse."

"I think the wives made it worse. It was a cat fight brewing."

"I've been thinking a lot about our future. I never wanted to work in an office, I don't want to work in sales, and I sure don't want to move to Newark."

"I couldn't agree with you more. (pause) What do you really want to do? If we're going to make a change let's make it a good one. Have you thought any more about becoming a veterinarian?"

"That's my dream. I'd like to work with animals and work with my hands."

"Well, let's do it! You go to college and I'll work to support us."

The decision was made, Bill would leave Federal Electric and we would move back to New Jersey. It was July so maybe he could register for the fall semester.

We drove to New Jersey that weekend and told our parents our plans. When we went back to Hartford, Bill gave notice at Federal. His boss was disappointed he was leaving. We also gave notice to Mrs. Franceour and I started packing. Before our lease

118

ran out, we rented a trailer, loaded it and moved our stuff to New Jersey.

We still needed to go back to Hartford for Bill to complete his responsibility to Federal. I had finished my last temp job and there wasn't enough time to take on another one. We rented a room in a city hotel that was barely bigger than the double bed it contained and its single window didn't allow much light. It was affordable temporary accommodations, nothing more. We were basically unemployed. We felt oppressed when we were in the hotel room and spent more time out than in.

Bill said his good-byes to his boss and some of his coworkers, and we loaded the week's laundry into our car. As we drove out of town we breathed a sigh of relief. Our spirits soared as we made the last trip over the Merritt Parkway, through New York City, and down the New Jersey Turnpike.

BACK IN NEW JERSEY
FAMILIAR FABRIC

Back in New Jersey we lived with both families, alternating two weeks in each home. It wasn't the best arrangement but it worked. Bill registered at Rutgers College of South Jersey. I was rehired at Owens-Illinois and he was hired at Sears.

We looked for an affordable apartment. Mr. C worked at Owens and told me they had a second-floor apartment they were willing to rent. The price was right and the location excellent. The only drawback was we couldn't have Penny with us because of Mrs. C's allergy to pet hair. Penny continued to live with Mom and Dad Cox. In lieu of furry pets, we had a parakeet named Puck and a fish tank with black mollies.

We attended church regularly and began to read the Bible together. Since we read in bed at night, whoever was reading was awake while the listener fell asleep. I don't remember how many chapters we read in Genesis but we didn't get very far.

Bill was working and going to college so I had time on my hands. I resumed leadership of the 4H Club Annie and I had before we married. The club was a pilot program. Instead of the usual home and farm based activities we focused on personal appearance and decorum. I know some of the other more traditional club leaders didn't take us seriously, but the girls enjoyed the club.

On Washington's birthday we were called at work. "You need to get home right away." Poppop had a heart attack. He died carrying a basket of eggs from the chicken house and was gone before he hit the ground. He was being carried out the door when we arrived. He wasn't outspoken about his faith but I expect to see him when I get to Heaven.

Two months later I discovered I was pregnant. We wanted children but this was sooner than we'd planned. Both sets of grandparents looked forward to their first grandchild. We did too but weren't sure how it was going to work out.

I made an appointment with Dr. L who had examined me before we married. I asked him about natural childbirth. I'd read about it and wanted to go that route. He was old school and didn't endorse it. I probably should have changed doctors right then and chosen one closer to home, but I didn't.

One day at work Kas Ale, Margaret Iles and I were discussing TV programs and how much time was spent watching TV. I said, "We don't have a TV." As soon as the words left my mouth, everyone began to laugh. There were comments like, "I guess you find other things to do!"

Dad Cox was considering leaving The Evening Bulletin to take a job with O. E. Szekely & Co. and Mr. Szekely was moving his company from Philadelphia to Commerce, Georgia to reduce costs. Dad and Mom flew to Commerce to look over the area. Dad was enthusiastic about the move. Mom was not. Not only was Barbara studying nursing at Cooper Hospital School of Nursing, but their first grandchild was on the way. All in New Jersey. They moved a couple of months before my due date.

We purchased a 28-foot Airstream trailer and moved it across the driveway from my folks' home. Buying the trailer cost less than renting the apartment. It was back from the road and nestled in front of evergreens. Bill added a small front deck.

Inside there was a sofa bed in the living room, an end table for our aquarium, and a small drop-leaf table with two chairs. The kitchen had all the essentials and plenty of cabinet space. You could stand in the middle and reach everything on both sides. The three-quarter bed nearly filled the sleeping area but there were built-in cabinets. Every possible space was utilized. The bathroom was unique! A shower stall fully lined with metal held a metal toilet and sink. You could hypothetically sit on the toilet and take a shower at the same time.

We lived in the country so Penny moved in, along with Puck and our black mollies. We also adopted a black female cat who we soon learned was also pregnant.

During the summer we took my 4H girls to Ocean City. We planned to spend the day on the beach and do the boardwalk in the evening. We packed a lunch, wore our bathing suits under our clothes, and took along dresses for the boardwalk. We had four girls in the backseat, Bill and I in the front seat and all our gear was in the trunk.

Bill was herding quite a group. We had a great time on the beach and enjoyed the sights on the boardwalk. I used the same suntan remedy I'd always used, baby oil and iodine. I normally got a little sunburn but then tanned. This time I felt the burn more than usual but figured it would soon feel better.

The ride home wasn't as much fun as the rest of the day. The girls were packed in tight and feeling the effects of the sun. They said that next time they wouldn't wear crinolines.

We took the girls home and I needed to do something about my sunburn. Bill anointed me with soothing lotion but it didn't help. When I looked in the mirror I saw a lobster staring back! I couldn't get comfortable in bed and finally stood in the bathtub while Bill poured tepid tea over me. Tannic acid is supposed to soothe sunburn.

There are lots of body changes when you're pregnant and evidently your skin can change too. I was as close to sun poisoning as you can get and never again relied on tanning up after a burn.

Those were exciting days. Except for mild morning sickness, cured with a couple of crackers, I enjoyed being pregnant. One negative was taking eating for two too seriously and gaining more weight than necessary. A positive was giving up smoking as soon as I knew I was pregnant. Dr. L never addressed either subject.

We enjoyed our little trailer until the heater stopped working during a cold spell. We moved into Nana's guest room until it was repaired. We didn't realize the heater in the fish tank also wasn't working so our molly colony froze. Puck had moved with us.

We had a couple of baby showers and the necessary provisions were making an impressive pile. If there were sonograms back then they weren't used to predict gender so it was a surprise when he or she arrived.

One special gift was from Nana. She kept the change from Poppop's pocket when he died. When she learned I was pregnant she gave it to the baby.

I gave notice at my job when I was six months pregnant. Women didn't work as far into their pregnancies as they do now. I believe it's better to work longer than I did. The positive was leaving Accounting. The negative was no job, no paycheck.

Nana used to make and sell cinnamon buns. I thought, "Maybe I could do that!" I made a double batch using her recipe. Bill took some to work and they sold immediately. I sent them to work with my mom and dad, same scenario. They not only sold but I received orders. I was in business.

As Thanksgiving approached, sales increased. With Christmas coming, I added cookies along with decorated gingerbread men. Braided buns and Christmas Stollen joined the cinnamon buns. Baked goods were spread out on my mom's dining room table. If a gingerbread man broke an arm, or was otherwise maimed, he was a reject making him fair game for passersby. This was extended to other cookies as well. I believe a cookie or two may have had help in becoming a reject though the crime was never acknowledged.

Keeping busy was good for me. Though my home business didn't bring in as much money as working at Owens, it helped. Bill was busy with college classes and his job at Sears. He and my mom and dad provided most of my orders and I found I enjoyed baking!

"God's in His heaven
All's right with the world!"
(Robert Browning)

MOM AND DAD COX MOVE TO GEORGIA

When Mom and Dad Cox arrived in Commerce they were wined and dined. This may have helped but Mom never completely accepted the southern lifestyle. She did get involved with a few of the women and even volunteered as a Gray Lady in the local hospital. She laughed when she told us how she had been assigned to water the plants in the lobby of the hospital. There was one plant she watered faithfully until she realized it wasn't real!

Mom was a voracious reader and a history buff. Moving to Georgia set off a flurry of reading about the Civil War, especially Andersonville. What she learned from books and local sources did not draw her to the south but made an even greater wedge. She coped with her surroundings but never embraced them.

Dad, on the other hand, enjoyed his community and his job.

He liked the slower lifestyle; sitting on the front porch, visiting with associates and neighbors. He was involved with the Lions Club and the country club, and occasionally played golf.

One neighbor's property was on the other side of a low fence. There was a fig bush on her side of the fence with branches that came through the fence into Mom and Dad's yard. When the figs began to form on branches in their yard she reached through the fence, tied strings to the stems, and pulled them back into her yard. She also rigged bedsheets to funnel the pecans from tree branches that hung over their yard. They had several pecan trees on their property so they didn't want or need more pecans.

Dr. Veal and his wife, Mary, were close neighbors. Dr. Veal was a pharmacist and attended the Methodist Church with Mom and Dad. Mary was one of Mom's closer friends but she attended First Baptist. Spouses there often attended different churches.

Bill and Barbara were in New Jersey so Mom and Dad were empty-nesters. Even though Mom wasn't satisfied with her surroundings she enjoyed being home instead of going out to work. She now had time to do things she enjoyed.

As a young married woman Mom made ceramic pottery and jewelry, and sealing-wax flowers. She was very talented. She did needlework and was an excellent seamstress. Dad was knowledgeable in tree identification and other nature lore. He did most of the repairs on their homes and some creative projects.

Both Mom and Dad were excellent cooks. Some of Mom's cooking was of German origin, influenced by her maternal grandmother. We have many of her recipes in her handwriting. Her lemon meringue and pumpkin pies are among my favorites. She introduced me to Stollen and Springerle. Because of her I now enjoy marinated herring, a new taste for me. She and I both enjoyed limburger cheese though I believe she liked the real thing, I favor pasteurized.

Dad taught me how to make vegetable soup. He used to make great club sandwiches, adding chips and pickles to the plate.

Little did they know when they taught Bill to cook he would help his bride find her way around the kitchen. All of us should be taught how to cook and take care of a house. One never knows when that will come in handy!

BUNKY ARRIVES
OUTING FLANNEL

Our baby was predicted to arrive on December 16. On the evening of December 15, I was rolling out yeast dough to finish cinnamon bun orders. I felt I needed to go to the bathroom and experienced a warm, wet sensation. *Uh oh, guess I waited too long. No, I hadn't waited too long!*

"Honey," I called to Bill, "I think my water broke!"

"Are you sure?" he asked.

"Pretty sure!" I replied.

Weezie joined the conversation, "Are you having contractions?"

"Just a little cramping. I need to finish up these buns for delivery tomorrow."

Weezie called the doctor. My Bill called his parents. Big Bill dozed in his chair. Nana said I should lie down.

Dr. L told Weezie, "There's no hurry to get to the hospital. First babies take a while. Let me know when the contractions are seven minutes apart. Then start for the hospital."

My Bill looked outside. It was a wintry night with light snow falling, "I don't want to take any chances. The roads are clear but we have an hour's drive."

I spread butter on a rectangle of dough, sprinkled on raisins and cinnamon, rolled it up and sliced it into rounds. The baking pans were ready to receive the buns. It was eight o'clock when I popped the last pans of cinnamon buns into the oven and set the timer. Bill brought my overnight bag out of our bedroom and set it by the kitchen door.

I was feeling contractions so I decided to recline until the buns were done. That didn't help. I felt better when I was working in the kitchen. When the timer went off I jumped into action. I guess I didn't jump, more like waddled to the kitchen. I turned the pans out onto aluminum foil, let them cool and wrapped them. Then I put them in the delivery basket with the cookie orders that were already packed.

We concentrated on timing contractions. It was easy to tell when they started and stopped. I'd read about natural childbirth, even though Dr. L wasn't interested, and used the breathing techniques I'd learned.

It was now after ten o'clock, Weezie called Dr. L when the contractions were steady at six minutes apart. Bill warmed up the car and Weezie accompanied us to the hospital. I looked forward to having something for pain.

Bill drove to the hospital entrance and an attendant helped me into a wheelchair. I was ready to give in to a little pampering. They took me upstairs to the maternity floor but Bill and Weezie were told to go to the waiting room. I hoped they could stay with me until I went to the delivery room. Not so!

After changing into one of those cute little backless numbers held together with a shoelace, I was examined and tucked into a hospital bed. The only light in the room was a nightlight. Maybe they wanted me to take a nap. Nap? I think not!

Feeling sorry for myself I wondered, "Have they forgotten me?" Time moved slowly. In fact, it seemed people moved slowly. Dr. L had been notified of my arrival but hadn't arrived. I'd been assigned my own personal intern. He was a nice enough fellow but obviously didn't want to be there. He sat at the bottom of my bed sipping a cup of tea.

"Have you had classes in natural childbirth?" he asked.

"No," I said breathing through a contraction. "I've read about it though."

"You're doing a good job," he answered. I reveled in his encouragement.

I had been examined several times when one nurse's head popped up with a startled look, "You're almost fully dilated!"

I hoped that was good. She hurried out of the room and returned with several other people. At this point I didn't know or care if they were male or female. Everyone had to look. They were all medical professionals, at least I hoped so. I felt like one of those chickens I used to poke when Nana was eviscerating them.

Evidently first-timers aren't supposed to dilate that fast. I guess I didn't get that memo but now everyone around me was in motion. I was whisked to the delivery room, arriving in a dead heat with Dr. L. Drugs were administered and the next thing I remember was waking up in a room with three other women.

My Bill and Weezie were finally allowed to visit me. They had seen William Franklin IV, his name was decided at the beginning of my pregnancy. If he was a girl she would have been Kathleen Louise. Our little guy scaled in at 7 lbs. 5 oz. and was 19.5 inches long. He had lots of black hair and was a handsome baby.

I was the only first-timer in the room. The other women quickly unwrapped their babes when they were brought to our room. They checked fingers and toes, and tickled and poked. I didn't unravel Billy's little cocoon until the second or third day.

I finally found his little feet because I was told to flick them with my finger to wake him so he would eat. That didn't help. I found out just before we went home they'd been giving him bottles in the nursery. No wonder he wasn't hungry when they brought him to me. Bottle feeding was the norm and nursing mothers weren't given much help. Dr. L told me to supplement with formula.

Unfortunately, my mother wasn't much help either. Dr. L told her that her milk wasn't nourishing so she fed us formula. I even asked Bill's mother and she said maybe I didn't have enough milk. I know Nana had a difficult time feeding my mother after one of her breasts was caught in the wringer of the washing machine. Her doctor told her to keep on nursing, blood and all. I can't even imagine what that was like.

My roommates were pleasant, one was very nice but went home the day after I arrived. The one across from me was around my age. She had a toddler at home. Her husband visited a lot and didn't seem to care that no one was to lie on the bed with the patient. The way they were cuddling I expected her to be back the next fall.

The day before we were scheduled to go home our baby was circumcised. Dr. L came in to tell me what he was about to do. He said it was a quick and easy procedure, and painless. I also remember hearing him cry in a room down the hall. Painless? The wound healed, but the procedure was not done well. The stitches left a little unsealed pocket causing ongoing problems.

Worst of all, I wasn't feeling that overwhelming love other mothers described. I thought he was adorable. I felt sorry for him when he cried. I even liked how it felt to hold him close. I just didn't feel connected. What kind of mother was I? I was sure he could have found a much better mother, one who could get him to breastfeed and knew what she was doing!

Just before I was released from the hospital, Bill told me he had dropped out of college and was working full-time at Patterson Oil Company. I was devastated! Not only had he stopped going to classes, he hadn't finished the semester, nor had he taken his exams. There wasn't anything to do about it but pick up the pieces and go on. I didn't agree with his decision but I'm sure he felt he did the only thing possible.

As we left the hospital and made our way across the Delaware River Bridge to New Jersey, excitement and apprehension were in a close race but apprehension was winning by a nose.

<O><

We started calling our baby Bunky shortly after we came home. It helped keep all our Bills straight! We settled him into his bassinet next to our bed in Nana's guestroom. We stayed for a few weeks until we could depend on the trailer heater.

I prepared a batch of bottled formula hoping to not need it. For two weeks I sterilized bottles and nipples along with trying to nurse him. I finally gave up and gave in to bottle feeding. He flourished and I was less frustrated. Years later I learned all the alleged reasons for my breastfeeding failure were false but not in time to succeed with our firstborn.

My sis-in-love, Barbara, came to my rescue and gave Bunky his first real bath. I gave him sponge baths on a towel because I was afraid he would slip out of my hands. That's a far cry from my later two babes who I soaped up and rinsed off under the kitchen faucet!

Living in the house with my parents and Nana presented problems. I didn't want to bother them and they didn't want to intrude. We should have done both! Bunky was a colicky baby. I believe it was brought on, at least in part, by my frustration. I have no doubt babies sense emotions, especially in their mothers.

There were diapers, lots of them, all cloth and needing to be washed. Wash 'n wear was not on the market yet so any cute little cotton outfits also needed to be ironed!

"Don't use pacifiers!" was the cry of people who supposedly knew, so we didn't. I believe Bunky would have enjoyed one. A pacifier might have helped him go to sleep on his own. By the time Karen and Matt came along I was willing to use one but neither of them were interested.

Bill's job at Patterson Oil required an hour drive to and from work. He made residential and commercial oil deliveries throughout Philadelphia. We were all concerned he'd fall asleep at the wheel coming home after midnight.

Residential deliveries could be challenging. Many were made at night and street lighting wasn't always good or nonexistent if the oil fill was in an alley. One of the worst scenarios was dragging a heavy hose across a yard full of dog feces. Then after completing the fill, dragging it back to the truck and wiping off excrement. Drivers made notes on the delivery tickets to warn other drivers about what they might find.

Some of the drivers boasted about their sexual exploits while making deliveries. Bill was unimpressed with their tales and thought it was wishful thinking. One guy was particularly unkempt. His clothing looked like he rolled in oil. Supposedly he was offered the lady's services in exchange for oil. Bill's reaction to situations like that was like Joseph with Potiphar's wife. *I'm outta here!*

Commercial deliveries were often sought by drivers. When they delivered to a chocolate candy company they were given samples. Tasty Cake was a stop Bill really enjoyed. Packages with inside out wrappers or blurred printing were given to them. Beer distributors got a thumbs-up from drivers who drank. Bill wasn't interested.

Bill and I both quit drinking, even socially, within the first year of our marriage, though Bill did have an occasional cold beer for a few more years. I stopped because I didn't really like liquor. I liked Screwdrivers but orange juice alone tasted just as good and never gave you a hangover. I'd already stopped smoking. Bill stopped later. We knew nothing then about secondhand smoke.

Mom and Dad Cox came up from Georgia for a visit shortly after we brought Bunky home from the hospital. We were surprised to find their first nickname for Bill was Binky. We weren't aware of that then, though later we saw it written in his baby book.

Christmas was upon us and a baby made it even more special. We settled into a routine with Bunky and he survived. We did too! Though it seemed like colic was going to last forever, it didn't.

In March we dedicated Bunky to the Lord in Hardingville church. Due to the church's Methodist roots babies were still christened with water when they were dedicated. However, it was not linked to baptism and was simply parents committing to bringing up the child in the faith. I kept the pressed glass bowl that Pastor Adams used and gave it to Billy when he married.

Baby 101 can be a tough course to master if you've had little or no previous interaction with a baby! Any baby! I babysat Charles Ale, but only changed one diaper and he slept most of the evening.

Growing up in a household with both my mother and grandmother available there wasn't much for a seven-year-old sister to do. I ran errands and helped entertain my little brother but that was pretty much the extent of my involvement.

The first born in a family carries a lot on his shoulders. He breaks new ground for himself and those who come after. The whole dynamic of the family changes and will never be the same because of his arrival.

Birth order is an interesting study but like most studies not every first-born, or his family, fits into the mold. Bill and I were both first-borns, with siblings of the opposite gender coming nine and six years after us. I've heard first-borns marrying each other can be unsuccessful but we proved that wrong. I think we were both compliant first-borns. If we had been more aggressive things might have been different.

Bunky was happy nearly all the time. He never knew a stranger and genuinely liked people, all kinds of people. He was a joy to take visiting because he minded well and delighted those we visited.

He loved to eat and it was fun to feed him. When I realized how much he enjoyed an egg for breakfast, I gave him two. Later I learned one egg is plenty for a toddler. The foods he enjoyed were eclectic. He loved stuffed peppers, corn on the cob, a roast chicken drumstick, just about everything we ate.

We'd ordered a Baby Butler before he was born and received it free because he arrived on his anticipated birth date. It was a high chair with a wide table and adjustable legs. He sat in it and watched me when he could sit up alone. Later he played with toys on it. He also watched Captain Kangaroo on TV while he ate breakfast.

He was always ready to play with other children, possibly because he was with adults so much. He was taller and bigger than most children his age but he was never aggressive. Sunday School was the only regular opportunity to play with other children. He would have benefited from and enjoyed pre-school, but that wasn't an option.

I loved reading and singing to Bunky and started as soon as we came home from the hospital. We both enjoyed cuddling and rocking. I sang songs to him that my mother and Nana sang to my brother and me, as well as those Bill and I enjoyed during our over-the-seas courtship, like *Dreamer's Holiday* and *Swinging on a Star*

When I put him to bed without rocking him he cried. Later I realized I should have let him cry, letting him get used to the idea. I didn't and when we finally did let him cry, he stood at the side of the crib and cried, and cried, then vomited all over the side of the crib and the floor. I surrendered and cleaned up Bunky, the crib, and the floor.

Score:
Bunky-1
Mommy-0

GEORGIA
RAW COTTON

In the spring of 1956 Dad Cox told Bill there was a job opening at O. E. Szekely. Instead of driving an oil delivery truck he could work with quality control and time management. It meant an increase in salary and there no more shift work!

We flew to Commerce to visit Mom and Dad and check out the job. We may have asked the Lord what to do but I don't remember spending much time being sure it was His choice. When Bill agreed, Mom and Dad were elated. Weezie and Big Bill were probably not thrilled but they understood.

Our lives were in overdrive: Bill accepted the position, Mom found us a house to rent, Bill gave notice at Patterson Oil, we sold our trailer and in August we were on our way!

This was the only move where someone else paid for everything. Most of what we owned was already packed in my parents' attic so the movers had nothing to pack. We just needed to box clothes, fill suitcases, and drive to Georgia. Though we didn't have many belongings, we had accumulated critters: Puck and Hamlet our parakeets, mama cat who had given birth to three kittens under Bunky's bassinet, and Penny! No fish were involved in the move.

Our baby travel bed took up half the backseat and Penny had the other half. When Bunky wasn't sleeping, he sat between us in his car seat or on my lap—no seating restrictions back then.

The birds were in their cage somewhere in the car. Mama cat and her kittens occupied a sturdy cardboard box with air holes. When we stopped for gasoline the kittens emerged and played follow the leader along the outside window ledge. We retrieved them and increased security.

The house we rented on Orchard Circle had a living room, kitchen, two bedrooms and a bath. Bill utilized an outside laundry room/storage closet for a workshop. It was on the edge of town, across the road from an abandoned orchard. We purchased our first TV, though reception was limited because of the power lines behind the house.

Mom's friend, Mary Veal, gave a coffee welcoming me to Commerce. A coffee was like a tea party but with Coca Cola as the primary drink. The women were pleasant. I particularly liked Mary's daughter but she was only visiting.

On our first Sunday, we attended the Methodist Church with Mom and Dad. The people were friendly and obviously thought we would join their church. The pastor's message was delivered in ministerial tones sometimes referred to as a holy drawl. He used one phrase several times, "We must open der winders!" We weren't sure why the windows should be opened but we knew it wasn't the church for us.

Mary invited us to First Baptist. The pastor was both interesting and challenging. We'd found our church home, much to Mom and Dad's disappointment.

We asked about joining the church and met with the pastor. We learned that baptism by immersion was required for membership and scheduled it for an evening in December. Mom and Dad didn't plan on going with us so Bunky stayed with them.

We arrived with a change of clothes and towels. Members helped us get ready. We had never even seen a baptism but the pastor led us through each step. As we drove home we talked about the experience. It meant more to us than we imagined. There was something special about being baptized like Jesus. We felt our commitment to the Lord had taken a giant leap forward and were inspired by what that might mean.

I enjoyed being a part of the church choir and the director asked me to sing solos, which I'd not done before. I even helped with VBS. I don't know what that church is like today but it was a good fit then.

Our neighbors were friendly folks so when Mom and Dad invited us to go to a country ham and egg supper we asked their teenage daughter to babysit. When Dad drove into our driveway we gave last minute instructions and left for the dinner. We were less than five minutes away when we realized we'd forgotten our tickets. Dad turned around and went back to the house. The neighbor family were all sitting on our front step with Bunky, who was crying.

We should have picked up our tickets and left, but we didn't want the neighbors to have to deal with his tears so we took him with us. Score another one for Bunky. If we couldn't take him, we didn't go. We didn't normally leave him with family, either in New Jersey or Georgia, because we felt we were imposing. It would have been better for him to get used to staying with others.

One of Bill's coworkers was a golf pro at the country club. They went golfing together a few times and Bill enjoyed the game. Bunky and I accompanied him around the golf course just once. Though there were few players that day, I was uneasy about golf balls. Yelling out "Fore!" didn't seem like much protection.

Though we had several friends who were of the country club set, we weren't into that scene. We also had friends who were factory workers. One had a son Bunky's age and our families got together on occasion. We had a lot in common, including our faith.

Penny liked her home on Orchard Circle. She went outside on her own and perused the field behind our house. However, when I called her to come in, even for her dinner, she hid in the weeds. When Bill called, she came without hesitation. So much for my winning her over! I was still the other woman.

Our cats also liked the area. Mama cat disappeared for extended periods of time, then left completely. She moved in with a family at the bottom of the hill. They were glad to have her and we didn't miss her. We still had the three kittens; two females and a male. One had white feet that soon became pink from the red clay. We renamed her Pinky. She eventually moved on with her mother.

We still had Blackie and Samantha. One morning we were playing with them on our bed before taking Blackie to see our veterinarian. Jack was going to castrate him. Much to our surprise, Samantha was not female, she was male! We called to let Jack know we were bringing two cats instead of one and Samantha became Sam. Bill assisted Jack with the surgeries and then was occasionally called to assist with other animals.

<O><

We only lived on Orchard Circle for two months when a young

man came to our front door.

"Miz Cox, I just stopped by to look at my house."

"Oh. Do you own this house?"

"Sure do. My daddy just bought it for me. Uh, how soon can you move out? We'd like to move in before Christmas."

Our landlord hadn't told us he had the house for sale and Christmas was only two months away. To top it off my family was coming for a visit at Christmas. Now what? We started looking for another house. One of Bill's friends told him about a house that was going to be available in the next month or so if we were interested. We contacted the owner and went to see it.

Bill B's house was also out of town and closer to where Bill worked. It was at the end of Hurricane Shoals Road which wound through a cotton field. They had just finished building the house when his company transferred him to Texas. They expected to move in November.

He showed us the house and told us they just finished building it when his company transferred him to Texas. They were moving the next month but another couple was living with them and he'd see how soon they could move out.

This house was different from the first one. It was a lovely rancher on a wooded lot with a stream below the back yard. It had a carport with a cement floor, and a full basement. The house had pine paneling throughout, hardwood floors, and built-in cabinets and bookcases.

We liked it immediately and told Bill B we were interested in renting. He said his friends would move as soon as work was completed on their new house. We went home and began to pack feeling sure we would move before Christmas. What a beautiful place to celebrate the holiday with our families.

Christmas was coming up fast and we were packed and ready. The couple in Bill B's house was not. The new owner of the house on Orchard Circle, as well as his father, came by to see when we were moving. We told him we were ready but the house we were going to rent was not. We were sorry to hold them up. We wanted to move also.

We talked with Bill B's friends and they assured us they were doing all they could. We finally realized we weren't moving by Christmas. I unpacked what we needed for the holidays. My parents, Nana, and my brother Bill arrived as scheduled and we had a great time. Celebrating Christmas isn't dependent on surroundings but it is enhanced by family.

We moved shortly after Christmas. We were delighted, as was our landlord. Not only was our new house less than a year old but we had plenty of room. It's the only house we ever lived where there were two unneeded kitchen cabinets! The cabinet over the refrigerator remained empty. The other one was a base cabinet where I kept some of Bunky's toys so he could play while I worked.

One of Bunky's Christmas gifts was a molded spring-mounted hobby horse. He loved riding it. One morning we woke to laughter in the living room. We went out to see what was happening. There he was riding his horse, stark naked except for his cowboy hat.

Bunky's first personal Easter egg hunt was along the edge of the woods on Easter afternoon. I hid the eggs and took pictures. Bill accompanied him with his little basket to find the eggs. We also took him to an Easter Egg Hunt at church. He was excited being with all the children. Instead of picking up an egg, he pointed to it as another child swooped in and picked it up. It didn't bother him. With our help, he finally got a few eggs in his basket. You sure can't blame a kid for sharing!

Hunting for Easter eggs when I was little was fun, as was hiding them for our kids. When I was growing up we didn't refrigerate those brightly colored hard-boiled eggs. They sat out for a week, but we were never sick from eating them.

I saved the kids' Easter basket grass from year to year, like my mother did. Sometimes I'd find a jelly bean from the previous year when I was refilling the baskets. No, I didn't eat it, though Bill would have. He loved jelly beans and marshmallow peeps! I freely shared them. Just give me chocolate!

Living in the house back Hurricane Shoals Road was a dream come true. Our driveway went through a cotton field and the setting was perfect. When it rained, a runoff from the cotton fields ran behind my clothes lines. It was quite a sight, a torrent of red-water rapids on its way to the stream below.

The house was beautiful with its natural pine paneling, woodwork and hardwood floors. However, we soon decided if it was our house we would paint some walls.

Being the first human inhabitants in a wooded area did present problems. The critters whose habitat we invaded were eager to move in with us. Instead of parging the outside of the basement walls, the builders made a trench in the concrete floor along the inside of the walls. Whether they came in through the basement or by other means, we did have some unwanted guests.

I found the first intruder one morning after Bill left for work. Captain Kangaroo was entertaining Bunky while he ate breakfast. I pulled the curtains across the living room windows to avoid glare on the TV screen. Lo and behold, there was a scorpion in a fold of the curtain! I captured it in a jar with rubbing alcohol and a tight lid. Then I called Bill at work and told him Bunky and I were going to his mother's and would come home when he assured me there were no more scorpions.

The next encounter was in the evening. Bill and I were sitting in the living room and Bunky was in bed asleep. There was a quiet clattering as a scorpion scurried across the living room floor, tail held high! This time Bill did the honors.

The last straw was the millipede nestled under my jewelry box. He was curled up tight, ready for a long winter's nap, or whatever millipedes do. This one was fully armored and not easy to destroy but the deed was done. We called an exterminator.

I nearly forgot the cockroaches. As soon as the light in the kitchen was turned off, out they came. Turn the light back on and they scampered out of sight. The exterminator got rid of them also.

Lest you think bugs were our only concern, copperheads sunned themselves in our back yard. Letting Bunky play outside wasn't an option. We never found one in the basement or next to the house, but I watched for them!

Besides the uninvited critters, we had critters of our own choosing. Bill knew I liked Irish Setters, so when he saw one advertised he suggested we go see her. She was two and a half years old, friendly, beautiful, pedigreed, housebroken and sort of obedient. We brought her home. We only had her a few months when she developed canine meningitis and had to be put down.

About this time, Penny came in heat and though we watched her closely, she was bred. We scheduled a caesarian section because of her broken pelvis. Six puppies lived. She developed eclampsia and seemed to be responding to treatment. One day she just disappeared. We searched but never found her. We believe she went off to die.

One dog came with the house. Her name was Princess, a friendly mixed breed. We fed her but she lived outside, until she sensed a storm coming. Then she asked to come in and went under the kitchen table. After the storm passed, she asked to go outside. When we moved, she stayed. It was her house and there were people to care for her.

<O><

One morning I was getting ready to go shopping. Bunky and I were in the living room when I thought I heard a freight train. My first thought was tornado! Nearby Gainesville had been severely hit a few years before. I got ready to go to the basement when I heard the train whistle, breathed a sigh of relief, and felt a little foolish.

<O><

Our home was only a couple of hours from the mountains. We enjoyed seeing them in the distance on a clear day and decided we should plan a camping/fishing trip. Bill gathered information from friends and collected equipment.

Early on a Saturday morning we dropped Bunky off at Mom and Dad's and drove north into the mountains. Bill found a spot along a stream that looked promising, so we set up camp and headed for the stream. It was a great place for fish though not so great for catching them. One good thing about fly fishing, it's an active sport whether you catch fish or not and it's a challenge to not get hung up in a tree!

We cooked over an open fire and ate well, though not fish. Bill used a shelter half to jury-rig a tent. We slept on army cots and used blankets in lieu of sleeping bags. Cleaning up after meals was fun. I put on my waders and sat on a rock in the stream to wash dishes and pans.

We sat around the fire before turning in. We didn't realize how cold it got at night and pushed our cots together to share body warmth. We wore every possible item of clothing and topped off our blankets with the floor mats from our car!

Seeing the sun come up in the morning was wonderful. We

finally began warming up! While we were eating breakfast, a ranger came by.

"Mornin' folks," he said as he got out of his vehicle.

"Uh oh," I thought.

Bill said, "Was it okay to camp here?"

"Oh sure," he confirmed, "I was wonderin' if you'd seen any bears?"

"We didn't realize there were bears in the area!"

"We see 'em once 'n a while. Just like to keep track of 'em and be sure nobody gets hurt."

"Thanks for letting us know. We'll be breaking camp in a little while."

"Y'all enjoy as long as ya like." He tipped his hat, got in his vehicle, and drove away.

We fished a little longer, then decided to pack up. It had warmed up so I put on shorts, a halter top and flip-flops.

Bill said, "I'll pack up the car while you check out those blackberries we saw along the road. I'll pick you up on the way out."

I took an ice cream bucket and walked along the road. I'd nearly filled my bucket when Bill pulled up beside me. I put the bucket in the back seat and climbed into the passenger seat. We were just leaving when we saw a car coming toward us. It swerved and stopped. Then it continued and pulled up next to us.

The driver leaned out his window, "I just ran over that rattlesnake up ahead. He seemed to be heading toward those blackberry bushes to catch a bird or two. Take care if you're picking." Then he drove off.

We looked at each other, then at the rattlesnake. It was a big one! We had more than enough blackberries and headed for home. They were the best blackberries I've ever eaten.

<O><

A year and a half into the job, Bill learned Mr. Szekely was selling his company. We were comfortable in our surroundings, our church, and being near family, but if Bill was laid off could he find another job in the area that paid as well?

There was also an underlying factor, we weren't comfortable with segregation. We didn't agree with whites-only water fountains, and restaurant owners who didn't serve people of color. I have never liked public restrooms, but it has nothing to do with skin color.

I enjoyed one southern perk, household help a few hours a week. Bill's mother had Sweetie and I had her niece, Johnnie. We picked them up in the morning and took them home after work, many folks didn't provide transportation. Along with cleaning and ironing, they liked helping with Bunky and he liked their attention. I don't remember what we paid them but we gave them more than the going rate. We kept that quiet because we didn't want to make it difficult for them.

While Johnnie was working, I got lunch ready. When I first invited Johnnie to eat lunch with us she was hesitant. It was even more difficult for Sweetie, probably because she was older. In time, Johnnie began to share more openly. She had completed eleventh grade in the colored school in Commerce but she had to go thirty miles to Gainesville to attend twelfth grade and graduate. She wanted to be a nurse. We didn't think it was right that Johnnie couldn't finish high school where she lived. Several years later we heard she was a nurse.

When we returned to New Jersey we realized there was segregation there, it just wasn't out in the open. At least in the south they were honest about it.

Bill contacted Mr. O, his old boss at Patterson Oil, so he had a job waiting for him and then gave notice to Mr. Szekely. I wasn't there when Bill told his parents but I wasn't surprised that Mom thought I had talked him into the move. Several days later I stopped by her house and we both said things we shouldn't have said. When Bill came home from work, I told him what happened and he went to see her. I didn't have further contact with Mom until we stopped at their house to say goodbye. Dad gave me a hug. Mom ignored me then and for the next year and a half.

Though it hurt, I knew it hurt Bill more. Gifts for Christmas and birthdays arrived for Bill and Bunky. When she wrote, she addressed the envelope to Mr. William Cox. Seeking forgiveness could have solved the problem but neither of us pursued it.

My son-in-love and daughters-in-love have hopefully profited from that shaky relationship. I am determined to be a good mother-in-law though I've missed the mark many times. I don't always agree with them but I love them. They have plenty to tolerate with me!

When we moved to Georgia the company paid for the move. Moving back to New Jersey it was our responsibility. Everything was packed and ready to go when the moving van arrived. The driver was going to hire someone to help him load so we hired on to cut expenses. This time our caravan included four puppies, two cats, and two parakeets. Is it possible we have gypsy blood?

We drove through the night and were exhausted. Neither of us could stay awake so my dad met us and drove the last few miles. We moved into Nana's guest room and put Bunky's crib in her sewing room. There were adjustments for all of us to make.

BACK IN NEW JERSEY, AGAIN
LEOPARD PRINT FLANNEL AND TWILL

Bill started work at Patterson right away. This time he worked in the terminal loading trucks and unloading barges. He was glad he didn't have to make deliveries but I'm sure he missed the Tasty Cakes.

Though he was not a strong advocate of unions, he joined United Mine Workers because it was required. He represented the employees at a meeting held in a hotel in Philadelphia. The union officials' agenda was ready for implementation before the meeting began. This did not improve his perception of unions.

Like his father, Bunky enjoyed constructing models. His were plastic and he began assembling them at the tender age of three. He used model glue that came in a little bottle with a brush. Yes, there were tiny parts but they weren't a problem, until he put one up his nose. Old Doc Harris took long-handled tweezers and plucked it out. It was precariously perched and could have gone into his trachea. Model making was suspended.

<O><

Jean Adams taught the names of the books of the New Testament in Sunday School. When we finished reciting Matthew through II Timothy, Jean asked, "Does anyone know who Titus is?"

To my surprise, Bunky raised his hand.

"All right, Bunky, who is Titus?" Jean and I waited expectantly.

"Titus is my turtle!" Bunky said confidently.

I confirmed, he indeed had a turtle named Titus.

Jean led us through the books of the New Testament, ending with Titus, then paused. "You don't have a turtle named Philemon, do you?" I assured her we did not.

<O><

Bunky was outgoing. He memorized quickly and didn't mind being in front of an audience. He sang with the Junior Choir, participated in children's programs in church, and engaged everyone in conversation.

On Easter Sunday, when he was about four, he wore a white shirt, red bow tie, a sport jacket and a fedora. He was a dapper young man. When it was his turn to recite, he confidently took his place in front of the microphone and removed his jacket. I wasn't sure what was coming next but he recited his piece perfectly. I miss those programs.

One Halloween we bought Bunky a leopard costume that did double duty as footed pajamas. It had a cap with ears and whiskers, as well as a tail. He wore those jammies until we had to cut off the feet to lengthen them. Not only did he wear them but Karen and Matt wore them also. They were threadbare when we tossed them out.

Bunky became known as Billy before he started Kindergarten. It seemed a good time to change to a big boy name. Since he was taller than most kids his age he looked like an older brother to his classmates. Unfortunately, looking older was sometimes a problem because people expected more of him.

Kindergarten was half days so I looked for part time work coinciding with his school hours. I applied for a job in the Guidance office at Delsea Regional High School and was hired. My half day finished an hour later than his half day but we thought it would work since Nana was there when he came home.

I enjoyed working with the full-time secretary. She was only two years out of high school and we worked well together. Her father was a Pentecostal pastor. We had many conversations concerning our faith and discussed some of the differences within the Christian community. One thing saddened me. She felt she was not as spiritual as those who spoke in tongues.

I didn't have to be at work until after lunch so I had all morning to get things done at home. That was great but meant I usually tried to fit more into the morning than it could hold. Bill's coworkers kept him updated on my hurried trips to work.

"Bill, I saw your wife today. She was moving right along in that truck of yours—just hittin' the high spots on the road."

I sometimes typed papers for Mr. Heimrath who taught special education. When I noticed the numerical tattoo on his arm, he told me he was in a World War II concentration camp. We sometimes discussed the circumstances surrounding the Nazi takeover of Germany.

I liked Richard Wagner's music, especially *Siegfried's Rhine Journey*. Mr. Heimrath had a different take on it because of Wagner's connection with Adolf Hitler. I found this information on the internet.

> *"Jonathan Livny is the head of the Israeli Wagner Society. His father, a Jew living in Germany, emigrated to Palestine. He was the only member of his family to survive. By founding the Israeli Wagner Society, he wanted 'to break the last symbol of hatred of Germans.' For his views, he says he has been spat at and received threatening phone calls. 'The more they threaten me,' he says, 'the more I want there to be a concert. The music isn't anti-Semitic.'"*

The music was not at fault, it's how people used it. Wagner's music brings me joy. It never caused me to feel animosity toward others.

Halfway through the school year we attended a routine parent-teacher conference. Billy's teacher shared he was doing well but she noticed a change in his attitude. After thinking through the possible reasons, we concluded it started when I went to work. I felt bound to finish the year but decided not to return in the fall. Billy was more important than my job.

BUILDING OUR HOME

Saving toward having a home of our own took longer than we'd hoped and finding the right home site was another problem. We looked at several possibilities but there was always something to hinder the purchase. Big Bill suggested we build at the back of their property. We would be off the road and at the edge of a wooded area. We accepted his offer and were deeded four acres and a wide driveway from the main road. Big Bill said we should own the driveway instead of having a right-of-way because we didn't know what the future held.

After looking at house plans incorporating our dreams, practicality kicked in and we decided on a rancher. Our local building code required homes to be at least one thousand square feet, so we added four feet to the length of the house. It had a fireplace, lots of windows and open areas, and we could add bedrooms in the future. Bill made a scale model so I could see it in three dimensions. He was good at visualizing, I was not.

It's a blessing being a do-it-yourselfer, most of the time. We seldom went shopping without thinking, "we can make that ourselves." Having lived through the depression, our families both "made do" or "made new." With that mindset, we often had things we couldn't have afforded otherwise.

Bill figured we could excavate the basement ourselves since the ground was easy to dig. He staked out the location of the house, we bought a drag bucket, and borrowed my dad's tractor. I drove the tractor and Bill manned the drag bucket. We made good progress until the tractor reared as I drove up and out of the hole. I pulled off to the side, got off the tractor and said, "Call Jimmy Zee," a local contractor. Being an understanding husband, and realizing he'd lost his helper, Bill called Jimmy Zee. Jimmy arrived with heavy equipment and dug the cellar in a day.

Bill installed batter boards and prepared the trench for the foundation. We mixed the cement and poured it. When I say we, Bill did the heavy work and I was his helper. When it came time for carpentry my dad helped.

We used twelve-inch cinder blocks for the basement walls. Bill laid them and I buttered them. When the walls were in place, I parged them with tar prior to backfilling. When it was done, we had a ceremonial burning of my work clothes. It was a dandy fire!

The house was special because it was ours from start to finish. We hired only a few jobs done: the tar and gravel roof, installing the large double pane windows, and pouring the basement floor.

Having the roof done was a good decision. We didn't have the equipment and Bill would have needed a different helper; I'm afraid of heights. The windows were special ordered so we had the company install them. The basement floor was poured by a contractor whose work could have been better.

Bill worked evenings and weekends on the house so it advanced slowly and consumed much of our time. When the outside was complete, the inside went even more slowly. As soon as we fulfilled the occupancy requirements we moved in, though the building inspector suggested we wait until it was finished. He was right. We didn't push as hard after moving in. A few things were completed prior to selling it fifteen years later. The man who purchased our home was a contractor and appreciated Bill's sturdy construction.

When we moved to Virginia we left the house we built and the home where we'd raised our children. Later moves were easier because my roots were shallower. As a wayfarer in this world, I appreciate that my home is in Heaven. I am not of this world, even though I am in it.

> *"This world is not my home*
> *I'm just a-passing through*
> *My treasures are laid up*
> *Somewhere beyond the blue."*
> (Jim Reeves)

Billy excelled in school until third grade. Then his grades started to slip and he began to make poor choices. When he showed interest in being a Cub Scout, we were told leaders were needed so Bill became his Cubmaster and I was his Den mother.

One of my favorite projects was learning about the Leni Lenape Indians who lived in our area. We made clothing, pottery, and faux leatherwork. We played their games, read about them, and made models of their villages. I enjoyed it as much as the boys, maybe more! We worked on merit badges, hiked, and had a great time! The boys presented their completed projects at monthly meetings, cultivating public speaking skills.

Our Cubs and Scouts collected food at the holidays for less fortunate families. Bill and the other leaders took some of the boys to deliver the baskets. Most families were appreciative and thanked the boys. A few presented a different attitude but the boys looked forward to doing it again.

MORE JOB CHANGES

Bill worked at Patterson for a couple of years when Mr. O told him he was changing jobs and asked Bill to go with him. The new job was with a chemical plant, just up the river. It appeared to be a good move but we soon found there were deadly aspects. One was climbing a ladder to check the gauges on top of chemical storage tanks. The height didn't bother him, he climbed the yardarm on destroyers many times. The danger was in the contents of the tanks.

Anhydrous ammonia is an unpredictable and caustic chemical. Basins at the base of the huge tanks confined spills but anhydrous is a gas and can't be seen. It can produce severe burns to the respiratory tract, eyes and skin. Several times Bill came down the ladder from gauging a tank and realized there was a leak. He ran across the basin and over the wall to safety. It wasn't hazardous during the day because there were other employees around. At night, he was alone.

Phenol was also dangerous. It was transferred by hoses under pressure from the river barge to the tanks. If the connection wasn't tight the spray could cut through one's body. A worker was killed months before Bill's employment. Bill talked with Mr. O about unsafe working conditions and Mr. O didn't think the company had plans to change anything.

We were all concerned for Bill's safety but he was reluctant to make a change. Big Bill apparently had a job change in mind. He talked with a friend who had an opening for an appliance repairman about fifteen minutes from our home. Bill was interviewed and hired.

Several years later the chemical plant experienced a huge explosion causing a six-alarm fire. Thirty people were sent to the hospital, two-thirds of the chemical plant was destroyed, and communities on both sides of the Delaware River felt the blast.

Bill liked the challenge of appliance repair though there are downsides to any job. Most calls were made during regular working hours but the boss sometimes intervened for friends. I was irritated more than Bill when he was called out on holidays for non-emergencies. One woman insisted her dishwasher be repaired right away on Thanksgiving Day so she could wash dishes between courses of her dinner party. You can imagine my thoughts about that!

One afternoon he went on a washing machine call, it wasn't spinning out. He was greeted by a terrible odor when he walked in the house. A large bag of dog food had dumped into the tub. They tried to run it through the rinse cycle instead of scooping it out. That didn't get rid of the dog food, but it ruined the mechanism.

Experience taught him that small dogs were often less trustworthy than large ones. On one call, two dogs appeared as he walked toward the house—one large, one small. The larger of the two wagged his tail and accompanied Bill to the back steps. The smaller one kept biting his ankle while the lady of the house assured him it didn't bite. He was glad he wore Wellington boots though teeth marks marred their appearance.

Bill serviced appliances for several years. He was a good repairman but moving large appliances worsened his back problems. He was given an assistant as often as possible and worked until the pain was unbearable. Then he made an appointment with Dr. Powell for an adjustment and spent a day or two lying on the floor. Because he was unable to work consistently he experienced bouts of depression. He needed to do something different, but what?

In the mid-60s he applied for a job doing industrial air conditioning at a large chemical company. The man who interviewed him was sure he would be hired since he was the most qualified applicant. Then came the phone call. The interviewer was sorry but they couldn't hire Bill because he wasn't black. We were disappointed but hoped the man who was hired did well. He wasn't responsible for what happened any more than Bill.

My dad mentioned Bill's situation to Jack, who was now Superintendent of Schools. Jack said he thought Bill should teach. He knew Williamstown High School needed an Industrial Arts teacher and felt Bill was a good fit. Bill was hesitant because he hadn't completed college but Jack told him he could teach on an emergency certificate, taking college classes while he taught. He applied for the position and was hired.

We were blessed again. Bill loved teaching. That might never have happened if he hadn't been refused the job due to his skin color. *God does all things well!*

WILLIAMSTOWN HIGH SCHOOL

"Start out tough. You can always lighten up. You can't toughen up if you start out easy." That's what the chairman of the Industrial Arts Department told Bill.

One tactic Bill used to get the students' attention was to lift a chair straight up from the floor by the bottom of one leg. He then encouraged his students to do the same. After seeing his physical prowess, they thought twice about challenging his authority.

Industrial Arts covered a variety of subjects and he liked them all: Metal, Wood, Automotive, Drafting, Mechanical and Architectural Drawing. Architecture was probably his favorite. About this time, Hardingville Bible Church was planning a new building. Bill drew up plans and built a scale model so people could see the project more clearly.

He volunteered to include special needs students in his classes. He had an innate ability to reach a wide range of students. He also welcomed young ladies and said, "Women make better welders than men, they have a more sensitive touch."

He developed a pilot program entitled Introduction to Industry where students were introduced to a variety of trades. A basket maker, a weaver, and other craftsmen were invited to demonstrate their crafts. I was apprehensive when he asked me to present pottery and ceramics but his presence in the classroom gave me confidence.

Automotive students entered a national design contest, making scale models of oil clay like the ones sculpted by professional designers. They didn't win prizes but it was a good experience.

Visual aids and hands-on involvement were his forte. When he wanted an automobile engine to show the internal workings to his automotive classes, he mentioned it to his students. The next morning there was a car sitting in the parking lot near his classroom. Bill suspected it might have been hot (misappropriated) because no one seemed to know how it got there. After several days, the principal suggested it leave the premises. Bill passed the word and it left as mysteriously as it arrived.

They built a go-cart from scratch in an automotive class. He told the students he'd drive it when it was finished. It was raining the last day of school, so he drove it down the hall of their wing, around the administrative offices, and back to the classroom, amid cheers. As he shut down the engine the phone rang in the classroom.

"Mr. Cox, did you just drive by my office?"

"Yes, I did."

"Well done."

He was popular with his students, even when he disciplined them. One time a fight broke out in the stairwell near his classroom. He tackled one young man, one of his larger students, and they tumbled down the stairwell. The young man apologized for fighting and kept in touch with Bill after he graduated.

In his second year of teaching he was assigned as advisor to the Class of 1970. He oversaw their meetings and directed their plays. I believe he enjoyed directing as much as teaching. We chaperoned their dances and sometimes had them in our home.

In 1972 Bill and three other teachers organized the Christian Life Club. The members were students who wanted to be a positive Christian witness to their friends and met for prayer before school. All four teachers began attending night classes at Philadelphia College of Bible, taking turns driving to the school's facility on Arch Street.

A friend soon joined them. Will had just purchased his first car and when it was his turn to drive he was overly cautious. Sensing his anxiety while driving through a rough section of the city they decided to have a little fun.

"Watch out for red lights. They'll strip your hubcaps before the light turns green."

"Better not go too slow past that boarded up building. You never know who'll jump out of that alley!"

Will was young and naïve, not used to their playful banter. He locked the doors, sped up, and ran a red light.

"Whoa there, you went through a red light!"

"But you said...!" Then he realized what they were doing and joined in their laughter. Bible school was serious business but they always found lighter moments.

Along with Bill's teacher friends, Pastor Joe and Ardeen Zearfaus had graduated from PCB and were influential in our spiritual journey. God used many people and situations when He pieced together this crazy quilt.

KAREN ARRIVES
CHALLIS AND BRUSHED FLANNEL

Our hope for another sibling was still just a hope and we began considering adoption. We wondered if a child of mixed race might be a good choice but we weren't sure how our family and friends might react. This was the early '60s. My blood boiled when I heard prejudicial comments. How would I react if they were directed to our child?

In late April 1965, I had flu-like symptoms and visited Dr. P, an osteopath whose adjustments helped Bill's back problems. Doc checked my vitals and did a test. When he came back to the examining room he said, "You're pregnant!" What? I went to see the doctor because I had a bad cold and instead we were going to have a baby. Maybe the adoption option works!

We were all excited. When our Cub Scouts found out they thought it was terrific! I finished off the season as their Den mother and they planned and gave me a baby shower with help from their mothers.

"Is it a boy or a girl?" I did have a preference this time. I wanted a boy. I was used to boys and didn't want a prissy-tailed girl. Okay, now you're wondering, "What's a prissy-tail?" To me it means a persnickety fussbudget. I'd seen girls like that and didn't want one. I didn't like the drama surrounding girls.

I enjoyed being pregnant. It was exciting being the vessel for a new life and this time around I thought I knew what to expect. Those first flutters of movement weren't gas bubbles. This was even more exciting than the first time.

Best of all, I loved this baby immediately. There was not a hint of hesitation! We decided I'd go to our family doctor in Elmer. We didn't want another cold and impersonal experience in Philadelphia. Visits to Dr. Mills were encouraging and Bill was happy knowing we were twenty-minutes from the hospital.

Shortly after I discovered I was pregnant my sister-in-love, Janice, found she too was with child. Jeffrey Michael had come on the scene three years before so this was her second as well. Since Janice was a nurse and lived right down the road, I asked if she'd be able to be with me during delivery. I was thrilled when she agreed.

Mid-afternoon December 2, 1965 I started into labor. Uh oh, Dr. Mills was deer hunting so his backup would deliver our baby.

My bag was packed and Billy was set to spend the night with my parents. When Bill arrived home from school we kept track of contractions and then were on our way. This time my Bill and Janice were with me, and our friend and neighbor, Evelyn Becker, was on duty in maternity. I was surrounded by loved ones.

The contractions were different than with Billy. Evelyn examined me and called in Dr. S. He checked me and said the baby was presenting facing backward. I hoped to have this child without drugs but he needed to sedate me to turn the baby and facilitate delivery. I was ready to do whatever was needed. Bill was having difficulty watching me in pain and left the room. I didn't care because I was in a drug-induced happy place.

Both Evelyn and Janice were with me in the delivery room. Janice was instructed to put the oxygen mask on me, which she did. I couldn't breathe and kept shaking my head. My hands were fastened at my sides so I couldn't reach up and pull it off. The pain meds were beginning to take effect so I wasn't thinking clearly. Everyone thought I was fighting the mask until Janice saw the oxygen wasn't on. I was smothering. We joked about it afterward but it was scary at the time.

When I woke up, Bill said, "We have a baby girl." I totally forgot I'd wanted a boy. Her name was Karen Louise. My first glimpse in the nursery assured me she wasn't a prissy-tail. I called her my little truck driver. She weighed in at eight pounds eleven ounces, had chubby cheeks like red apples, and an abundance of black hair.

When they brought Karen to me, she latched on and her free hand pulled me toward her. She also grabbed hold of my heart. We were meant for each other. Who needed another boy anyway! (Sorry, Matthew, just not then!)

I shared a semi-private room with a mom who had also birthed her second child. Rooming together was like being on vacation. We sat on the sides of our beds facing each other for meals We enjoyed the food and didn't have to cook it! Our families visited regularly but we weren't lonely when they left. I can't imagine a better situation. We stayed in touch for several years but eventually lost track. The last I heard her son was doing well and his big sister liked having a little brother.

Being in a small country hospital was wonderful. The maternity staff at Elmer Community was the best. The nurses were helpful and brought our babies when they were hungry or if we wanted them. In case you're wondering, I wasn't afraid to unwrap my child. On this trip home, we were several notches up on the confidence ladder. There would be new learning experiences but we could do this!

<O><

At home things were going well but fifth grade was not a good year for Billy. He was in an accelerated class: half from fourth grade, half from fifth. It sounded like a great plan but it wasn't working and it was a while before we knew how bad it was.

We received notes from Billy's teacher stating he wasn't turning in his homework. We knew he did it and he told us he'd turned it in. I received telephone calls from Mrs. G suggesting we get help for Billy because he wasn't well adjusted, ostensibly because he felt displaced by his baby sister. It seemed like she always called in the evening when Bill was attending classes. She told me she was a single mother with a son Billy's age. Our conversations started with her concerns about Bill but the focus always seemed to turn to her problems.

Billy told us Mrs. G had taken his new birthday wristwatch and hadn't returned it. Was he paying too much attention to it in class? We sent her a note asking her to send his watch home. She wrote back saying she didn't have it. We weren't going to get to the bottom of this without meeting with Mrs. G so we made an appointment to meet with her after school. She seemed glad we had come. We talked with her for a time, asking about the watch and homework papers. She denied having them. We'd heard from other parents that their children knew Billy's watch was in her desk.

We felt she wasn't forthright with her answers. Since we weren't making progress, we went to the principal's office. Bill explained the situation and asked him to intervene. I don't remember when he looked in her desk but he found Billy's watch as well as a quantity of homework papers—Billy's as well as others. The clincher was she wasn't dismissed. We felt that was bizarre. We asked the principal about it and he told us it would be too difficult to find a teacher with her credentials to finish out the year. We asked to have Billy moved from Mrs. G's accelerated class to a regular classroom. His teacher was now Mrs. Hall, a tough but loving teacher. The remainder of the year went well.

Billy was now in Boy Scouts and his dad was the troop leader. Being the troop leader's son meant making sure your ducks were not only lined up but fit and ready to march! One of the requirements was to climb twelve feet up a tree. This was a problem because Billy was afraid of heights. With a lot of encouragement, he finally made it to just twelve feet.

When he built a fire with one match to pass a test, he did it outside during a snowstorm. He didn't have to do it then but he wanted to complete the requirement. He built it outside our dining room window so we had a good view. He did it with just one match and his smile was brighter than the fire.

<O><

With Karen the blessings continued. She didn't have colic, she was eager to nurse, she slept for impressive periods of time and was content when she was awake. Does it get better than that?

Bathing her was fun. When she outgrew her little tub, she graduated to the kitchen sink where she loved being rinsed with the sprayer. She never once slipped from my grasp. My fears were gone.

There was one concern. When I changed Karen's diaper I thought she might have diarrhea. She was fine otherwise but we needed to find out if anything was wrong.

At her first checkup, Dr. S was pleased with her progress. I mentioned my concerns about her loose bowel movements. He said I could try giving her skim milk. I didn't realize breastfed babies have looser bowels and obviously Dr. S didn't know either. When I started adding bottles, my milk production diminished. When she was just three months old I admitted defeat. I cried—

no, I sobbed. Those times together were so delightful and I didn't know how to get them back. I later learned it can be done, but too late for Karen.

She flourished and was an absolute joy. Billy loved showing her off to friends. She had captivated our hearts.

Her cousin, Brian, was born three months after her arrival. We like to say he was present at her birth, though we couldn't see him.

<O><

We took on a newspaper motor route as a summer job. Bill did it when he wasn't taking classes and I was his backup. When he went back to teaching in September, Karen could sleep in the car while I delivered newspapers. It seemed like a good idea but Karen didn't buy it. Nana went with me to hold her but that didn't work either. I finally asked Gloria Wright if she would keep her while I delivered newspapers. Gloria liked having her and Karen liked being with Gloria, but it didn't take an accountant to figure out this wasn't the job for us. By the time we paid a sitter and figured in gasoline, and wear and tear on the car, it wasn't helping financially. We gave notice and were done before winter.

One of my final delivery days stands out. It was fall and I was on a back road where we had only a few deliveries. Ahead of me was a driveway where I needed to pop a newspaper into a tube. Just before I got to the tube a young woman in a blue sedan pulled out of the driveway and into the path of a man driving a pickup truck. He couldn't avoid hitting her and was visibly shaken when he got out of his truck. He kept saying, "I didn't see her."

I jumped out of my car and ran to the young woman's car. I wasn't sure what to do. She wasn't moving, nor did she seem to be breathing. She had a deep dent on her forehead and it wasn't bleeding. I called to a man coming out the front door, "I can't find a pulse!"

By this time, others had arrived. They called the police and an ambulance. There wasn't any more I could do, so I left my name and phone number and finished delivering newspapers. I wasn't surprised to hear she was dead.

Occurrences like that tend to stay on in our memories. I didn't know her but I'll never forget her. She was a lovely young woman. I wonder if she knew Jesus.

CERAMICS

While I was pregnant with Karen, Weezie and I took a class in ceramics. We enjoyed working with clay and continued after classes were finished. We made gifts and even sold some pieces. Friends asked me to teach them so I started classes in my home. Our instructor sold me materials at wholesale prices and fired our greenware. The money I received for classes paid for a kiln. It was a tidy little business.

I believe everyone has some artistic talent though it's not always discovered and seldom nurtured. My youngest student was Karen. When she was about three she made an abstract tiger from a lump of clay. It's one of my treasures. My oldest students were my Nana and a student's mother, both in their eighties.

Naomi DuBois often produced better work than mine. When we slip-painted dogwood on a vase, hers was beautiful! It's a joy to see a student excel. A teacher should encourage students to do their best and then celebrate their accomplishments.

<O><

It's important to be attentive with a young child around. We'd been antiquing manger scene figures. To facilitate clean-up, I used little paper Dixie cups to hold mineral spirits.

It was late afternoon and my students had gone home. Ginny Schneeman was helping me clean up. Karen awoke from her nap and came to the kitchen. She saw the Dixie cups on the table and, thinking they held apple juice, she drank one. I vividly recall her eyes rolling back in her head as she said, "I drinked it."

I knew immediately what she'd done and called the hospital. They told me not to make her throw up. We left a message for Bill at school and we were on our way to the Emergency Room, praying all the while.

This was another of those times when God's presence was evident. We had one car and Bill wasn't home yet from school. Ginny was there to drive us to the hospital. The ER attendants pumped Karen's stomach and I never again used Dixie cups for anything but juice. Thank you, Lord!

Is that the end of the emergency stories? No! Two weeks later I was on the telephone in the kitchen and Karen wanted me to pick her up. I hoisted her up on the kitchen cabinet. I was right next to her but within seconds, she fell, injuring her arm. Off to the ER again!

The attendants recognized me. I even mentioned being there two weeks before. This was before the tough scrutiny of Child Protective Services but I was uneasy about what they thought. I tended to be overprotective but my child was in the ER twice in two weeks! I even wondered about me.

Karen sustained a hairline fracture in her forearm. They put on a removable cast and tied on a sling to keep it in place. Slings back then were constructed from unbleached muslin. To make her slings fun, I made several from cute fabric and stopped using the plain one. Karen found the sling was a handy carrier for everything from stuffed animals and dolls, to a puppy!

I'd like to say there were no more trips to the ER but not so. Several years later she was playing with Sharon DuBois in the haymow of their barn. She stood up under a beam and a protruding nail gashed her head. Scalp wounds bleed profusely so she was quite a sight. They ran to the house and Sharon's mom, Naomi, cleaned her up and called me. I picked her up on the way to the ER where they stitched her scalp. That was her last trip to the ER on my watch.

OILS ON CANVAS

Shortly after Karen was born Bill thought I needed to get out and do something for myself so he arranged for oil painting lessons. A half-dozen of us sat around a large table in our teacher's basement. We were all at different levels of experience.

I had previously tried oil painting with no success so I was uneasy. We worked from photographs or pictures. I brought several possibilities with me for my first class. We chose a harbor scene. I painted at home, and in class my instructor helped me over the rough spots. When it was finished, Bill built a frame out of barn wood. I loved painting.

My second painting was Mirror Lake in Yosemite National Park, from a National Geographic photograph. My third was a log cabin near a stream. In an art exhibit in Virginia, the harbor scene won first prize, Mirror Lake won second prize, and the log cabin won honorable mention.

Years later I painted a copy of the harbor scene for Dad Cox. Frances showed it to an art dealer and he was impressed. I wonder if she sold it after Dad died. I started a third copy but it's unfinished. Maybe someday.

If it hadn't been for Bill, I doubt I would have painted. I miss his inspiration and encouragement. I also miss his creative criticism, I trusted his judgment.

My grand-girl, Morgan, shared a gem of wisdom. One of her art teachers told his class, "Never get rid of any of your work." I wish I'd learned that sooner. We gave away or sold most of our artwork over the years which I don't regret. However, there are a few pieces I threw away because I didn't think they were good enough. I realized recently they were probably worth keeping. Too late.

<O><

Years ago there was an adorable cartoon thumb character who had a captivating smile. He said, "I'm thumbody 'cause God don't make no junk!" I always liked that little guy. He was right!

When we complain we don't like our body build, our voice, even our talents, we're saying God made a mistake when he created us. Not true! He created us the way He wanted us to be.

God made us who we are. Yes, we need to take care of what He gave us but the basic me is just fine. You are too! Rather than complain, we need to be better stewards of what we have and not always want to be someone or something we aren't.

I'm thankful God hasn't given up on me! How about you?

FAMILY CAMPING

Our first family camping trip was with my brother and his family. They were seasoned campers. We didn't own a tent, they loaned us one. We didn't have sleeping bags, we used blankets. We took precautions against rain, they were inadequate. We got wet the first night and spent the next day drying out. We had a great time but needed to improve our equipment.

The summer of '65 we spent three weeks at a campground near Trenton State College while Bill attended classes. We had a wall tent affording us plenty of room. I got the cot because I was pregnant. Bill and Billy slept on the ground, assuring me it was no different than Boy Scout camp. I didn't argue.

Problem: trips to the restroom at night.

Solution: portable facility in tent.

Problem: Bill said, "Even animals don't go where they sleep."

Solution: Bill built a canvas enclosure, snug up to the tent.

We took our church youth group camping with Rich and Margaret Iles. By this time, we were a family of four. The weather was wet and cold. Margaret opened the back door of their borrowed camper and called, *Are we having fun yet?* Camping wasn't her thing but she was spunky.

We survived without the bacon that was forgotten, but we weren't sure we'd survive the yellow jackets. They were everywhere. Karen was about to bite an apple when a yellow jacket landed on it. It was close but she wasn't stung.

We camped in Elk Neck State Park along the Chesapeake Bay and watched the big ships across the waterway. Even more entertaining was watching people launching their boats. Some were adept, some were not.

A rather pompous man wearing a captain's hat nearly lost his truck while launching his boat. When his boat was finally in the water it drifted toward a roped-off swimming area. As he was bellowing directions, a Girl Scout leader quietly and efficiently directed the launching of her troop's canoe. It was quite a show!

Late in March, 1968, we rented a cabin at Parvin State Park. It was cozy and right on the lake. We had bunk beds, a little kitchen, and a fireplace. It was more convenient than tent camping and a very special weekend.

We also camped at Parvin since it was only an hour from home. We set out when Billy got home from school on Friday. He set up the tent and Karen and I arranged the rest of our camp. Bill came directly from school. They were good times.

Later tent camping adventures were in campgrounds providing raised platforms. It was great not dealing with rocks and tree roots. In the early '70s we purchased a pop-up camper. It had a bed at each end and a built-in kitchen. By now, Matt had joined us but Billy liked a separate tent so we fit nicely.

In the '70s we spent a week at a campground near the seashore. Billy had a job so he stayed home. We purchased a screened canopy to keep bugs and other critters out. That didn't deter a marauding squirrel. Time after time bread and marshmallows were moved or missing. We finally saw the culprit carrying off a bag of hot dog rolls. He chattered his indignation at our interrupting his routine, and improving our security.

We enjoyed camping at Hickory Run State Park in the Pocono Mountains and visited a unique natural attraction there. Boulder Field covers an area of about sixteen acres. The rocks are ten to twelve feet deep and range from just inches to twenty-six feet in length. Were they deposited by glaciers? If so, why is there no sand or debris between them? Maybe God provides mysteries for our enjoyment!

We had a large rock garden at one end of our home. We often brought home interesting rocks from our travels. Along with the rocks there was a stone baby which was originally on Aunt Grace Godefroy's grave. When I was a little girl Nana put flowers on family graves and I put a little bouquet in the baby's hand. When the baby was removed from the cemetery, Nana put it on her front porch. When she died, it was given to me. We left the stone baby when we moved to Virginia. The new owners had lost a baby and they felt it was right for their garden.

As for the rocks, maybe someday a geologist will try to figure out how they came to be there. A random glacier?

MATTHEW MAKES THREE
A TINY PATCH

E velyn Becker's oldest son Robbie was in Bill's scout troop. He had a horse named Alice and sometimes rode over to visit. When Karen showed an interest in Alice, he boosted her onto Alice's back. From then on, she wanted a horse.

The Beckers also had a pony mare who was bred with a cart pony. They asked if Karen could have the colt. We accepted their offer. Shortly after he was born, Nipper and his mother lived with us until he was weaned.

It was obvious that Karen not only loved horses and ponies, she also loved dogs, cats and most things furry or feathered. She is her father's daughter.

Karen had a pony but now it began to look like she might have a new sibling. In late spring 1968, I thought I was pregnant again. Though I wanted twelve children, Bill wasn't completely on board with that. Three sounded good to him. Dr. Mills no longer took maternity patients so we decided to try a popular OB/GYN in Pitman. Bill drove me and waited in the car.

Nothing prepared me for this man. He did an internal exam as I expected. He was gruff, which I didn't expect. His bedside manner was lacking. Then it got worse. He held up a bloody gloved hand and said, "Well, if you were pregnant, you aren't now!" Without another word, he left the room!

I felt like I'd been kicked in the stomach. When I got in the car, Bill asked what was wrong. I explained briefly. He wanted to go in and talk with the doctor. I wanted to go home. Was I pregnant? Was I not pregnant? I just wanted out of there.

We made an appointment with Dr. Mills. Though he wasn't taking maternity patients he was still our family doctor. He examined me and said I was pregnant. He suggested names of several OB/GYN doctors. The only one still practicing at Elmer Hospital was Dr. L. so we made an appointment with him.

Karen and Billy were looking forward to a little brother or sister. We had no preference since we had one of each. Bill was busy with school, college, and church activities. Life was good.

The pregnancy went well except for early pelvic floor pressure; uncomfortable but not painful. In late November I experienced mild cramping and spotting. Dr. L advised me to stay off my feet so I took up residence on our couch.

Do other people plan major overhauls at illogical times? I'd like to say Bill was the culprit but it was both of us. We piled project upon project and then wondered why our lives were in disarray. This time we decided to repaint the interior of our home. Bill and Billy said they could get it done because of Thanksgiving vacation and I didn't need to be involved.

Saturday night we stayed with my folks to avoid the paint fumes. I woke at sunrise on Sunday with cramping, spotting, and dampness. Nearly a month before the due date this little Cox seemed anxious to arrive. When Bill called the hospital, a nurse said, "Bring her in."

Dr. L met us at the hospital. Bill stayed with me but my contractions stopped. Was it false labor? Dr. L suggested I stay a while longer. Bill was scheduled to teach Sunday school so he left.

Nurse Janet wheeled me into the delivery room. I was on a not-so-comfortable delivery table, thinking I should go home. Dr. L and Janet were chatting. All signs indicated it was time, so they induced labor. More waiting. Then, one whopper of a pain and a baby boy popped out into Dr. L's hands. He arrived at eleven a.m.—just in time for church! He weighed in at just five pounds five ounces. Jaundice was a concern but easily corrected.

We named him Matthew Duval. Bill liked Matthew or Luke so I cast the deciding vote. Duval was Mom's maiden name.

The hospital was phasing out maternity so there were only three of us on the floor This time my roommate was younger and not the fun friend I had with Karen.

I hadn't planned to sign and address Christmas cards on a hospital bed so we'd chosen a lovely snow scene highlighted with glitter. By the time I finished the cards there was glitter everywhere. The nurses referred to me as Sparkle Plenty.

Karen was my truck driver and Matthew was my bag of bones. He needed more time in the oven to plump up. I checked him out thoroughly which was good because the next time they brought him in, it wasn't him! The nose was more prominent. A nurse hurried in apologizing profusely. *The nose* belonged in the next room.

When I nursed Matthew, Karen sat beside me on the couch and fed her dolly, just like mommy. Matt dined every two hours because his tummy needed small, frequent feedings. This time I was better informed. He was fourteen months old when we both knew it was time to switch to a cup.

When Billy was little he ate jarred baby food and baby cereal, then junior foods. We started table food earlier with Karen, and Matthew never had baby food.

Not only did Matthew have the audacity to keep me away on Karen's third birthday, but his birthday is the day *before* hers and she is three years older than him. She has probably forgiven him for arriving when he did, but she still likes to remind him that he was an interloper!

HOMEGOINGS
MOM COX

Both Barbs and I were three months pregnant when we went to Georgia for Mom Cox's funeral in 1968. The first time Bill spoke at a funeral was his mother's.

We were aware Mom dealt with diverticulitis but had no idea her death was imminent. After she was gone, Dad was despondent. He went to work but at home he brooded. A concerned neighbor called Bill but there was little we could do.

Dad's friends encouraged him to date, so he invited a friend's widow to go to dinner. I'm sure he looked dashing when he arrived at her door. Mrs. B met him with a drink in one hand and more than dinner on her mind. He made his excuses and left quickly.

Frances Benton was Mom's friend in Commerce. She was a widow of fourteen years with a fifteen-year-old son. In August, Dad called Bill and Barbara to tell them he was marrying Frances the following weekend and there was no need to come to the wedding. When Grandfather Cox married quickly after his first wife died, Dad and Mom were stunned. Now Dad was doing the same thing. I doubt there's a gene for that, but Bill told me if there was one it was skipping his generation.

We first met Frances when she and Dad visited us in New Jersey. Later we visited them in Georgia when they were getting ready to move to a new house. Bill and I sat on the steps to their attic to go through old family photographs that were destined to be thrown away. We later made copies for the rest of the family.

The next time we visited them in Georgia was in their new house. Dad and I sat across from each other at the dining room table one morning, laughing at how we were always the last ones still eating. He was dealing with cancer but doing well.

He said, "I've had two good wives. Many men don't have one."

It was on this trip we met Princess, their Shih Tzu. She was a cute little dog. She was a good companion for Dad and sat with him in his recliner. However, her attitude left a lot to be desired and she had an obvious dislike for young males.

Frances's son was nicknamed Biff. Dad didn't often comment about him. I'm sure Frances dealt with Biff and being the stepfather of a teen-aged son was probably not easy. We met him a couple of times. The last time was at Dad's funeral.

Dad and Frances visited us in Skeetrock in 1976. They let us know when they were a couple of hours away and we drove to Clintwood so we could lead them to our house. We parked where we had a good view of cars as they arrived in town. As we watched the cars going by we realized we were seeing the same cars over and over. This was nightlife in Clintwood. Though most drivers were young, there were also adults! Watching the cruisers furnished lots of laughs and time passed quickly.

Finally, we saw Dad's car. Bill waved and he pulled in next to us. Their trip was lengthened because they accidently cruised through a little coal town off the main road. We had a good visit. This was the only time Dad heard Bill preach.

DAD COX

The next time we saw them was in March. Dad was battling prostate cancer and was in the hospital. Bill wanted to talk with him about his relationship with the Lord but every time he was alone with Dad, Frances showed up. We prayed God would work it out. The three of us walked toward the hospital elevator to go

168

up to Dad's room but Frances turned into the gift shop. Bill got into the elevator and I stayed with Frances. In the time they were together, Dad told Bill that both he and Mom had accepted Christ when they were young. Bill was relieved!

The next time we went to Georgia was for Dad's funeral in April 1977. Bill spoke at his service. Sometime later, Bill was notified his great-great-grandfather's tool chest and secretary desk were willed to him. Karen, Matt and I stopped in Georgia to pick them up on the way home from a visit with Billy and Kathy. Frances took us to an Alpine Village in northern Georgia where we saw a dinner theater presentation of *The Sound of Music*. She was very hospitable.

When it was time to load the furniture, Frances asked if Bill would trade the secretary desk for a new table saw Dad had never used. I knew Bill would enjoy the saw but doubted he'd trade a family heirloom for it. I suggested we call him. His answer was as I thought. Thanks, but no thanks.

After Dad died, Frances and a friend had a little antique and craft shop. We invited them to bring their crafts to a Dickenson County Craft show. They did well and we enjoyed their visit. I mentioned to her friend that I wasn't sure if Frances wanted to stay in touch with us. She assured me she did and I tried to stay in touch. We sent gifts at Christmas and occasional notes, but never heard from her. After a while I gave up. I learned of her 1996 death while doing ancestry research.

NANA GOES HOME

On a frosty February morning in 1972 my Nana fell and broke her hip. The doctors stabilized it but surgery wasn't an option. She was mentally alert before the fall but during her hospitalization she seemed to develop hospital delirium. I thought staying with her might help keep her connected with reality. I sat with her, held her hand, and talked to her. Weezie couldn't visit because she was sick, and my brother stayed with her when he could.

For some time Weezie and I thought Nana had something wrong internally but she never talked about it. Years before, she told me Grandmother Rainey had cancer and didn't tell her children. Now Nana was doing the same thing. They grew up when there wasn't much that could be done. Did they now simply accept what came their way?

A urologist examined her internally while I was there. He began without even speaking to her and it was obviously painful. He found Nana had fistulas between the bowel and urinary tract, bearing out what Weezie suspected. He determined nothing could be done. I determined I'd never choose him as my doctor.

After two weeks we were told Nana could go home if she had sufficient care. Bill agreed we could take her home with us. She seemed pleased. Others thought she should go to her house and we'd take turns caring for her. I reluctantly agreed.

The day before she was due to go home, Weezie was finally allowed to visit her. We were both there when she went into cardiac arrest. We had a Do Not Resuscitate (DNR) order in place but when the end comes it's still hard. We stood at the foot of her bed holding hands. It was best to let her go but her departure left a hole in our lives.

Now, Weezie needed to dispose of things to combine two households. When we looked through Nana's house we discovered a lot of things had already been sold. We knew about her pump organ and other large items, but hadn't noticed the glass and china disappearing. This happened even before Poppop died because their income from social security and the farm was very small.

Bill and Janice suggested having an auctioneer appraise and sell. Weezie and I didn't like the idea, though time revealed we were wrong. Instead we had a huge yard sale. We researched prices but didn't really know what we were doing. Knowledgeable buyers attended the yard sale and quickly bought up the best items. They weren't interested in attending the auction we had later. I shouldn't have attended the auction. Seeing family memories selling for close to nothing was devastating.

When Nana's platform rocker came up for bid I cried out, "NO!" I saved the chair but my outburst disrupted the auction. There was little momentum before my outburst, and it slowed even more.

We used the platform rocker for years and then it went to Karen. It was recovered several times and refinished at least twice. Now it's gone.

Though I enjoy browsing a yard sale, I don't enjoy putting a price on my stuff. We had a yard sale prior to moving to Virginia and friends took care of sales. I stayed out of the way.

Did you notice I referred to "my stuff"? For years, I put too much stock in things. For me it had to do with emotional worth, rather than financial worth. Those things were connected to people I love, places I've been, memories I cherish. I confronted this obstacle each time we down-sized and it became increasingly easier to conquer. I'd like to say I no longer embrace things. That isn't completely true, but I can honestly say I've improved!

"Set your minds on things above, not on earthly things."
(Colossians 3:2)

I believe that all I own isn't mine, even my life, it all belongs to God. I am His because He created me, and then He redeemed me (saved me) with His blood.

"The earth is the LORD'S, and all it contains,
The world, and those who dwell in it."
(Psalm 24:1)
"In Him we have redemption through His blood,
the forgiveness of sins, according to the riches of His grace…"
(Ephesians 1:7)

The platform rocker is no longer with us, but someday all our possessions will be gone. It won't matter how much you love them or how much they're worth.

"…the elements will be destroyed by fire,
and the earth and everything done in it will be laid bare"
(2 Peter 3:13)

WRITING

Death may bring about surprising changes. After Nana died, an opportunity came my way. For years she wrote a weekly newspaper column for three local papers. She wrote it in the careful cursive peculiar to a bookkeeper.

Every week she called our neighbors gathering information for the Hardingville News. Though the news wasn't earth shattering it kept us aware of what was going on.

Folks were encouraged to contact Nana with their news but they seldom did. Calling people had a two-fold purpose, to gather news and to show someone cared. After Nana died we realized how many people were encouraged by her phone calls. Too often we are so involved with ourselves we don't know what's happening around us.

I called the editor of the Sentinel and asked if I could continue to write her column but do something more than just the news. He didn't sound excited but said I could give it a try.

We titled the column Hardingville and Roundabout; my first venture into creative writing in a long time. I had written a few short children's stories but my writing reflected what I'd read as a child and it didn't fit the needs of the current market.

This time I wrote about common everyday events with a twist. Before long I heard folks looked forward to reading my column. I didn't call people for their news like Nana did but included some each week.

One column that caught a lot of attention was about Sally's, a fabric shop in Clayton. Sally had big bins of fabric remnants. Rather than purchasing fabric by the yard, it was weighed and sold by the pound. Buying fabric this way made home sewing less expensive. My sis-in-love, Janice, introduced me to the store and several of my friends also shopped there.

To find enough of the right fabric you pulled yard upon yard of fabric from the bins. Since the remnant pieces were random in size, finding just the right piece was a treasure hunt. Seldom was there a piece big enough to complete a project so finding enough was like putting together a jigsaw puzzle. I made nearly all of Karen's clothes, some of mine, and even a few things for Bill and the boys so I often spent hours at Sally's. My sewing machine was busy!

The humorous piece I wrote for the newspaper elaborated on the hunt for treasure at Sally's. Two days after the column was published, there was a knock at our front door.

"Delivery for Pat Cox," said the driver of the florist shop van as she handed me a lovely floral bouquet.

I returned a surprised, "Thank you!"

I put the vase on our dining room table and looked at the card. It was from Sally. She thanked me for the great piece in the newspaper and hoped I enjoyed the flowers. The flowers were lovely but the recognition was even better!

Writing for the newspaper continued until we moved to Virginia. It also stirred my desire to write. When we were missionaries in Virginia my writing was useful for prayer letters. It was helpful in college and served the Lord writing scripts for the puppet ministry in Bumpville.

Though writing hasn't been lucrative financially, it has enhanced many areas of our lives and afforded an outlet for creative expression. Most of all, I hope my writing will honor and glorify God. As with everything, it all belongs to Him!

"...that you may with one mind and one mouth
glorify the God and Father of our Lord Jesus Christ.
(Romans 15:6)

SPIRITUAL CHANGE

When Billy was quite young, Bill was asked if we would be youth leaders at Hardingville Bible Church. As youth leader, Bill decided he should stop smoking cigarettes. He wanted to be a good example. He still smoked a pipe but he soon gave that up and tossed all his pipes into our burn barrel. He said they were a temptation. It was a little sad because he had purchased several while overseas.

We were growing spiritually but it was slow. We were active in the church but our walk with the Lord was at arm's length rather than close and personal. At various times, Bill was a trustee on the church board, Sunday School Superintendent, sang in the choir and even directed it. I taught Sunday School and sang in the choir. I still wanted control of my life and wasn't sure what God might ask me to do if I surrendered my life to Him. Some of you may identify. Others may think, "How silly." I'm telling you how it was for me.

I spent little time reading the Bible except when preparing for a class. I often resolved to spend daily time with the Lord but it didn't last. My prayer life was active but not consistent and we didn't have regular family devotions.

One Sunday morning when Karen was a baby I stayed home from church with her because she had a cold. Bill and Billy went without us. I was still in my bathrobe and Karen was sleeping. Unexpectedly I realized I was being rebellious to Almighty God and had an overwhelming desire to give Him all of me. I cried out to Him and threw myself on His mercy. The ensuing sense of peace and relief was stunning.

When Bill and Billy arrived home from church, I wanted to share what happened, but they couldn't wait to tell me what happened to them. After the morning message, they both went forward to rededicate their lives to Christ. The Holy Spirit was working in our church and in our home with all three of us at the same time.

I'd like to say from that time forward I always did what God wanted me to do and never again had issues with faith and trust but that wouldn't be true. Even so, it's a precious patch in my quilt.

Hazel and Ben Richards, along with others, had been praying for someone from our church to go the mission field. I began to wonder if God wanted Bill to be in full time ministry. My mentioning, more than once, that I wondered if God wanted him in ministry may have bordered on nagging. To his credit, he didn't call it that, but he told me he didn't want to hear any more about it. I took the hint and asked God to show him what He wanted.

One day after church Pastor Joe asked Bill to preach for him when he was going to be away. Bill was a little uneasy but glad to help. His message was well received and he filled in several more times. Then Bill told Pastor Joe he wanted to share a message on how we shouldn't presume we will always have the privilege of openly worshiping God in our church. Also, to show what could happen if we no longer had access to the Bible or our hymnals. Yes, this was even a concern over forty years ago.

Only a few knew the plan. Pastor Joe opened the service as usual but just before the message a local policeman interrupted it. He was in uniform, walked into the church, went to the front and appeared to arrest the pastor for preaching the Gospel. People were stunned but only one older man stood and wanted to physically stop the policeman from taking the pastor out in handcuffs. It was Joe Jones. He didn't know it was a setup. In my eyes, he was a hero. What would you have done?

Shortly after that service, Gerry Hobart and his wife visited Hardingville Church. They were with National Home Missions Fellowship. Missionaries are often thought of as going to foreign countries but the NHMF represents missionaries here in the states. Bill and Gerry got along well and they had several in-depth conversations about ministry. Bill soon shared with me that he knew God was calling him. We just didn't know what or where. I asked God not to send us to a city.

Through this I learned a valuable lesson. The Holy Spirit is sometimes referred to as *The Hound of Heaven*. When he is pursuing someone, He doesn't require help. It's best to let Him do things His way. My intruding hindered rather than helped. I'm glad He showed me I should back off and keep quiet.

Pastor Joe asked Bill to fill the pulpit from time to time and Bill jumped at the opportunities.

One day he told Joe, "Any time you want me to preach I'll be glad to do it."

With a smile on his face Joe replied, "Get your own church!"

We laughed about it but saw the handwriting on the wall. Bill would get his own church in God's time. From then on, he was preparing messages, even when he didn't have an invitation to speak. That continued until he left us on assignment in Heaven.

Note on *The Hound of Heaven*:
The term isn't scriptural but the inference is
there. It's from a lengthy poem written in old
English by Francis Thompson, depicting how God
pursues us relentlessly.

FAMILY TIMES

When Karen and Matt were little they cooled off on a hot summer day with a tubful of toys and soap bubbles. When they were older they played outside in a kiddie pool. They played trucks together, crayoned and painted together, rode ponies together, played with Barbie and GI Joe together, and did barn chores together. They sometimes played with Brian and Jeff, as well as the Zearfaus kids.

They didn't always choose who came to play but we told them they should be willing to play even if they weren't fond of the kids. Bill had stacked window sash at the edge of the woods behind our house, planning to use them to build cold frames. Matt and a visiting lad threw rocks at the glass, resulting in a lot of broken glass. When Bill found out, he reprimanded them and I concurred.

While writing this, I decided to go right to the horse's mouth and asked Matthew what happened on that fateful day. With his permission, here's his take on the incident:

> *"Allow me to bring you up to speed on my actions that involved the boy that I was required to play with that regularly broke my stuff. We were down by the barns where Dad had a lot of junk (treasures) stored. We were playing but not with my toys.*
>
> *We decided to play SWAT or Emergency, both popular programs with young impressionable boys. In order to save victims trapped in a burning building it was necessary to break out the glass in the windows.*
>
> *I thought the windows were there to be thrown away. In real life, they would have had a parade for me honoring such a heroic act by such a young boy, instead I got busted by my folks for destroying the tops to the cold frames."*

Now isn't that a better tale? I don't believe I've been clued in often enough to the heroic actions of my children. I dare say the world truly is a safer place because of them. Had I known the whole story that afternoon I would have at the very least gone to bat for Matt. To the unskilled eye, Bill's treasures could have been mistaken for junk.

Bill often saw treasure in what other people called junk. Throughout our married life he accumulated things other people saw as scrap, planning to use them to produce something useful. He was constantly creating and building in his mind and on paper. He could have done it but his projects were far too many to accomplish.

Back to the kids! One of their favorite activities was playing with toads. At our house, they were found in our window wells. At the Raineys' there was a big excavation in their backyard for a while and the kids made cliff dwelling homes for the toads. I have no idea how many toads lived or died but I do know the kids had a great time! It's evident that getting warts from toads is an old wives' tale. If it was so, they would have been covered with warts.

Billy didn't enjoy climbing trees but Karen, Matt and their cousins did. There was a mulberry tree at the bend in our driveway where they spent a lot of time. It was good for climbing and mulberries tasted good. They also stain kids and their clothing.

There is a scary memory of Brian's leg impaled on a sharp branch on the mulberry tree. It broke off leaving part of the branch imbedded deeply in his leg. Karen was above him and couldn't get down so they sent Matt for help. Visions of infection danced in my head. I called his mom and she took it from there. He healed without infection. Thank you, Father!

Bill did most of our auto repairs until the manufacturers started using computers. One day he was working under our car, concentrating on what he was doing, when he heard a voice, "Whatcha doin' Unca Bill?" There was Brian, hunkered down, peering under the car. I can hear Bill muttering, "Oh no!" Brian was always interested in what Bill was doing which was not always timely but often provided a good laugh.

<O><

For a time in the early 70s, Bill and I were hired by our church to clean the buildings and mow the churchyard.

Back then we still threw rice at weddings. Even though it was thrown outside the church, some always showed up inside. When I found rice while vacuuming I prayed for the bride and groom. Church cleaning can be a ministry.

The church cleaning job was okay, but the mowing job was great! The churchyard wasn't large and quickly finished. The cemetery was challenging and fun. The grave stones weren't in any order, nor were they installed with the idea of getting a riding lawnmower between them. After mowing a few times, you knew where you could move quickly and where to slow down.

You could also sing as loudly as you wished and no one could hear you. The residents certainly couldn't. Bill said he did some of his best singing and preaching on the riding mower.

<O><

Karen thought since you learned your ABCs and numbers when you went to school, why learn them before you go? Brian could rattle off his ABCs and numbers and even tie his shoes before he hit Kindergarten. Karen was unimpressed and learned later. I wonder if she shares that with her preschool students.

She did well in Kindergarten. Her teacher was Mrs. Walls, an excellent teacher. She was a Christian but didn't talk about her faith unless a student asked.

One evening Karen and Matt were in the bathtub while I folded clothes nearby.

"What's Hell like?" Karen asked.

That certainly wasn't expected! I assured her it was real and a bad place to be.

"Is there really fire?" she asked.

Wondering where all this was coming from, I stopped folding clothes, went into the bathroom and sat down next to the tub. Karen was serious, she wanted to know about Hell. One of her classmates had asked Mrs. Walls about Hell and she wanted to know more.

I went over what the Bible teaches about Hell. When I finished she said, "I don't want to go there. I want to go to Heaven."

After I explained how she could be sure of her destination, she asked Jesus into her heart and life. When we later told her daddy, he quipped, "She could have been baptized. She was already in the water."

It was obvious Karen was serious about this salvation business. The first thing she did was tell Matthew, "You need to do it too! You don't want to go to Hell, do you?" He agreed but didn't remember later—he was just three.

Matthew may not remember Karen's plea to be saved, but he does remember responding when he was six years old. Dale and Opal Linebaugh held meetings at Hardingville church. When Dale gave an altar call, Matthew tugged on my sleeve and said, "Will you go with me?" He was normally very shy so this was out of character for him. I went forward with him, and Dale asked Opal

178

to talk with him. He accepted Jesus as his Savior. Years later he followed in Dale's footsteps at Miracle Mountain Ranch. What a wonderful God we serve!

The next day following her bathtub conversion, she told her cousin Brian he needed to be saved. She didn't want to go to Hell and wanted everyone else to avoid going there.

<O><

After having a great teacher in Kindergarten, Karen's teacher in first grade was a different story. Karen missed a lot of school in first grade. She had chicken pox, mumps, strep and scarlatina all in one school year. Mrs. K belittled Karen for her frequent absences and said she would not be promoted to second grade. Her grades were good and we provided notes from our doctor. Though it didn't help Karen, Mrs. K didn't return the next year.

Both Karen and Billy had negative experiences with teachers, though just one each. The others were fine, some even exceptional. We wanted to come alongside the teacher to help our children learn. We also wanted to give them the benefit of the doubt until we knew all the facts. Balancing that with upholding our children can be tricky. I'm glad our children are grown but I am concerned what may be ahead for their children, and even their children.

Note to self: God IS in control!

MAINE
BUCKSKIN AND BEADS

In the early 1960s Big Bill and Weezie went to Maine on vacation. They stayed in a cabin owned by friends. They liked the area and when a one-room schoolhouse went on the market they bought it. It hadn't been a school for years but had been used for grain storage and finally as a hunter's camp. They worked on it on vacations and holidays. They installed siding, replaced the roof, replaced doors and windows, painted, put in a drop ceiling, refinished hardwood floors, and went sightseeing.

Indoor plumbing? They bathed in a wash basin. Laundry was done in a wash tub, the town laundromat, or hauled home. Weezie did dishes with water carried from a nearby spring and heated on the stove. Drinking water came from another spring.

Toilet facilities? May I introduce you to the inside-outer. Maybe the outhouse was separate from the building at some time, but it was connected at this point. It had a lidded toilet seat and tissue holder. It looked like a normal bathroom until you saw the bag of lime sitting on the floor or lifted the seat cover.

They encouraged us all to visit. Both our Billy and Jeff Rainey visited with them and enjoyed the camp. The first time we visited as a family, Matthew was a toddler. We were meeting my parents for a few days, then staying a few more days by ourselves.

It was a beautiful day for travel. We stopped for gasoline and I changed a diaper on the tailgate of our station wagon. Several miles down the road we saw a toll booth ahead. I reached for my wallet and couldn't find it. When we left home, we put all our money in my wallet though we'd never done that before. Bill stopped along the side of the road. When was the last time I had it? At the gas station! Bill gave it to me after paying for the gas and I put it on top of the car so I could finish the diaper change!

Bill said, "Let's look for it!" He was calm. I was not. We went back to the gas station and retraced our route. We prayed, we looked, still no wallet. We found a dime on the floor of the car. We weren't sure if we had enough gas to get us to our destination and we knew we needed more than ten cents for tolls. Why didn't we call? No one had cell phones and there was no phone at the camp.

The gas station attendant accepted Bill's chronograph watch as security for a loan of twenty dollars. We planned to redeem it on our way home. When we arrived at camp, Weezie and Big Bill loaned us money for our return trip. You can be sure we never put all our money in one wallet again!

Is there Biblical advice here? It's a stretch but ...
"Divide your portion to seven, or even to eight,
For you do not know what misfortune may occur on the earth."
(Ecclesiastes 11:2 NASB)

Weezie and Big Bill took us to Presque Isle along the Canadian border. We drove through the paper company forests. Their log trucks rumbled south on Route 19 right by the driveway. We also visited a nearby beaver pond and hiked to the top of a hill where we could see Mt. Katahdin in the distance.

The next time we visited Maine was several years later, on Easter vacation. Karen was seven and Matthew was four. It was spring in New Jersey but we packed snowsuits and snow saucers. We hoped for signs of snow as we drove north but not a flake in sight! A gas station attendant in southern Maine said the snow was gone.

Farther north we finally saw snow in the edges of the woods and when we reached camp we barreled through a drift in the driveway. The next day the kids bundled up in snowsuits and used their snow saucers. After time on the slope, they had rosy cheeks and were glad to warm up by the wood stove. We had one good day in the snow. Warmer weather arrived so we enjoyed signs of spring and sightseeing.

This was our second trip to Maine and we still hadn't seen a moose. We joked that there was one moose traveling between Canada and Maine but it was never in Maine when we were there. We saw tracks and scat but no moose. Big Bill often saw moose when he was hunting. He told us how they tilted their heads to go through the woods without slowing down.

We again climbed the hill to see Mt. Katahdin. This time the field had been seeded by plane with pine trees. We also found the meadow we'd visited with my parents. We parked the car and walked around the pond. The wet ground showed lots of tracks: bear, deer, and smaller animals.

We were a distance from the car when we saw fresh bear scat! Bill said, "Maybe we should start back to the car." He didn't mention to the kids that it was fresh. We didn't see a bear, but we did see the beaver dam and where they cut down trees.

We visited the coast of Maine and saw some of Acadia National Park. We enjoyed the rocky coast and the tidal pools with all their sea life. We drove through Baxter State Park for a closer look at Mt. Katahdin, though the roads up the mountain were still closed. We saw black bears and people who, disregarding the warnings, got out of their cars and offered them food. We were content to watch from inside our car with the windows closed.

One thing we encountered in the park wasn't in our travel plan. As we were driving through Baxter, Karen said, "Mommy, I itch."

I turned to look and she was covered with chicken pox! It wasn't difficult to diagnose. We were near the end of our stay and it was obviously time to leave for home. We knew the pox was destined to be with us for a while since Matthew was with her in the back seat throughout the trip. His spots showed up right on time.

Early in the trip we attended church in Holton and met Sam Fast, missionary to the Passamaquoddy Indians. We heard about his ministry and took his suggestion to visit the reservation. We did a drive-through on our own and it was depressing.

We told Sam we were interested in coming back the next summer to help if he could use us. We were to get in touch with him when we got back home. As we were driving home from Maine we saw Mt. Katahdin in our rear-view window and looked forward to working with Sam. We wrote asking for more details but didn't hear from him.

When we visited Maine several years later we saw Sam at church.

"Do you mind if I ask why you didn't answer our letter?" Bill asked.

"Not at all but I never received a letter from you. I wondered why you didn't answer my letter," Sam replied.

Bill was now a pastor so we weren't free to join Sam in ministry. God must have intervened in our exchange of letters. We trusted God to show us what He wanted us to do by stepping out in faith. He redirected our path toward a different goal than we had in mind.

"Trust in the LORD with all thine heart;
and lean not unto thine own understanding.
In all thy ways acknowledge him,
and he shall direct thy paths."
(Proverbs 3:5-6)

In the early 1980s we took our last family trip to Maine. We planned to be there for one week but it stretched to two weeks. As we drove from Bumpville to Maine, we knew something was wrong with our car. The transmission gave out just as we arrived at camp. With a neighbor's help, we arranged to have it fixed in Smyrna Mills and the garage loaned us a car. Parts were ordered from Bangor and when they were a long time arriving, we drove to Bangor to pick them up.

Our usually pleasant Karen was the picture of doom and gloom. She wasn't excited about the trip because she left a boyfriend at home. She had nothing good to say about the trip in general and especially the state of Maine. She was sure we had been kidnapped by the state and would never get home. She even took exception to the wording on Maine license plates: VACATIONLAND.

Though we weren't happy about the transmission it gave us extra time to enjoy some special adventures. We saw not one but three moose.

Late one afternoon Bill, Matt and I went into Patton to get supplies. Miffed at Maine, Karen opted not to go. As we were driving along Route 19 a young moose came out of a logging road. He stopped before stepping onto the macadam, looked both

184

ways, and walked across the road while we watched. Though he was young he was huge! He seemed to move in slow motion. His gait was both ungainly and graceful. Karen missed seeing him. There are consequences for our decisions.

The other two moose offered an exciting adventure. We all went to the beaver dam. The terrain was always different, depending on the season. Bill and the kids walked on ahead of me. They saw a moose and her calf browsing in the marshy edge of the pond. Karen and Matt went down to the water's edge for a good view. Bill followed the path along the edge for a better photograph. The calf ran up the bank on the other side of Bill, putting him between it and its mother. The mother crashed through the brush startling a black bear who had apparently been sleeping and it ran off. Bill and the kids saw the moose and her calf, Bill saw the bear. I heard what was happening but didn't see a thing. I suspect the moose and bear also had an adrenaline rush.

As Big Bill and Weezie grew older the long drive to Maine became more difficult. Trips became fewer and there were years instead of months between visits. On their last trip, my brother needed to drive up to bring them home. Big Bill was unable to drive.

Times change and people change. When they first purchased the camp it was safe even when it was vacant, but in the 90s there were break-ins. Some things were stolen and there was damage. We talked with Weezie about selling and she agreed it was best. Bill and I drove from Virginia to New Jersey where we picked her up and then continued to Maine. We pulled a flatbed trailer to bring home what she wanted to keep.

Since the springs where we used to get water were no longer safe for drinking, we filled milk jugs with water from home and loaded them on the trailer. We were driving north on Interstate 81 when a state policeman flashed his car lights and yelped his siren. Bill pulled off the road.

A trooper came up to Bill's side of the truck, "Mr. Cox, may I please see your driver's license and registration?"

Bill retrieved his wallet from his pocket while I rummaged through the glove compartment to get out the registration. He continued to talk with Bill while a second trooper came to my window.

185

"How are things in Clintwood?" he asked.

"Just fine when we left," I replied.

Our conversation continued, mostly about the Clintwood area and where we were going.

The first trooper asked Bill, "What do you have in the trailer?"

"Jugs of water. We're going to New Jersey to pick up my mother-in-law to take her to Maine. She has a cabin with no running water. We're taking water from home so we don't have to buy it when we get there."

"Do you mind if we look?" he asked.

"Of course not," Bill answered.

Bill and the trooper went to the rear of the trailer.

"Do you mind if I check the water?"

"Not at all," Bill said as he reached for a jug.

"No, not that one. How about one over there?"

Bill handed him the jug he'd indicated. The trooper unscrewed the top, sniffed the jug, replaced the top, and handed it back to Bill.

By this time, I'd gotten out of the truck and walked to the back where we all stood together. The troopers explained that they ran our tags when they saw the jugs. When they saw we were from Dickenson County it was a red flag. It seemed our county was known for its production and sale of moonshine. They were cautious but polite and we were impressed with how they handled the situation.

When we realized why we were stopped all we could think of was the possible headline:

MISSIONARY TRANSPORTING MOONSHINE ON I-81!

We continued to New Jersey and then on to Maine with Weezie. It was a nostalgic trip for her. We brought back a few treasures. We tried to dig up some little evergreens from around the building. The ground was frozen so they were bare rooted. We planted several in front of our home and the rest went to family. When we moved from Virginia in 2008 they were twelve feet tall.

I loved our Maine trees.

LATE 60S AND EARLY-70s
KHAKI AND TARTAN

Life in the Cox household was always busy. Our lives revolved around school, college, Boy Scouts, and church. The only time I remember going on a date was annually for our anniversary. Dates always involved going out for dinner, not finding a movie we wanted to see, buying magazines, and taking ice cream home to eat with our kids.

I volunteered with Child Evangelism Fellowship, teaching Good News Clubs. I believe having a summer 5-Day Club in our backyard was the motivation. Ardeen Zearfus and I held weekly clubs in the homes of Rich and Margaret Iles, and John and Esther Smith. I usually led the singing, prayer time and the Bible lesson. Ardeen presented the missionary stories. We learned Bible verses, which I still remember today. It's now more difficult to memorize Scripture! We had a wide range of ages and there were several unchurched kids. I remember one little girl who asked for prayer for her dead frog!

In the spring of 1969 our scout troop prepared for hiking a section of the Appalachian Trail in Virginia. They took several preparatory hikes to qualify, including two overnight trips. Billy was one of fifteen scouts who participated and Bill was accompanied by three hiking leaders. Another leader met them periodically to replenish supplies.

Bill experienced quite an adrenaline rush one afternoon on the trail. They were moving single file along the face of a mountain and were attacked by a swarm of bees. A couple boys took off running. There were no guard rails and Bill saw a turn ahead. He bellowed, "Halt!" which had the desired effect.

While on the trail, the leaders stayed in Adirondack shelters, sometimes sharing with other hikers. One group stopped with them for a second night. They said, "We feel safe with you guys. Bill's snoring keeps the bears away."

The boys slept in tents. One boy kept rolling out at night so they tied a rope around a tent peg and the other end to his ankle to keep him safe.

When Billy was a teen he sang with the Camp Ha-Lu-Wa-Sa choral group. (Ha-Lu-Wa-Sa stands for Hallelujah What a Savior) They sang in churches and at other events. He was also involved with Youth for Christ and played in a Christian band. There were several from that group who had a positive influence on his life.

There were local boys who were not a good influence and had a stronger hold on him than his Christian friends. I believe one young man set him up as a scapegoat, though he never said so. He did some things that were wrong and made restitution. In later years he said, "I am responsible for my choices, no one made me do anything."

Though sometimes rebellious, he never was disrespectful. One incident that took place when he was twelve or thirteen comes to mind. I was standing in front of him in the middle of our kitchen giving him what-for and shaking my finger at him. It became apparent to me that he was a head taller but was just standing there taking my tirade. I tried to suppress a giggle then burst out laughing. He looked confused, then laughed with me.

Another time, I was reprimanding him rather vigorously. To make a point I thrust the corn broom in my hand to the kitchen floor, bristle end down. When it hit the floor, it bounced up on an angle and broke a window in the back door. You're right, it was my anger that broke the window! I'm thankful that's no longer a problem.

When Billy was in senior high school I stopped getting up with him in the morning, by mutual consent. He got himself ready and left the house at seven. Senior high classes started early in the morning, making it easier for students to get part time work. I think he liked the independence. When I heard the front door close, I got out of bed. I felt guilty not seeing him off but he preferred it that way. I got up with the rest.

Our oldest son was good at floating an idea and watching for a reaction. He was a junior in high school when he came home and told me he was interested in a girl at school. I figured that was normal and didn't pursue the subject. He seemed to want to tell me more. Finally, he said, "She's black." I said, "That's nice. What's she like?" I guess he expected me to react to the girl not being white. When I didn't, she was never mentioned again.

He was involved in musical productions. In his sophomore year he was Mr. Lundy in *Brigadoon*. That was a speaking role, though he also sang with the chorus. In his junior year, he was Horace Vandergelder, the male lead in *Hello Dolly*.

In 1974 Billy graduated from Delsea Regional High School. Immediately after the ceremony he brought his diploma to show his dad it was real. Though he was gifted with intelligence, he put little effort into most of his classes. When he wanted to do something, he excelled.

Billy was born into a Christian family but our spiritual growth was stagnant and lacked depth. We were spiritual mugwumps, trying to sit on the fence with our mug on one side and our wump on the other.

I need to speak for me on this. I nearly left off the last phrase in the verse below because it wasn't money or riches that was my problem, it was self. It may be a stretch, but the word mammon is a Semitic term for "the treasure a person trusts in." Putting self before God suits the definition of mammon.

"No one can serve two masters;
for either he will hate the one and love the other,
or else he will be loyal to the one and despise the other.
You cannot serve God and mammon."
(Matthew 6:24)

OUR SIBLINGS

"A family is a unit composed not only of children
but of men, women, an occasional animal,
and the common cold."
Ogden Nash

While we were busy with our lives, our siblings' lives also continued to go forward. Bill's sister Barbara visited friends in Cape May and met Michel Andre Remy. After graduating from Glassboro High, she graduated from Cooper Hospital with her RN in 1958. They married in 1959.

My brother Bill graduated from Glassboro High in 1955. He met and dated Janice Ware while in high school. She became an RN through West Jersey Hospital. Bill spent six months in the Army, then worked for DuPont. They were married in 1960. Bunky was the ring bearer in their wedding and I was a bridesmaid.

The Rainey clan lived near each another so we got together for holidays and birthdays and our kids often played together.

We enjoyed visiting the Remys in Cape May. Barbs said they were the only family not overrun with relatives during the summer season. We should have visited them more often.

One weekend we attended a large church near Cape May. We had our children and three nieces and nephews with us and an usher suggested the children might want to go to children's church.

"No thank you, they'll stay with us." This was mainly because our kids didn't like being separated into strange classes with kids they didn't know.

Most of the pews were filled so he tried to find someplace we could sit together. The front row was empty so we started to go there.

"You might be more comfortable near the back."

"No, we usually sit in the front row in our home church."

He said, with a concerned look, "The service will be broadcast, so you'll need to be quiet."

"We'll be fine." We were quiet and didn't ruin the broadcast.

<O><

During the '60s Shelly and Suzie visited us for a week or two each summer; usually when we had Vacation Bible School at our church. Michel came barreling up our driveway, his car loaded down with luggage, bicycles, miscellaneous stuff, and the kids. We enjoyed having them.

The boys are younger than the girls so Mark came only once to spend a week and Steven never made it. I have a picture in my head of little Markie in his footed pajamas. He was a cutie.

The deal was everyone helped in the garden in the morning and we went to Richie's Lake in the afternoon. I'm sure the girls thought they were slave labor but we stuck to the rule, most of the time.

One summer they were with us for the green pea harvest; English peas if you're from the south. Commercial harvesting machines picked and shelled the peas in the field. We purchased them directly from the harvester. Back home we washed them in large tubs and readied them for the freezer. If it was a warm day, the kids wore bathing suits. It was work but they sure tasted good in the winter.

<O><

Michel and I never quite measured up to Mom Cox's expectations, so we referred to ourselves as the out-laws. Bill and I couldn't have asked for a better brother-in-law.

He was born in France. His parents were in the French underground resistance during World War II. The Germans executed his father and his mother later married an American serviceman. He came to the states, leaving all he knew and loved and lost contact with his family in France, especially Aunt Marie-Louise who raised him.

Michel didn't plan to return to France because he thought his family was gone. When Steven married Cecile, a French citizen, that changed. They tracked down the Remy family, including Aunt Marie-Louise. Michel and his family had an exciting reunion. He was the only child of the only son in his family! While there, he visited the memorial to his father and others who worked in the resistance movement.

Marie-Louise died shortly before Michel made another visit to France. When Michel realized his death was imminent, he instructed his ashes be taken to Le Thillot and buried in the family cemetery. Steve carried out his father's request. His memory remains in our hearts!

GOD CALLS
GOSSAMER AND DENIM

We joyfully anticipated Bill's graduation from college, though he decided not to attend the ceremony. Finally, a summer without attending classes. What a great time to install an above-ground pool! We ordered one from the Sears Roebuck catalog.

Severe abdominal pain was not in our plan. Dr. M thought it was caused by his gall bladder and referred him to Dr. K for evaluation. Tests showed stones in his bile duct and his gall bladder needed to be removed. Bill didn't need urging to sign up.

His surgery went well but the night before his discharge he was feverish. He was afraid the fever might delay his going home, so he was restless and unable to sleep. As he lay praying in his hospital bed, he saw a light in an upper corner of his room. There was no feasible source for the light but it increased in size and intensity. Bill was certain God wanted his attention. He told Him that he would do whatever He wanted him to do, and go wherever He wanted him to go. The fever broke and he slept.

Soon after breakfast he was dressed and waiting for Dr. K to remove a drainage tube. It was late afternoon when the doctor checked him over, yanked out the tube, signed the release, and left the building. Yes, you read that correctly. He pulled the tube as you might pull the cord to start a lawn mower. Bill told me, "I felt a shock wave that shook me to my core." He explained to the nurse that the pain was coming in waves. She tried to contact Dr. K but he was on his way home. We picked up Bill's pain pills, went home and waited. When Dr. K called, he assured Bill the pain would subside. Bill said it was the worst part of the procedure.

Unlike today's laparoscopic surgery, Bill had an impressive scar on his abdomen. The scar lasted, and so did his commitment to the Lord. It wasn't something he promised and then forgot. He didn't know what he was to do but he knew God would show him.

While recuperating from surgery at home, he received a call from a missionary our church supported in Virginia. The Hemonds had a children's ministry in southwest Virginia and several other states. Hank wanted someone to pastor his church during the summer while he traveled to meetings. When he asked our pastor if he knew anyone who could help him out, Joe said Bill might be available. It seemed this is what God wanted Bill to do, at least for the summer. He told Hank we would be there.

Remember the swimming pool? We ordered it, but delivery was delayed because of a glitch at their warehouse. We called and canceled the order. We weren't going to be home to enjoy a pool.

We planned to take our pop-up camper and camp on the way to Virginia. We also planned to stay in it all summer since Karen and Matt's dogs, Horatio and Teddy, were going with us. Billy was working so he'd take care of the house. Everything was falling into place. We were excited.

Though we didn't know Hank and Joyce well we'd met them several times. Pastor Joe and Ardeen had worked with them in camp ministry. When the Hemonds heard about our camper, they insisted we stay in their home. They would only be there for two weeks and the rest of the time we would have it to ourselves. They assured us our dogs were welcome.

Our trip south was fun. We were excited to see mountains from a distance and then we were in them. After going through Clintwood, we traveled eight miles of winding road with no guard rails to get to Skeetrock. It took nearly a half hour.

We arrived on Wednesday night, just in time for prayer meeting. I had on shorts and wondered if I should change but was assured I was okay. We attended prayer meeting and the men helped Bill carry our stuff down the trail over the rocks.

The Hemonds lived in a brick house next to the main road. The church was up behind them on the hill. Joyce left notes telling us where things were and to use whatever we needed without going to the expense of buying supplies.

Bill learned the men wanted to do renovations in the church and hoped for his help. I wonder if they knew his skills or just *got lucky.* We don't believe in luck so it seems God stepped in again.

The church was a one-room then a two-room schoolhouse. They were currently using one room as the sanctuary. They planned to install new windows, put in a drop ceiling and panel the walls in the unfinished room, then move the sanctuary there. It was ambitious but well within Bill's level of expertise. Bill was told it was a surprise for Hank and they hoped to have it well underway by his return in mid-summer. We later heard Hank wasn't totally in agreement with the proposed changes.

Bill brought hand tools and power tools from home. He rarely went away without them. The men, and some women, got to know one another by working together. The owner of a local woodworking shop allowed Bill to use his shop and equipment to make the door and window frames—a money saver.

THE BILLY KIM CRUSADE

I'd been privileged to lead children to the Lord but not an adult. During the Linebaugh's meetings, Dale encouraged us to focus more on sharing our faith. He challenged us to make a commitment to share our testimony, seeking to bring someone to the Lord during the next year. I made a commitment to share Christ with an adult. During the following year, I often thought about it, but it hadn't happened. Did I miss my opportunity?

Soon after we arrived in Skeetrock we heard about the Billy Kim Crusade. Along with others from the church we attended counselor training sessions. We'd never heard of Billy Kim though his name was well known in Dickenson County. Our training was like the training for Billy Graham's Crusades. Maybe this was my opportunity to lead an adult to Jesus.

Billy Kim was born in 1934 to a poor Korean farm family. Carl Powers from Dickenson County was stationed in Korea and helped Billy come to the States. He enrolled him in Bob Jones Academy where he received Jesus as his Savior. Billy earned top grades in college, preached in small churches on weekends, was ordained and received his master's degree. He returned to Korea with his wife where he had a thriving ministry and translated for Billy Graham's 1973 Crusade.

We wore name tags showing we were counselors and were spread throughout the seats on the Ervinton football field. We enjoyed the music and Billy's message. When the invitation was given, I watched for a woman to stand. An oriental girl moved forward so I followed. Imagine sharing Christ with someone whose roots were from the other side of the world. When people stopped coming, we questioned as instructed.

"We're glad you're here this evening and hope to be of service to you. Do you mind telling me why you came forward?"

"No, of course not. I want to meet Billy Kim. We may have mutual friends in Korea."

Well, that wasn't the answer I expected! We talked for a bit and it was obvious she just wanted to meet Billy Kim. I took her to an area where she could meet him and called it a night. So much for my first adult convert. That doesn't sound right! Even if she had been interested in accepting Christ as her Savior she was His convert, not mine!

The next night an older woman with two young children went forward. I followed them to the front. Maybe this time? I asked her why she came forward and she told me she was a believer but her grandson had some questions about whether he was really saved. We talked for a while, shared scripture, and he went home assured of his salvation.

The last night of the crusade there were 2,000 people in that little mountain stadium. During the week, Bill was involved with two men accepting Christ as Savior and one who rededicated his life. I shared with folks but I didn't fulfill my commitment to bring an adult to the Lord.

Sometimes we try too hard to do something *for* the Lord instead of simply allowing Him to work through us, in His time and for His purposes.

"Be still, and know that I am God;
I will be exalted among the nations,
I will be exalted in the earth!"
(Psalm 46:10)

We were comfortable living at the Hemonds. They told us to use whatever we needed for food. There was a big metal storage can full of flour. Joyce said to be careful to remove the bay leaves, they helped discourage weevils. She also said to sift the flour to remove any that weren't discouraged. I figured if any of the little fellows remained they just added protein.

Sorghum molasses was a new commodity for me. Joyce used it in cooking. I used it a lot until I realized our systems weren't used to that much molasses. It tasted good but I cut back!

We participated in Vacation Bible School and met folks who weren't a part of the church, like Cody, a neighbor boy. He was disobedient. I saw him kick his teacher and intervened. When he didn't comply, I took him by the arm and walked him across the churchyard. I knew his grandfather was bush hogging a nearby pasture.

"Take yer hands offen me. I'll tell my dad. He'll give you what for. Don't you touch me."

"You aren't scaring me, Cody, I'm sure your grandfather doesn't want you to kick people."

The church was on top of the hill and Ernest and his tractor were at the bottom of the hill. I pulled Cody along because he wasn't coming willingly. I wondered what his grandfather would say. Would he tell me to stop manhandling his child? Would he say Cody couldn't come to VBS?

We paused at the edge of the field. Ernest stopped and climbed down from the tractor. Cody tried to get in the first words but Ernest wasn't having it. He told Cody to hush and asked me what was wrong. I explained that we couldn't tolerate his behavior but wanted him to come to VBS.

Ernest's response was even better than I'd hoped, "Boy, you need to obey your teachers!" Cody hung his head, this wasn't going the way he hoped. He kicked his toe in the dirt. I'd released him as soon as Ernest stopped the tractor. He showed no sign of running though he threatened to do so.

Ernest apologized for Cody's behavior. He gave me permission to do whatever was needed to keep him in line and then said, "Let me know if you have any more trouble from him."

We were blessed with many new friends that summer and when the men of the church asked Bill to return as their pastor we were honored. However, Bill had already signed his contract to teach the next year and we needed time to pray. Was this God's will?

"See then that you walk circumspectly,
not as fools but as wise,
redeeming the time, because the days are evil.
Therefore do not be unwise,
but understand what the will of the Lord is."
(Ephesians 5:15-17)

We enjoyed our trip back to New Jersey and again camped along the way. We were excited about the possibilities but not sure what we should do. That's the good news, but it wasn't all good news awaiting us.

We knew about the sump pump not functioning and the basement floor being flooded. Billy got rid of as much water as he could but things were ruined. Yes, they were just things but also cherished possessions. My Poppop's Morris chair and several spun cotton Christmas ornaments from the 1800s were among them. I salvaged the strings of blown glass beads from my Nana's first Christmas tree. They no longer have the silvery inside coating but the colored glass is pretty.

We discovered something else in our basement. I had a lot of houseplants and Billy cared for them while we were away. He told me a friend was growing plants I might like and he was going to raise them. I was glad he was taking an interest in something like that and looked forward to seeing them.

When we were inspecting the basement for water damage we found a large plywood box lined with aluminum foil with a light over it. Though we had never seen a setup like that, we'd read about them. It didn't take a rocket scientist to figure out someone was growing marijuana in our basement! When I was giving the house a thorough cleaning I found some interesting literature tucked away on a book shelf, information on growing marijuana.

Maybe you've thought, "That could never happen to us." I've thought that also!

There were other bumps in the road as well. Karen was having migraines and medication to alleviate pain put her to sleep. She was scheduled for a brain scan. Bill took us and everything went smoothly but the radiologist noticed a shadow on the scan. She was scheduled for a second one, this time with contrast.

The first time had been easy so I wasn't concerned when Bill couldn't go with us the second time. I soon realized I didn't comprehend what it meant to "use contrast." As I filled out the necessary forms, more extensive than the first time, I thought, "Is she allergic to shellfish? I don't think so. I'm not sure she even likes shellfish."

Karen was sitting next to me watching what I was writing so I reacted internally, "Wait a minute! She could die from contrast? I have to sign something that says they can use something that could kill her?" I talked to Bill in my head, "I need you here with me to sign this. I can't do this alone!"

I told Karen to sit tight. I found a nurse and expressed my fears. She said the percentage of problems was miniscule. She'd never even seen one. Back I went to Karen. As I was signing my name to the waiver I talked to the Lord, "Please, Father, don't let anything happen to Karen. Take away her fear, and mine too!"

A nurse took the signed papers and led us to an examination room where Karen was situated on a hospital bed. Someone in the next cubicle was screaming. Our curtain was open and a nurse walked by with a large syringe. Karen's eyes opened wide. "They aren't going to stick that in me, are they?"

I answered, "Of course not!" but thought, "Surely not!"

I was directed to the waiting room but the nurse soon reappeared, "Come with me." It seemed when Karen saw them approach *her* with the large syringe she tried valiantly to be brave. However, the nurse sensed her concern and asked, "Would you like to have your mom here with you?" Karen replied, "Uh huh!"

The big syringe just held the contrast and a tiny butterfly needled was inserted in Karen's arm. We held hands during the rest of the preparation. She was great and followed instructions. Best of all, the contrast didn't affect her and the shadow they saw on the original scan wasn't even there. Another happy patch in our quilt.

Our doctor suggested she take Periactin, an antihistamine that can prevent migraines in children. She took it for a year and didn't have migraines for years. Sadly, it only helps children and not menopausal women.

After our move to Virginia we were notified Blue Cross had covered all but $235 of the costs of the scans, but we owed the balance. We wrote to the hospital and asked to make payments. The hospital responded by forgiving the balance and wishing us well in our ministry. We thanked the hospital and praised God!

Karen's migraines were controlled but she was feeling weak in mid-afternoon. It seemed to be due to low blood sugar. A glucose tolerance test showed she was pre-diabetic. We monitored her at home. At school, she and Brian went for mid-afternoon snacks together. Her symptoms eventually went away.

Life moved forward with normal bumps in the road. We were back to evening Bible school and regular commitments. We had family all around us. We were comfortable. We were actively involved in local ministries but soon knew God wanted us to move to Virginia. We accepted the call.

The next step was putting our home up for sale. There were few people interested and one offered less than half our asking price.

We also needed a place to live in Virginia so Bill made a trip to see what was available. He tried to find something we could afford but there was nothing in our price range. We had no idea how God was going to work this out!

<O><

One evening our telephone rang and Bill answered, "Hello!"

A male voice asked, "This Bill Cox?"

"Yes, this is Bill."

"This is Al Branham. Heard yer lookin' fer a place in Skeetrock."

"You heard right."

"Well, Prudy wants ta move in ta town so she don't hafta drive the curvy road in the winter. We're gonna sell our trailer. Thought ya might be interested."

"How much are you asking?"

"Asking for what?" I wondered.

"I figure $18,000 is a fair price. There's 'bout an acre 'round it."

"We might be interested but we have to find out what we can do. Give me your phone number and I'll get back to you."

"OK. I'll be waitin' to hear from ya."

Bill's face revealed his surprise and I was eager to hear what was happening.

"That was Al Branham," he said. I looked puzzled. "The guy that lives in the trailer behind the church."

"The one who drives his truck across the church yard?"

"That's the one."

After praying about it and having the folks at the church look it over, we felt it was a good plan. Marvin Senter talked to the bank and vouched for us. They worked out a loan until our house in New Jersey sold. This was God's doing.

Al wasn't a believer but he accepted Christ several years later.
"And we know that all things work together for good
to those who love God,
to those who are the called according to His purpose."
(Romans 8:28)

OFF TO VIRGINIA

Waiting isn't easy and can causing doubting. We were closer to moving and our house wasn't sold. When our six-month contract was over we changed realtors.

To complicate matters I had fibroid tumors. My doctor said I could have a D&C, which might solve the problem, or a hysterectomy which would solve it. We were getting ready to move to an area with unknown doctors and hospitals. Though it meant not having another child, after considering Matthew's early arrival we decided for a total hysterectomy. The surgery went well. I followed my doctor's orders explicitly. I had no symptoms of menopause then or later. It was a good decision.

As I regained strength, I continued packing. We gave stuff away and prepared for a yard sale. Bill and I priced everything, but we had volunteers who dealt with the customers. It was best for me, and others, that I was not involved!

"I don't think I'll need my sewing machine cabinet. I can set it up on the dining room table." *Yes, but...*

"The kids may need the World Book Encyclopedia but where will we put it?" *Under the bed?*

"Honey, I hate selling the coffee table you made but there's no room." *Mistake! Bill made it and it was a great table!*

Decisions, decisions! All were made thoughtfully but not all made well. I do have emotional attachment to things that were in our families. I've had to work through this and am still learning to just let it go, as my daughter tells me.

BICENTENNIAL 1976

Along with getting ready to move, preparations for celebrating the bicentennial of our country were underway. Elk Township planned a parade, quite an undertaking for a rural area. Karen and Matt prepared costumes and decorated their bicycles with red, white and blue streamers woven through the wheels.

Karen made Uncle Sam hats for her and her dog, Horatio. He rode in her bicycle basket with his feet perched on the front, enjoying the attention. They won first prize in their division.

Matt was dressed as a lad from 1776 complete with tri-cornered hat. He won first place also but a boy in a similar costume retrieved the prize before Matt got to the judges' stand. We asked the judges about it and they said Matt won. We didn't protest.

My dad drove his riding lawn mower decorated with red, white and blue. He was dressed appropriately. The parade route went along route 538 so we had front row seats. I'm sure other areas had more elaborate celebrations but ours was exciting.

Our move took place on Saturday, July 3, 1976. That was not planned, just the way it worked out. We often seem to need just one more day before we leave on a trip.

ON OUR WAY

Though still not sold, we cleared the house for its future owners. We rented the largest van available. Bill drove it, pulling their largest trailer. I drove our station wagon pulling our travel trailer, both filled to the gunwales (pronounced gunnels). We had plenty of help packing but it was apparent we needed another vehicle to pull an additional trailer. Eldon Sheppard volunteered.

There was a mix of tears and smiles when we pulled out of our driveway. We looked like a gypsy caravan. Bill led the way in the big truck and trailer, I came next with our station wagon and camper, Eldon brought up the rear with their station wagon and the other trailer.

My vehicle had an interesting load. The back area of the station wagon could be pulled up into side seats, making a well. Bill lined the well with heavy plastic and lots of hay. That's where our goats, Theresa and Sandy, rode. One little guy, in a car passing us on the highway, tried to tell his mother there was a goat in our car. She ignored him. I should have honked the horn to get her to look!

Along with the goats I had our cat. We didn't have a carrier so he was loose in the car. Soon after we started out he climbed up behind the glove box and stayed there with his tail hanging down. I wondered how to get him out if he died. When we arrived at our destination, he came down off the glove box.

We also had two hamsters our kids got from the Rainey kids. Janice said they were both female so they were together in a cage. They found a way to escape and were loose in the car. The cat didn't know or didn't care.

We also had one Siamese Fighting Fish, a Beta. He was in a jar with a lid. I took the lid off to give him air when we stopped at Hardee's and the jar dumped over on the floor. It had been raining so I used his jar to scoop up rainwater from the gutter, snatched him up and popped him back in his jar. This all took place under the glove box where the cat was hiding. The fish lived on.

A friend moved Nipper and Chubby down in a horse van so they weren't in the original caravan. The kids switched between vehicles. They were with Bill in the truck, me in the station wagon, and with Eldon and Janice. It was a long ride.

We left the interstate after dark and traveled over winding roads in heavy fog. Bill turned up a hill and realized it wasn't the correct turn. He backed down with Eldon on the road holding a flashlight. We finally arrived in Skeetrock very late at night or, more correctly, very early in the morning. We bedded down wherever we could and tried to get some sleep before Sunday School and church. It was Bill's first time to preach as their pastor. We ran off church bulletins before we left home and found out they didn't normally have bulletins and apparently didn't want them. I kept one as a memento.

FIRST SUNDAY AS PASTOR

Sunday morning came early. Along with the usual congregation, there were several visiting missionaries from Camp Bethel. Bill was encouraged by their comments as they left after the service.

One comment was unexpected. When the former pastor shook Bill's hand he said, "Well, you can't be Billy Graham every Sunday." We weren't quite sure how he meant it, as it could have been taken several ways. Though it was puzzling, there wasn't time to dwell on it because we had a busy day ahead.

Both Bill and I loved sailing ships and had looked forward to seeing the tall ships televised on the holiday but our TV wasn't set up. We spent the day getting as settled as possible and were thankful we had arrived.

We still had a mortgage on our house in New Jersey. Though it was low by today's standards, it was a lot for us. We were purchasing a house trailer with no money to pay for it until our house sold. We were receiving a small salary from the church, a small monthly check from Hardingville Church and had a couple of supporters. No wonder some thought we were crazy!

We had the bare necessities and we were where God wanted us. We were never without food and always paid our bills.

Jehovah-Jireh– God provides.

SHEPPARDS

Billy knew the Sheppards before we did. He and their son, Barry, were friends. They met while participating in musical theater in high school. Barry told me recently, "We covered a lot of ground together bicycling around Hardingville."

Eldon and Janice also had two daughters, Sandy and Carol. They raised Newfoundlands and Yorkshire Terriers. When Billy said they were looking for a good home for a male Yorkie, Karen wanted him. We assured them he would be well cared for and Captain Horatio Hornblower joined our family. He became Karen's constant companion and stole our hearts.

Through the Sheppard family, Billy became involved with Civil War reenactments. They were Union and Billy was Confederate. They were all appropriately uniformed. Barry was a cavalry officer and retired just a few years ago.

We only attended one reenactment. It was in Elk Township during the time of the Bicentennial. The battle was interesting but visiting the encampment was even more so. Walking through the camp was like being transported back in time. We even admired the working cannon that Eldon built.

Billy made his own uniform with very little help from me. It was gray wool, uncomfortably hot in summer. I watched him craft his canteen. It was made of wood strips, then waterproofed. He carried an antique gun reproduction and wore a kepi.

There was an area of Janice's life that concerned me, Spiritualism. She and some other professing Christians attended meetings, like séances. One friend stopped going when she felt someone, or something, sit on her lap and there was no one there.

We prayed Janice would see the error of the teaching and escape it. We had no idea how God would answer.

When the Sheppards arrived in Virginia they liked the area. Eldon was between jobs and believed he could find work. They returned to New Jersey, packed their belongings into a bus he'd renovated and moved to Virginia. They set up their bus/camper at the bend of our driveway and our kids started school together in the fall.

Eldon quickly found employment in construction at the new elementary school and then at Breaks Interstate Park. They gained a good worker.

While they lived in Skeetrock they attended church with us. They were Christians before we met. Janice was just caught up in one of the enemy's ploys. As followers of Christ, we must be wary of Satan's schemes. There is danger in astrology, palm reading and Ouija boards. Sorcery can pull you into the occult. I am sensitive to this because of my background but also because of God's Word! The Apostle Paul speaks of this in Galatians chapter 5 and many places in the Old Testament.

When Eldon found permanent work near Pulaski, Virginia, they moved there. They were active in church and Eldon became a deacon. Years later, Eldon called to let us know Janice had died. He asked Bill to preach her funeral. Later, their children asked Bill to preach Eldon's funeral. He felt honored in both cases.

When we prayed for Janice to leave the Spiritualist movement, we never dreamed they'd move with us to Virginia. God hears our prayers but has His own way of answering them. It is humbling to be used by Him but be ready. His way may be different than what we expect!

BILLY AND KATHY

Though the Sheppards moved to Virginia with us, Billy did not. It wasn't long before he said he'd like to come down to look for work. We were pleased. He was hired as a carpenter on the new school building. Sadly, the carpenters were laid off after his being on the job for just a couple of weeks and weren't needed until the next spring.

He then was hired to work at Haggee 2 Mine, several miles

from home. Working in a coal mine can be a challenge when you are 6 ft. 5 in. The mine was low coal so he spent a lot of time on his knees. There was unrest between union and management, in fact it seemed to be perpetual. A few times Billy arrived ready to work but learned a strike had been called.

He had a part time job as a bouncer at The Golden Pine, a roadhouse in Pound. It was a busy place because it was a short distance from Jenkins, Kentucky, which was dry. His physical stature was a plus but his working as a bouncer wasn't exactly what we'd hoped for him.

In early January 1977 Billy rented the old Branham home place from Orville Branham. It was across the churchyard from us and had been empty for years. The house was in disrepair, but Billy hoped to fix it up. The inside walls had been covered with cardboard and newspaper, water came from a bucket well near the front porch, and a path led to the outhouse. It was heated with a small wood stove because the fireplace and chimney weren't safe. He had his civil war rifle over the mantle and reveled in nesting.

A friend joined him to help with expenses. Just two weeks after moving in, Billy was at Artrip's store talking with Theta when they saw smoke coming from his house. Theta called Clintwood Fire Department and Billy ran to the house. We saw smoke billowing beyond the churchyard and hurried over to see what was wrong. Karen and Matt followed us and Theta took them to her house.

Billy rushed into the burning building to rescue his belongings. We quickly realized there was no water except from the well. Orville was upset and stood at the edge of the cliff, about twenty feet above the fire, holding his garden hose that barely reached to where he stood.

Bill hauled bucket after bucket of water from the well house but he couldn't keep ahead of the blaze. There was only one bucket so I couldn't even help by filling it. When the wooden roof of the well house caught fire, I feared for his being trapped inside.

The fire trucks arrived as quickly as possible but the house was like a tinder box. They did all they could to prevent sparks from reaching Orville's or the Artrips' homes.

Bill had difficulty breathing from exertion and smoke. A

member of the Rescue Squad said he should go to the hospital. Theta invited Karen and Matt for supper. I rode with Bill in the ambulance as it careened over winding roads with the siren blaring. Bill's eyes were wide with fear which I thought was because of the siren. I asked them to turn it off and they did. Now I believe his long-standing dread of suffocation was the problem.

We were in the emergency room briefly and he was admitted to the hospital. We called Theta who offered to keep the children overnight. They ended up staying for two nights and Theta and John took care of our animals. Don't feel too sorry for Karen and Matt. Theta was a fine cook and doted on our kids. She even made cream puffs for them. It was a blessing that Karen and Matt were comfortable with Theta, and we knew they were safe. She and her husband John often took them to feed their cattle back our dirt road. The Artrips obviously loved children and our kids loved them.

At the hospital, Bill received good care. He shared a room with another man who was a smoker and annoyed that he couldn't smoke because Bill was on oxygen. In that area, smoking was allowed in hospital rooms. He complained constantly and even tried to light up a couple of times. I'm sure he was glad when Bill was discharged. We were too!

Though Bill recovered from his encounter with smoke inhalation, it was a long time before he was back to normal. Even then, he was more prone to bronchial irritations.

We later learned the young man may have allowed the stovepipe to get too hot. Billy was careful because it went through flammable walls. Remember the cardboard and newspaper? Even if he had been careful, it was an accident waiting to happen. Orville was devastated because the family homestead was gone. We felt sorry for his loss.

Billy saw a Navy recruiter and joined on February 24, 1977. Lack of work and the fire were major contributors to his decision. We took him to Abingdon to meet with four other men travelling by plane and bus to Great Lakes Naval Training Center. His original company was 056 where he was appointed Recruit Master at Arms. When he was transferred to 608K, which he jokingly referred to as fat man's club, his Commanding Officer told him he was a good leader and he hated to lose him. He also said to use him as a reference for a Petty Officer position in his new company.

In a letter home, he mentioned that his rack (bunk) always passed inspection. He commented, "Strange that I never could make it at home!"

Company 608K was for recruits who were in a holding pattern, like his dad's experience. Some needed to lose weight, others hadn't passed physical training or were non-qualified swimmers. He needed to lose weight, though he consistently passed physical training, and swimming was no problem. In 608K he was Recruit Petty Officer Chief, in charge of all recruits.

By the end of March, he was assigned to Company 078 and on his way to graduation. He was 1st Platoon Leader and was nominated for Honorman.

> "S. R. Cox (Seaman Recruit) has displayed an uncanny ability to handle men in his assigned task as Educational P. O. (Petty Officer). This is obvious in the fact that only one test failure resulted from Test II. His military bearing is impeccable and his attitude toward the Navy is outstanding. He exudes an aura of pride that reflects itself on all hands with whom he comes in contact. He is a perfect example of a young American bluejacket and I will be proud to serve with him in the fleet."

Graduation from Boot Camp was in May. We drove out but weren't in time to attend the event. We did spend time with Billy. I'd prepared food at home and heated it up in our motel room. I didn't know if that was allowed and hoped I wouldn't get in trouble.

After graduation, he was a Company Commander's Aide for six months. Part of the time he worked as Night Officer of the Deck, like military police. He was on legal hold several times because he busted recruits for using pot, smoking in unauthorized areas, assaulting other recruits and a Junior Office of the Deck. He appeared at Captain's Mast and Court Martials as a prosecution witness.

Billy wasn't one for writing letters. However, he wrote several long ones during his time away. It was obvious he was lonely. He especially missed his sister and brother. He came home for two weeks leave in October. One afternoon I was preparing dinner when he came into the kitchen with a young lady. He was all smiles, but she seemed uneasy.

Without a moment's hesitation he said, "This is the girl I'm going to marry!"

I don't think I dropped anything but that was unexpected! They met at the Golden Pine on October 30. They wanted to be married when he had leave in a month!

Our first concern was they barely knew each other. Then we asked if Kathy was a born again Christian and she assured us she was. We also realized if Bill didn't perform the ceremony they would probably go somewhere else. They planned their wedding for December 3, 1977, right after Karen's and Matt's birthdays. Billy drove 600 miles back to base on his motorcycle. He also had his future lined up as a Navy hospital corpsman, though not in San Diego as he'd hoped.

November was a busy month. We had a wedding to plan. Scheduling the church wasn't a problem. We invited close friends and family, and planned a reception to be held in the church. My mom and dad came from New Jersey. We prepared a buffet to feed the troops and there were troops! Three of Billy's Navy friends were part of the ceremony. Two were groomsmen and one was a bridesmaid, all in uniform. His longtime friend, Barry Shepherd, was his best man and Barry's sister, Sandy, was Kathy's maid of honor.

Billy flew into Tri-Cities Airport the day before the wedding so they could get their marriage license. He was asleep at his destination and no one woke him. When he woke up he was in Roanoke and the airport was closing for the night. He and another passenger caught a clerk at the car rental counter just as he was leaving. Billy dropped his car-mate off and drove on to Clintwood where he met Kathy, and they got their license. Another generation cut it close! The Navy personnel and Shepherds arrived in plenty of time.

We met Can and Nettie Baker for the first time the morning of the wedding. We talked a while in our living room, then went over to the church together. We were all uneasy about this full-speed-ahead wedding but hoped for the best.

"We're glad Kathy seems to have a good head on her

shoulders with finances," I shared with the Bakers.

They looked at me with questioning eyes. "Our Kathy?"

"Oh! I guess we need to pray a lot!"

The wedding and reception went off without a hitch. The entire wedding party spent the night in a motel in Pound before Billy and Kathy left for Illinois in her Mustang.

Their marriage endured pleasant pastures and rocky roads.

"...to have and to hold, from this day forward,
for better, for worse, for richer, for poorer,
in sickness and health, until death do us part."

MOUNTAIN WINTERS

Before we moved to Virginia we asked what the winters were like and were told, "They're not bad. It might snow a little but it melts right away!"

That is not how it happened in the winter of 1976-77. We had snow and ice that stayed for weeks. Dickenson County schools were closed from early December through much of January. The temperatures stayed well below freezing. It was difficult to get into town for supplies and folks in some areas were stranded.

The school administration attempted to make up the days missed by having half-days on Saturdays. It didn't work. Teachers couldn't stay on track because there were so many absences. The state finally forgave some of the missed days.

We survived that first winter and were told it would not happen again. The next winter was nearly as bad.

"That which has been is what will be,
That which is done is what will be done,
And there is nothing new under the sun."
(Ecclesiastes 1:9)

OUR MOUNTAIN HOME

Sleeping arrangements in Virginia weren't great at first but we figured we could adapt until we added bedrooms. Bill and I had the larger bedroom with a queen-sized bed that came with the trailer. Karen and Matt shared a small bedroom with a three-quarter bed that covered most of the floor space.

Unpacking presented problems due to limited storage areas. We had some room in the pump house out back but that filled rapidly. Though we had downsized, we should have done more. We utilized every available area: under beds, under the couch, behind the couch and chairs. The trick was remembering where we put it.

We also found water was in short supply. We had a nice dishwasher but couldn't use it. Baths were at a premium. Instead of skipping baths we shared water by age meaning Bill was the last one in. Maybe that's why he later enjoyed long soaks.

NEVER A DULL MOMENT

A few weeks after our arrival there was a startling incident. In the wee hours of the morning Karen bounded through our bedroom door. She neither slowed nor missed a step but ran up between us on the bed crying out, "Something hairy is eating Matthew!"

We jumped out of bed! She said she'd heard squealing. She had! One of the hamsters was giving birth! So much for both being female. We also found our cat, Samantha, under the bedcovers. She was the hairy something, but obviously not eating Matthew.

The Raineys were due to visit us the next weekend. We posted a sign on our front door announcing the birth of our hamsters. Big Bill and Weezie also visited. Having family around helped us feel at home. Weezie was protective of my time and ran interference on the telephone and when visitors arrived at the door. I sometimes needed to dampen her fervor, though I appreciated her intent.

My dad did what he did best, he got to know the neighbors! No matter where we lived or visited, he soon knew everyone in the area. If there was a road crew working, he got to know them. If the telephone or electric company linemen were working on the lines, he got to know them. We learned a lot we wouldn't have known otherwise and it never hurts to make friends. He quickly joined the older men in the neighborhood in Artrip's country store and knew many of them before we did.

We went to Camp Bethel for their Friday night campfires. John Henry, founder and director of the ministry, put on quite a show. Though his messages might be different they always finished with Elijah and his battle with the priests of Baal. John was an animated preacher and kept the attention of young and old alike. He had a deep voice and made good use of it when Elijah shouted to the pagan priests. Each week we were on edge of our seats as he hurled insults at Baal and set the stage for the finale. When Elijah called for fire, it came shooting down from above, igniting a huge bonfire in the center of the arena.

Even when we knew the fire arrived via a steel wire, crashing into a fuel-soaked stack of wood, it never lost its appeal. This reenactment of one of God's miracles is a wonderful memory.

One time we went over to camp to attend services and Bill was caught unprepared. Their scheduled missionary was unable to speak and Bill was asked to fill in. He hadn't taken his Bible and had to borrow one. From then on, he not only had his Bible but he had a message ready to go!

John Henry had a mischievous side when he showed folks around camp. Part of the area had been strip mined and the camp had its share of hills. When John took Bill and me for a tour he drove his Jeep to the top of a steep hill, then drove down rapidly. We later heard he delighted in watching visitors as he attempted to frighten them. Did we disappoint him by enjoying his shenanigans?

SOLD

Our home in New Jersey sold for our asking price. The buyers were perfect for the house and the house was perfect for them. Mr. L was a contractor and appreciated Bill's workmanship. He was impressed that Bill always opted for the best way to build and the layout of our home suited their family. They had three sons. Two had muscular dystrophy and were in wheelchairs. The open room arrangement and wide doorways suited their needs. They even liked the stone baby in our rock garden because they had lost a baby girl.

FIRST SNOW — THEN FLOOD

The infamous flood of '77 took place in April. The winter's snow and ice melted and Flanagan Dam barely held the water. The Pound River was so full it looked like the high bridge at the bottom of Skeetrock hill was floating. Low lying areas were devastated. Without a photograph of the water nearly touching the underside of the bridge, I'd think I'd imagined it. Schools again were closed, this time due to flooding.

BUILDING AGAIN

We fenced in an area for our animals. Then we were given an old barn. All we had to do was take it down, move it, and put it back up. Easy for me to say because I didn't do the work. Big Bill and Bill took it down, transported it, and rebuilt it. It provided shelter for all our animals and was indeed a blessing.

With our home sold, it was time to add rooms to our trailer. We used a plan for a vacation home and it made a fine addition! It was an A-frame with windows and sliding glass doors facing south, providing passive solar heat. The doors opened onto a cantilevered open deck. There was a large family room on the first floor, along with a bedroom and storage closet. A spiral staircase led to an upstairs loft where there were two more bedrooms overlooking the family room.

Bill prepared the foundation for the frame building. He planned an entry from the trailer's back door to go through a utility room accommodating our washer and dryer. Weezie and Big Bill came to help with the structure. The floor was finished first. Then the walls were built on the ground and raised into place. The raising of the walls was an experience. Bill and my dad constructed them and directed the raising of the walls. I drove our garden tractor pulling the walls into position. Weezie prayed!

Matt remembers a day when he went with Big Bill to pick up lumber. Matt made a comment against the current president of the United States, Jimmy Carter. Big Bill looked at him sternly and said, "He is your president! Respect him." Matt was repeating negative comments he'd heard from his Democratic grandfather but was rebuked about talking against a Democratic president by his Republican grandfather.

Along with passive solar heat we had a wood stove. Bill chose the Jøtul for efficiency, but it was also attractive. It doubled as an airtight stove and an open fireplace. He built a brick hearth and at Christmas we hung our stockings on the mantle. When there was a power outage we used the top for cooking.

Bill cut and welded the metal for the circular staircase by looking at photos. Our kids enjoyed climbing up on the outside as well as the inside. Later our grandkids did the same.

The high ceiling in the family room allowed for very tall Christmas trees. We cut down cedar trees from along our driveway for several years. They weren't our favorite tree but they were tall, and free! We stood on the staircase to decorate the top branches.

Abundant light accommodated large houseplants. We had a six-foot Norfolk pine, a five-foot palm tree, and a very large schefflera. Bill moved them in before frost and out in the spring, until he wasn't able. Then Matt or Paul did the honors.

ANGEL ON THE RIVER

We never seemed to have time for camping while we lived in Skeetrock. A bi-vocational pastor, especially one who teaches school, doesn't have much free time. But, we did sometimes do fun things.

We rented a boat with an outboard motor so we could fish and explore the Pound River. We took precautions to protect ourselves from the sun and even took a camera to preserve the memory. We did not think to take an extra container of gasoline. I don't know if the outboard motor was a gas guzzler, or if we just cruised up one too many tributaries, but the motor sputtered and stopped quite a distance from the marina. It was late afternoon so Bill manned the oars and we were making way slowly when a larger craft stopped by.

"Hey there! Are you in trouble?"

"Out of gas. Guess we didn't plan ahead."

The other boat came closer, "Here, take this. It should get you back okay."

Bill filled our gas tank and returned the container. "Thanks! How much do we owe you?"

"Not a thing. Glad to be of help." With that they were on their way.

As we started back to the marina, this time under motor power, Bill rubbed his arms. "Glad I didn't have to row all the way back! It's been a long time since I've used those muscles!"

Do angels sometimes ride in motorboats?

214

SKEETROCK
CALICO AND BLUE JEANS

Skeetrock Bible Church had a diverse congregation. Not only were we from different areas of the country but many occupations were represented. There were several coal miners at first but that changed as mining became less profitable. We admired those who went down into the mines and prayer for their safety was an ongoing request at prayer meeting.

Skip and Paula Dobis' daughter Amy was five years old, a bright little lass. One Sunday Bill gave an invitation for salvation. Amy raised her hand and Bill asked me to talk with her.

Amy and I walked hand in hand to the Sunday school area.

"Amy, honey, why did you raise your hand?"

"I want to be saved. I don't want to go to hell."

"Good! Let's look at some Bible verses together, okay?"

She nodded affirmatively.

"Romans 3:23 says, 'For all have sinned and come short of the glory of God.' Amy, have you ever sinned?"

She shook her head firmly, "No!"

"Haven't you ever done anything wrong, honey?"

"No!" she said as she shook her head vigorously.

I tried to help her understand we all have sinned, starting way back with Adam and Eve but she had already drawn a line in the sand and wasn't going to budge. We walked to where her mom and dad were waiting. "Maybe we need to wait a while."

Several months later, Amy raised her hand again and Bill asked me to talk with her. "Oh no," I thought, "I'm afraid this won't go well."

People of any age are saved through the working of the Holy Spirit not because of anything we do or say. This time Amy understood and was smiling when we returned to her mom and dad.

Bill was asked to baptize her. Amy asked, "Pastor Bill, when you dunk me down in the water are you going to preach?"

"No, Amy, I'll just say a few words as you go down and come up!"

Amy was visibly relieved, "That's good!"

Jerry Gray, a local lawyer, and his wife Denise came to our church and though we were poles apart on some issues we began a friendship that has lasted over the years. When he was about three, their son saw the collection plate go by with cash in it. He said, "Wow, I'm gonna be a preacher like Pastor Bill."

We had good times with Jim and Elly Childress. One afternoon we played Wiffle ball in their side yard. I've never thrown straight or batted well. When I did connect with the ball I had no idea where it would go. After going down the embankment through brushy and possibly snake-infested undergrowth for the umpteenth time, Jim finally said, "Pat, maybe you should just not bat." I was relieved to be relieved!

Shortly after we moved to Skeetrock we looked for a different vehicle. Jim offered to sell us his blue 1973 Silverado pickup truck at an excellent price. We cashed in Bill's NJ teacher's pension to purchase it and a chest freezer, both practical investments. That was the nicest truck we ever owned. The freezer lasted well also.

Jim's father raised a huge turkey gobbler named Virgil who reigned over all the adjoining properties. The hound dogs kept out of his way and only ate after he was finished. There is a good story about Virgil, and Elly gave me the straight scoop:

> "Virgil protected our kids while they waited in the shed for the school bus. They seemed to be the only ones Virgil liked. If anyone came around the kids Virgil would flog them.
>
> "Virgil didn't like Jim and the feeling was mutual. I was afraid of Virgil as I'd seen him flog my sister-in-law, Donna.
>
> "One time Jim saw Virgil sneaking up on him. He had a PVC pipe in his hand and whacked him on the head. Virgil fell to the ground, blood dripping coming from his beak. I yelled, 'You've killed him for sure.'

*"Jim picked up Virgil's head and started rubbing
it. Up Virgil jumped—mad as ever and after Jim! He
was just too mean to die."*

<O><

Skeetrock Bible Church grew out of children's ministry. The Hemonds, Sutherlands, and Senters refurbished the old Skeetrock School. Jim Childress and the Senters' sons helped with the physical work. They held Vacation Bible School in July 1969 and it was so successful they started a Sunday School. Most area churches believed children were too young to understand the Bible, so Sunday Schools were scarce. Skeetrock Sunday School changed folks' thinking.

We had many good times during the six years we lived in Skeetrock and many revolved around the church. On Old Timey Day we dressed as folks did a hundred years ago. Many of the men, including Bill, wore overalls.

There was a frog jumping contest and a turtle race. If you want to have fun, just try those! When they had the hog calling contest it's a wonder hogs didn't come from miles around! There was also a greased pole with a $5 bill on the top. Several tried, including Matt, but no one retrieved the prize.

My Bill and Bob Phipps took the youth of the church on an overnight hike along the ridge of Pine Mountain and were treated to a lightning and thunder storm. Another time they hiked Mt. Rogers, the highest natural point in Virginia at 5,729 feet above sea level. On this trip, they had a young man who was diabetic. When they hiked to the peak he didn't have his supplies with him and Bill carried him back to camp on his back.

Some of the pastors in the area tried to get together to encourage and learn from one another. There were a couple of meetings and Bill looked forward to the fellowship but it never happened. There was a heated discussion about which Bible translation should be used and they never got beyond that.

I say we read it in the original text. Wait! I don't read Hebrew or Greek, do you?

SKEETROCK NEIGHBORS

Pine Mountain separates Virginia from Kentucky and we could see it from our front porch. There are few gaps in the ridge and years ago there were no roads, let alone highways. John and Elsie

Branham told us how their people went across the mountain ridge with wagons to haul goods. A team pulled the wagon to the top of the mountain. They were then hitched to the back of the wagon to let it down on the other side. The Virginia side is steep but the Kentucky side is steeper. Is it any wonder they produced most of their food and necessities!

When we moved away from family in New Jersey we missed family times. John and Elsie loved to have the kids stop by for a visit. Elsie introduced us to dried apples as well as leather britches (dried beans). Her dried apple pies were superior to fresh or canned apple pies. She dried the beans on her porch. When I tried, mine molded.

Speaking of beans, soup beans were a staple in the mountain diet. They were served with cornbread, made with white cornmeal. Coal Miners often took cornbread soaked in milk in their lunch pails.

Orville Branham, John's brother, lived at the end of our driveway. He was a retired teacher and lived alone with his little dog, Pierre. For exercise, he rode his bicycle around the churchyard with Pierre riding in a handlebar basket. Orville attended church on special occasions. He had a drinking problem and thought he wasn't good enough to be saved. Bill and others tried to explain that none of us are good enough. God wants us just as we are and He will do the changing. Sadly, another neighbor told him he had to clean up his act before he could be part of our church.

Bill Branham's pasture adjoined our property. He was John and Elsie's son. His brother, Al, sold us the trailer where we lived. Matthew liked helping him feed his beef cattle and several times asked him to come to special services at church. I remember one time he told Matt he'd be there. Matt waited for him at the door of the church but he didn't show up. Matt was disappointed. It was a hard lesson for a young lad.

We prayed for Bill Branham for over thirty years. Matt even wrote to him a few years ago but he didn't respond. Recently, I heard he was saved! His adopted son accepted Christ and shared his testimony. Bill Branham finally made the most important decision of his life. We must never give up praying for the unsaved!

A man from Ramey Flats used to tell my Bill he'd get saved after he lived his life the way he wanted. Then he'd ask Jesus to save him. Bill asked, "What if your brakes go out when you're coming down the hill on the other side of the river and you aren't able to make the turn. When you're going over the hill into the river, will you be asking Jesus to save you? Or will you be trying to figure out how to stay alive?" He didn't answer. Years later we heard he had decided not to wait any longer.

Bill got to know the families of the children he transported to and from Awana Club. He was cautioned that one father, Mr. W, didn't allow uninvited folks on his property. It was said he operated a still. There was a chain across the driveway and a no trespassing sign. The children were well behaved. One evening on the way to AWANA his daughter said, "Pastor Bill, my father says you can come over and get some wood for your wood stove. Just let him know and he'll take down the chain."

Not only did he take the chain down and give us a pickup load of wood, but we were invited in for fresh baked fruit bread and coffee. We were blessed several more times and enjoyed their fellowship. Was there a still in the woods? We never knew. We were thankful to reach their children with the gospel and extend God's love.

Another family lived back a narrow dirt road. Their mother brought them out to the main road to be picked up. When it was dark she met them with a lantern to light their way home. We heard the father was out of work so Bill visited to see how we could help them. While they were talking, some plants caught his attention. Cannabis. Several years later we heard their oldest son was in prison. I don't know his offense but I remember a fine young fellow who took good care of his siblings.

We never found folks in the mountains to be standoffish. Our immediate neighbors were friendly from the start. I often wondered if arriving with our farm animals helped us to fit in.

GRANNY VIRGIE

Dorsey Phipps owned and operated a little store in Skeetrock. She was a member of Skeetrock Bible Church and a close friend. Bill and I enjoyed coffee in her home and she always served delicious homemade delicacies to go with it. She was an avid reader and we had discussions about everything from gardening and cooking to books and world events. We also discussed the Bible.

One Hallowe'en our church used Dorsey's barn for a Haunted House as a youth activity and an evangelistic outreach. Later, when her store went out of business, we used that because it was on the main road. Groups were ushered through a variety of presentations, finishing with a scene portraying a man in a coffin. The man looked dead but sat up at the appropriate time in the message. It was an attention-getter! I'm not a fan of outreaches like that but folks heard the Gospel message.

We never knew Dorsey's husband, Cecil, since he passed on before we moved there. We did know her son, Bobby, his wife Jewell, and their children. They were members of Skeetrock Bible Church until Bobby reopened the church his father built, hoping to reach families in the area who were reluctant to come to a church with so many outlanders.

Granny Virgie was Dorsey's mother-in-law. She didn't take kindly to preachers visiting her. She lived in a little cottage back the road beyond Dorsey's. Dorsey was concerned there might be some supernatural unrest there. Bill and I visited Granny together the first time. Bobby told Bill not to dress like a preacher or carry a big Bible. She met us at the front door carrying a shotgun.

Some mountain folk tended to look away and not make eye contact. That wasn't true of Granny Virgie. Her eyes bored into ours and held a disconcerting glitter. We introduced ourselves and asked if we could come in. She opened the door and led us into her living room. She motioned us to sit down, poked the coals glowing on the grate in the fireplace, and settled into her chair.

"You don't mind if I smoke, do ye?" Her fingers pressed Prince Albert into the pipe she'd plucked from her pocket. Striking a match, she drew the flame into the bowl of the pipe.

Her eyes closed for a moment, "Nothin' like a good smoke."

Our first visit was cautiously friendly. On my next visit, I noticed a child's rocker in the living room with a doll seated in it. At first glance the doll looked like the dolls I had as a child, right down to the messy hair. But her eyes seemed to follow me when I moved around the room. Granny referred to her as her little girl.

When the Linebaughs held meetings at our church, we had a ladies meeting in Dorsey's home. After the ladies had gone home

Dorsey told Opal about Granny Virgie and our concerns. Opal and I visited her the next day and she welcomed us. We sensed hostility, though not from Granny.

We visited her several times after that. Each time she was more approachable and during one of my visits she permitted me to read to her from the Bible. She listened without comment.

Not long before Granny died she asked Jesus to be her Savior. We weren't there but were thrilled to hear of her decision. Bobby said Bill was the first pastor she welcomed into her home. He was honored to preach at her funeral service.

Several days after Granny's funeral, Dorsey and I were having coffee together at her kitchen table. "Pat, doesn't Karen collect dolls?"

"Yes, she does," I answered.

"Well, we found some little ole dolls in Granny's things and I thought Karen might like to have them."

"I'm sure she would," I replied, "only I don't want that one in the rocking chair in the living room."

Dorsey paused, obviously in thought. "You know, I don't know where that doll got to. I don't remember seeing it when we cleaned up."

"That's fine with me. That doll gave me the creeps. I don't want it in the house."

A few weeks later, Dorsey and I were again chatting over coffee. She said, "You know, we looked all over for that doll and no one's seen it. It's just disappeared."

We looked at each other, and shook our heads. The little dolls given to Karen were small and quite old, a nice addition to a collection. Before they came into our house, we prayed over them and asked God to show us if they were safe.

I've wondered what happened to that other doll. Maybe Granny Virgie disposed of it.

LIFE IN SKEETROCK

Karen cried out, "Dad, Mom, come quick! Matthew can't get up!"

Dr. Pat had been treating Matthew for a stubborn strep infection. The first medication she prescribed didn't work so she tried something stronger. He was getting better but randomly lost the use of his legs. Sometimes at school, or even playing at home, his legs just gave out. Since he couldn't attend school, one of his teachers brought his lessons and he kept up with his class.

Unable to find a reason for his problem, Dr. Pat suggested we take him to a hospital in Bristol. They proposed exploratory surgery. No way! Back to Dr. Pat and she agreed. She then suggested we take him to the University of Virginia Hospital in Charlottesville.

This was January 1978, our second snowy winter. Bill and Karen stayed home in case school resumed. Matt and I started north on Interstate 81 in a snowstorm increasing in intensity. We arrived safely and were settled into a room.

I remember two doctors who saw Matthew though there may have been a third. The first was a neurologist. He arrived in the room on rounds with a bevy of medical students. He told Matthew to sit on the edge of the bed while he did a cursory examination. He then told Matt to get off the bed. Matt was hesitant because he didn't want to fall. The doctor held out his hands seeming to encourage him. Matt fell to the floor when the doctor withdrew his hands. I was shocked and unable to speak. He and his entourage left as quickly as they came.

We then saw a psychiatrist. He asked questions about our family and was very interested when he learned Matt's dad was a pastor. It was obvious he had little time for God. I thought I could see where this line of questioning was going.

"Do you have any unusual practices in your church?" he asked.

"Are you referring to snake handling?" I countered.

"Yes," he came back rather eagerly.

"No! I've read about it and have seen it on television but nothing like that happens in our church."

He told me we needed family counseling. I told him we would go. Forgive me, Lord, for lying. I didn't realize we could just walk out and was afraid they might stop us. As soon as we were released, we were on our way home.

We saw Dr. Pat. She said, "Of all the families I know you are the least likely to need family counseling!" It felt good to hear her say that! Maybe I didn't lie after all. I checked with Dr. Pat.

After reviewing the situation, Dr. Pat said she believed the second dose of stronger antibiotics had adversely affected Matt. His steady improvement seemed to prove her theory. It wasn't long before he was back to school and doing well.

<O>

That year was also a challenge for the Coxes at Camp LeJeune. In December Billy was working in the base wood shop, building furniture for their home. The guard wasn't in place on the table saw and the blade caught his wedding ring. He lost both the little and ring fingers on his left hand, his dominant hand. They retrieved the fingers but couldn't restore them.

He recovered well but was encouraged to take a medical discharge. He wanted to stay in the Navy so he proved he could do his job and stayed. I'm sure there were many things he had to learn but he seemed to handle them well.

He and Kathy looked forward to having children. They didn't give up easily. Billy's being in the service made it possible for them to do all the needed testing. It took a few years but their determination paid off.

The night Kathy went into labor. Billy called and told us he wanted to deliver their baby at home, himself! I have no doubt he could have done it in an emergency, but we told him he needed to get Kathy to the hospital right away! He did.

Rebecca Coetta Cox was born January 12, 1982. Her name means "captivating victory." She captivated our hearts when we met her several weeks later. She is our first-born grandchild.

"Children are the rainbow of life.
Grandchildren are the pot of gold."
Irish quote

<O>

Ernest's farm was back our dirt road. He was a widower. We knew him through several means: his grandson Cody, horses, and farming. He needed someone to help raise Cody so he married Lily.

When they'd been married a couple of years Ernest blushed when he told us they were expecting a baby. What would people think? Bill assured him no one could think poorly of him since babies are a natural byproduct of marriage. Lily gave birth to another boy. Now she had two children and Ernest to care for.

Our relationship with Cody got off to a rough start but he seemed to thrive on tough love and visited us often. On one occasion, he was going roller skating with our AWANA group and arrived at our front porch with his roller skates on. He had skated from his house to ours on the gravel road. He was proud of his new skates but we wondered how long they'd last. Lily later shared she thought he would lose his shoes at the rink and figured it was better to wear the skates than lose the shoes.

Cody's practice on the gravel road gave him confidence but a rink surface is different than a gravel road. He spent a lot of time on the floor, as did others. We were amused when they hurried onto the rink, fell, got up, skated a little way and fell again. Nothing deterred them.

When Bill taught Agriculture at the high school he was often called to help with veterinary questions. We didn't have a vet in Dickenson County and people liked to stay in the county. Ernest knew Bill had experience with horses so he came to him.

Two instances come to mind. The first was when his stallion was caught in barbed wire and received a nasty gash on his flank. Since the gash was deep they decided to clean and treat the wound, then allow it to heal from the inside out. This should prevent proud flesh. It took a while but healed well.

The second was with the same horse. He broke a leg and had to be put down. Ernest raised him from a colt and couldn't do it so he called Bill. He was a beautiful animal but in terrible pain and nothing could be done except release him from his misery. It was one of the most difficult things Bill ever had to do. He was no stranger to putting down animals but this was someone else's treasure. The shot went true, the horse went down, we all cried.

When we moved back to Skeetrock from Bumpville in 1990 Cody showed up on our doorstep again. He had not been living at home for a long while.

Matthew was out of high school, completed some college, worked in a supermarket, and counseled a summer at Miracle Mountain Ranch. He helped us move back to Virginia and planned to go back to the ranch for their apprenticeship program.

Cody was full of questions, especially about Matt. He told Matt he had some friends in Clintwood who would like to meet him. From other comments, Matt put two and two together and realized his friends were not ones he was interested in meeting. Cody had taken a turn away from what the Bible teaches about relationships. He had looked for acceptance and found it, but at a price.

Did he recall what he'd been taught when he was a young fellow in Sunday school and AWANA?

"Study to shew thyself approved unto God,
a workman that needed not to be ashamed,
rightly dividing the word of truth."
(2 Tim. 2:15)

<O><

Jim and Sheila attended Skeetrock church with their children. God brought Sheila into my life to fulfill a need. She was my friend during those difficult times in the church, encouraging me.

In the last year of our ministry there, Jim experienced the full effects of a widow-maker while cutting wood. This near-death experience brought him to the Lord.

There are things in our lives we regret and cannot undo. One of mine pertains to Sheila. She wrote a beautiful account of Jim's accident and conversion and asked me to look it over. Instead of giving it back to her with verbal comments, I proofread it and red penciled it. Why didn't I ask her if she wanted me to do that? What I did was thoughtless. I apologized but the harm was done. Our friendship was never the same but I am thankful God brought her into my life for a time.

CLINTWOOD ELEMENTARY SCHOOL

Moving to Virginia meant Karen and Matt changed schools. This can be difficult or a blessing. With us it was both.

Matthew was placed in Janie Bise's second grade at Clintwood Elementary. Mrs. Bise was a gem. She knew just how much to push her students without discouraging them. Matthew was shy but thrived under her instruction. His transition was seamless and positive.

Karen did not fare as well. In Aura School, Karen was with the same peers since kindergarten. She was a good student. This fifth-grade class was cliquish. Some teachers in Clintwood seemed impressed with their position in the community and that carried over to their children, several of whom were in Karen's class.

Paddling students was new to us but we weren't against it if the punishment fit the crime. One of Karen's teachers was quicker with the paddle than we felt necessary. Intimidation is a nasty tool.

In October we were introduced to the Halloween Queen contest. The girls in each class made and sold goodies. The one who sold the most was the Queen and runners up were princesses. We weren't pleased with this school fundraiser but Karen wanted to be involved and we hoped it might help her feel a part of her environment. She made caramel lollipops, a lot of them. It looked like she might even be Queen. A popular boy asked Karen to pick him for King if she won. He was cute, and nice, so she told him yes.

I'm sure other girls wanted to be Queen but one *really* wanted to win. Karen was ahead in the competition and a threat to her plan. Just before the final tally the girl's mother arrived at the school and gave them a check, taking her daughter over the top. She won. Karen was disappointed but happy to be a princess. Bill and I were stunned at the payoff.

Karen told us she needed a gown. A gown? We couldn't afford to buy one and she didn't have anything like that to wear. I looked through my stash of material. There wasn't enough of any color to make the dress but I had enough white! I stayed up most of the night to finish the dress and it was ready to go to school the next day. Karen looked lovely.

As instructed, she took the dress to the library and left it with the librarian who accepted it without comment. Later in the day she was told she couldn't wear her dress because only the Queen could wear white. She hadn't heard that and was discouraged when she brought the dress home. I was too. She wore her only good dress, a plain peasant style that looked nice but it wasn't a gown. I'm sure she felt like Cinderella before her fairy godmother waved her wand.

It was obvious there was a caste system and we abhorred that stuff. When Bill applied to be a substitute teacher and people realized he had credentials, attitudes began to change. They needed substitute teachers so I was also hired. Karen noticed the elitists were now willing to accept her. Too late. We were willing to let bygones be bygones but wary of friendships with folks so shallow.

<O>

Though we qualified financially for free lunches, we chose not to sign up. A high percentage of students had them and there didn't seem to be a stigma attached. We just didn't feel we should.

One day the principal questioned me, "It seems you might qualify for free lunches. Is that so?"

"Yes," I answered, "I'm sure we do but we believe we have chosen our lifestyle and no one else should pay for it."

He nodded, "I understand, but did you know it helps the school financially when we have more students in the free lunch program?"

"No, I didn't know that."

"Well, think about it and let me know what you decide."

I told Bill of our conversation. "What do you think?"

He pondered the idea, then said, "I don't have a problem with it and if it helps the school, why not?" We signed up.

<O>

Karen was troubled with strep infections. Dr. Pat suggested a tonsillectomy and it significantly improved her health.

Teachers can be influenced by other teachers. Karen was pegged a lackluster pupil and began to see herself that way but sixth grade was a little better than fifth. When she entered seventh grade she had teachers who acknowledged her ability. Beth Baker was especially helpful and I credit her with getting Karen back on track. Lester Phipps was a positive influence and she enjoyed his classes. Sarah Mullins was also a fine teacher. It was a good year!

Karen's grades in high school improved dramatically and she was elected to the National Junior Honor society. Once again, she was her normal happy self. It was good to have her back!

THE MIDGETS

We first heard of the midgets when we visited in 1975. They lived on Mullins Ridge, one ridge over from us. The term was a misnomer since none of them were midgets. One had a type of

227

dwarfism, the other two were normal size. We wondered how we could reach out to them.

Bill was coming home from town one day and saw one of the women along the side of the road examining a wheel on her wagon. She had been pulling it up the hill from South's store filled with dog food. Thinking he might be of help, he stopped.

The woman appeared frightened so he assured her of his desire to help. He assessed the situation and told her he would take her and the dog food home, then take the wagon home to fix the wheel. She cautiously agreed.

Bill loaded the wagon and dog food into the back of our truck and took the woman to her house. He carried the dog food in, going through a fenced yard filled with dogs of all sizes. Most were just excited but his years in appliance service made him wary of others. The yard was liberally embellished with canine deposits.

Two women timidly came to the door. He assured them he would return the wagon when he fixed the wheel. On his way home, he thought about how God made it possible to meet the women and wondered how we could help them.

"What's in the truck?" I asked as he came in the house.

"A wagon I'm fixing for the midgets but they're not midgets. Only one is short."

"I'm sure God set this up. Now I need to figure out what to do next. Will you go with me when I return the wagon? I think it might be better with a woman along."

"Sure! I'd love to go!"

"You need to be ready for what you'll see, and smell. I don't know how many dogs there are, at least twenty or thirty. Most of them are outside but there were several inside too and they obviously aren't housebroken!"

I wondered what we were getting into but replied, "OK, I'm in!"

Bill fixed the wheel and cleaned up the wagon. We went to their house, picked our way across their yard and knocked on the door. Dogs were barking inside, dogs were barking outside, I wondered if they could hear us knocking.

The door opened a crack and a woman peered out. Her clothing was stained and her hair hung in tangles. The smell was overwhelming. I looked at her bare feet and saw feces oozing up between her toes. We stayed on the front step. She murmured thanks to Bill for fixing the wagon.

I'd brought a Wordless Book and offered it to the woman. I told her the significance of the colored pages and she took it with quiet thanks. I asked if we could come again and she nodded. We picked our way through the yard and went home.

Through further visits we learned more about these women who were treated as outcasts. The oldest of the three was Claudie. She was my age, forty-four, and the slowest of the trio. Her sister, Edith, was a little younger and the shortest. Claudie gave birth to Jeannie, the tallest, when she was thirteen.

They were born and raised near Princeton, West Virginia and lived with Claudie and Edith's parents until Mommy died. When their father died, they were moved to Clintwood, possibly to be closer to family. Much of what they told us showed a close family relationship. Their father read the Bible to them and they held both Mommy and their father in high regard.

Jeannie was an avid, though not accomplished, reader so a Wordless Book wasn't necessary but they liked it. They also enjoyed comic books. Claudie didn't read much. Edith had poor eyesight making reading difficult. She, however, was intelligent and sensible. They all had a quirky sense of humor.

Not only was there an abundance of canines, over fifty when the dog warden counted them, but there were also more cats than we could count. Some were in the house, some were outside and many were in a shed that they called the cat house. They ranged in age from nursing kittens to full grown cats. Many were inbred and sickly but they were well fed.

We found they were on public assistance and talked with their case worker. Together we worked on helping them make their house more habitable. Their assistance covered rent for the house they lived in but the landlord never made repairs. The toilet in the bathroom didn't flush so they used the outhouse. The bathtub and sink didn't work so they couldn't wash themselves or their clothes.

They bagged up the trash and cleaned the floors, particularly in the kitchen and living room. The men of our church took truckloads of trash to the dump. They had to choose just one or two dogs and cats to keep and the dog warden picked up the rest.

Before we met them, we'd heard rumors that they ate dogs. We didn't believe that but it was even more outlandish when we learned how much they loved animals. Their dogs and cats were rescued from where people discarded them, local dumpster sites or along the road. Not only didn't they eat dogs, a significant amount of their monthly allotment went to feed them.

They also lived in fear. They were targets for all the drunken sots in the neighborhood. The same men who ridiculed them weren't above trying to use them for their own ugly purposes. Several times Bill intervened when local ne'er-do-wells shot at their house or otherwise frightened them. They had a phone in their house and called us in an emergency. When the phone lines were cut, Jean walked a quarter mile to a local pastor's home to call.

After the floor was free of trash, Bill asked Jean to scrape it and pick out linoleum for the kitchen. Imagine our surprise when she picked white! The store put the linoleum down. When she proudly showed it to us we saw a few lumps but it looked better than before.

We invited them to church and picked them up on Sunday mornings. We asked them to wash and wear clean clothes. They tried the best they could. Some folks took it in stride. Others moved as far away from them as possible. Having the ladies, as we came to call them, attend church had not endeared us to some of our congregation.

They had accepted Christ years before but hadn't been baptized. Bill reviewed with them what they believed and assured them, and himself, of their relationship with the Lord, then baptized them in Camp Bethel's lake.

Their monthly food shopping trips were prearranged with the local taxi service but the woman in charge of their finances sometimes asked me to take them shopping. When we went to Piggly Wiggly, folks stopped and stared. At first I was uneasy but I quickly got over that and enjoyed our trips. Truth be told I was just waiting for someone to say something out of turn!

I was often surprised by their purchases. They had definite likes and dislikes. One area always caught their attention in The

Pig or Singletons, a nearby dry goods store. It was the toy area! They loved trying out as well as purchasing toys!

A while into our relationship they invited Bill and I to lunch! We weren't sure what to expect but were pleasantly surprised. Claudie made soup beans and they were very good! Jean said Claudie's secret was extra black pepper. The dishes they used weren't always clean so they purchased two new bowls and two new cups for our use.

We brought them to our home several times so they could bathe and wash their hair. The first Christmas we knew them we invited them for Christmas dinner. Bill picked them up and they dressed up for the occasion. They brought a gift for Karen and Matt, TinkerToys. Their table manners were fine and it was a blessed experience.

Their case worker finally found a house for them with running water, indoor plumbing, and a washing machine. Having these necessities enabled them to better care for themselves. Clinchco was their new community and a church there reached out to them. Jeannie even attended GED classes.

Edith was the first to pass away. Claudie moved into the nursing home in Clintwood. I visited her when we were back in the area. She died several years ago. Jeannie is in an assisted living facility. We exchange Christmas cards and notes.

JOB OPPORTUNITIES

In fall of 1977 Bill was offered a job teaching in the agriculture department. Harry Lee Strouth was the department chairman and taught the agriculture classes while Bill taught the shop classes.

When Harry Lee retired, Bill was offered his position because there was no one certified in Ag. He taught for a couple of years when he was told a young man from the community had graduated with a degree in agriculture and would be taking over his position. I believe the administration knew Bill was an interim but didn't tell him. We didn't see it at first, but God was at work again.

Bill next worked for Dickenson County CETA (Comprehensive Employment and Training Act). He never had a problem finding a job. His work ethic preceded him. His office was in the courthouse on the same level as the jail. He hoped to have a ministry to prisoners and this put him in a good place. He provided GED training as well as Christian counsel.

One thing I know our kids remember is the stash of treats in his desk drawer, wherever he worked. Jelly beans were his favorite. He shared when they visited.

On his way to work, he took the kids into town with him so they didn't have to ride the school bus. Matt liked that because he was prone to bus sickness. Bill was not above a clandestine stop at Hardee's for coffee and a bun. He smiled at Karen and said, "Don't tell your mother." Matt missed out because the elementary school was located before they reached town.

The four of us met after school in the Jennie B. Deal Library, my all-time favorite library. The librarian, Sheila Phipps, always helped me find something to read for pleasure after I finished a semester at college.

When the CETA program ended the County Extension Agent asked Bill to come across the street and work for them as county 4H agent. Karen and Matt were already active in 4H. One summer they all attended a week of 4H camp. That was the first time I was ever home alone overnight. I wasn't fearful, but I woke at every sound.

Both kids participated in a horseshow. We didn't have a trailer so they rode Brandi and Socks seven miles to the arena, the longest ride they'd ever taken. They went on a less traveled country road and we followed in our truck. All went well until some curious cows came to the fence. Socks was a prima donna and reacted so Karen had her hands full. The herd had moved on by the time we returned home.

The horse show was a good experience. This was our kids' first show and they performed well. Brandi had been in shows before so she strutted her stuff and Socks was great for a first timer.

There was stiff competition between Matt on Brandi, and a girl on a black horse. As with many events involving children, the parents may be involved more than they should. We applauded and called out encouragement, but we didn't yell at our kids or make remarks about the other contestants.

When we arrived at the bottom of the last hill on our way home, Socks refused to go further. When Karen dismounted she was fine; under mount she limped. Socks played the system.

During Bill's term with 4H he introduced Sermon on the Mount to all the schools in Dickenson County. Lew Sterrett, director of Miracle Mountain Ranch, was just starting the SOM ministry and this was their first time taking it on the road. Now it's known throughout the United States and around the world. Also on our twisting and turning roads Lew discovered car sickness isn't always alleviated by being behind the wheel.

Lew brought along two students from the Camp Apprenticeship Ministry Program (CAMP) at the ranch: Greg Pike and Dan Cooper. We enjoyed having them with us. Matt was about eleven. None of us could have dreamed that Matt and Dan would someday be in the ranch ministry together. Nor would we have thought two of their children would marry each other. God knew!

MOUNTAIN CULTURE

Moving to the mountains meant moving to a different culture. I no longer live there, but the area and its people are dear to my heart. Most folks know little about the people of the mountains. They were isolated for years. Partly due to terrain, partly because they liked it that way. The people are generally independent and strong-willed. Anyone less wouldn't have survived. Even the terrain combines beauty with toughness. They were primarily Celts, with some English, Welsh and Germans. Some of their speech hails back to the 1600s, reminiscent of Shakespeare. I was sometimes called Mizres Cox which may have come from an Old English pronunciation of Mistress.

When we arrived in the mountains I noticed the people pronounced Appalachia differently than I did. I pronounced the stressed third syllable with a long 'a' sound (as in hay). In the mountains, it was pronounced with a short 'a' sound (as in latch). I started using the short 'a' because the people living there certainly knew best how to pronounce the name of their home.

During our first summer, we traveled from Clintwood to Wise with several young people. They convulsed with laughter when I incorrectly pronounced Dante, a nearby town. I pronounced it like Dante's Inferno. They pronounced it as *ant* or *ain't* preceded by a D.

When they asked me how I pronounced H-a-y-s-i, that was easy. Hay followed by a Spanish si. Got that one wrong too! It's

233

pronounced Hay-sigh. I provided lots of laughs and learned a few things.

Colloquialisms can also be different. One that nearly caused a problem for Bill was used by Jim Childress.

Bill said, "Jim, how about we make up food baskets for folks at Thanksgiving."

Jim answered, "I don't care to."

Bill was taken aback but thought maybe they'd tried it before and it hadn't worked. Figuring Thanksgiving baskets were dead in the water he dropped the subject.

A couple of weeks before Thanksgiving Jim asked, "Bill, shouldn't we get started on those Thanksgiving baskets?"

Bill was nonplussed, "I thought you didn't want to do them."

Jim replied, "What made you think that?"

"Because you said you didn't care to."

Jim laughed, "I didn't mean I didn't want to do it. I meant I did."

Though we speak the same language, we don't always understand each other.

We were impressed by the well-mannered boys and girls in the school system They addressed Bill as sir, and me as m'am. School teachers were appreciated and adults were treated with respect.

Back then the area was about twenty years behind the outside world. The arrival of television brought the outside world into homes and easier access to transportation made travel easier. Along with positive advancements, folks were no longer sheltered from negative influences.

Some local entrepreneurs found the rugged mountain terrain made a likely place to grow marijuana. Though difficult to find on foot, airplanes and helicopters soon leveled that playing field.

Mountain folks may have been slow to embrace *furriners* since outsiders sometimes took advantage of them. I've read that land with mineral rights sold for as low as ten cents an acre. Since local folks probably couldn't have mined the coal efficiently, a case can be made for both sides.

Timber has been a valuable resource. There are two sides to that also. Some don't want to lose the forests. Some say they grow again healthy and strong. Bill and I didn't like to see trees cut down and then covered over without utilizing the wood. It might not have been profitable for lumber but it could have been used for heating.

Change is certain to occur. The English language has changed since the time of Chaucer. The world at large has become more accessible with modern technology. What we do with those changes makes a difference.

The best changes in my life came when I paid attention to what God was teaching me and put that information to good use. Most of His teaching came through habitually reading His Word daily. Good habits bring forth good changes.

<O><

While we were enjoying our home, we were completely unaware of trouble lurking in a brushy area along the edge of our property. It was left by the former owner and we had lived with it for several years without finding it. That was about to change!

There was a knock at the front door.

"Mrs. Cox? I'm from the Department of Health," the woman said as she handed me an official looking paper.

I looked it over quickly. "I'm afraid I don't understand."

"May I look at the area in question?"

"I guess so. Yes, of course!"

Our neighbor, whose pasture bordered the cliff side of our home, had registered a complaint against us. Sewage was leaking into his pasture and he was concerned about his cattle. Why didn't he tell us about it? Not only didn't he tell us, but his brother was the previous owner of our property.

Instead of putting in a septic system, they buried an old refrigerator on its side. That was the holding tank for household waste. We didn't have a home inspection when we bought the place, though we obviously should have.

We contacted a contractor who got on it right away and gave us a good price. He had to blast rock to put in the holding tank but the drainage field worked well and the holding tank didn't need to be pumped for over twenty years.

COLLEGE DAYS

Before we married, we assumed I'd be a stay-at-home mom. When Billy was in Kindergarten we tried to change the plan, but it didn't work. Now Bill was working full time, as well as pastoring a church, and they were both demanding jobs. If I helped financially he could quit the outside job and spend more time on ministry.

I was surprised when I was accepted as a substitute teacher. One thing in our favor was that we talked like the television which evidently meant we used correct English. Bill subbed in high school and elementary school, and I subbed in elementary.

The first morning I was called to sub I was nervous! I'd taught all ages in church but this was different. I prayed as I drove to school. The teacher's lesson plans were easy to follow and I had a teacher's aide who could have done the job herself. I thanked her, letting her know how much I appreciated what she did.

One sweet memory is the hanging basket Karen gave me after the first day I subbed in her class. The card read: "To Teach with love!" I enjoyed subbing in her classes and Matt's as well.

The biggest drawback with substituting was not knowing if I would be called so it was difficult to plan my day. Knowing ahead of time was best. After a while teachers asked for me when they knew they needed a sub. I was working close to full time and realized I'd make twice the money if I had my degree. We discussed it and Bill called a family meeting.

"You know we've been talking about Mom going to school. We want to know how you feel about it. It means you both need to take on more responsibility here at home."

Karen smiled, "Gonna be a real teach, huh?" I smiled remembering the gift and card she gave me.

"Will you go away to school?" Matt asked.

"What do you mean, Matt?"

He had been mulling. "Will you come home on weekends or just for Christmas?"

"Oh, Matthew, I'll live at home. I'll go to school in the morning just like you do and probably come home about the same time you get home."

Matt was obviously relieved, "Good. I'd miss you if you went away."

As soon as my dad and mom heard what we were considering my dad offered to pay for my tuition and books. An unexpected blessing!

I visited Clinch Valley College in Wise to get information and was on my way. My advisor told me mature students usually do very well. I wanted to pursue English and teach in high school but he said if I really wanted a job I should pursue Elementary Education. There was a higher turnover in elementary schools. He also suggested taking C.L.E.P. (College Level Examination Program) tests dealing with general information covered in the first two years of college. I tried English and Humanities and passed them with flying colors. He also signed me up for a summer course, Children's Literature.

My Kiddie Lit professor was an older lady and a creative teacher. The class was K-7 so in one section we acted out nursery rhymes. Our group staged Three Pigs of Diminutive Stature and made our own costumes. My piggy costume was a pink flowered bedsheet covering a hula hoop. Karen and Matt attended the presentation.

I scheduled all my classes on Tuesdays and Thursdays for my first semester. In the two and a half years I was a student, my schedules were usually family friendly.

CVC had a high percentage of commuters and older students. We gravitated toward one another but also mingled with the younger students. We were not only accepted but often sought out.

I always sat in the front row of the classroom where there were fewer distractions and I could focus on the instructor. I took careful notes because I had to combine listening with writing to retain what I heard. I even took notes at home while reading.

In one history class there was a young woman on the basketball team who missed classes because of game schedules. She asked me to share my notes with her and we sometimes studied together before tests.

Math 101 was my most difficult subject. I didn't have Algebra in high school so I was originally assigned to Remedial Math. Several days into the class the instructor told me if I worked hard in Math 101 I should be able to pass the course. I transferred. I'm not sure it was the best move. I barely understood a concept when we moved on to a new one. I passed it but never learned it.

Working hard meant I spent a lot of time with my algebra book, pretty much ignoring everything and everyone around me. More than once my kids came by my study room and asked, "Are you coming out soon?"

"I'll be out in a little while, honey. I just need to finish this page."

One evening I was in the kitchen cooking dinner when Bill stopped by the stove. "We need to talk!" His words took me by surprise. We came to an agreement on how much time I should spend on homework, specifically math homework. I began putting family before my grades. In math, I just hoped to survive but I did want to do my best, perhaps at the cost of being prideful and selfish!

With the patient guidance of Wayne Edwards, my instructor, and Pat Large, my tutor, I passed the course with a C. That's the lowest grade I received and to this day I am proud of it! I worked hard for that C.

Mr. Edwards stopped me in the hallway early in the second semester, "Would you consider tutoring Math 101?"

"Mr. Edwards, do you remember me from Math 101?"

"Of course I remember you," he replied.

"I barely passed your course!"

He smiled, "Students who have had difficulty with math make the best tutors."

I shook my head in wonder. "I am honored you'd even consider me as a tutor but I'm afraid I can't invest the time."

Surprisingly, I enjoyed history. I didn't like history until I met Bill. He was a history enthusiast and I guess it rubbed off. I stumbled onto Dr. Ed Henson for my first history class. He was an older gentleman with a sense of humor. He was a professing Christian though his theology and take on history were quite liberal. By carefully manipulating my schedule I took all three of my history courses with him.

Attending a liberal arts college challenged my belief system and made me think about what I believe. I was thankful for other students who were believers. We encouraged one another.

English and literature were my forte but in World Literature I was confronted with what I considered smut. Think me prudish but I can't imagine any useful reason for some of those books. The class was made up of a few young English majors and a handful of older Elementary Ed majors. At least two of the older women were also believers so we told our professor we would appreciate not having to discuss the more offensive portions of the required reading in class. He never embarrassed us. I burned those books when the class was over. OK, now you can add book burning to my sins or achievements, you pick.

I pulled off a coup in that class. I achieved the only A+ Dr. B had given in several years. I don't remember the book I critiqued but I recall tearing it apart and evidently proved my points. I kept the paper for a long time but must have thrown it out during a purging of files.

My paper on censorship received an excellent grade but I'm not sure if I'd write the same words now. Banning is subjective and even the Bible is banned in some countries. When we lived in New Jersey I sent Bible portions to Christians in countries where the Bible was banned. It was exciting to be part of the Bible underground.

College wasn't all book learning. I used to watch my parents play tennis when I was a little girl but never played until my final year in college. We were coming down to the wire and I needed physical education credits. Tennis 101 was one of the few available courses that fit my schedule. At forty-nine I was the oldest in the class. I never got the hang of directing a serve or a return and I still don't understand scoring. The class was pass/fail. I passed if I showed up. I showed up.

The other PE class was Conditioning. I had no idea what that was but I wasn't the only one. Several El Ed majors were also on the roster. We were introduced to machines that I enjoyed, once I figured out what to do.

Though there were other activities, the one I remember best was running laps around the gym. I was never a runner but what I lacked in expertise I made up for with persistence. We were on the honor system to keep track of laps. A fellow El Ed major, much younger than me, questioned me on my report when I turned in my total for the day. I was sure I had counted correctly but told her I'd be happy to have her track me in the next class. This turtle just kept on chuggin' and even passed my young friend. She was surprised. I was delighted!

My least favorite class was an invitational honors class in philosophy. I don't remember what it was called, maybe because I'd like to forget it existed. The class was small. Oneidah and I were the only females, and the only Christians. The other four were males of atheistic or agnostic persuasion. I wish I'd been more outspoken about my faith. I doubt I could have impacted them but the Holy Spirit could have!

The professor was obviously in line with the pagans. Earlier he had been my economics professor. Though I wasn't fond of economics, faith had not been an issue. I learned one important fact in economics that I still use on occasion: everything costs something! There are no free rides. Someone pays. Even when we refer to salvation as free, it cost Jesus a horrific death.

I enjoyed most of my classes. One English professor suggested I stay another semester and graduate with a double major. It was tempting but I had all the credits for my Elementary Education degree and was ready to graduate and get on with life.

Not surprising I'm sure, my favorite classes were art and I took as many as I could. One was pottery where I used a wheel for the first time. I produced a nice little pot but it was more difficult than I'd expected. Karen and Matt attended a few of those classes with me and they brought up a pot on the first try. At least my children are gifted in throwing pots.

It wasn't practical to ride the county provided bus to college so most of the time I carpooled. Oneidah Stanley and I shared a ride for a couple of semesters. She had recently graduated as class valedictorian from Clintwood High School. She was a history major and said she'd learned as much history from well-researched historical fiction as from classes and textbooks. We shared the same beliefs, making for great conversations.

CVC was known for not closing its doors due to inclement weather but one day it began to snow and accumulated rapidly. It was announced school was closing. I was the driver so I put our new front-wheel-drive Citation to the test.

We had no problem on the highways, but when we reached the bottom of the big hill up to Clintwood we saw pickup trucks in the ditch. We looked at each other, prayed, and started up the hill. The front tires gripped the road and climbed past the trucks and into town. I dropped Oneidah off and drove home. I loved that car!

240

I did my student teaching in fifth grade at Longs Fork under Doug Dotson. He was a great mentor. I enjoyed his students and it was difficult to leave them.

My classes were finished at the end of 1981 but graduation was not until May 1982. I was hired at Clintwood Elementary to teach Remedial Reading until the end of the year. I again had a wonderful aide and I hoped to be offered a position for the next school year.

Time for graduation! My mom and dad came from New Jersey. Bill, Kathy and Becky came from Camp LeJeune, where Bill was a Corpsman in the Navy Hospital. I was not quite 50 when I graduated, the oldest in the Class of '82. I received an award for top education major, an introduction into The Darden Society, and graduated Magna Cum Laude. Gaining knowledge is good but should be kept in perspective.

"The fear of the Lord is the beginning of knowledge..."
(Proverbs 1:7)

Age isn't entirely a state of mind but it shouldn't keep us from reaching beyond our perceived limits and trying new ventures. It's been thirty-five years since my graduation and I still believe that's true.

A DIFFICULT PATCH

This section was difficult to live and harder to write. I believe the story must be told to achieve my goal of bringing honor and glory to God through all facets of our lives. I thank and praise Him for being in control and knowing what we needed even when we didn't understand. It's not my desire to cast stones, nor do I want anyone to take up an offense. In His time, God brought great blessing out of adversity!

Bill was commissioned by our home church in New Jersey and we arrived at our place of ministry excited to see what God was going to do. It wasn't until later we learned the former pastor was not in agreement with the decision to call Bill because he hadn't graduated from Bible college and wasn't ordained.

I need to reaffirm that my memories are not in chronological order. There was a honeymoon period when everything seemed fine. Then, at a deacons' meeting, it was brought to Bill's attention there was a problem, and I was it!

During a ladies' Bible study, someone suggested we have

communion on Sunday evenings so non-believers or the backslidden wouldn't feel uncomfortable. I said I believed serving communion in the evening service was fine but not for that reason. The local church meets for the edification and equipping of believers, even to evangelize non-believers, but certainly not for their comfort. Some didn't agree but no more was said.

Recently a friend reminded me, "We had some wonderful times and there were new people and youth attending. Satan likes nothing better than to destroy or distract when God's work is thriving." That is true.

Some thought Bill acted like a dictator. This surprised us because he felt the membership of the church should step up and take a more active role in conducting church business rather than having a few be in charge. Years after we moved, those same folks told us they realized what he was attempting to do.

When Bill asked if they had a board of trustees, most didn't know. With others, there was reluctance to share the information. It turned out there were three trustees: one active member, the founding pastor, and a former member who lived in another state and no longer attended the church. We believed trustees should be active members elected by the congregation.

Some folks were put off by Bill's demeanor in the pulpit. I was concerned that his photo gray lenses didn't allow the congregation to see his eyes. I believe seeing a person's eyes is crucial to effective communication. He was very serious about his teaching, which I'm sure was evident. However, he was also apt to joke and maybe that wasn't always understood.

He sometimes stepped on toes. Too often folks in the pew believe the preacher is speaking about them personally when he is relaying the Word of God and the Holy Spirit is the one speaking to them. I've had my toes stepped on by every pastor I've heard, including Bill, and rightly so.

Bill was a natural leader from his youth. He never sought leadership but God had other plans. He took his role of pastor seriously. Though people call the pastor, his call is primarily from God. He knew he answered to God for not only himself and his family, but also for those under his care in the church.

There were several accusations, though not made directly to us. I don't remember them all and it serves no purpose to bring them up now. It was often an "everybody's saying" situation, with no one taking personal responsibility. We felt it best not to try to find out who those were who were making the complaints unless they came to us themselves.

There were several meetings from which we were excluded. We heard that one person said, "You can't talk with Bill." That took us by surprise since just a year before the same person wrote in our guest book, "It's so wonderful to be able to talk with you— you really understand." What happened?

Having a revered former pastor still a part of the church intensified the situation. Many denominations do not allow that, for good reason. It's certainly not entirely the fault of a previous pastor when things go off course. Some may go to the new pastor and then to the old pastor looking for what they want; rather like a child will go to one parent then to the other. Even legitimate issues can't be resolved unless they are made known to the presumed offender.

For most of his ministry in Skeetrock, Bill drove the church van for AWANA. He enjoyed listening to the children and talking with them. One night he returned home in a joyful mood. He said he'd been singing all the way home. I was surprised because there didn't seem to be much to sing about. Most people realize Bill tended to be a pessimist and I was the optimist.

The next day I sat at our piano and toyed a bit with Bill and Gloria Gaither's *The Song.* I began to sing as I played and soon knew why Bill sang. God is worthy of our praise and any pain we experience is nothing compared to what Jesus suffered on the cross. Nor does it compare with the hurt our Father experienced when He saw His Son undergo such degradation, humility and pain.

Because of the church's affiliation with a nearby Christian camp we often were blessed by having visiting missionaries. They provided good fellowship and were often scheduled to speak in our services. We also scheduled special services, known in the area as revivals. Two men come to mind: Jack Yost, a traveling evangelist from Berwick, Pennsylvania, and Dale Linebaugh from Miracle Mountain Ranch in Spring Creek, Pennsylvania. Though neither were aware of our situation before they came, they were quick to sense the unrest. Each stayed with us in our home which gave us time to share concerns and pray together. This was positive encouragement for both of us.

Jack said he knew of several churches where Bill could candidate. All we needed to do was let him know and he'd make the arrangements. One was in an urban area. None of us were overly enthused about that but the kids perked up when we said sidewalks meant they could have skateboards. A church in Alaska caught our attention. Now, I'm not sure if I would have dealt well with the short winter days.

When the deacons presented Bill with ministry guidelines he shared them with several respected men from outside the area who had ministry experience. They gave him good counsel. He kept Dale Linebaugh's reply in his Bible until the day he went Home to be with the Lord.

Where does a pastor go for counsel? Easy to say he should go to the Lord, but there are times when he needs another human being. Though Bill and I shared most things, sometimes a man needs input from another man. I'm thankful that over the years we were blessed with wonderful men of God who encouraged and edified. I can only imagine how difficult it was to preach to a congregation where some have turned you off. Perhaps Bill's years of teaching high school helped, even more so God's grace made the difference!

When Bill was given opportunity to present his view on the guidelines he responded and backed his points with scripture. A few averted their eyes but we were thankful for those who listened.

We were concerned how this might affect our kids. Another move? Another uprooting of our family? We talked with them and shared what they needed to know. They accepted the situation well. We were thankful for their understanding and knew God was taking care of His precious lambs.

Sheila asked, "Have you put out a garden?"

"No, haven't had time."

True, but a weak excuse. Why use precious time to plant a garden when we may not be here to harvest it?

Sheila says she'll be glad when we plant our onions. She knows we'll be staying. I've told her she

244

can help me shop for them.

It's hard to make plans involving the future. Right now, it seems there is no immediate future.

(from my journal)

A vote was scheduled to determine if Bill should be relieved of his responsibility as pastor. Days before the vote a few families got together at a nearby campground and we were invited to their campfire. They wanted to reassure us of their concerns for the church, and for us. We sang. We prayed. We laughed. We cried. How sweet and healing Christian fellowship can be! This gathering gave us a glimmer of hope.

The deacons have announced another called meeting after church. An announcement is to be made. It seems I just get on with the business of 'being' when I'm jolted back to the reality of the problem we're living through. Am I unrealistic? Am I an ostrich hiding my head in the sand? Oh how I long to hide; not just my head!

I've been reading through Psalms in my quiet time. I can identify with David. My adversaries, our adversaries, are fellow Christians. David's adversaries were his countrymen, even his own son. That must have hurt even more.

(my journal)

The vote was held after a Sunday morning service. I was proud of Bill's ability to lead the service and bring the morning message. The vote was by secret ballot. When the votes were counted and the outcome was announced, I was sitting in the front row of the church and naively said, "It's over!" In a sense that was true. The vote was over. Those who wanted Bill to stay outnumbered those who felt he should leave.

Some might say since the vote wasn't one hundred percent in favor of Bill's staying we should have left. We considered that but God gave us no indication we should leave so we stayed and trusted God to work out the details. We knew there was still opposition to be faced but at least some of the problems were out in the open. An open wound heals more quickly when it's exposed to light and air. The former pastor and his wife left the church to attend another church. Sad, because there was no resolving of differences.

> *Romans 5:3 says to glory in tribulation? Really?*
> *Looking deep inside there is resentment to be dealt*
> *with. Bitterness. Anger.*

(my journal)

Most of my negative feelings were quickly resolved but it was several years before I completely dealt with all the fallout from that time. Forgiveness is a powerful healer.

We spent six years there, most of them after the vote. I'm thankful those years produced more fond memories than discouraging ones.

On a spring morning in 1982 Bill and I were having coffee together in our family room, enjoying a slow start for the day. We were finishing our sixth year of ministry. I was enjoying the freedom from college classes and looking forward to teaching in the fall.

We discussed our plans for the day. Bill sat stroking his beard, obviously deep in thought. His hand paused, then fell resolutely to the arm of the chair. "I believe it's time to move on. I don't know what God wants us to do next but we'll find out when He's ready to let us know." He wrote a letter of resignation saying he was stepping down as pastor in April. Making the decision to leave was difficult but when it was decided we had peace.

Endings are fraught with emotion; sadness for what will never be again and anticipation of what lies ahead. We accepted the fact that we weren't going to live there for the rest of our lives. Our major concern was, "But, there's so much to be done!"

We mentally gathered all those special ones with whom we'd been working so closely and presented them to the Lord. "What about these folks, Lord, how can we leave them now?"

The ones I was most concerned for were the ladies. How would they fare? The realization that these precious ones were not mine but His allowed me to turn them over to Him. He takes care of His own.

That was perhaps the greatest lesson I learned. No matter how involved we become in the lives of others, they are not ours! That includes our children! God will care for them far better than we ever could.

Would I want to go through it again? No way! Am I glad it

happened? Yes! God used that time in our lives to grow us in a way that was necessary for what He had for us in the future. Did I realize that during the unrest? Not always.

A month after our decision to move on, Bill had several offers to candidate. Within a short time, we were on our way. Our next ministry was healing for us and our new church home. It wasn't perfect but we were blessed. What we learned from our first ministry was immediately useful, and when we later joined Bible Club Movement (now known as Bible Centered Ministries) the experience was even more useful.

Through it all, God knew what He was doing! He still does.

ON OUR WAY AGAIN

We readied our home for sale and were blessed with friends willing to help us. They helped physically and financially to make the move less stressful. We'd hoped to sell by advertising privately and word of mouth but that didn't happen.

Billy, Kathy and Becky lived there for a while after he was discharged from the Navy. When they moved to Kentucky he came back to check on the property when he could.

We never followed up on trying to sell it, but we rented it twice. I use the word rent loosely. The first renter was a mother with two children. Her home in Kentucky had burned and she wanted to live closer to her mother. She was on public assistance so arrangements were made through her case worker. We wanted to help her and were naïve. She was to pay us directly but that never happened. Later we found we could have been paid by her case worker but by then it was too late.

I don't remember how long she lived there but it was long enough for her, her boyfriend, and her children to do considerable damage. We had to replace broken windows and repair several holes in walls. When they moved they took the wagon wheel ceiling light fixture from our dining room, electric baseboard heaters—everything they could move. They only got the 700-pound Jøtul woodstove as far as the door.

Sometime later we heard the woman moved back and forth across state lines using and abusing those who tried to help her. We were happy to *git shed of 'er*, as they might say in the mountains.

A young couple was interested in purchasing the property and did repairs in lieu of rent. They lived there a couple of months, but when their grandmother died and left them her house, they didn't need ours.

Do you think God didn't want us to sell?

BUMPVILLE
FLEECE AND TAPESTRY

We never learned the origin of the name Skeetrock, but when we moved to Bumpville we discovered the origin of that name. We sure can pick 'em!

Bumpville was named for Reuben Bumpus. He joined the militia in 1776, serving as a Minute Man for four years. In 1806, while hunting, he came upon a likely spot to live. He purchased fifty acres at three dollars an acre and settled there with his wife, Phoebe. The couple was childless but Reuben loved telling stories to children. His tales of adventures were called Bumpus stories and young lads liked the ones involving his longbow and Old Saxon, his gun. Reuben and Phoebe are buried in Bumpville Cemetery.

Bumpville Church had been without a pastor for several months when we arrived. The ministry thrived under the last pastor but their relationship with him did not end well. The folks at Bumpville asked Paul Carlstrom if he would consider being their pastor. He believed God wanted him to stay at Miracle Mountain Ranch so he suggested they contact Bill. After candidating on three separate occasions he was called to be their pastor.

Family and friends helped us move. Moving household and personal possessions is one thing but moving animals is another. Besides our family of four we had: Brandi and Socks (our mares), Nod and Nikki (our milk goats), Horatio and Teddi (Karen and Matt's dogs), as well as Samantha and Angel (our cats). The goats had traveled in our station wagon from New Jersey to Virginia, but we no longer had the station wagon. We also had nothing to move horses. Lew Sterrett from MMR offered to pick up our farm animals on his way home from a Sermon on the Mount presentation.

The night before they were due to leave, Socks got into a bag of chicken feed and developed colic. She was in danger of foundering, which can be fatal. Transporting her was not advisable but the only way to get her to Pennsylvania. Lew did his best and we prayed!

Jesse Gardner was aware of our situation and contacted an old Amish gentleman who was good with horses. When Socks arrived, it was evident she had foundered. They tied her in a stall with wet clay on the floor to cool her feet. Then she was tied in the stream behind the Gardner's barn to continue the cooling process. Bill sat down by the water for long periods of time to be sure she was all right. We had high hopes for the treatment but weren't sure if it would be successful.

The next step was putting leather soles on the bottoms of her feet, after filling the frog with pine tar. The treatment took several months but it worked. The only long-lasting effect was that her hooves required frequent trimming.

Several years later she was sold to an MMR apprentice and she used her for barrel racing. This is not only a testament to the old Amish gentleman's expertise but a wonderful demonstration of God's grace.

When Crystal no longer could keep her, Socks was purchased by an older couple who liked seeing a horse in their pasture. She had been a stubborn young mare but brought joy into our lives and finished out her years in pleasant retirement.

Moving day arrived. Billy and Kathy came from North Carolina to help. It took all day to load so by evening we were weary and still had a long drive. Jim and Sheila insisted we stop at a motel when we got out of the mountains. They provided for that and dinner as well. We felt refreshed after a night's rest.

Again, we looked like a gypsy caravan. Bill drove the big truck with Billy alternating as the driver. Kathy drove their vehicle, I drove our car, and Karen drove our pickup. We traveled convoy style, in sight of each other. Karen was nearly attached to the back bumper of the big truck. She wasn't about to get lost. Since Kathy didn't drive as fast as the rest of us, we sometimes lost her but she was always found.

Somewhere in Pennsylvania after dark, we lost our way in heavy fog. Bill pulled off the highway and into a roadhouse driveway. We followed him, along with several other vehicles. He went in and got directions. When he came out he learned the other cars were also lost. We finally arrived in Bumpville in the wee hours of the morning to find welcome notes, bedding and food.

LIFE IN BUMPVILLE

Being close to the church was a positive. Folks dropped in for coffee and the youth sometimes ate with us. One Sunday I'd cooked a big batch of spaghetti and tried to pour it into my largest colander. The colander wasn't quite big enough so some landed on the floor. Russell Carrington, one of the youth, was standing next to me. He scooped it up, rinsed it and put it in the bowl! I poured on the sauce and we all lived to tell the tale. Thanks, Russ!

After one Sunday evening service, we'd locked the church and were enjoying the cold starry night as we strolled home. The phone was ringing when we walked in the door.

"Pastor Bill, would you go over to the church and see if Freddie is under the last row of seats? We didn't realize he was missing until we dropped off the other children and herded ours into the house."

Bill went back and sure enough Freddie was sound asleep. Bill called to me, "He's here! I'll stay with him until they pick him up." I told Freddie's parents he was fine and he never even roused when they took him home.

The church was at the top of a long hill. The parsonage was bordered on two sides by cow pasture. The cows sometimes came to the fence, curious about what we were doing. A windmill would have done well in our backyard.

The hill was a challenge when snow plows hadn't come through. Many a neighbor found it an invitation to prove his vehicle. We enjoyed watching them back down and try again and again. They didn't give up easily.

Soon after we arrived in Bumpville a reporter stopped by. He was surprised to find Bill in jeans, a plaid flannel shirt and a peaked cap working on our truck. Karen and I were pinning laundry on a clothesline in the back yard. I guess we weren't what he expected. People often have preconceived ideas of what a pastor and his family should look like. He wrote a nice article, complete with photographs.

251

Our kids were in walking distance of friends' homes. They ice skated and played snow games in the winter, and swam and fished in the summer. When we couldn't afford hospitalization insurance we told the kids to enjoy themselves but NOT break any bones!

There was a large storage building behind the trailer that accommodated Bill's tools. We seldom locked our house or storage shed unless we were going to be away for several days. We'd always trusted our neighbors so didn't see the need. We learned the hard way that not all neighbors are trustworthy.

Bill had an array of tools. They were in the storage shed along with miscellaneous building materials. It didn't occur to us that the contents of the shed might be interesting to someone looking for metal to sell until he realized his anvil was missing. It had been his father's. We suspected, but couldn't prove, who took it and locked the shed.

We preferred to err on the side of trusting folks but that's not always prudent. Years ago, churches didn't lock their doors and people could stop in any time. Now, insurance companies insist doors be locked. Rules are necessary because there are people—more people, more rules. That just the way it is.

NORTHEAST BRADFORD SCHOOL

Matt expressed concern about our move to Bumpville, "Nobody knows us there." He was right. After his first day at school he asked if I could teach him at home. Back then I didn't know anyone who did that. I assured him it would get better and it did.

Karen and Wendy Carrington became close friends. Though Wendy was a year older and attended a different high school her friendship was a blessing. Karen especially enjoyed art classes, something she'd missed in Clintwood. She attracted the attention of Burr, a senior boy. This was good for her self-esteem but presented us with a whole passel of problems. He finally showed his true colors when he went to college and brought a new girl home on break. Karen was ticked off. I was relieved!

Matt did well in school. He was disappointed that Northeast Bradford didn't have a football team. He opted not to play basketball in eighth grade but embraced it the next year. He played junior varsity and then varsity all through high school. He spent more time on the bench than not, but his devotion to the team was noticed by the coach. He made him co-captain during his senior year and the lessons learned were positive.

I learned from Matt's basketball years that what a basketball coach in Virginia told me about sports injuries is true. A medical website states "participating in contact sports such as basketball or hockey" is one of the main causes for a broken nose. Imagine that, basketball and hockey in the same sentence! Protective gear is worn in football, not in basketball. Of course, Matt's dad broke his nose while wearing a football helmet.

Matt sustained a nasty blackened and swollen right eye during practice when a fellow player, and good friend, was making a jump shot and his hip connected with Matt's face. Another time the cartilage in his nose was broken during warmup before an away game, producing a lot of blood! I'm not sure how many times he strained or sprained an ankle. All of this happened in high school. While playing volleyball in college he sprained his ankle and spent time in physical therapy. Not too many years ago a chiropractor found his back had been injured, probably from basketball or possibly a later bucking mule injury.

Recently, Matt and I were reminiscing about his injuries and he recalled a dear older friend, Kern Sanford, saying, "If I knew I was going to live this long I would have taken better care of my body." Good for all ages, but especially for the young!

Parenting an athlete may also provide learning experiences. My thoughts toward a coach who insisted on practice over the Thanksgiving holiday were neither thankful nor kind. He did have winning teams and in Matt's senior year they went to state finals.

Thinking on those state finals brings forth a not-so-stellar memory. It was obvious some of the referees' calls were skewed in favor of the better-known team. Some of us may have been a bit vocal about this during the game. After the game, several parents were waiting for our young men to finish showering before we drove home. The refs left the building as we were starting toward our vehicles. Our perhaps louder than necessary conversation may have criticized some of the refs' calls. Security guards arrived on the scene as we casually entered our vehicles. Not exactly a praiseworthy moment.

Were we sore losers? I don't believe so. If you lose fair and square that's one thing. To lose because of biased calls is something else. Should we have been less vocal with our comments? Absolutely!

Lord, make my words sweet because
someday I may have to eat them!

On our first Christmas in Bumpville we went to New Jersey to spend the holiday with my parents, and brought Billy, Kathy and Becky home with us for a visit. We encountered falling snow as we traveled north. When we reached North Rome, the roads were barely passable and turning toward Bumpville, driving was even more difficult. Bill drove about a quarter mile, then he and Billy pushed while I steered. We came to a stop near Paul and Judy Yager's house. They called our neighbor, Caleb, who pulled us up the hill. Then we drove across a level area to the bottom of Bumpville hill. Since our car was front wheel drive, Caleb attached a chain to the rear and pulled us up the hill backwards. Apart from the snap of the 180 turn, it was an easy ride.

We didn't learn the best part of the story until the next day. Anna and Clarence Crain had a large picture window fronting on the road. Anna was watching the snow fall as well as the lights gathering at the bottom of the hill. Then the lights came up the hill and past their home.

"Clarence," she called. "Come look at this. Pastor Bill has figured out how to come up the hill backwards! He's coming by right now!"

Yes, Anna did see our car going by backwards. What she didn't see was Caleb's tractor pulling us. Who says life in the country is uneventful!

Clarence and Anna were our closest neighbors. Clarence was one of Bill's deacons and a dear friend. He was short in stature but tall in character; a man of few words with an ever-present twinkle in his eyes. He had a quirky sense of humor and a penchant for a practical joke. He used to start up the wood-stove in the church basement for Sunday morning services. When he was away, Bill filled in. It frustrated Bill that he couldn't get the fire started as quickly as Clarence. One morning he was looking for matches when he found Clarence's secret—a jar of corn cobs soaking in kerosene. Bill told Clarence he was on to him. Clarence just

254

smiled.

When the church toilet wasn't flushing, Bill and Clarence worked all morning digging up the drain pipes. The trench was waist deep and the pipe fully exposed. They were in the trench and had just opened the pipe to search out the problem when one of the church youth stopped by. As he went into the church they called to him, "DON'T flush the toilet." They heard the toilet flush and barely made it to safety. They both laughed about it later but the young man was fortunate they remembered WHO they represented before they laid into him.

'Steel Magnolias' was a movie about strong southern women but they aren't only in the south. Anna Crain was a quiet woman who had those barely perceptible steel qualities. She was gentle in speech but you knew there was an edge there. She was delightful.

We stayed with the Gardners, Jesse and Cora, when Bill was a pastoral candidate. They had downsized and moved from the family dairy farm but Jesse needed something to do so he started back into farming with a cow or two. Soon, he was maintaining a small herd.

Cora was a professional cook, played the organ, wrote poetry and at least one hymn. I wanted to ask them to dinner but was apprehensive because she was such a good cook. I found she was elated to be invited. They received few dinner invitations, probably for the same reason I was hesitant to invite them.

I've always liked cows. When we lived at Shipley School Farm I liked to visit the cow barn. I liked the smell of the barn. I liked the sound of cows chewing their cud and their soft lowing. I liked to hear the milk ping as it squirted into the pail. I even liked their rough tongues when they licked my hand.

When we lived in New Jersey I wanted to see our cow give birth. My dad said I could watch but Bonnie was a sly one and didn't let anyone know when she was ready. No matter how quickly we arrived, we missed the grand event. I told Jesse that I'd like to see a calf born and he said he'd try to make it happen.

One morning when I arrived at the Gardners' to lead a ladies' Bible study I was greeted by Cora. She said, "Jesse says to come straight to the barn. There's a cow in labor."

I went into the living room and said, "Good morning

everybody! Go ahead without me. I'm going to witness a calf being born!"

With that I was out the back door and headed down the grassy slope to the barn.

Jesse smiled as I hurried into the barn, "She won't be long now."

The cow was lying down in her stanchion. Her intermittent mooing reflected her discomfort and two little hooves had just appeared.

Jesse was holding a chain. I had no idea what it was for but realized soon enough when he fastened one end around the extended feet and handed me the other end!

"Take a steady strain," he ordered.

My excitement overtook my apprehension and I did as I was told. The calf was gradually slipping out through the birth canal.

Then he said, "Now! Pull as hard and steady as you can!"

My feet firmly planted on the cement floor, I leaned back and gave it my best shot. This was hard work! Was this hurting the cow and her calf? Then the calf burst out onto the straw covered floor with Jesse gentling its fall.

I laughed and cried simultaneously! It was a beautiful moment. That little calf had left a safe warm place and entered an alien environment. From living dependent on its mother, it was breathing on its own.

I stayed long enough to see the mama begin to clean up her babe, then went back to our Bible study to share the miracle of birth. Only in the country! I thanked Jesse for allowing me to help with the birth, and will always treasure that special time God provided for me.

HOUSE TOO BIG TO HEAT

We were comfortable in the trailer across from the church. We had a garden in the summer and were right in the middle of downtown Bumpville—just us, the church, cow pasture, and woods. It was good.

Then, Keith Crain told the men of the church that we could use the farmhouse at the bottom of the hill. The farm was in foreclosure. Keith was renting the acreage and barns but had no use for the house.

Karen was now a student at Messiah College. Sometimes

people joke about moving while their children are at college. Our move was only half a mile down the road but we did it while she was gone.

Only Bill knew that I always wanted to live in an old farmhouse, which we jokingly called a house too big to heat. Not only did we have the house but there was a little barn for our goats and we were closer to the barn where we kept our horses. There was a little stream running down past the house and barn, so we often saw muskrats and other wildlife, as well as the Muscovy ducks that came with the house.

I was elated moving into a house with so many rooms! The living room was spacious, easily accommodating our furniture. We held prayer meetings there during the winter to save on heating the church. I delighted in being able to stay at home.

Remember how I said I wanted a big old farmhouse that was too big to heat? We got it! During the coldest winter days, the first-floor temperature never went over fifty-six degrees. The second floor was colder but bundled up in bed we were fine. We heated with wood and the wood furnace had seen better days. The biggest problem was the fire died down during the day while we were at work and it took a while for it to warm up when we got home.

Upstairs we had four bedrooms. Karen's was lavender with feminine wallpaper but it had a problem. The sun coming in the window warmed the room up on cold days. Good, right? Except the warmth brought out big fuzzy house flies that lived in the walls. There were always dead flies to sweep up.

Matt's room was on the other side of the house. The existing wallpaper looked more masculine. It wasn't a bright room and had a small door accessing the attic, but he didn't have flies!

There was another bedroom that must have been a nursery because it had Winnie the Pooh wallpaper. That was our guest room. It wasn't guest décor but guests had their own room.

Our bedroom was at the back of the house. I don't remember much about it except we had a telephone next to the bed. An enclosed porch opened off the bedroom. That was my writing workroom. Karen was home for the summer and in lieu of a summer job we paid her to take care of the house while I focused on writing. I planned and wrote but didn't sell a thing.

I did receive a lovely rejection from Guideposts Magazine. The printed notice said my submission was too late for their Christmas edition. There was also a handwritten note saying I should try elsewhere because it was well written. I never submitted it again but did use it several years ago for our Christmas newsletter. It was a true story from our time in Virginia. I don't regret giving writing a try that summer and learned from the experience. One thing I learned was I give up too easily!

We enjoyed having guests, especially those who made themselves at home. Lori Baker came home with Karen from college one weekend. We enjoyed watching her flying down the hill on Brandi. Though Brandi was a safe ride she could shift into high gear with little encouragement. I'm not sure Lori knew where high gear was but she found it.

We hosted Thanksgiving for all the family and we all fit around the big dining room table. There was plenty of room for folks to enjoy being together.

I hugged my dad when they left that weekend. I remember the hug well and can see his face clearly. He had on his black faux fur Russian Cossack hat and red plaid wool jacket. I pushed aside the thought, "...this might be our last hug." It was.

Christmas was exciting! What a great place to decorate. The living room was perfect for a big live Christmas tree and shouted, home for the holidays!

Later in the winter we encountered a big problem. We were getting ready to go up to the church for the evening service when Bill smelled something burning. There were no burners lit on the kitchen stove, no candles, what could it be? Then we saw smoke coming from under the kitchen baseboard and we knew! The chimney was on fire!

Bill began putting it out and was soon joined by Clarence, Vern and Ben. Linda Crain had seen the smoke and alerted them. When they tore out the wall encasing the chimney the cause was evident. There were spaces between the stones where cement had crumbled allowing sparks to ignite the dry timbers. We later learned Jim and Linda Crain put out two chimney fires when they lived there before us.

Here was another instance of God's grace. He continued to have His hand on us. We were thankful it happened when we were still at home or the house could have burned down.

Within a few days, the chimney and wall were repaired. It would have taken a lot of money and manpower to put the house back in good shape, but we enjoyed our time there. I no longer want to live in an old farmhouse that's too big to heat—been there, done that.

BIG BILL LEAVES US

You may remember my mentioning we had a phone in our bedroom. We received a call from my brother very early on a December morning saying our dad had experienced a myocardial infarction (MIA) and was in the hospital. I left to go to New Jersey. Bill and the kids stayed behind until we had more information.

Big Bill was in ICU when I arrived. We spent the day in the waiting room, going in separately for short visits. Speaking was difficult because of the ventilator but he could communicate with his eyes. He'd enjoyed good health most of his life, other than a kidney stone incident a few years earlier. He didn't tolerate sickness well in himself, or others.

While Big Bill was resting, we went home for dinner. It was only fifteen minutes away so we could eat and be back in an hour. We had just finished eating when the hospital called, "You need to come right away." He'd had a massive heart attack and was gone when we arrived. At least I'd been able to see him, hold his hand, and tell him I loved him. Tests showed he'd had several previous heart episodes but he'd never complained.

He left us on December 11, 1984. He would have been eighty on January 13. He always said thirteen was his lucky number because that was the day he was born. The Aura School Christmas program was dedicated to him. The printed program said the word that best described him was dependable. A fitting tribute.

As soon as we knew the timing of events, Bill and our kids drove to New Jersey, and Billy flew in from Florida. While we were sitting around Weezie's living room after the funeral, Weezie said she had two tickets for a bus trip the next weekend. She asked Billy to go with her and he did.

Weezie was always the one who preferred to stay home. Big Bill was more gregarious. She told me later she realized she needed to be more outgoing, even if it meant pushing herself. I was proud of her. When my Bill left us, I remembered what she told me.

I was blessed to have my dad for over fifty years. I still miss him and think of him often.

THE BLUE ROOFED HOUSE

During the eight years we lived in Bumpville we lived in three different houses, all within a mile of each other. We started in the trailer at the top of the hill, then moved to the farmhouse at the bottom of the hill. When we were told there were different plans for that house, we needed to move. There was a house just around the corner for rent. It was smaller but Karen and Matt were both in college so we could adapt to less space.

The house was across the road from the barn where we kept our horses. It was one of two called the blue roof houses. Ev and Pat Cook owned the other one and we already knew them.

This time we had a non-resident landlord with a higher and unrealistic opinion of the property. We worked out an arrangement that satisfied both of us and told him we might be interested in buying since we planned to stay in the area.

Moving is moving no matter what distance is involved. You need to pack everything and get it to where it's going. The space we moved into was limited so we needed to downsize again. We joined with friends from church in their yard sale. Some things we sold weren't missed. Some should have been kept, like the antique stereopticon viewer with its many slides. It sold way too quickly.

Bill made me a wonderful wooden porch swing as an anniversary gift. We looked forward to sitting there in the evenings. The hooks in the overhead beam held tight but the floor of the porch was rotted so we couldn't get to the swing to sit on it. Our landlord wasn't interested in paying for repairs even though Bill offered to do the work, so the swing hung there until we moved.

This seemed a good time to take my mother and Karen to Florida to visit family. To help cover travel expenses I sold my piano. I seldom played it at home and there wasn't room for it in the living room. It was good to see Billy, Kathy and Becky, as well as others. We enjoyed the trip.

There's not much to tell about the blue roofed house. It was not a memorable house, but there were memorable events. One

260

was being adopted by Max, probably our all-time favorite cat. Matt wanted to bring him home from North Rome church and I said, "No more animals." Within days he was walking by with a neighbor, stopped at our house, and gradually worked his way inside.

We could see the blue roofed houses across the fields from the church. The pasture behind the house sloped up to a ridge at the top of a hill. One evening we were standing outside the church and looked over to the ridge. There was an animal silhouetted against the sky. It was moving slowly. We first thought it was a cow. On closer inspection, it was a bear!

Neither we nor the Cooks experienced problems with bears but several nearby beekeepers were visited by them. We never saw one nearby again, but we were careful going outside after dark.

<O>

One summer afternoon a young man r his horse to the school and tied it to a tree while he went inside. Bill looked out the window and saw the horse trying frantically to pull free. He ran outside to calm the horse but when he got there he realized the horse was being attacked by wasps. As he tried to free the horse, he was stung multiple times. The custodian came to his assistance and an ambulance was called.

A vet was called for the horse, but it was too late. It died from anaphylactic shock. The young man didn't see the wasp nest when he tied the horse. When the horse moved around the wasps were agitated. We were thankful he was treated and recovered but grieved for the young man and his horse.

FERDINAND

Jesse Gardner kept one Guernsey cow with his Holsteins to add butterfat to the milk. He gave us one of her calves to raise for our freezer. We named him Ferdinand after the children's book and movie. You should never name your meat!

Ferdinand lived in the blue roofed barn. Bill and Matt cared for him but they also played with him. This eventually became a problem for Karen and me because Ferdinand pinned us to the barn wall just being friendly.

We knew Ferdinand was meat for the table but it didn't fully sink in until it was time for him to be butchered. I rode with Bill to the slaughter house. I had taken goats to be butchered and wasn't keen on it but somehow it was different with Ferdinand—maybe it was because of the song from the movie.

Ferdinand, Ferdinand the bull with the delicate ego
Ferdinand, Ferdinand, the heifers all called him amigo
Ferdinand, Ferdinand he'd curtsey and greet them politely
He knew how to tango and dance the fandango
but he never learned how to fight."

He was unloaded and we were ready to leave when I jumped out of the truck and headed for the office. A big man with bulging muscles was standing in the doorway. I thought to myself, "He must be the executioner."

"Are you the one who kills the steers?" I sputtered through tears.

"Yes," he answered hesitantly. I wonder what he was thinking.

"Pease make it quick … and don't hurt him. He's a good boy."

I hurried back to the truck. Bill was shaking his head when we pulled away. Even I wondered what I was thinking. Can you kill a steer without hurting it? At least the man had a unique tale to tell at the end of the day.

As for the meat in the freezer, we were back to, "Who is this?" at the dinner table. Yes, it is never a good idea to name your meat.

<O><

We buried pets in the yards where we lived. The blue roofed house is the final resting place for Horatio and Teddy, Karen and Matt's dogs. They lived long lives but it was still hard to lose them.

We also had a bred mare we were purchasing from Lew Sterrett. Her name was Buggs. As part of the purchase deal we were to breed her twice and give the foals back to MMR. She was a gentle mare but blind in one eye and didn't do well in a herd. I was thrilled to have a horse I could ride. For our first ride together, Bill rode Brandi and I rode Buggs. We rode up Bumpville hill and by the time we reached the top I was in pain. Riding astride a horse aggravated the arthritis in my hip joints and I was miserable.

Buggs gave birth to a foal we called Peanut. She was a good mother. We transported them to the ranch to deliver Peanut and breed Buggs again. We knew Peanut never belonged to us but it was hard to give her up. Buggs was bred again but it didn't take. However, Socks was bred and we were excited in anticipation of her foal. She was due to give birth soon when we were to visit family in New Jersey. We weren't sure we should go but our neighbor said he would watch her. The night we returned home there had been heavy rain. We saw Socks in the pasture and there was a small mound on the ground. She had given birth but the foal was dead. We never knew what happened. This was her first foal. Maybe she didn't know what to do? We tried to breed her again but that didn't take. With Job we could say,

"Naked came I out of my mother's womb,
and naked shall I return thither;
the Lord gave, and the Lord hath taken away;
blessed be the name of the Lord."
(Job 1:21)

Socks and her foal were His to do with as He saw fit. We grieved the loss, but the foal wasn't ours to lose.

MORE BUMPVILLE FOLKS

We have been blessed with many friends. Most we would never have met if we hadn't moved from New Jersey. Some friendships have continued over the years. It's a gift to meet an old friend and pick up where you left off the last time you were with them. Bill wasn't one for 'going out with the guys' and I shied away from 'hen parties.'

Bill liked being alone or with family. He seldom opted to be in groups or crowds. Strange for a pastor? God's choices don't always fit our preconceived criteria.

"... My thoughts are not your thoughts,
nor are your ways My ways,
declares the Lord."
(Isaiah 55:8)

Vern was one of Bill's deacons and his closest male friend in Bumpville. They spent little time outside of church together but their friendship was solid. They traveled to a men's meeting and found they had one very different personal preference. They stopped for coffee, and probably a doughnut if I know my husband!

263

Bill ordered while Vern went to the restroom, "Two black coffees."

Vern returned, took one sip of his coffee, grimaced and sputtered, "This is cold!"

Bill replied, "I had them put in a little ice so we could drink it right away!"

Vern never let Bill order coffee again.

Vern's wife, Connie, was head deaconess when we arrived in Bumpville. In some congregations, the pastor's wife heads up all women's activities. I was never expected to do that because the deaconesses did it. Bumpville church was a well-working entity when we arrived so we just joined in.

Vern had an aversion to having his photo taken. I knew this but without thinking I took his photo. He didn't say a word but I quickly realized I had stepped over the line when he left immediately. He later forgave me. Several years later we went back to Bumpville for a visit and stayed with the Pecks. Before we left we were taking photos and I asked if we might have a photo of the three of them. He graciously consented and even smiled for the photo.

Bill and Vern died within months of each other. They prayed for each other as they battled cancer.

Alice was a widow. Her son, Leslie, lived with her. Leslie had limited motor skills but worked in a sheltered workshop. One Sunday afternoon we were invited to have dinner with them. Following the meal, Alice suggested we join them on a walk through the woods behind their home. It was a beautiful day. We noticed Leslie was lurching along over the branches and uneven ground while Alice seemed oblivious to his situation.

"Should we wait for Leslie to catch up?" I asked Alice.

"No, he'll be along," she answered brightly.

She was encouraging Leslie to do his best. He wouldn't have come as far as he had if she had coddled him. She simply expected him to push himself. There's a lesson there for all of us. How often do we fall short because we don't push ourselves? Do I live like I believe what the apostle Paul says?

"I can do all things through Christ who strengthens me."

(Philippians 4:13)

Arden and Sue loved to shop for bargains. They gathered unlabeled cans and marked down items from the supermarkets and often give us a grocery bag full of surprises. There were packages of meat and close-to-outdated or dented food items. The most exciting gifts were the cans with unknown contents! You shook the can to guess what was inside but until it was open you didn't know. You might have hash, peas, or even dog food!

They also visited yard sales. Arden liked old books. He gave Bill a little black book printed in the 1800s. It was a handbook directed to young preachers. The author admonished preachers not to include personal experiences in their sermons. Bill often connected Scripture with true anecdotes from his own life. Bill's comment, "I guess I wouldn't pass muster!"

Abe and Betty had a dairy farm. Since Betty found wearing pants practical for working around their farm, and their church didn't allow women to wear pants, they became members of the Bumpville church.

Dan and June came to our church on advice from their pastor. June was divorced as a young woman, before she was saved and prior to meeting and marrying Dan. Because she was divorced their areas of service in that church were limited. Their pastor felt they would be a good fit for us. He was right.

Geraldine was a bird-like energetic widow. She raised nine children and had an abundance of grandchildren and great-grandchildren. She had a heart of gold and took care of her mother until she died. Though her lot in life was difficult, I never heard her complain.

Mr. R was a gentleman who could have gone unnoticed by the casual observer. He had been a widower for years and was rather reserved. Beneath that quiet exterior were multiple talents. One of his paintings hung in the church vestibule. He also played the saw, an uncommon talent, and had a fine sense of humor.

We occasionally had a Sunday evening service when folks were encouraged to bring a poem, or a song to share. I was at the piano when Mr. R stepped out of the pew, walked by the piano, and said with a twinkle in his eye, "Play Jesus Saves, and swing it." I don't know if anyone saw my startled expression but I was delighted. God's gems are not always where you expect them.

265

One Saturday morning a group of ladies were sorting through clothing we were sending to a missionary. We tossed donations that weren't useable into a pile. One lady arrived a little late and before we could explain the discard pile, she pulled out a pair of well-worn pants and a shirt with a torn sleeve and said, "These are good enough for the missionaries!" Not a word was said. We just kept on sorting and after she left we made sure the discards were discarded. From then on, we made it clear that we shouldn't give anything if we wouldn't wear it ourselves.

Frugality is one thing, health issues another. During Vacation Bible School one of our ladies insisted we wash the foam cups used for the children's drinks and use them again. She didn't seem to understand it wasn't healthy and maybe even illegal. We finally let her wash them but threw them out when she went home.

Little churches and big churches have one thing in common— people! A little church is a microcosm of a big church. Each one has folks who are dedicated to the Lord and others who are dedicated to themselves. In a large church, there are more of each kind but with staff to spread the responsibility. Things weren't always rosy at Bumpville but life isn't always rosy. What was special was we worked together, with Christ at the center. We were family.

We hoped the church in Bumpville would grow in number and be able to fully support a pastor. There are many small churches in that position. If someone isn't willing to pastor them what will they do? I believe God loves His little churches just as much as His big churches. Bill had a heart for little churches, and I share that love.

ORDINATION

When Bill accepted the call to pastor Skeetrock Bible Church, he was licensed by Hardingville Bible Church. Licensing provided legal documentation in lieu of ordination. He then stood before a judge in Virginia so he could legally perform weddings

After pastoring Bumpville Union Church (later Bumpville Bible Church) for over a year, the Board of Deacons suggested he be ordained. While we were at Hardingville Bible Church for meetings in October 1983, Pastor Mark Franklin expressed a desire to be part of the ordination proceedings. From that point on Mark worked closely with Bill and the BUC deacons to bring about an ordination council. Bill prepared an extensive doctrinal statement which included:

His Conversion and Call
Doctrine of the Scriptures (Bibliography)
Doctrine of God (Theology Proper)
Doctrine of Christ (Christology)
Doctrine of Holy Spirit (Pneumatology)
Doctrine of Man (Anthropology)
Doctrine of Sin (Hamartiology)
Doctrine of Salvation (Soteriology)
Doctrine of the Church (Ecclesiology)
Doctrine of Angels, Satan, Demons
Doctrine of Last Things (Eschatology)

There were twenty-six members on the council representing three states. The questioning lasted three hours. He was ordained a minister of the gospel on May 18, 1984 at the unanimous recommendation of the council.

Years later Bill was invited to sit on an ordination council. He had met the man to be ordained but didn't know him well. There were only three pastors on the council. He was surprised when he was asked to sign the ordination papers without examining the candidate. Instead of complying, he made his concerns known. They then questioned the candidate and he answered everything doctrinally to their satisfaction. I'm not sure how the others felt about Bill's stand but I know he wouldn't have signed his name without finding out if the man was qualified. He later sat on several other councils.

Ordination does not make a man a pastor or preacher. God calls the man and the ordination council confirms His choice.

There is a quote by an unknown source summing up the call to preach:

> "If you can be happy doing anything else,
> then God has not called you to preach."

OUR BACKPORCH

When Dale and Bernie began attending Bumpville Bible Church, they told us about a unique program for kids. It was like a popular TV show but taught Christian values. We sent for information and watched a video presentation. It was just what we wanted but the cost was more than we could handle. If this ministry was God's will, He would provide the funds.

In the sixth chapter of Judges, Gideon sought confirmation from God by 'putting out the fleece.' This should not be used to seek God's will but to confirm it—just what we needed to do.

We set a date for a special offering. If cash and pledges covered the initial cost, we would begin work. The amount sought was a lot for a congregation of our size but with God all things are possible. (Mark 10:27b)

After the offering was taken and the tally was in we had received exactly half of the required amount. It seemed the program was not for us. Had we been wrong about His will? Now what? A meeting was set to determine our course.

The group around our dining room table was dejected.

"Looks like we can just forget anything that special."

"I guess we were crazy even thinking we might be able to have something like that in a little church like ours."

"I 'spose it's back to the old BJYP (Bumpville Junior Young People)."

"That wasn't so bad."

"I know, but this would have been great."

We knew there was the possibility of a moment like this when we decided to throw out the fleece. Were we willing to proceed on an altered course?

"Have you thought of creating our own program? Don't let the idea die before it has a chance to prove itself. We could write something ourselves and adapt it to be more in line with our needs. The action could take place on a farm, or in a backyard, or even on a porch. Our kids would identify more with that setting than with a city street."

"Oh, I don't know..."

"That sounds like a lot of work."

"Do you really think we can do it?"

"Where will we get the puppets?"

"What about the puppet stage?"

"Who will write the scripts?"

"We've never done anything like that before."

"How much will it cost?"

"It might be fun to be a puppeteer."

"Our Backyard – that's sort of catchy."

"I like Our Backporch better."

"Hmm, Our Backporch—I like that."

While Our Backporch was being conceived, Bill was sketching a tentative set.

"What do you think of this?" he asked, holding up his sketch.

"That's really neat!"

Bill offered, "I'll figure costs and write up a bill of materials."

"The Carlstrom family from Miracle Mountain Ranch are puppeteers. They make their own puppets. Maybe they could show us how they do it."

I said, "I've never written a script before but I'm willing to try."

Dale consented to be the director and others offered to be puppets.

None of us had done anything like this before but we wanted to improve our Junior Church program and reach kids for Christ. What we lacked in know-how, we made up for with determination and enthusiasm.

Bill drew up plans. The porch was of 2x4s and plywood. A door, window frames and pillars were donated. Somewhat damaged white siding was purchased. The roof was shingled and window curtains were provided. The fence was rough lumber. Many hands were involved.

We decided Our Backporch should debut at our annual Christmas program. The story for the first script was to be about sacrifice. A puppet would give up something special to obey God.

Names for the puppets and human counterparts were chosen by the puppeteers. Each presentation had three people involved. Each person was to be on stage part of the time as a person and part of the time as a puppet. We talked about tentative personalities but learned the puppet's personalities developed on their own.

Our audience was primarily children from church families. They were familiar with most of the Bible stories, so we taught godly living through life situations. This gave them what they needed most, practical application of Christian principles. We also brainstormed future themes and planned to use Our Backporch for junior church beginning in February.

Our puppet workshop was successful. The Carlstroms gave us a crash course on all aspects of puppetry. We cut, sewed and stuffed, producing a variety of unique puppets. The puppeteers tailored their puppets to their characters. The Carlstroms taught us how to hold and move the puppets—it's not as easy as it looks.

As for the actors, Vern became Uncle Oscar, a wise leadership authority. His puppet was Otie, a hand-in-the-cookie-jar kind of kid.

Dale was Hank the Handyman and wore a tool belt. Hank was resourceful and easy-going. His puppet was Rusty, a jokester and instigator.

Bernie was Barbara, a bubbly homemaker who loved to cook. Her puppet Bridget was a self-indulgent girl from a wealthy family, trying to be more Christ-like.

Matt took on the name of Max. He was a young man not unlike himself: wry sense of humor, basketball enthusiast, All-American boy. Marty, his puppet, was a good lad but had occasional outbursts.

Later actors: Joy's southern drawl lent itself to Tara, Jon was a natural for Ernie, Paul was Skippy, Ben brought in the old west with Pecos, Karen was a little black girl named Angel, Ron was Melvin and Holly was MaryAnn.

Before long, I knew how each character reacted in any situation. They seemed to play in my head as I wrote. When the actors began to ad lib during rehearsals, they made every episode better than it was written. It was fun and I loved doing it.

Teaching children in church and Bible clubs was helpful in choosing themes. Sometimes just listening to children pointed me in the right direction. We based each week's presentation on a Bible story or principle and then used real life situations to bring home the teaching.

Since we used Our Backporch for Junior Church we needed a new script every week. This was sometimes a challenge since I was working full time. When it was necessary to cut back, a friend offered to help with the writing. That was a learning experience for me. Having someone else handling my baby didn't always set well. I needed to learn to let go and back off. Our Backporch was not my ministry! It was God's and He would take care of it.

One evening they were practicing a skit and I inwardly took

exception to how my co-writer was handling a situation. It wasn't even my skit. I hurried (stormed?) out of the church before I said something better left unsaid. As I went through the front door I missed the step. Down I went, spraining my ankle, feeling silly, and in pain! Bill took me to the emergency room.

When Bill and I were in Dr. A's office for the last follow-up on my ankle I said, "I have pain in my hips. Advil helps but not for long. I've read about hip replacement. Do you do it and will it help me?"

After a preliminary examination he said, "Let's make an appointment for additional tests. Then we can talk about it."

On my next visit, he showed us the x-rays of my hips. "It's easy to see why you're in pain. Your hip joints are rubbing bone on bone. Hip replacement is probably in your future."

"Is it something I should do soon?" I asked.

"You'll know when it should be done. Give me a call and we'll start the process."

He was correct. I knew it was time when I couldn't walk my students across the yard to their outside activity area.

Good things can come from not-so-good situations. I haven't come close to losing my temper since then. Until now, only Bill and I knew the cause of my fall. Now you know!

OBP LESSONS TAUGHT

Though the scripts were directed to children, adults were often convicted and as the writer I was the first to experience it.

In one script we taught about minced oaths. I first heard the expression in a message from Gerry Hobart, of National Home Missions Fellowship. Prior to that I'd not thought about what those mild expletives meant. They were sanitized versions of expletives and many were about God Himself! It took more than one sermon and a puppet skit to break my habit.

"You shall not take the name of the LORD your God in vain,
for the LORD will not hold him guiltless
who takes His name in vain."
(Exodus 20:7

Another script had to do with the power of the tongue. We all need to watch what we say because words can hurt, intentionally

271

or unintentionally. Spreading gossip is one way this can happen.

"Even so the tongue is a little member
and boasts great things.
See how great a forest a little fire kindles!"
(James 3:5)

We also need to be careful of idle or careless words. Our words show what is in our hearts. A clean heart produces clean words. What goes in, comes out.

"But I say to you that for every idle word men may speak,
they will give account of it in the day of judgment."
(Matthew 12:36)

Undoubtedly the most memorable script had to do with child abuse. I always hoped that our scripts were Spirit-led but that one seems obvious. I had no inclination of what was coming when it was being written.

We'd heard news stories about children who had been molested by family members, trusted family friends, even teachers. It seemed an appropriate subject to address so I waded into the unknown. I didn't have anyone specific in mind, not even a news story. Though the subject matter was difficult, the story line seemed to flow. When it was finished I presented it to the rest of the team and they were on board.

On the Sunday we presented it in Junior Church we alerted the parents to the sensitive nature of the material so they could understand any comments their children might make. They could even choose to have them not attend. The children watched and listened attentively and participated in the usual question and answer period following the presentation.

That afternoon we received a call from the mother of three young sons. Her ex-husband was in the military and stationed in the southwestern United States. Though she had the boys with her most of the year, they visited their father for a couple of weeks each summer. They had expressed a desire to not visit him during the upcoming summer but she didn't pay much attention because they weren't ever keen on going.

The boys began asking questions about what they'd seen and heard in Junior Church that morning and it wasn't long before she realized they had good reason not to want to visit their father. Bill encouraged her to get in touch with law enforcement which she did. That set the wheels in motion and local officials worked in conjunction with the military. Bill and two of the boys' school teachers were flown to Albuquerque, New Mexico for the father's court martial. He was found guilty and sentenced to significant time in Leavenworth.

Bill was impressed with how the court handled having the children testify in their dad's presence. They legally had to confront him and were fearful but an impressive man in uniform talked with them before they went into the courtroom. He assured them he would protect them and he always stood between them and their father. The authorities were sensitive to the boys' needs and did everything possible to put them at ease.

Since Bill had never been to the southwestern states he looked forward to visiting the area. They were housed and fed by the military and an effort was made for them to see as many local sights as possible. Bill wanted to see the Native American culture but they had to share transportation and the rest were more interested in aircraft. He was also never a fan of spicy food so was unimpressed with the restaurants chosen by the majority. Even so, he enjoyed the experience.

They stayed in Albuquerque for a week and Bill was more than ready to set his sights on home. Winter storms were causing problems around Chicago and the northeast so we watched the weather reports and prayed. They were on the last plane out of Chicago before the airport shut down. He was due to come into Binghamton, New York where Matt and I were meeting him.

It started snowing in Bumpville and I was happy to have Matt drive. Just before we left for Binghamton we got a phone call that Bill's plane was rerouted to Elmira. We were relieved when his plane arrived, just as that airport shut down.

Besides the three lads, another young fellow shared with his mom that his birth father had been inappropriate with him. These were different and unrelated incidents and the boys had not had an opportunity to share information. No criminal charges were involved in the second case but the father lost visitation privileges.

God is able, no matter how heinous the situation.

BUMPVILLE JOBS

Shortly after we moved to Bumpville, Bill heard about a teaching position with BLaST Intermediate Unit #17 in an alternative school in Monroeton. He submitted a resume and went for an interview. He wasn't very optimistic when he came home.

"I doubt I have a chance. I talked with the other applicant while we were waiting and he's far more qualified than I am. I also figure my being a pastor may not be a positive. That came up several times during my interview."

Imagine our surprise when he was asked to return for a second interview. He was asked even more questions about his faith by the supervisor, Mr. J. He was hired! When Bill talked later with Mr. J he learned that he was a believer. He also explained the reasoning behind his decision.

"We've tried just about everything to get through to these kids. Maybe it's time to bring God into the mix. I believe you can do that. We need to get these kids going in the right direction so do whatever you need to do."

Bill was the lead teacher but shared teaching responsibilities with Miss M who taught English and the arts. They taught students in grades seven through twelve from Bradford, Lycoming, Sullivan and Tioga counties (BLaST) who had been "unsuccessful in their home school programs." They were often discipline problems. In some instances, the school in Monroeton was their last chance before deeper involvement with the juvenile justice system.

One seventh grade girl was referred because she attacked her teacher with a pair of scissors. This was not her first offense and was only the tip of the iceberg. Another girl acted out at school but at home was being molested by her stepfather. When one young man turned eighteen the police showed up to take him into custody. Several were at risk for suicide. Bill spent hours sitting on the back steps of the facility counseling students.

The mother of one of Bill's potential students couldn't understand why her daughter was moody and depressed. After listening to the mother, the truth became clear. Her aborted baby's birthday was close at hand. She was grieving the loss of her child. The parent had insisted on the abortion—there are no easy fixes.

Bill did not just teach academics but also tried to find ways to get the students to think about others instead of focusing on themselves. One way was having them clear and maintain a walking path along a nearby section of the Susquehanna River. He also devised ways to overcome their poor reputations in their schools and communities. He defended them whenever he could but didn't hesitate to discipline.

<O><

I hoped to find a teaching position when we moved to Bumpville but there were no elementary jobs available. We signed up to substitute. After substituting several times, I was offered a long-term sub position in the English Department for a teacher on medical leave.

The principal was wonderful, the teachers were great, and I liked my students, especially the work study students. They were a challenge but probably not the way you're thinking. I wanted them to succeed. I bent over backward to get them through every quiz, every test. There was potential for behavior problems but they knew I cared about them and policed themselves.

As for the rest of my students it didn't hurt that Matt was on the basketball team. They also recognized me as Mrs. Cox whose husband was Mr. Cox, a force to be reckoned with. Balance of power is great when you're on the right side of the equation.

When the regular teacher was unable to return, I was asked if I wanted the position. Of course, but I didn't have the right credentials. I was an Elementary Ed major, not an English major. If only...not going there!

Since my teaching career appeared to be at a standstill, I looked for work in another area. Vern said The Daily Review, which he called The Daily Disappointment, was looking for a Circulation Manager. I seemed to fit the job description so I submitted a resume, was interviewed, and hired. I told them up front I wanted to continue to look for a teaching position.

When I reported for work, I was ushered into the main office, shown my desk and introduced to my coworkers representing accounting and advertising. B spoke up, "This woman is a pastor's wife so you'd better watch your language."

Perplexed I said, "You don't need to clean up for me." I wished I'd added, "That's between you and God."

B claimed to be a Christian, but *her* language didn't fit the label. I wished she wouldn't tell anyone she was a Christian because it was negative advertising.

Though the office staff had some rough edges, and complained a lot, they were friendly and did their work well. Attitude in the workplace makes a difference in getting along with others. I made sure mine was positive, and ignored their comments.

My job was to make sure the newspapers were delivered. Since it was a morning newspaper it went on the street in the early morning hours. Deliveries were made on foot in town and by motor carrier to stores and rural areas. If a carrier didn't pick up his papers, it was my responsibility to make sure they were delivered. This meant doing it myself if I couldn't find someone else.

We delivered a newspaper in New Jersey so this was not completely uncharted territory and that helped my relationship with my carriers. They knew I'd been there and understood.

I was also the complaint department. Some folks have definite ideas about how and when their papers should be delivered. The language in the office was nothing compared to some I heard on the phone. Each complaint was a challenge but I appeased the customers and never lost my temper, though I did take a little walk after a few phone calls.

Our bedroom telephone again came into play. About two a.m. I received a call that one of my carriers hadn't picked up his newspapers so I called him.

"Hello, this is Pat from the Daily Review. Jimmy hasn't picked up his papers. Where is he?"

His girlfriend answered, "I can't get him up. I guess he had too much to drink."

This wasn't a surprise and probably why this was his primary job.

"Tell him I'm on my way over to get him up! I want those papers delivered!"

With a full head of steam, I dressed and drove to Towanda! Jimmy's girlfriend met me at the door. He was already delivering his newspapers. Maybe the thought of me getting him up provided incentive. He was a likeable guy and one of my better carriers. I had him stop by the office, and we had a little chat.

Before Karen had a car, I drove to Messiah College on Friday afternoons to pick her up for the weekend. The flexibility of comp time and the amiability of my boss made this possible. It was a lovely drive, a relaxing finish to a hectic week.

There were aspects of the job I enjoyed. I created a cartoon character and blatantly illegitimate paper money with his face on it for a carrier promotion. Setting up special events to encourage our carriers was fun as well. One was at an amusement park and another was for a big-league baseball game.

Laura knew I still hoped for a teaching position. Eager to entice me to stay on, she hired additional help. This meant I had fewer of the mundane aspects of the job, like filling in for a no-show carrier. It also allowed time for working on special projects.

The Review was a Monday through Saturday newspaper. I helped with laying the groundwork for delivering a Sunday edition. This had to be accomplished before other newspapers in the area could do it first. I was sworn to secrecy and helped with laying out the motor routes. Bill helped me install delivery tubes so we got to see a lot of the area we'd never seen before.

Then I heard about a one-year fifth grade teaching position at Northeast. The regular teacher was taking a sabbatical. I thought this might get me in the door.

I told the principal, "I bring the wisdom of age with the fresh approach of a recent graduate." I was hired.

Laura was happy for me but not with my leaving. She even tried crunching numbers to match a teacher's salary but It didn't work.

TEACHING FIFTH GRADE

To say I was excited to finally be teaching is an understatement, though my excitement was infused with apprehension. Is it possible to be confident and fearful at the same time?

Karen helped me prepare bulletin boards for my classroom. The regular teacher left a note telling me where she kept supplies and encouraged me to use anything I needed. My mother took me shopping for comfortable shoes. All the new teachers for the upcoming school year were taken on a school bus tour of the area and welcomed with a luncheon. I met the other fifth grade teachers. Mrs. A was assigned to be my mentor. She was an older woman who had been teaching for years. We met once before the first day of school. From then on, I was on my own. I found her intimidating.

There were thirty students in my fifth-grade homeroom. One lad was in my homeroom but his regular classes were special needs. The students had classes with all three teachers so I had contact with all of them. Their average age was ten to eleven but their social and emotional development was all over the spectrum. Some still played with dolls and trucks. Some girls talked about older boyfriends and I was concerned. Some were from stable loving homes, some were not.

We had a get-acquainted time prior to the first day of school. One mother shared her son's concerns. He was a stocky lad who appeared to be cocky rather than anxious. Looks can be deceiving. She shared their earlier conversation.

"What if I don't like her?" he asked his mother.

"What if you do?" she replied.

He stood by his desk in a far corner of the room. His demeanor was more defiant than concerned. We got to know each other, a little at a time. I can't say he never presented a problem but he never challenged my authority and we ended up getting along well. In one instance, he and another boy got into a disagreement in the classroom coming close to physical contact. After listening to both sides of the situation I gave them some firm suggestions.

Then I said, "I don't want you to just say you're sorry but you are to ask forgiveness of each other. Then shake hands."

The boys' eyebrows flew up, as did those of the onlookers. Surprise can be an interesting equalizer. The apologies weren't enthusiastic but relatively genuine and they shook hands. There were no more near-fighting incidents, but I used the forgiveness factor several more times. It was interesting to see Biblical principles at work in a secular atmosphere without even mentioning the Bible.

In the '80s we were told God shouldn't be present in the classroom. However, children do ask questions and they are always curious about their teachers. I kept a Bible on my desk though I never read or opened it in class. Several students told me they attended Sunday school. J told me he was a believer and occasionally asked questions in class that led to Biblical answers.

One day I told the class about a troublesome mouse at home. He thought it was hilarious and shared the tale with his mother. J gave me a homemade Christmas ornament, a little stuffed mouse with its tail caught in a trap.

I have fond memories but it was a tough year. Standing outside on playground duty was painful. Instead of moving around the room I sat at my desk. That was even noted on one of my evaluations but I never mentioned my pain.

That wasn't the only problem. My mentor wasn't mentoring. I should have shared my concerns with the other fifth grade teacher, Mrs. B, since I knew her teaching style and mine were similar. I missed a golden opportunity.

There were days I cried on the way to school. I felt like a failure. I thought the world of my students and wanted them to succeed. The good news is most were doing well. The bad news, I needed help and didn't ask for it.

We heard Mrs. A was retiring partway through the school year. She was worn out and didn't need the added stress of mentoring. Mr. C was hired to finish out the year and applications were received for the next year. I applied without expecting to be hired. When I was interviewed for the position the principal told me he was hiring Mr. C. Was I disappointed? Not really. I knew Mr. C was the best choice.

Then the principal said he believed I would be well suited to teach a position opening in kindergarten. I appreciated his suggestion but knew I couldn't physically handle the job. Instead of sharing the obvious physical reason for not applying, I told him what I previously thought to be true, I felt more comfortable teaching older students.

The year was a positive, though sometimes painful, learning experience. I should have accepted the fact I needed help and been willing to ask for it. I could have asked Mrs. B or even my principal.

What came next demonstrates that God has a plan even when we can't see it. Wouldn't you love to see His lesson plans? Or, maybe not!

CROSSROADS

While Bill was teaching in the alternative school he heard a female teacher was needed for a new program named Crossroads. It was being planned by IU17 in partnership with Bradford County Action. The motivation was to encourage pregnant and parenting teens to complete their education. Bill told Mr. J that I was looking for a teaching position and he told Bill to have me submit a resume. I did. He interviewed me, as did the partner organization, and I was accepted.

At the same time Karen landed a summer job with Bradford County Action. She taught needed skills to men and women reentering the workforce. Though we didn't work together we had the same Action supervisor and it was nice having Karen nearby.

Crossroads was within walking distance of Bill's school. I was given a tour of the building while renovations were underway. The classroom accommodated a large table, chairs, and cubbies for the students' belongings. There was also a computer room for student use and a small office for me. Adjacent to the classroom was a nursery with a play area, sleeping area, and kitchen facilities. I was under the jurisdiction of IU17, the preschool teacher and two assistants were under Action.

Since I was involved with setting up the academic area and helping to select the necessary equipment and furniture I started work right away. I'd never done anything like this before but Bill was helpful and Mr. J was a good resource. I asked for help!

My biggest problem with the building was its lack of windows. This probably was fine for the previous tenant, a meat market, but being closed-in does not make for a good learning situation. Some might say there are fewer distractions without windows. Fortunately, they weren't the ones planning my classroom. Putting a window in a cement block wall was costly so I asked for a large mural, a scene overlooking a mountain lake. It covered the entire outside wall of the classroom and was framed like a window.

The plan was to accommodate a dozen young women and their children. Their sending school teachers provided lesson plans for me to follow or in some cases the students studied for the GED test. Every day they traveled via Endless Mountain

Transportation Authority (EMTA) with their books, children, car seats, and diaper bags. Attendance was usually good but we followed up closely on absences.

Some in the community thought the program was a waste of time and money. If they had gotten to know the girls, they might have changed their minds. They weren't all success stories but there were positives.

I taught group lessons whenever possible. One of the girls had an assignment in her literature book that required studying the Biblical book of Job as literature. I asked permission to use the book of Ruth and taught it to the whole class. It was more appropriate and they enjoyed it. We did art projects, craft projects and wrote papers. We tackled science experiments and did research. Algebra was a challenge but we even survived that.

For a project that fit a series of lessons, I allowed them to bring a pet to school. They told me what they wanted to bring and I scheduled the date. The only pet I remember was a tarantula, probably because I said no several times before agreeing. I dislike spiders, especially big spiders. I touched it but it didn't crawl on me.

We had a small field near the school and the girls and their children went outside when weather permitted. Sometimes we had combined activities with Bill's students. We walked over to their school and played softball or volleyball. We celebrated birthdays with cake and ice cream. We had baby showers. We had picnics. We worked hard in class. We shared joys and sorrows.

A nurse provided by Action taught physical, emotional and sexual health issues to the girls. You might be surprised at what they didn't know. They were provided with colorful condoms regularly, though they seldom took them home. The preschool teacher and the nurse taught parenting skills. The girls ate lunch with their children and were encouraged to play and spend time with them whenever possible.

Most of the girls lived with a parent. Some had close contact with the fathers of their children. Some did not. The youngest of the girls was married to the baby's father and they lived in an apartment in her parents' home. She was fourteen and in seventh grade when I met her. Her baby was several weeks old.

One of my girls had been in Bill's school until she got

pregnant. We had a rule that no girl could stay if she had a second child. Not only did this girl have a second child but was pregnant with her third when I left the program. Sometimes rules need to be stretched. She and her children were high risk. I don't know what happened with her but being familiar with her background I'm not confident that it was good.

Many of the girls were manipulative. They had learned how to work the system as a survival technique. Most days were uneventful but there were times when hormones and poor choices had to be confronted. A few times it was necessary to step in and physically restrain someone but I never felt personally threatened.

There were no normal days at Crossroads. One morning I arrived early, as usual.

That phone again! Seems like no matter how early I begin... "Good morning, Crossroads." No reason to take it out on the caller.

"Hi, Pat, this is Tammy." I recognized the voice of the EMTA dispatcher and I wondered who hadn't shown at the pickup point, or which van was going to be late.

"Yes, Tammy, what's up?"

"Just wanted to let you know that the valley van will be a little late. The girls will be in just as soon as the driver can get them there. Diane's in labor."

"Diane's in labor? On the van?"

"Right. They're five minutes from the hospital and her contractions are one minute apart," she laughed.

"Is she o.k.?"

"Sure is!"

"How about the driver?"

Fortunately, the driver was a level-headed lady, not quick to get her feathers ruffled. I rather doubted "transporting person in labor" was in her job description though.

One young woman who was a loving mother found she was pregnant for a second time by the same guy. She lived at home with her parents. She had a bright sunny disposition and worked hard in school. She wanted to keep the second child but her parents believed she should have an abortion. She was resolute; her parents were persistent. They even woke her at night to try to change her thinking. Eventually they won. She had the abortion. She was never the same. In the months that followed she was morose, even hostile. This is a byproduct of abortion that some don't want to talk about.

My time at Crossroads was a wonderful experience. It was full of laughs and joys, as well as heartbreaks and tears. It was exciting to watch the little ones as they experienced new situations and the mothers as they completed their classes and even put new parenting techniques into practice. Did they use them when they weren't with us? Maybe some did.

I heard from a few of the girls after we moved. One young woman wrote several times. She and her toddler's father were planning their wedding. She was getting involved with a church and she sounded as though she might have a relationship with the Lord. The last note I received from her was appreciative and joyful.

Then I received a newspaper clipping from her mother. Her daughter and grandchild were involved in an accident. The toddler lived, her mother did not. The father and grandmother planned to raise the little girl together. My heart still breaks over what might have been but I have a glimmer of hope that I may see her in Heaven.

A TOUGH DECISION

Tough decisions came in bunches. Bill felt the church needed a different pastor, a younger one with more energy. When a local man who pastored in another area returned to Bumpville, Bill hoped they might join forces. Bill was discouraged when that didn't happen. He wanted to be sure he did what God wanted him to do and considered it prayerfully. He set a time when he ceased being the pastor but was willing to help if needed.

I put the finishing touches on a casserole of broccoli and cauliflower au gratin, to take to the fellowship dinner at the church. When we walked down the stairs to the fellowship hall we were greeted with crepe paper festoons, balloons and a horseshoe-shaped spice cake decorated with flowers and the words, *"Thanks for the Memories!"* Gifts and cards surrounded the cake. We had no indication this was a special time set aside to thank us. What a great surprise!

After a meal of many of Bill's personal favorites we were invited to open gifts but the best gift was yet to come. Vern was master of ceremonies and many of those attending gave personal testimony as to what our ministry of seven years meant to them. Cora Gardner shared through poetry and some told of specific experiences. We were touched and humbled by what they shared.

Helen Crain gave him a thoughtful and unique gift. She listed the accomplishments of the church over the time he was their pastor. Briefly, Bumpville Union Church became Bumpville Bible Church and now belonged to the membership instead of the community at large. Many improvements were made to the church's interior and exterior. They had their first missionary conference, began a nursing home ministry and a puppet ministry, as well as a men's Bible study and a discipleship class.

Helen mentioned the wooden cross Bill crafted and hung behind the pulpit. He also made a sign for the front of the church:

"Come now, and let us reason together, saith the Lord"
(Isaiah 1:18)

I don't think Helen knew he crafted a cross behind the pulpit in each church in which he was involved. In Hardingville he constructed a large glass-block cross in the wall at the front of the church, framed it in wood and lit it with hidden neon tubes. In Skeetrock it was a wooden cross in front of a window. The meaning of the cross was inscribed on his heart and it was his desire to share it with others.

HIP HIP AWAY

Bill taught at the alternative school for three years. He saw positive outcomes, but it was a constant drain on him. His decision to leave the program was difficult. Even though he wouldn't teach full time, I would continue at Crossroads. He would substitute and we should be able to manage financially.

Then our landlord told us he wanted to sell the house we were renting. We could buy it or move out. We considered the possibility of buying but the price they were asking was more than the house was worth, considering all the needed repairs. We looked at several homes in the area because we didn't want to move away. Nothing seemed to work out, every path was a dead end.

I was noticing major changes in my mobility and walking was increasingly painful. I made an appointment with Dr. A and he agreed it was time for hip replacement. Rather than having two surgeries, I opted to have both hips done at the same time. Since we would soon not have a home we decided we should move back to Virginia but have the surgery done before the move while I still had hospitalization.

Life in the Cox household was busier than ever. We were packing and getting ready to move back to Virginia as well as preparing for my surgery and recuperation. We were also finishing up the school year and getting ready for someone else to take over our positions.

Hip replacement surgery usually requires a lot of blood and there was a scare that the blood supply was contaminated. My brother gave blood in New Jersey, Bill gave, as did Vern. Their blood didn't meet the requirements because I had something in my blood called Anti-E. I gave blood once but later was refused because I had a cold. Dr. A told us they would collect the blood resulting from the surgery and use that, a procedure called cell salvage or autotransfusion. We trusted God to take care of my blood supply. He did. I didn't need blood other than my own.

Setting the surgery just before Memorial Day weekend seemed best. I wanted a smooth transition for my girls and the substitute teacher finishing out the final two weeks of the school year. We also needed to be sure my hospitalization covered costs.

I was admitted on Tuesday, May 21 and on Wednesday morning, May 22 I had bilateral hip replacement. What a way to celebrate our 36th wedding anniversary! According to my doctors the surgery was textbook perfect but my recovery was not what they expected. I was in post-op all afternoon. I talked with people but had difficulty waking up and fell asleep during conversations.

I have a vivid memory of one incident in post-op. I was in a bed close to a nurse's station. I think there were other beds circling the station. It was dark. I awoke and needed to go to the bathroom. I tried to get out of bed and got tangled in the sheet. I couldn't find my way out and lost control of my bowels. I was terribly embarrassed and apologized to a very sympathetic nurse. I was afraid if the doctor found out he wouldn't let me go home.

On Thursday I was in a regular room. Billy called to talk with me as a nurse brought me my food tray. I remember holding the telephone in my left hand and in my right hand I had a forkful of green beans. I didn't know what to do with the fork. I remember hearing Billy talk but couldn't speak. That memory snapshot is clear as crystal. What happened next was told to me. When I didn't respond, Billy called the nurse's station on another phone and told them they'd better look in on me.

Dr. A told us he was going away for Memorial Day weekend but I don't know when he left. The staff didn't notice my decline until Billy alerted them. That evening I was put in the intensive care unit (ICU) where I stayed for two days.

When a doctor shared my situation with Bill, the prognosis wasn't good. No one knew if I would be normal again. Being in a vegetative state was a possibility.

Karen remembers her dad calling her. He was crying and frightened, "I took my best friend into the hospital and I'm afraid I won't ever see her again." Later Bill told me he prayed all the way home, telling God he'd care for me even if I never was me again.

Karen came from Lancaster. She told me recently she wasn't sure what to expect. "It's hard to explain but you were just not yourself. I could tell that even before you spoke. I didn't see Mom in your eyes. Not one of my favorite memories."

Wendy Carrington came with Karen and I said Wendy was a better daughter because she didn't move away and leave her family. I have no idea where that came from. Was it some buried resentment over her not living closer to us? We certainly missed having Karen at home but were happy she had a good job and good friends.

I journaled about my hospital stay shortly after returning home.

Being in ICU was like viewing a movie. I felt disconnected from everything going on around me.

Someone told me it sounded like how people describe an out-of-body experience. Whatever it was I was glad when it was over.

When I reentered the real world, I remember a male nurse talking with me and helping me sit up. I know his body strength was comforting and I realized how male nurses are a great addition to the medical community. Soon after that I was released from ICU to a regular room.

The doctors later told me they believed a fat embolism from my bone marrow went into my bloodstream, coating my lungs and obstructing my oxygen supply. They thought it was more apt to happen when both hips were replaced.

I was supposed to have physical therapy in the hospital. One time my meal tray had just arrived so the therapist said he would come back later. Another time I had visitors and he said he would come back later. He didn't return either time. I had one session prior to my going home. I walked down the hall using my walker to where there was a set of portable steps. I went up and down once and then back to my room. When I looked at the hospital bill I saw my insurance was billed for therapy sessions. I should have reported the lack of service but didn't. I faithfully did the exercises the doctor gave me, slept with a pillow between my legs for weeks, and refrained from any positions or movements that might be harmful. I am still careful.

Weezie came from New Jersey to help us. Bill set up a cot for her and a hospital bed for me in our living room. Though she was nearly eighty she was wonderful. She cooked, kept things tidied up, and cared for me.

Matt was in the apprenticeship program at MMR and Marcia Carlstrom brought him to visit. I'd just come home from the hospital when they arrived. By then I was back to normal.

We survived another close call. God's grace was certainly evident during this time. He was in the operating room, the recovery room and ICU. Then He watched over my recuperation. The decision to have hip replacement surgery was a positive one. It gave me quality of life.

Early in July Bill and I made a pre-move trip together. Dr. A gave permission for me to go if we stopped often so I could get out and walk around. We did as he said because we understood the danger of post-surgery blood clots.

At one rest stop I stepped out of the vehicle and used my walker to go to the restroom. Bill waited to walk me back to the truck. On the return, I didn't need the walker so I carried it in one hand.

Bill took my other hand in his and asked, "Why are you laughing?"

"I wonder if it looks like I've stolen this from a little old lady."

CARRY ME BACK TO OLE VIRGINIA
GINGHAM AND CORDUROY

Vern, Connie and Ben Peck helped with the main move of furniture and belongings. It was a long day and we traveled into the night. Just as we entered Pound, Virginia, we had an encounter with a bridge.

Connie remembers:

"We were following you and Bill. As you came to the bridge the right rear tire on the trailer caught the bridge. The tire came off and dropped the side of the trailer. I remember seeing the sparks flying when it dropped. Scared me to death!"

Bill drove the truck and trailer into the parking lot of a little convenience store. We asked the manager if we could leave the trailer until morning when we could get help to move it. He told us it was in the way of his breakfast crowd and insisted we move it right away. Then he called the police. Our trailer was damaged but the bridge was barely scratched. Would we be issued a ticket?

The town police officer arrived and imagine our surprise when we recognized him! It was Phil Stanley, a member of Skeetrock Bible Church.

"Hey, Pastor Bill, haven't seen you in a long time!"

Phil greeted us warmly, much to the astonishment of the store manager. Phil suggested we call Skip Dobis who came right over. They offloaded some of our things from the trailer to his pickup truck. The four-wheeled trailer had two axles so they tied up the twisted axle and we continued our journey using the undamaged axle.

Around the time we moved back to Virginia, the Carlstroms moved from Miracle Mountain Ranch to North Carolina. They were going to work with Equip, a ministry preparing missionaries for serving in third world countries. Our move south was not coordinated, but we lived about the same distance from each other there as we did in Pennsylvania.

In August, Matthew graduated from Miracle Mountain Ranch's Camp Apprenticeship Ministry Program. We attended his graduation, along with Karen and Becky. It was an exciting time but some of the excitement took place before we arrived.

We were not aware Matt and his buddies were riding in a rodeo the morning of graduation. Matt survived riding a bull, but a bucking mule was his nemesis. The mule tossed him into the air and he landed on his tailbone. When we arrived for graduation, he came out to meet us moving very slowly and carefully. He assured us he was fine but it was difficult for him to sit through the graduation dinner. He hasn't ridden a bull or mule since, but he does ride a longhorn steer. It doesn't buck.

Bill and Matt made trips from Pennsylvania to Virginia before and after the final move. On one trip Bill and Matt had Brandi, Socks and Buggs, our mares, as well as Nipper, our pony, in a horse trailer. The trip took over twelve hours so Bill and Matt checked on them several times. They realized Brandi hadn't urinated and was showing signs of distress. Taking her out of the trailer didn't help. They finally found a grassy spot in Virginia and she relieved herself. Maybe she was waiting for the green, green grass of home. After all she was a native Virginian!

We were back in Skeetrock but several of our closest neighbors were no longer around. We were surrounded by empty houses. Elsie and John Branham were no longer with us. John and Theta Artrip had moved to a home out on The Flats and Dorsie Phipps had gone on to be with the Lord.

We hoped to secure teaching positions. That was not the case. What on earth were we thinking? Bill was sixty-one and I was fifty-seven. The job market was not our friend.

We had no jobs, no income, and our home needed repairs. Karen was living and working in Lancaster. Billy and his family were living in Florida. Matt had finished the apprenticeship program and was trying to decide what was next. Bill and I had no idea what we were going to do! We just knew God wanted us back in the mountains.

I don't know how we managed financially those first months. I have a memory snippet of one lunch when I made a sandwich for three of us to share. We had two pieces of bread and one piece of bologna. We also had mustard for the sandwich, and applesauce for dessert! That is an extreme memory. Obviously, we didn't starve.

We all did substitute teaching. This was a first for Matt and he did well. He stayed with us through Christmas and then traveled to a friend's wedding with the Carlstroms. Scott suggested he go to Grand Rapids, Michigan to look for work. He did, and lived with Scott while working at Zondervan. While he was working at Zondervan he realized God wanted him at the ranch. He returned in 1991 to be the ranch's farmer. This suited him well because he was serving the Lord while spending time outside and on a tractor.

There were many positives about returning to Virginia. We loved the area and the people. We were well known. Our neighbors said they were happy that we had returned. We had been accepted before but now we were folks returning home. And, we didn't have rent payments!

I was hired to teach a GED class, filling in for the regular teacher. Teaching adults who want to learn is a delight and this class was no exception. There were about 15 in the class: a married couple, a teenaged male, two men, and the rest were women of various ages. The class was in the evening and the only negative was the class was an hour from home.

The class composition was interesting. The husband dropped out rather quickly, as did one of the other men. The young male and one older man completed the scheduled classes, as well as most of the women.

One evening only women were in attendance and they shared their hopes and dreams. A few said they couldn't talk about how they were doing in class because their husbands didn't like it. Instead of being happy about their wives getting an education they belittled what they were doing.

One young woman was a very good student and obviously intelligent. She told us she wanted to be a teacher. I encouraged her to go to college when she received her GED but she didn't think her husband would let her.

I'm sure there were many reasons for this type of thinking. Macho male feels threatened by successful female? Husband fearing his wife won't need him? Admittedly I only heard the women's side of the problem and never heard directly from the husbands. After that evening I considered what we were trying to achieve and prayed it would be positive for everyone involved.

Bill helped with the construction of a large log home just a couple of miles from us. This was something he enjoyed. He loved working with his hands. On this job he worked with, and for, two good friends, Phil Henry and Bob Phipps.

I taught first and second grade in a Christian school for several months to finish out a school year. Teaching youngsters can provide laughs, often at personal expense! One day I was sitting on a little chair reading to the first graders clustered on the floor in front of me.

A boy pointed to my legs and asked, "Mrs. Cox, what's that all over your legs?"

I looked where he was pointing and to my chagrin it was hair! Since I had been wearing stockings I hadn't bothered to shave my legs, evidently for some time. Who would have thought anyone would be close enough to see my hairy legs?

I smiled, "That's hair. Someday you will have hair on your legs too."

Then I continued reading the book. Don't ever think children aren't observant!

Though our outside employment was sometimes spotty, we were always busy. When we weren't working on the house and grounds, we were producing crafts, leading Bible studies, meeting with people. Our lives were full.

When Bill turned sixty-two we decided to apply for Social Security. We needed the income and the lower amount would balance out over the years. The bad news was his income was low the last couple of years. This brought down the figures they use to compute what your check will be. Even with the negatives, God took care of us.

In 1993 Bill started teaching courses in automotive, small engine repair and welding at Equip. He enjoyed teaching there, though it was only once or twice a year. We also enjoyed spending time with the Carlstroms. It was a double-barreled blessing.

One of Bill's students was a young woman who was deaf. She read lips and used sign language which worked well until she and

Bill were working under a car. He forgot she had to see his lips and turned his head. She reminded him with a sharp nudge and a flurry of hand signals. She was a great student and not at all handicapped. Through fellowship with Equip, and other ministries, we have met folks from all over the world we would not have met otherwise. Another blessing.

When you change anything in your life it has far reaching effects. If we had not returned to Virginia, our lives would have taken a radically different direction. God's hand directs in ways we least expect. I am thankful He puts the quilt pieces together in accordance with His plan and not mine.

CLINTWOOD BIBLE CHURCH

It would have been convenient to walk across the churchyard to Skeetrock Bible Church but we believed it best to find a different church home. After a few visits we decided on Clintwood Bible.

Bill felt a kinship with Pastor Theo Yates and James Taylor, both Navy veterans. *Once a sailor, always a sailor* sums it up. Theo served in the Pacific during World War II and saw combat aboard the USS Terror. James served in the Atlantic fleet during the Korean War. Theo and Bill came home after their enlistments were completed. James completed twenty-one and a half years. They often sat together at church functions.

A few called CBC the rich man's church. Some were blessed financially but they were generous to the church and community. We were never interested in the size of someone's bank account. Our friends always ranged from well-off to barely-making-it.

When I taught GED, spiritual matters came up naturally. One young woman asked where I went to church because she and her husband were looking for one. I invited her to CBC. They came one Sunday morning but didn't come back after the first visit. It had nothing to do with how they were treated or even the message they heard. Her husband was a Union man and we had several men in management. She said she was sorry but he wouldn't return. Prejudice rears its ugly head when you least expect it.

Theo sometimes asked Bill to fill the pulpit, which Bill thoroughly enjoyed. Even when he was no longer a pastor he was planning messages. Several times folks asked Bill if he was interested in pastoring again. He told them God was no longer calling him to be a pastor but he was always willing to preach or minister.

When God called him to minister with Bible Club Movement, CBC supported us financially and in prayer. They even gave me a shower to outfit me for this new phase.

The odometer on our pickup was racking up numbers and repairs were becoming more frequent. It had done us well and we hesitated to get rid of it, but the folks at CBC encouraged us to consider more reliable transportation.

Ethel Hughes was concerned after she went to Florida with us and a tire came off on our way home. God provided a Christian pastor to help but Ethel figured it was time to find a better vehicle. Linda Childress wrote a letter sharing the need.

We were sent to Johnson Chevrolet to look at possible vehicles. We knew a couple thousand dollars had been collected so that was the price range we kept in mind. We picked out one that looked like a possibility but Sam Patton suggested we look at others that cost more. We did but said we wouldn't go in debt.

When we asked Sam for his suggestion, he showed us a gray Astro van. We took it for a test drive. The color wasn't my preference but the van was perfect for us. The price was more than the funds collected but we were told to sit tight. The next Sunday in church we were presented with the van. The church made up the difference. We only paid the sales tax and license fee!

About this time, Pastor Theo retired after twenty-seven years as pastor and a search committee was formed. I only remember one candidate. There could have been more since we were often out of town. He was a young man with a wife and child and made a positive impression on most, not on us. We voiced our concerns but were the only negative votes so we yielded to the majority. Since he was our pastor, we did our best to support him. We grew to appreciate him personally though we never embraced his style of preaching. His wife was a wonderful asset with children and music.

The church discussed bringing our ministry support closer to the level suggested by our mission. We were asked to name a figure that would do it, so we went over our finances to produce a sensible budget. It's always been difficult for me to be realistic yet not seem greedy, but we settled on a figure. The church voted for the full amount!

Before the end of Pastor S's first year we knew there was dissension but weren't aware of the reason. The situation came to a head and a meeting was called to dismiss him. Some of our close friends decided to leave the church. We weren't in agreement with the way the situation was handled and wondered if we should leave. God didn't give us freedom to do that. We stayed and were glad we did.

A pastor is subject to the same sins as any man but is held to a higher standard because of his calling, as he should be. If he repents he will be forgiven by God and should be forgiven by those around him. Did he repent? God knows. I hope so.

A split in a church is painful for everyone. It's like a human losing a body part. It causes pain and should be avoided when possible. However sometimes a split is necessary for pruning and good for the overall body. Hopefully wounds were healed through offering and receiving forgiveness. Holding on to grievances is never an option for a believer.

Pastor Theo's son, Mike, became our pastor. He and his wife, Anita, have been our friends for many years. Over the 18 years we were members there we enjoyed serving in a variety of ways. We sang with and led the choir, taught Sunday school, and were involved in Vacation Bible School. Several years I played piano for services, enjoyed ladies' Bible studies and retreats, as well as trips to special events.

In 2005 I approached Anita and Pastor Mike asking if they thought we could have a special class for teen-aged girls concerning modesty and sexual purity. For a while I'd felt someone needed to address the young women in our church and finally realized I might be the one to do it. I trusted parents had already broached the subject but sometimes it's good from an outside source.

With Pastor Mike's blessing I approached the parents of the girls for their permission, explaining what I planned to teach and what I would be sharing from our lives. Bill was in accord. It took courage for both of us because we shared part of our lives that only we knew. The first time was the most difficult but if exposing our sin keeps someone from going astray, it's worth it.

You may wonder if the class was successful. We started with four, and two left by the end of the second class. Two stayed with me and seemed to enjoy our time together. Was the class helpful? Only the girls and God know. I just know they blessed me.

When we moved from Virginia to North Carolina, our van was showing its age and the transmission needed to be replaced. We purchased one from a salvage yard. Then Pastor Mike asked if we would be interested in another Astro. It was close in age but with fewer miles. We accepted the offer.

After Bill left, I no longer needed a van and began praying for a smaller vehicle. One day my pastor at the Christian Missionary Alliance Church in Marion told me that he and Janet wanted to give me their 2000 Toyota Camry. That was seven years ago and Runwell (she was named before I got her) has been running well ever since. She has taken me thousands of miles on trips, through twelve states, and is still going strong.

CBC continued to support us financially even after Bill's cancer made it necessary for him to retire from BCM. Later, when my needs were being met, their financial support was no longer necessary.

Clintwood Bible Church "gave with liberality" to those in need, whether to the strangers who came to the door or by distributing "to the needs of the saints." (Romans 12:8 & 13).

The rich man's church? More so they are rich in sharing.

POUND LADIES' BIBLE STUDY

In the early 90s I attended a retreat in Pikeville KY with a group of ladies from Clintwood Bible. Doris Bowman from Pound Independent Baptist was part of the group. Doris had been leading a Ladies' Bible Study in Pound for several years. Now she and her husband were preparing to move to Cedine Bible Mission in TN and she was looking for someone to take over the Bible study.

While we were at the retreat, God prompted me to accept the challenge to lead the Bible study. Doris hadn't directly asked me so I hoped I wasn't being presumptuous. The ages in the Bible study were diverse and we had great times together. We learned from each other and there was an atmosphere of trust, allowing for sharing.

We studied a variety of Bible books and themes. The book of Ephesians stands out in my mind. I don't remember how long it took us to go through it, we went verse by verse. It continues to be one of my favorite books. Each time I read it I think of those women. Of course, in preparation for teaching, the teacher is the first to learn and be challenged.

Doris is an exceptional speaker. She combines truth and wisdom with humor and often does little skits in costume to make a point. Even with her giftedness, she has always been ready for any task set before her. One of her responsibilities at Cedine was to clean the bathrooms for retreats. As she knelt before the porcelain thrones she prayed for all those who were coming to the retreat, that God would use the time to provide for spiritual and physical needs. I'll never forget her willingness to serve in any capacity. May we all be that willing to serve others.

MIRACLE MOUNTAIN RANCH WILDERNESS CAMP

When Vern's father died we purchased his pickup and camper from his widow, Ruth, a lovely woman. Ed had taken good care of it and Ruth gave us a good price. We had all the comforts of home along with not having to search for restrooms.

For several years we spent a couple of weeks each summer at Miracle Mountain Ranch. At first, we were missionaries of the week and stayed with a family or in a guest trailer. Later, when Bill helped run Wilderness Camp, we lived in our pickup camper.

In Wilderness Camp the kids stayed in a wooded area away from the main camp. The first day they worked as teams building their own dwellings using black plastic tarps and rope. Bill shook his head and laughed as he recounted the day's activities.

> *"The hardest part is getting them to build their shelters so they have a place to sleep. Most of them just want to climb trees and cut down saplings.'*

Bill was involved with Boy Scouts for years, and spent many nights outdoors, but he found few of these young fellows had any idea what to do, including the counselors. Only one or two of the counselors even wanted to be in the woods. This meant

297

not only keeping the campers directed, but also their leaders.

"We knew there was rain coming in. We showed them how to ditch around their shelters so the water wouldn't flood them out. One group built their shelter right over a gully and wondered why they got wet."

The first year there was a week for boys and another for girls. Bill said,

"The girls' campsite was a different story. They built their shelters right away and then added paths and landscaping complete with flowers! Girls like to nest! One group even had a foundation of logs under their tarp."

Girls' Wilderness Camp was canceled after the first season to the chagrin of the girls and their leaders. It has now returned, stronger than ever.

Both boys' and girls' camps followed the same format. Each had group devotions in the morning and evening chapel around the campfire. They had one trail ride a week, as well as other activities. They came into the main camp mid-week to shower and showered again before going home.

After the 1995 camping season Bill was notified Wilderness Camp was being discontinued because the Executive Director felt it was straying too far from the intent of the ministry. Short term, Bill was saddened for the boys who were looking forward to the next season. Long term, he was disappointed that his vision of packing out with horses wasn't going to happen.

Thankfully, Wilderness Camp again became a part of the MMR ministry in 2010. Though they have not added packing with horses, they do have several weeks of Wilderness Camp including one week for girls and a week of paintball camp. There are now young men who enjoy roughing it and come to the ranch specifically to work in Wilderness Camp.

In 2016 they had the first Absolute Bearing Camp. Participants learned the basics of survival and orienteering and then went on an overnight canoeing trip on the Allegheny River. Bill would be pleased.

PAUL SPEAKS

When we returned to Virginia from Pennsylvania, we thought Paul Speaks might be a viable ministry. The seed for Paul Speaks may have been planted in 1975 when Bill dressed and spoke as a shepherd for VBS at Skeetrock Bible Church. I believe that was the first time he did a message in costume. He studied Paul's life in depth, Biblically and historically. All the messages were based on scripture but not word-for-word.

The first presentation of Paul Speaks was for an evening service in Bumpville. The setting was the dungeon of Rome's Mamertine prison where the apostle was held near the end of his life. Paul wrote Timothy to encourage him. The dungeon setting, chains on his wrists, and the parchment scroll lent credence to the setting.

Another early message was Paul standing before King Agrippa describing his Damascus Road experience. That costume was of finer fabric than the rough prison clothing.

The circuit riding preacher was presented at several churches. The preacher was a composite of several historic figures and wore a black frockcoat and a tri-corner hat. Bill also dressed as a mountain man from the late 1800s for MMR Wilderness Camp.

My favorite character was originally intended for young people. His name? Tersius. Bill dressed in Biblical attire but spoke in the present. He taught about Paul, and the environment of his time. He used his knowledge of history and geography tied in with Scripture while interacting with the audience.

Do you know who Tersius was? Look at Romans 16:22. There he is! He penned the letter to the Roman church as Paul dictated. It was common for Paul to use an amanuensis (scribe or secretary) and this time we know his name. Ministry needs people behind the scenes and in Tersius we meet one of the early ones.

John the Baptist was the last character to join the cast. Pastor Mike Yates encouraged Bill to do John. He arrived in the church auditorium shouting, "Repent!" Bill had a fondness for the theatrical and The Baptist commanded attention!

Bill did presentations at a Christian school, a missionary training facility, several churches, and two Christian camps. Walt Brannen, a friend with a mission church in the Pocono Mountains, hosted Paul Speaks at his church and facilitated presentations at other churches in his area. It was well received in some but didn't take off as we thought it might. God had something else in mind!

"A man's heart plans his way,
but the LORD directs his steps."
(Proverbs 16:9)

BIBLE CLUB MOVEMENT

Walt mentioned a possible ministry opportunity with Bible Club Movement. He said Dave and Lois Haas were at a nearby camp and he suggested we meet them. Dave was director of USA ministries. We agreed to listen to what they had to say.

After friendly introductions Dave told us he was looking for a Regional Director for the southeastern United States. He wanted someone in closer contact with the missionaries as a liaison between them and headquarters. He laid out the qualifications for the position and what would be required.

The possibility was interesting but imagine my surprise when Bill said, "I'm your man!"

Just a minute! Shouldn't we talk this over?
Have we prayed about this?

I didn't say it out loud but it went through my mind! Bill was decisive but I never saw him make a snap decision like that before! He knew immediately it was what God wanted him to do, so he said, "Yes!" Remember the hospital room? The circumstances were different but the call was the same.

We still needed to go through the application procedure and be approved by the mission. Dave and Lois came to Virginia and met with us to go over the details. BCM is a faith-based ministry so we needed to raise support. Since we were receiving Social Security we were partway to our suggested goal.

While Dave and Lois were with us they took us to visit two of the missionaries who would be in our care, Joanna Gerhardt and Mary Lou Weber. They were stationed in Jenkins, Kentucky, only an hour from our home.

We filled out a lengthy application. The questions helped us to consider our personal beliefs. Bill had done this for his ordination but it was all new to me. We didn't compare answers until we were finished. As soon as we were accepted, we began seeking financial support for the cost of orientation and our future monthly income.

BCM orientation was in late summer. There was an overlap

with our weeks at MMR so BCM permitted us to miss the first part of our training. As soon as Bill finished Wilderness Camp, he set the camper on jacks and we were on our way.

Our orientation at Traber Center was exciting. Our class was multicultural. Some hailed from the USA. Others were from Trinidad, Ghana, Guyana, Holland, Ivory Coast, India, Spain, Dominican Republic, Brazil, and St. Lucia. We came from diverse backgrounds but bonded as a group. We were brothers and sisters in Christ.

Together we attended classes, studied, helped prepare meals, cleaned up after meals, swept floors, scrubbed bathrooms, took tests, laughed and played together. We also shared concerns and prayed together. We came to know each other well.

Everyone pitched in except one young man from the Ivory Coast who avoided taking part. Larry, from a neighboring country, told us J was from a prideful tribe who felt it was beneath them to do manual labor. J was a likeable young man, a barber by trade. He cut my hair and did it very well. He was always eager to share his faith when we were out in the community. He finished orientation but didn't follow through with his commitment to the mission.

When I first met M I was wary. It had nothing to do with him personally, but much to do with what I'd read, and heard firsthand, about how men from the Middle East treated their wives. I knew a young woman who met and married a man from the Middle East while they were in college. They had two sons. He treated her with respect until their sons were older, then his attitude changed. When they visited his family overseas she was increasingly ignored, not only by his family but by him. Then he illegally took his sons to live overseas and didn't allow her to visit them. She was devastated but was working with a rescue organization to facilitate their return. I don't know the outcome but I do know I saw M through the lens of her situation.

My Nana said her first impressions always stuck with her. That has not been the case with me and this is a good example. I told M my concerns. He assured me he was not like that. After observing him for a time I realized that was true and asked him to forgive me for jumping to conclusions. He did.

M knew Bill enjoyed coffee and invited him to join him in a

cup of his special brew. He had a brass coffee pot that made one cup of coffee and the preparation was complex, requiring boiling and preserving the froth on top. He used a finely ground Turkish coffee. Bill's appraisal of the coffee? It reminded him of the espresso he had overseas—too strong.

We enjoyed getting to know M. We learned a lot about his country, and what it's like to live where it's dangerous to be a Christian. He took part in all our classes but was never officially a student. His death was possible if officials knew what he was doing. He owned a company and was officially here on business. When we parted, he gave Bill and I a papyrus with this verse:

"The Lord shall preserve thy going out and thy coming in
from this time forth, and even for evermore."
(Psalm 121:8)

We displayed it in our home by our front door. We haven't heard from him but continue to pray for his safety.

The mission provided several field trips in the Lancaster area as part of our orientation. They were probably mostly for the foreign candidates but we all had a grand time. We attended a patriotic musical presentation at The American Music Theater and enjoyed the seemingly endless buffet at Shady Maple Smorgasbord. We also visited the Green Dragon, a farmer's market in Ephrata, and toured an old building where a variety of craftsmen displayed their wares.

The highlight for Bill and I was shopping with Ron from Guyana, Larry from Ghana and J from the Ivory Coast. Their delight in the merchandise at the Green Dragon was so much fun. The best part was they continually shared their faith! It didn't matter where we were or who we met, they asked people if they knew the Savior and talked with them.

These men lived out what the Bible tells us to do and in doing so they showed us how we fail in carrying out the mission.
"...always being ready to make a defense
to everyone who asks you to give an account
for the hope that is in you,
yet with gentleness and reverence."
(I Peter 3:15)

302

BCM orientation classes are still held here in the States but also in locations overseas. I'm sure the change is positive in many ways, but we were so blessed by getting to know Christians from many different countries.

After orientation we were welcomed into the mission during Annual Conference. Over twenty years has elapsed and we remain in touch with some, hear about others, and pray for many. Our time together was precious.

We enjoyed attending BCM Annual Conference. It was a good time to connect with other missionaries and before returning home we could spend time with Karen and Kent, and their girls.

The trip home was a long one so we decided to get groceries the day after our return. Just as I was getting in the truck the next morning, I decided to go back inside for a cup of coffee to take with me. I hurried up the front steps and sprawled onto the porch. I didn't feel any pain but knew I should when I saw my right foot! The sole no longer was facing away from my body. My foot had swiveled sideways at the ankle with the sole facing to the side!

"Bill, I need you!"

As soon as he saw me he called for an ambulance and found something he could use for a splint to immobilize the ankle. Marvin Senter and Hank Hemond came over from the church where they were working and assisted. I wish we'd taken a photo. The position of my ankle is difficult to describe.

Marvin and Hank suggested we see Dr. U, an orthopedist they knew did good work. The ambulance crew left the homemade splint in place and loaded me, but they couldn't shut the ambulance door! The board was too long, so Bill removed several inches with a handsaw. He followed the ambulance to town.

When we arrived in Clintwood we were told I had to transfer to another ambulance that could cross the county line into Wise County. That didn't take long and we were on our way again.

By the time we arrived in the Emergency Room I needed a bathroom. I tried to wait, figuring the doctor would be there any minute. Bill located a bedpan and helped me on it just as Dr. U arrived. He didn't even seem to notice what I was trying to do. There I sat (I use the term loosely) and with Bill's help I covered myself discreetly. There was another doctor with him and they discussed my situation.

While they were talking, Dr. U yanked the ankle to its proper position. It all happened so quickly I didn't have time to feel pain! He said I had a total dislocation of my ankle and needed surgery to secure it. He planned to operate later that day. And he was gone. He was like a tornado blowing through town. At least the ankle was in a better position and I finished my task on the bedpan.

They took me to a room and Bill stayed with me. X-rays were taken, it was confirmed the tibia was fractured and I was given pain meds. Around supper time, Dr. U talked with Bill. He said he wanted to put off the surgery until the next morning. He had been in surgery all day and he was tired.

"Mr. Cox, if she was my wife, I would want her to have the best care possible. Tomorrow, she will be my first surgery."

Bill thanked him and agreed it was best to wait. I was given something to help me sleep and I don't remember anything until after surgery the next day.

When Dr. U visited me following surgery, I found he had a great bedside manner. He fully concentrated on me and ignored everything else. He later shared that he believed in focusing on the patient with him and wasn't concerned about time. This was evident when we were in his waiting room on follow up visits. We never minded waiting because we knew I had his undivided attention when it was my turn.

I went home with a cast on my lower right leg. I was instructed not to put any weight on the leg and stay off it completely. Recovery time was estimated to be three months! Three months of staying put, really staying put!

Bill set me up in our little guest bedroom with an adult potty chair beside my bed. He took care of the household completely. I did whatever I could while staying on the bed. After a few weeks I could maneuver around the bed and reach whatever I needed on my own, if it was within arm's reach. Bill was an excellent nurse. I already knew he was a good cook.

Occasionally a friend visited making a nice change in routine. Some brought meals and that pleased us both. Since I had a window facing the front yard, I didn't feel totally closed off from the world.

When Dr. U removed the screws from my ankle and released me, he told us if anything happened to that ankle he would fix it free of charge. He was very confident. I never had a bit of trouble with the ankle.

During our several visits, he and Bill sometimes discussed faith. He knew we were Christians because we gave credit to God for guiding his hands during surgery, as well as my recovery. We were thankful we connected with Dr. U. I could not have asked for a better doctor!

Of course, I'm glad I haven't needed to call on Dr. U to repair his work. He moved back to India!

God provided the right man at the right time!

FIVE YEARS WITH BCM

The five years we spent with BCM were good ones. Being regional director was like being a pastor and our missionaries were our congregation. Missionaries are people and have the same trials and joys we all have. Some were easy to know; others not so much. Many were retired, though in name only. They continued ministering even though they had an (R) after their name.

Florence was the first missionary to greet us when we joined BCM. She sent us a note, saying she was glad we were onboard and looked forward to meeting us. She worked with Africa Inland Mission and lived in their Retirement Center in Minneola, Florida.

Bill and Eileen were on staff at a camp in Tennessee. Both Bills had many of the same talents and interests. They visited us in Skeetrock where we had a great time playing Mexican Train, along with Jo and Mary Lou. That was one of the few times I saw Bill enjoy playing a table game.

Shortly after we joined the mission we attended a SE missionary retreat at Camp Sunrise in north Georgia. There was a large indoor amphitheater with a planetarium and a museum where I enjoyed browsing the rock and mineral collection. All information was Bible-based and scientifically sound. There we met many of our southeast missionaries, among them Jim and Lois. They lived and ministered in Georgia. Though Jim lost his skirmish with cancer, he won the battle and is now in his heavenly home. Lois continues serving the Lord here in the states and overseas.

When we visited missionaries in Florida we visited Billy and his family in Gainesville and traveled from there. Since we didn't have a cell phone back then, Billy loaned us his. It was good to have it with us but we seldom needed to use it.

Another couple in Florida works with college students and internationals in the Tampa area. Jeff has gained the respect of many Muslims. Bill and I felt his ministry was admirable, but the full effect may take years to be revealed. I smile when I remember his wife Martha using a pole to knock grapefruit from the tree in their front yard so we could take some home.

Minnie ministered to children in the city of Wilmington, North Carolina. Bill presented her with a plaque commemorating her many years of service with BCM.

We knew the missionaries in Kentucky better than most as they lived close by. Donna Dudte and Hazel Huff were a little farther than the gals in Jenkins. Brian and Sarah Hampshire were in Kentucky for several years. Sarah was great with Weezie and sometimes stayed with her.

There is a bittersweet memory. Sarah, Jo and I were having breakfast together in Clintwood on September 11, 2001, joking and laughing as we ate. A handful of people were watching TV and the waitress called across the room, "Listen up!" We looked at the TV and saw why she called out. Flames engulfed one side of the north tower of the World Trade Center.

We joined the others clustered at the counter, bewildered. Was it real? Could it be another *War of the Worlds*? No, it was real. Our country was under attack! We watched the south tower explode when another airliner crashed into it and both towers were on fire. In dismay, we saw the towers crumble and fall.

Before leaving, we apologized to the others in the restaurant for what appeared to be disrespect. We took leave of each other in the parking lot, and went home more quietly than we had arrived. We prayed for the families of those directly affected and for our country.

Many of us believed the attack was a wakeup call to turn back to God. For a while there was a surge of revival among Christians, and an awakening among unbelievers. There was even a groundswell of patriotism. It was grand to be American.

Though there was some positive change, repentance was lacking. It's a modern version of the parable of the sower's seeds found in the synoptic gospels. Some of the seeds for change fell on the berm of the road, some on rocky soil or among thorns. We hope some fell on fertile soil and grew to maturity.

Paul writes to the Ephesians:

> "...Awake, sleeper, and arise from the dead,
> And Christ will shine on you.
> Therefore, be careful how you walk,
> Not as unwise men but as wise,
> making the most of your time,
> because the days are evil.
> So then do not be foolish,
> But understand what the will of the Lord is."
> (Ephesians 5:14-17)

ONGOING HOME RENOVATIONS

"Where do we start?"

"What's our top priority?"

"What can we do without spending money?"

We encountered these questions and more when we relocated to Skeetrock. Billy said he thought we should get rid of the trailer and add on to the addition. He was probably right but that meant putting in a kitchen and bathroom right away and we couldn't handle that financially.

We did the most urgent repairs first. Renovations began in 1990 and weren't completed until just before we sold in 2008. With the help of family and friends we rebuilt the trailer and the addition. I will only touch on the highlights and a few of the folks that were involved, in little or no order.

In October 1991, a work team came from the ranch. Chip Hungerford and Ralph Magill headed a crew of CAMP students from MMR. It was a coed group and they did a great job of enclosing the trailer and putting on a new roof. Two crew members missed the first part of the week because they were on their honeymoon, Matt and Jenni! They stopped by for a few days on their way back to the ranch.

Matt and his family came annually for vacation. Merriam-Webster defines vacation: "time a person spends away from home, school, or business usually to relax or travel." They traveled, but relaxed?

Landscaping was an ongoing project. Bill did the heavy work and I took care of planting and upkeep. We found raised beds were best for both vegetables and flowers.

Over time, the back deck and front porch were rebuilt. The entire foundation of the building was enclosed; floors were rebuilt; vinyl and porcelain tiles were laid; carpet was laid; new doors were installed; ceiling fans were installed; brick hearths were repaired; everything was painted; trees and bushes were trimmed and removed; new roof was put on the addition; the driveway was graveled.

When I planted English ivy to cover one wall at the end of the trailer, Paul asked me if I was sure I wanted to do it. Of course I did, then. It climbed on wood panels and found its way into our pantry. It became a problem. When we took it off it left its little footprints to be sanded off. After they were assigned to remove it, Hannah and Megan will probably never plant English ivy on their homes.

We had lots of volunteer help and couldn't have done it without them. A friend told us about a local young man who was a good worker and we hired him as much as we could afford. He was a tremendous help. He worked with Bill and with me. He even worked with Jenni on the roof. He was a native of the area and we learned a lot from him. I can't imagine having a better worker or a more enjoyable friend. Thank you, Phane.

Besides MMR we had other work teams. Paul Carlstrom brought teams from both the CMA Church and Equip in Marion NC. He and Marcia came many times. During one of their visits, Fred and Karen Sauls came to help. James Taylor repaired the brick hearth in our sitting room and other folks from Clintwood Bible Church helped with a myriad of projects. Among them were Mike and Anita, and Palmer and Mildred. During the final push to the finish, my brother Bill installed our new front door and Janice power washed the porch.

Our neighbor DJ Brooks was a tremendous help to Bill. He mowed our lawn when we couldn't and did all kinds of needed repairs. He was a man of few words and just showed up. We often didn't even know he was outside working.

You may or may not be familiar with the term paraclete but it fits perfectly here. Spiritually the term paraclete often refers to the Holy Spirit, our Comforter or Helper. It comes from the Greek paraklétos meaning *one who comes alongside.*

It is impossible to mention all those who helped us. I have mentioned only a few. We could never have accomplished the work on our own but God provided the help we needed through family and friends. Sometimes through folks we barely knew.

"God is our refuge and strength,
a very present help in trouble."
(Psalm 46:1)

NEW CHALLENGES FOR A NEW MILLENIUM

God used a BCM contact to help Bill through a medical problem. He had two episodes in Virginia. The first one happened around 1980. Though alarming at the time, it's foggy now. We thought he had a transient ischemic attack, better known as a TIA or mini-stroke.   Karen, Matt and I remember him being unresponsive.

Twenty years later he had a similar episode. He was sitting in our family room after eating dinner. He began to feel dizzy and his pallor was poor. He felt bloated, but vomiting didn't give relief. He was extremely weak, broke out in a cold sweat, and couldn't speak. I gave him an aspirin crushed in honey and insisted we go to the ER. The attendants noted his poor color when they helped him out of the van. On the examining table his color began to return and the symptoms diminished. He wore a portable electrocardiogram for forty-eight hours and was referred to a cardiologist.

At the Heart Center they tried to do a heart catheterization but were unable to get the catheter to his heart from either groin. Some arteries were 100% blocked, another was 75% blocked. The good news was his body had built up collateral vessels allowing his blood to continue circulating. These collateral vessels are known as natural bypasses and can be built up by endurance exercise training such as running, bicycling, swimming and hiking.

God made great bodies for us and He built in a way for them to recover from our lack of care. We may block arteries with poor diet but our bodies can build up collateral vessels to bypass those obstacles. I wonder when Bill's body pressed those smaller vessels

309

into service. When he played football? He was a young man. Maybe when he took Boy Scouts on hikes? Whenever it was, we were thankful they were there.

His diagnosis was silent ischemia. He took medication to slow his heart and another to cut down cholesterol. He had nitroglycerin pills to take if he felt a heart attack coming on but with silent ischemia there is no pain to signal an attack.

We learned a lot from Bill's being a heart patient. One nurse told us, "If you have one problem with the vascular system, there are probably more that haven't surfaced yet." Also, his blood pressure was different depending on which arm was used to take it. That's common with vascular patients.

He knew he needed to follow doctor's orders but had difficulty trying to figure out what he should and shouldn't do. Though he wasn't the most cooperative patient at times, he did try to avoid anything that making his situation worse.

This is when a friend we met through BCM stepped into the picture. Norris and Dottie Bunn lived on Smith Mountain Lake in Virginia. We visited Dottie's father, Jim Hutchinson, who lived in an apartment in the Bunn's home with his second wife, Lillie. Dottie's mother died some years before we met. The Hutchinsons were BCM missionaries.

Though we hadn't seen him for some time, when Norris heard about Bill's heart episode he sent him a helpful note. Bill trusted what Norris said, partly because he was a retired surgeon, but more so because he had been living with cardiac problems for years.

"I walk slower and work slower than I ever did before … what gets done gets done, and what doesn't get done doesn't get done. Perhaps there will be another year in which to do it. Obviously it won't get done if I drop dead.

"Don't be afraid to stop everything—sit right where you are and rest if you feel tired. After resting, leave the tools and go inside. You can always pick them up tomorrow if you don't kill yourself today.

"God keeps us going one heartbeat at a time. When we realize there is no reason to expect the next heart beat to occur, something we all take for granted, God begins to teach us the

meaning of faith and true dependency on Him."

Norris's note gave Bill practical advice and hope. In a note back to Norris, Bill quoted a verse that meant a lot to him.
"Fear not for I am with you;
be not dismayed, for I am your God.
I will strengthen you, yes, I will help you.
I will uphold you with my righteous right hand."
(Isaiah 41:10)

WEEZIE'S BIRTHDAY MOVE

Early in our marriage, Bill and I agreed when our parents couldn't live on their own they could live with us. We knew some of the pitfalls and were hopeful we could adapt. Weezie and I were close and kept in touch regularly. When she visited us, she stayed a week or two, then was ready to go home. Jeff and Linda Rainey lived next door and Bill and Janice lived down the road. She had good friends in her church and community.

One concern was her driving. My mother loved to drive. One of her dreams was to drive a tractor trailer. Now she had glaucoma affecting her peripheral vision, and macular degeneration taking her central vision. I wonder why Weezie's eye doctor didn't tell her she shouldn't drive? Did he know she was still driving?

One day my brother was driving to Glassboro and saw Weezie coming toward him, on his side of the road. He called me, "We need to do something." We talked with her and she agreed to give up driving though it was a blow to her independence and her world was growing smaller. Janice took her to the grocery store, my brother picked her up for church, friends took her to other activities, but it wasn't the same.

When she visited we discovered she saw things no one else saw. One day we were driving home from town and she said, "Aren't those flowers lovely? It seems late in the year for them to be blooming." There were no flowers. After several similar experiences, I researched and found Charles Bonnet Syndrome (CBS). It is linked to macular degeneration. Weezie's seeing things had a name!

CBS is phantom vision, like our Billy's phantom pain after his leg amputation. It was first thought to be rare but now is considered common. It was discovered by Charles Bonnet in the 1700s. Macular Degeneration is most often the cause, but there can be other factors. Visual hallucinations appear as sight diminishes. The scenes are normally pleasant. Weezie saw horse drawn carriages, people strolling through the Piggly Wiggly parking lot, rocking chairs on large front porches, and often there were flowers.

One morning in Clintwood Bible Church she leaned close and quietly asked, "Do you see those people in white robes going toward the front of the church, or are they one of my illusions?" I told her she was the only one who saw them, though I confess I did wonder if she was seeing something beyond my temporal vision.

Since CBS is more prevalent in people who have restricted social interaction, Weezie was a perfect candidate. I doubt she mentioned her illusions to her doctor but I think patients and their families should be made aware of the possibility of CBS.

Weezie finally agreed to move to Virginia and we drove her home with us on her ninetieth birthday. I went to New Jersey to help her pack. We hoped integrating her furniture with ours would make her transition into our home easier. We gave her our dining room as a sitting room and encouraged her to take the larger bedroom, but she insisted on the smaller one.

She wanted to help around the house but it was difficult to find things for her to do. She folded towels and other laundry for me. I sometimes brought out a pile of dish towels and bath towels that I unfolded so she could fold them.

She enjoyed her new church and pastor and was happy to become a member. She sometimes sat with a couple of the older ladies for special events. She sang along with the congregation even when she couldn't see the words in the hymnal. Though her voice didn't have the richness it once had, it aged far better than mine.

She listened to television in her sitting room but tired of it when she could no longer see it. Books on tape were great. She enjoyed some from the Mailbox Library. One time, when the kids were visiting, Weezie was listening to a book I'd not heard before. Jenni called my attention to the content, which was quite racy.

Weezie was sitting there shaking her head and fiddling with the buttons. "I can't turn the darn thing off!" From then on, I was more careful with the books we ordered.

All was well for a while but we began to see signs of dementia, like those my brother saw before she moved with us.

My Bill and Weezie always had a good relationship. When she became demanding or berated me he showed remarkable restraint. He didn't intervene but there were some stressful times. Her tone could be accusatory, "I know I had chocolates. You've been taking them." There were times we had to deal with a different Weezie, the polar-opposite of the one we knew and loved.

One day I needed to pick up a prescription from our doctor. I thought she could stay in the car while I went into the office. It was a nice day and she seemed comfortable. When I went back to the car she was trying to climb out through the window. We realized she couldn't be left alone anywhere, even when she seemed to be doing well. Gracious friends stayed with her so we could go to appointments. Among them were Leona, Sarah, and Anita. We will always be thankful for them.

Seven months after Weezie came to stay with us, Bill had a colonoscopy. The report showed he had colon cancer. When he was scheduled for surgery, we knew we needed someone with her while I stayed with him in the hospital. We talked it over with Weezie and arranged for her to enter the nursing home for two weeks, giving us time to get Bill home and settled before she returned. It seemed to be a reasonable plan.

After surgery Bill needed a regimen of chemo and radiation. Weezie was going to be in the nursing home longer than we planned. She took the news in stride. I hung photographs on the wall next to her bed. One was of her in her wedding dress; the other was one with my father. I wanted her caregivers to see her as more than just an old lady who couldn't take care of herself.

She had several roommates during her stay and most were okay. Only a couple were unpleasant but there was one who was a special blessing! She was about my age and lived with her mother and father. She was there for rehab after surgery. They became good friends and Weezie was sad when she went home. I was too. She and her mother came back to visit Weezie several times.

Most of the staff were good. Jean Kendrick became friends with Weezie, and me. She was a bright spot in Weezie's day. There were a few aides I wish hadn't been there but overall her care was fine.

She had Physical Therapy. The PTs were wonderful and one young man made quite a hit. During a visit Weezie told me she had good news.

"I'm getting married," she said with a smile.

"Really?" I responded, not knowing what else to say.

Had a resident approached her? I'd never seen a man around her. After my father passed, a friend suggested he knew someone who might be interested in getting to know her. Her response, "I am not interested!"

"Do I know this man?"

"You've met him," she said with a shy smile.

"Well, who is it?"

"Tim."

Wait a minute! That was one of her physical therapists. He was in his mid-twenties and engaged to a lovely young woman.

"Isn't he a little young for you," I asked.

"Age doesn't matter."

"So, where are you going to live?"

"With his parents," she responded.

Have you thought what you would say to your 93-year-old mother who says she's going to marry a 26-year-old man and live with his parents? It had never crossed my mind. I changed the subject and we enjoyed the rest of our visit. The next time I talked with the therapists, I asked about Weezie, being sensitive to Tim's embarrassment. He took his job seriously and was gracious to his patients. I assured him I understood his predicament and thanked him for his kindness to my mother.

I think Tim's telling Weezie about his girlfriend helped because talk of marriage dwindled and she was no longer planning her wedding. He did put up with some teasing from his fellow workers but that too passed.

We passed by the nursing home on our way to and from Clintwood. On Sundays we picked her up for Sunday School and Church, then took her out for dinner. Chicken from Long John

Silver's was one of her favorites. She also liked dinners at church and the folks were great with her.

There were good days but there were also days when she wasn't herself. She sometimes called me from the nurse's station, disoriented or concerned. In a journal entry from 2003 I wrote:

"Pat, I don't know where I am.
I think I'm supposed to go somewhere
but I don't know where."

She was upset. We talked a while and she settled down.

She fell on the floor trying to get around the sides meant to keep her from falling out of bed and fractured her hip. Afterward, while in a wheelchair, she slipped under the restraints and fell to the floor.

When I visited I asked, "Weezie, why did you get out of the wheelchair?"

Her answer was with a smile, "Because I could!"

I wasn't the only one to visit Weezie in the nursing home. Bill went with me until he couldn't go. Pastor Mike and folks from church visited her. Bill and Janice visited. Karen, Morgan and Kensey visited, as did Matt and Jenni and their girls. The Coxes sang to her and quite a crowd gathered in the hallway to listen.

This has been a tough chapter to write, but then it was tough to live. I had determined to never put a loved one in a nursing home. I learned that 'never say never' has the ring of truth. I've told my children that if they need to put me in a nursing home they have my permission.

BILL'S FRIEND RAY

Ray was Bill's closest friend in the Navy and best man at our wedding. He married a short time after we did. Ray was excited about his upcoming marriage to his pretty bride-to-be. We attended the wedding and it was lovely. The reception featured lots of delicious food as well as an abundance of alcohol. We acted as designated drivers since we weren't drinking.

We wanted to give them a nice gift but finances were limited. Since our entertaining wasn't going to be formal, we re-gifted them a lovely silver plated covered vegetable dish.

Several weeks after their wedding we were invited for dinner and Ray's wife was using the silver cover as a saucepan lid.

Though it was no longer my cover I was sad to see that it had slipped socially from the dining table to the kitchen stove.

Ray and his wife produced a son a few months after our Bunky was born. I don't know if she wasn't ready to accept the responsibilities of a family or was simply immature. She became involved with another man and left Ray and her baby son. After a time, their marriage was annulled. Ray's mother and sister helped Ray, and Little Ray was well cared for. When Ray and his family visited us on the farm, Little Ray and Bunky enjoyed playing together. Both were surrounded by adults and had no siblings.

When Ray remarried, we were out of touch with him for several years but reconnected when we moved back to Virginia from Pennsylvania. Ray's job required extensive travel so he stopped in and spent a few days with us when he was in our area. When his wife died from cancer and he retired, he came for longer visits. Bill and he discussed spiritual truths, especially concerning the Bible's teaching on a personal relationship with Christ.

Ray was lonely and wanted a companion so he got a little Shih Tzu and treated it like a child. She came with him when he visited and got along fine with our Labs. She was a welcome guest and not at all like Dad Cox's Princess.

We liked our dogs and let them lick the bowl clean after we were finished eating ice cream. However, they never ate from the bowl with us and certainly didn't lick the ice cream while we were eating it. Ray and his dog shared ice cream!

One evening Ray called Bill to tell him he had good news. He had a girlfriend. They'd gone to high school together but hadn't seen each other in years. Anne's husband had been in the military, stationed in Hawaii. She worked there during his enlistment and stayed on after his death. Ray met her again through mutual friends when she was home over the holidays.

"I'd like you to meet Anne. Could I bring her down for a visit?"

"Sure," Bill replied. "Anne can use the guest room, and you can bunk in the sleeping loft."

Weezie was always fond of Ray and liked Anne. After they married we visited and enjoyed their company. Unfortunately, Ray developed leukemia. This was difficult for Anne because she lost her first husband to cancer. Sadly, Anne soon found she had cancer and died before Ray.

Ray did well financially, partly due to parental guidance but he was a hard worker and his second wife was an excellent money manager. He donated several times to our ministries. We were thankful for his gifts but concerned he thought giving put him in a better position with God. Bill wanted him to understand our position with God has nothing to do with what we do but everything to do with what He has done.

We visited Ray in the hospital shortly before he died of lymphoma and we met Little Ray for the first time in many years. We saw photos of his wife and children. He is in law enforcement. His father was proud of him. His grandparents would be also.

Long-lasting friendships are precious. Bill's friendship with Ray is a good example.

MORE ABOUT BILLY

In 1994 we spent Thanksgiving in Florida with Billy, Kathy and Becky. Karen and Kent joined us but Matt and Jenni couldn't because of Hannah's impending arrival. We celebrated Christmas together, beginning a family tradition allowing families to be in their own homes for Christmas.

Billy hoped we would retire to Florida but we liked the change of seasons and didn't relish the hot summers. We spent time with them when we visited Florida missionaries.

We enjoyed visiting some of the area attractions with Billy's family. We saw our first Renaissance Fair, the Cedar Key Seafood Festival, an old fort and the lighthouse in St. Augustine, and Matanzas Beach where we drove our pickup camper on the beach.

In the summer of 2001, Billy said he'd like to come to Virginia for a while. We told him we would love having him and he could even spend time with Weezie. Later we realized he probably couldn't have made the trip. In early fall, he called and said he'd like us to come to Florida. Bill didn't think we could take time away. Now I believe he needed help but didn't ask.

He dealt with Type 2 diabetes and had neuropathy in his feet. One leg had already been amputated below the knee. He wanted to have the other one amputated rather than deal with the problems it presented. Not only were his lower limbs affected, but his eyes were a concern. He was apprehensive about laser treatments for retinopathy. These problems were at least partially caused by his blood sugar levels not being controlled—he allowed them to run high.

In early December his foot went through the hallway floor, injuring his good leg and infection set in. He was hospitalized and it looked like he would lose the good leg. Matt made plans to go down and build a ramp for him to use on his return home.

Just before Matt left, Billy called us. He was about to go into surgery so our conversation was short. He was in pain. That was the last time I heard his voice. Kathy called to tell us he went into cardiac arrest while they were moving him to surgery. He was in a drug induced coma to rest his heart and allow it to recover.

Though the coma was induced there was no assurance he would come out of it. I talked with Mike Yates, our pastor, and told him of my concerns for Billy. He accepted Christ as his Savior when he was a young lad. In fact, he prayed on several occasions to be sure. His adult life didn't always reflect those beliefs.

"Pastor Mike, I'm just not ready to let Billy go. He has so much to offer but he needs to get back in fellowship with God. If only I was sure he would go to Heaven …"

Mike had spoken several times with Billy on the phone and believed he still embraced his Christian convictions. I remembered back to when Billy was actively involved with Christian activities as a youth. He was also right at home in the little church they attended in Florida when they first moved there. He knew truth even when it seemed he had turned aside from it. I had turned away and God hadn't given up on me! God is faithful and persistent.

"Lord, my hope is you will heal Billy and allow him to return to us. However, if it's time for him to leave, then give us the strength to accept whatever comes."

As I copied those words from my journal I noticed I asked God for strength. Now I would ask for grace.

We called the Carlstroms and told them about Billy, as well as our concerns about taking care of Weezie. They graciously offered to have her stay with them.

Matt met us in Florida. When we arrived, we found Barry and

Tilly Flitcroft, of Equip International, had paid for rooms for us for as long as we needed them. Matt and Bill started working on the hallway in Billy's trailer, as well as doing other repairs. I stayed with Billy in ICU all day. Bill came when he could. Matthew stayed with him at night.

When I was with him I prayed, talked to him, and sang to him. When I wasn't doing that, I read. I asked Matthew to sing Pass It On with me. That song had special meaning to me. I loved hearing Billy sing the harmony. He had a fine voice but no longer sang.

When he was moved from ICU to a regular room we knew he wasn't going to be needing a ramp at home. Spending time with him helped me to accept his death. I was constantly aware of his breathing, even when I was reading. It slowed, then stopped. I knew when he was gone.

I went out in the hall and called for a nurse. A sweet Latino gal came and checked him. We clung to each other, cried together, and prayed together. Not yet knowing what happened, Bill and Matt were on their way to pick me up for dinner. Did we eat? I don't remember. Matt went back to the house and continued to work. Bill and I waited for Kathy and Becky.

When they arrived, we thought they needed time alone with Billy so we waited in the hall. I've wondered since if we should have gone in with them. Every situation is different and you don't get to have a dress rehearsal.

Billy was to be cremated so we planned a memorial service in the hospital chapel when the rest of the family arrived. Karen and my brother flew down. Kent stayed home with the girls. Jenni took their girls to her parents' and flew down. Airport security was heightened due to 9/11 and everyone was patted down and searched. Loui and Bill Thompson drove from Tennessee.

Even at a funeral, families can enjoy being together. Our time in the motel was good. We talked about serious things but also reminisced. Billy would have appreciated it. He would also have liked our going to his favorite Chinese restaurant, where he first introduced me to sushi.

On Christmas Eve afternoon, Bill again spoke at the memorial service of a close family member. Several people shared how Billy had been a help to them. He had a big heart and was quick to help anyone in need.

One of Billy's friends shared something he told her. *"My dad would probably be surprised at just how much I believe the way he does."* This was a comfort for me and I thanked her for sharing his words.

After the service, Matt and Jenni left for home to pick up their girls on Christmas day. They celebrated Christmas on the 26th. My brother and Karen arrived home late Christmas Eve. Karen's girls were relieved to have Mommy home and had separation issues for a while. Mickey and Bill left for Tennessee. Then it was just us.

We invited Kathy and Becky to join us for dinner on Christmas Day. We had trouble finding a restaurant that was open. Matt and Jenni said open gasoline stations were few and far between on their way home.

A wise man once said:

"There is an appointed time for everything.
And there is a time for every event under heaven—
A time to give birth and a time to die ..."
(Ecclesiastes 3:1-2)

CANCER

When we joined the ministry of BCM in 1995, we sought a family doctor to have the required physicals—our first in years. We both felt comfortable with Dr. M.

Bill later commented, "We were just fine until we saw a doctor!"

Hindsight indicates we would have found Bill had high blood pressure as well as high cholesterol and triglycerides sooner if we'd seen a doctor. I wasn't totally off the hook because my cholesterol and triglycerides also needed to be lower. Ignorance may be bliss but there is a reckoning.

We went to doctor appointments together except when we had internal exams. In doing that we both knew what was going on. What one might miss, the other heard, and we kept each other accountable; at least we tried.

Even with regular physicals the subject of a colonoscopy never came up. Bill preferred to ignore his rectal bleeding, though in the mid-80s he did mention it to a doctor in Towanda. With no examination, he was assured it was bleeding hemorrhoids. Bill grabbed hold of that bit of information and embraced it.

The same doctor treated my ingrown toenail. Without

numbing the area, he ripped along the outer edge of the nail as he asked, "How high is your threshold of pain?"

"Not quite that high!" I gasped.

During a regular checkup, I mentioned to Dr. M that Bill had bleeding hemorrhoids. He hadn't found them, nor had the urologist Bill was seeing for an enlarged prostate. Dr. M sent Bill to see a gastroenterologist, Dr. G, who scheduled a colonoscopy. When Bill was fully awake following the procedure, Dr. G talked with us.

"I can't say for sure until we get all the results, but right now I'm nearly 100% certain you have colon cancer."

I was concerned about his bleeding but this was a shock! He explained the situation and suggested a surgeon, Dr. B.

I commented, "I'm glad I mentioned Bill's problem to Dr. M."

Dr. G looked me in the eye and said, "Have you ever had a colonoscopy?"

Oops! "No, I haven't."

"Then you need to schedule one."

I did and proceeded to ask friends, family, and strangers at the pharmacy counter if they'd had a colonoscopy. They are important.

Dr. B and Bill got along well, though I was overwhelmed by him at first. He was just the right blend of expertise and friendliness. After his examination, and more tests, Bill was scheduled for surgery at Holston Valley Medical Center in Kingsport. Dr. B assured Bill he would do everything possible to avoid his having a colostomy bag.

The Carlstroms came from North Carolina and we met for dinner the night before Bill's surgery. We all stayed in a nearby motel. It was a pleasant evening and a somewhat restful night.

Bill was admitted and prepped early in the morning. We stayed with him until they wheeled him out for surgery.

Bill asked, "Do any of you have a Bible?"

"What scripture do you want?" Paul questioned.

"Isaiah 26:3." Marcia quoted it from memory, "Thou will keep him in perfect peace, whose mind is stayed on Thee."

Paul led us all in prayer before we left for breakfast. Back in the waiting room, we prayed, read, and talked. Sooner than expected, Dr. B arrived, noticeably shaken. He said when he opened Bill up, he found an abdominal aortic aneurysm the size of a grapefruit. It was the largest one he'd seen that hadn't already burst. Marcia knew immediately what he meant. I had little understanding of the danger but soon learned!

Though now a general surgeon, Dr. B had been a cardiovascular surgeon. He immediately stopped the surgery. If the aneurysm had burst Bill would have been dead in moments. The day before surgery, Bill wanted to get heavy work done so he pushed 4x8 sheets of ¾ inch plywood up a ladder using his abdomen to assist in pushing.

Dr. B said there was a cardiovascular team in the adjacent surgical bay and they were taking over as soon as their current surgery was finished. The colon cancer had to wait—the aneurysm was a greater threat. The cardiac surgeon neutralized the danger by inserting a stent and reconnecting the aorta.

We were comforted to hear the cancer still seemed to be contained in the colon. It was a blessing to have Marcia with me to better understand what we were told. God knew I needed her, and He knew Bill needed that cardiovascular team.

I went in to see Bill in recovery as soon as he awakened. He had been anesthetized for the first surgery, kept under while waiting for the second surgery, and then for the duration of the second one. It took a while for him to stay awake in recovery. He was then taken to the Coronary Care Unit.

The recovery from surgery was difficult, not just physically but emotionally. Dr. B said depression was common following any surgery involving the heart. Bill told him about his depression years before and they determined he could fight it without drugs.

I've read that this type of depression is like post-traumatic stress disorder. This surgery and recovery was the most difficult of all; including his cholecystectomy (gall bladder), and the later colectomy (colon), and liver resection.

You may have heard the quote "God works in mysterious ways." Though it's not Scripture it is true. Here's a quote that is in the Word and it suits the situation well:

"Oh, the depth of the riches and wisdom and knowledge of God!
How unsearchable are his judgments
and how inscrutable his ways!"
(Romans 11:33)

I often tell people that cancer saved Bill's life. We had no idea he had a time bomb in his abdomen. God's activity throughout our lives continues to amaze me.

Bill began seeing his oncologist late in 2001. Dr. M oversaw our cancer journey for over six years and became a dear friend. He sought wisdom from God each step of the way and prayed with us after each visit.

Because of the cancer we retired from BCM. That brought another blessing, Ken and Faith Grubb. They stopped by to introduce themselves and left us confident that Ken would do well pastoring the SE USA missionaries. Ken was faithful keeping in touch with Bill, and when Bill left us he checked on me. I especially enjoyed their annual visits when I lived in their district.

On Valentine's Day 2002 Bill had surgery to remove the cancer. The cancer had metastasized to his liver and was now stage four. When the physician's assistant at the cancer center explained that the cancer was in Bill's liver she said, "Colon cancer loves the liver!" We were told the average life expectancy for someone with stage four colon cancer is about five years. He had both chemo and radiation. Chemo was the worse of the two. Drugs that kill cancer cells also harm healthy cells. He was nauseous, lost his hair, lost weight, was fatigued and discouraged, but never gave up.

Dr. M was baldheaded. He and Bill joked about being bald. Bill told him, "I'd rather be bald than nauseous!"

The first time we were told there was no sign of cancer I shouted, "Yahoo!" as we drove home from the Cancer Center. I never did it again. Living with cancer makes even an optimist wary. Not detecting the presence of cancer doesn't mean it's not there. Five years with no sign of it is good and may mean it won't return, but there is no guarantee.

Though his quality of life wasn't always what we would have liked, there were many good times. He preached occasionally and even did a few presentations of Paul Speaks. He was always working on his next sermon. He loved teaching the Word. We visited family, and they visited us.

Hoping to remove the cancer from his liver, Bill had a resection in April of 2004. We planted a rosebush under our bedroom window commemorating our 50th Wedding anniversary and hoped we could attend the repeating of our vows in May.

Bill recovered from the procedure well and we traveled to Hardingville Bible Church where we had been married. He even did much of the driving. Family and friends came from near and far, including our nephew Steven Remy from France. We didn't have to limit numbers this time.

Several of the original bridal party were there: Barbara Cox Remy, Bill Rainey, Bob Ormsby and Ray Pental. This time our grand-girls meandered down the aisle with us, handing daisies to the congregation. Our oldest grand-girl, Rebecca, carried the youngest, Emily. Lydia stayed close to her Poppop, or did her Poppop stay close to her? Hannah, Morgan and Megan charmed the crowd. I walked with Kensey who was overly enthusiastic with the daisies. The procession was a lot more fun than the first one.

Pastor Bill Adams, who married us in 1954, presided and challenged us. The Coxes sang several numbers. I read my vows and Bill improvised his. The recessional was lively and Bill did a little jig as we started to the back of the church.

Bill and Janice hosted a lovely reception with a wedding cake decorated with daisies *and* red roses. We were gifted two weeks at a beach house. One week just for us. We could see the beach and ocean from the back of the house and listen to the waves at night. Bill never liked the sandy beach but loved the ocean. He also liked watching the traffic on the waterway and bridge from the front porch.

The second week with our kids and their families didn't work out quite the way we expected. We hoped they could all be there at the same time to have fun together. Schedules didn't allow that.

On the journey, we were thankful for the positives and trusted in God's grace for the negatives.

WEEZIE FLIES AWAY

In August 2004, the nursing home called to tell me Weezie was in the ER. This had occurred several times and she was fine when I arrived. Not so this time. I spent our last hours together holding her hand, sharing memories, singing to her, and praying aloud.

Many of the songs I sang were ones she sang to me when I was a little girl. One was this lullaby:

All aboard for blanket bay,
won't get back 'til the break of day
Roll her all up in her little white sheet,
'til you can't see her little pink feet
All aboard little sleepyhead
snuggle up tight in your trundle bed
Bless Mommy and Daddy and sail away
All aboard for Blanket Bay

The ER doctor asked, "Are you sure you don't want us to try to resuscitate her?"

Why did he ask? She made the decision years before and we had agreed. His question made me wonder if I was doing the right thing. Now was not the time to change our plan. Weezie was ready to go to her heavenly home where she would no longer be trapped in a deteriorating mind and body. God would make the call.

The ER was quiet. The nurses checked in occasionally. I kept my Bill and my brother Bill aware of what was happening. Her breathing began to slow, stopped, another breath, another—then no more.

I called the nurse, my brother, and Bill. Weezie wasn't with us anymore. She was in Heaven with my dad and her Savior.

I cried, but not for long. There was no reason to cry. She was again the vibrant woman I remembered from my childhood. If there is a chandelier in Heaven, she could kick it! Her spirit had left us. Just her body, her shell, remained.

I had plenty of time to follow through with the preplanned final arrangements but I wasn't thinking. I didn't comply with the instructions from the funeral director in New Jersey. We knew the folks in Clintwood and they did what I asked them to do. Weezie's body was soon on its way to New Jersey. We packed the van and were also on our way to New Jersey.

"I wonder if we'll see the funeral home vehicle on I-81?" I asked Bill. "We could have saved money by taking her ourselves!"

We exchanged dubious smiles.

"I think she would have liked that. She enjoyed road trips."

Bill looked over at me, "Can you imagine what would happen if the police stopped us like they did on our way to Maine? What would you tell them when they ask what we have in the back of the van?"

"A merry heart does good, like medicine,
but a broken spirit dries the bones."
(Proverbs 17:22)

Family and friends attended her memorial service. Some told how she had impacted their lives. Those were comforting words.

At the graveside, I asked those who knew All Aboard for Blanket Bay to join me as a final farewell. I'd heard it sung to me, sang it to my kids, then to Billy and Weezie during their last hours but my mind went blank! Matt and Karen began and I joined in.

Another funeral, another mini-reunion. Wouldn't it be great if we didn't wait for funerals to get together?

One final word. In case anyone would have reason to see her remains in the future, we put a note in her coffin:

"This is the body that housed our mother's soul/spirit. We know that she has gone on to Heaven and no longer dwells in it. However, we don't know if someday someone may view these remains so we have placed some meaningful objects within this coffin to let you know who she was and direct you to the only true God. In Jesus' love, the family of Gertrude Louise Reichner Rainey."

We put a faux wedding ring on her finger and tucked away the real one.

CANCER—QUITE A RIDE

We continued dealing with good days, not so good days, and just plain day to day living. In 2005 Bill said, "I have cancer, but cancer doesn't have me."

I usually wrote our prayer letters with input from Bill but he wrote this one and included an epitaph from a tombstone in London, England:

"Beneath these clouds and beneath these trees,
Lies the body of Solomon Peas;
This is not Peas, it is only his pod;
Peas has shelled out and gone Home to God.
(authored by S. Peas)
"No, I'm not writing my epitaph and, Lord

willing, I won't need one for a while. However, each day I get older making me closer to the end of my time here on earth. That is so whether or not I have cancer.

"Peas' epitaph makes me sort of wish my family name was Peas! More importantly, I am reminded that this body I inhabit here on earth is just a temporary residence for the real "me." Since I know Jesus as my Savior, the real "me" will go Home to Heaven when I'm finished with it. What if I didn't have that assurance? I'd sure check out my options.

"Since today is my 76th birthday, it's been a time for reflecting—am I really this old? I've been through a lot over the years, some good and some not so good, but God has been right there with me. Through it all He has blessed me with the most important things in life: faith in Him, a loving family, and the fellowship of good friends.

"By the way, there are only 2 options – Heaven or Hell

It's easy to go to Hell – just don't do anything.

It's also easy to go to Heaven, certainly a better option!

Recognize that you're a sinner, just like me (Romans 3:3, Romans 6:23)

Know that Jesus died for all our sins, yours and mine (Romans 5:8)

Repent and ask Him to forgive your sins, I did (John 1:12)

Remember, He does it all—we just accept the gift of salvation. (Eph. 2:8-9)"

In March I wrote in my journal that we had been talking a lot about Heaven. It all started with Billy's leaving, my mother struggling with dementia before she left us, and Bill's ongoing battle with cancer. Though certainly wonderful beyond anything we can imagine, Heaven is an unknown. Life here is known, even with its problems. Heaven increasingly looks better.

When Bill went to church it wore him out but he was glad to

be there and I loved having him beside me. He still taught on occasion and that blessed him. In May the lesions on Bill's liver reduced in size and there was no active cancer showing in his body. He was in remission through summer and fall.

Even though cancer was often the focus of our lives, there were happy times. Our daughter-in-love Jenni wrote and published her book *What Can I Give Him*, a memoir of how they changed the focus of Christmas in their home from gift-getting to giving to the One whose birthday we should be celebrating.

We also made a big decision. We should move to an area closer to family. Bill wanted to be sure I would be cared for when God called him Home. We loved our home in Skeetrock and were heavily invested in it, but Bill knew I couldn't keep up the property alone.

Though we discussed moving before, now it was time to act. We considered moving to Pennsylvania but housing in the southeast was beyond our means and the snowy northwest didn't seem practical.

Paul and Marcia knew what we were considering and showed us several areas on their property where we could put a double-wide. We accepted their offer and began looking for used homes.

We began to downsize in earnest. This was difficult for both of us but more so for Bill. We were savers with a depression mentality. The term "waste not, want not" was repeated often in our growing up years and we kept things to be recycled or saved for a rainy day.

In the fall Bill officiated at a 50th wedding anniversary celebration, led congregational singing in Clintwood Church, and taught and preached on occasion. We celebrated our family Thanksgiving/Christmas at our home and loved having our chicks under our roof. Paul called to tell us the well for our new home was ready and capped off. Pastor Paul Adelgren and folks from Equip helped him with it.

In November a scan showed tumors in Bill's liver and lungs. We met with a doctor at Duke and he said surgery was not an option. When people asked Bill about the return of cancer he said, "I'm disappointed but I'm not discouraged."

In BCM candidate school we memorized II Corinthians 4. Verses 7 and 8 became increasingly meaningful.

"...we have this treasure in earthen vessels, that the excellence of the power may be of God and not of us. We are hard-pressed on every side, yet not crushed; we are perplexed, but not in despair..."

We always hoped for a longer or permanent remission. Would we have liked God to send a miracle and erase cancer forever? Of course! Could He have done that? Absolutely! Did we lose faith because He didn't? No!

God is God and knows what's best in every circumstance. Only He knows the big picture and we can count on Him.

2006

Bill often used his Navy experiences as illustrations when he taught. Many said he should write them down. I suggested he tell his stories into a cassette recorder. This seemed like a good time to do it but he couldn't concentrate.

During one series of treatments in 2006 he had abdominal cramps, nausea and vomiting. He didn't want to sip water or suck on crushed ice and became severely dehydrated. This led to his spending six hours on IV fluids one day and four hours the next at the Cancer Center until he was rehydrated.

We got to know most of the personnel at the Cancer Center quite well. At least two nurses started going to church after talking with Bill. We also got to know other patients. One man talked with Bill in the treatment room and the waiting room. His wife said she was pleased because her husband didn't even talk with her about his cancer. We were blessed to be a part of their lives.

Bill enjoyed watching football on television. I enjoyed watching it with him and he didn't mind explaining the game to me. You'd think after all those years I would have figured out more, but he was patient. He taped the 2006 Super Bowl without watching it so he could share it with Matt when he visited. Though he knew the outcome, he looked forward to their enjoying the game together.

We visited the Carlstroms and attended church with them just before the Super Bowl. Pastor Paul's message was timely for the game, and for us. He asked us to visualize a football field, with goals at both ends. What's in the middle? Yardage, just yardage. What happens in the yardage only has significance when the ball crosses the plane of the goal line. Sometimes you lose yards; sometimes you gain yards. You don't make a touchdown on every play.

Pastor Paul compared the football field to life. Our goal is Heaven and life's circumstances are yardage. There are ups and downs; gains and losses. We can let circumstances hinder us or we can keep running the ball toward the goal line.

With Jesus as our Savior, circumstances and yardages don't determine the outcome. Our goal is assured. He's waiting to welcome us Home. This message comforted both of us—we were headed toward the goal. Bill had the ball and was running with it.

As often as possible we went to church together, sometimes I went alone. Occasionally we needed to stay away from people when Bill's immune system was weakened, so we attended *bedside Baptist* together.

We again experienced remission in the spring. Bill worked on repairing and maintaining equipment, mowing lawns, sorting and reorganizing in preparation for moving. Our home was not on the market yet but we were pressing toward the goal. We figured we would be in our home for another year.

"Those who wait on the Lord shall renew their strength;
they shall mount up with wings like eagles,
they shall run and not be weary,
they shall walk and not faint."
(Isaiah 40:31)

During the summer there were no signs of active cancer. Bill's hair grew back thicker and curly! He wanted to exercise but neuropathy made walking difficult so he tried swimming. We went to Breaks Interstate Park to swim and he did short laps, resting in between. Bob Phipps invited us to use their pool, until the weather turned cool.

In the fall the cancer was back in Bill's liver and lungs. They also saw what appeared to be an aortic aneurysm measuring 5.1 cm so we met with Dr. K, the surgeon who had repaired his aneurysm.

He told us, "There's a bit of a flap, broken free from the previous surgery, but there is also a small aneurysm near the original one. I can't see the stent but I know it's still in place. We'll keep an eye on the aneurysm and see you in a year."

"How do you know the stent is still in place if you can't see it?"

"You're not dead!"

We spent New Year's Eve alone and were in bed before the ball dropped in Times Square. We looked back on a roller coaster ride with cancer but it was a good year. We saw old friends when we visited Hardingville Bible Church and both churches Bill pastored in Pennsylvania. Karen was teaching three-year-old children in preschool and Matt was managing the horse herd at Miracle Mountain Ranch.

"Hope is the thing with feathers that perches in the soul,
and sings the tunes without the words and never stops—at all."
(Emily Dickenson)

We had hope, not assured, for the immediate future. We had hope assured for our eternal future.

"Being confident of this very thing,
that He which hath begun a good work in you
will perform it until the day of Jesus Christ."
(Philippians 1:6)

2007

T. S. Eliot said, "Humankind cannot bear very much reality." He was partially right. Without God we can't bear much reality. A man named Matthew wrote about that:

"Therefore do not be anxious for tomorrow,
for tomorrow will care for itself.
Each day has enough trouble of its own."
(Matthew 6:34)

Sometimes Bill's problems came in bunches: protein in his urine, swollen ankles, diarrhea, nausea, fatigue, hair loss. But by early summer 2007 everything was looking better. Throughout our cancer journey we were surrounded by prayers of family and friends. We even had a church in the Philippines praying for us. When Bill was asked how he was doing he said, "If I was doing any better I couldn't stand it."

By summer he was in remission but there were still those persistent tumors in his liver and lungs. Dr. Miller gave Bill a two-month respite from chemo to allow his body to recover. Karen and Jenni and our six grand-girls spent a week with us helping with projects. We also had a fun time at a friend's pool.

Bill's vacation from chemo went by too quickly. The first month he was recovering; the second month it was hot and humid. However, we were delighted with how our home was shaping up.

"The Lord has done great things for us; we are glad."
(Psalm 126:3)

We attended Nettie Baker's funeral in Kentucky. She was our daughter-in-love Kathy's mother. Nettie accepted Christ as her Savior in the last months of her life and we prayed her testimony would have a positive effect on unsaved loved ones.

In October the tumors in Bill's liver and lungs increased by 20%. The good news? No new tumors and the aneurysm was stable.

The last book Bill studied and spoke from was Habakkuk. I wondered why he was so interested in that book. Charles Swindoll in his comments may shed some light:

"The book of Habakkuk offers us a picture of a prideful people being humbled, while the righteous live by faith in God. It reminds us that while God may seem silent and uninvolved in our world, He always has a plan to deal with evil and always works out justice . . . eventually. The example of the prophet Habakkuk encourages believers to wait on the Lord, expecting that He will indeed work out all things for our good."r

Bill brought his first message on Habakkuk at Clintwood Bible Church. He had two more messages on the book that he planned to use later.

"For the earth will be filled with the knowledge of the glory of the Lord, as waters cover the sea."
(Habakkuk 2:14)

Exciting News

Matt and Jenni were expecting our eighth grandchild. Boy or girl? Big sisters wanted a little brother. We were happy with either but quietly hoped for a boy. It would be nice to have our branch of the family tree continue.

Matt and family were with us for a week. Jenni helped Bill

downsize and organize his shop, not an easy task. We had our final yard sale and gave away a lot of stuff.

When Bill was first diagnosed with colon cancer we were told there was a five-year average for survival. We had reached that point and were living beyond the average. He had no active cancer in his liver and the lesions on his lungs had diminished significantly. We knew better than to get too excited.

"Happiness does not come in boulders generally, but in pebbles, so I think we all ought to be thankful when we receive such a pebble; and how much more delightful to give one!"
(Gail Hamilton, author)

2008

Again we slept through the changing of the year and 2008 arrived on the scene with little fanfare. We were living moment by moment and not making plans too far into the future. It wouldn't be easy to leave Skeetrock but we were sure it was what we should do. This was our family home to our grandchildren, the only one they knew. Some still long a bit for that home.

IT'S A BOY!

A sonogram showed that grandchild #8 was a boy and his name was to be Jonathan William. Matt and their four girls were in the room when the sonogram was done so they could discover the gender together. Emily was disappointed that the sonogram didn't look like a baby and wasn't even in color!

WHEN ARE WE MOVING?

By now we were on our second realtor. The first one was a personable young man and we liked him but saw no action. When contract time was up we tried another. We had a couple of nibbles but it was too far from town. Our new realtor contacted an assessor due to the unconventional nature of our home. That's us—unconventional.

"We have a God who delights in impossibilities."
(Andrew Murray)

Although Bill was weak he used the riding mower in April. He brought the morning message on Palm Sunday at Clintwood Bible. He also filled in for the pastor at Skeetrock Bible on Easter Sunday but was unable to complete the message due to an episode of weakness and disorientation. It didn't last long but was scary.

Bill's sister Barbara, and our niece Shelley, spent a few days with us. Barbara's son Mark brought her down for a visit earlier in Bill's cancer journey.

Even on a journey such as ours, life continued around us. I helped with backdrops for VBS, planted outside flower beds, and we planned to attend the Relay for Life Walk where they light luminaries in honor or memory of cancer patients. Our cancer nurses served breakfast and patient families helped by contributing food. We contributed food but couldn't join the walk.

On May 27th Jonathan William arrived, the first boy of this generation in both families. He brought joy to all our lives.

More good news and bad news. The tumors in Bill's lungs appeared to be dying from the inside out and were not large. However, the persistent tumor in his liver increased by 25%. He also developed gout.

Finally, someone came to look at our home. When it was shown by the realtor we had to leave the premises. We arrived back home while the realtor and prospects were still there and parked at the end of the driveway. I thought they liked it because the wife waved enthusiastically as they drove away.

Sure enough, they made an offer. It was less than but close to our bottom line. We called Paul to see what he thought. Both Bill and Paul believed we should stay with our bottom line but I was the one who had to call the realtor. I was fearful it wouldn't sell and accepted the offer. I should have listened to wise counsel instead of giving in to my fear, which certainly wasn't from God. We could even have countered their offer and met half way but ...

Since the buyers' home was already sold, we needed to find a home quickly. Settlement was scheduled for July 8.

"The effective, fervent prayer of a righteous man avails much."
(James 5:16)

We focused on collecting boxes and packing. When Paul said they had some good leads on double-wide homes, we loaded the boxes that were ready in our van, along with some potted tomato and pepper plants, and filled the back of our van.

Paul cleared part of his shop for our stuff. We loaded the

shelves and then concentrated on finding a home. We looked at a couple of repos but people had deliberately trashed them before moving out. They were so badly damaged, Paul felt it was too costly to make them livable.

We looked at several new double-wide homes but they were out of our price range so we decided on a single-wide. Paul wasn't sure a single-wide would fit on our plot but said he could work it out. He also offered to add on a room to give us more space.

On our way back to Virginia, we talked about our options. When we arrived home we called Paul, "Maybe we should reconsider the repo. Neither of us feel comfortable with a single-wide."

He replied, "Let me think about it. I'll call you back."

When he called back he said, "Marcia and I want to help you get the new double-wide. We're certain it will better meet your needs. We've gone over the figures and will give you the difference between the cost and what you can pay. You can repay us when you're able."

We were overwhelmed by their generosity. God once again provided through the kindness of His people.

Now we were packing in earnest and disposing of stuff with gusto. The folks buying our property said they would be glad to have any shop leftovers. They ended up with a huge assortment of hardware, metal and wood.

They also asked us to leave our porch furniture. Though we liked the furniture we had nowhere to put it. A wooden love seat glider and chair glider were especially difficult to part with since they were built and given to us by James Taylor. We also left our washer and dryer because we thought the double-wide included them. We should have checked. It didn't.

We scheduled inspections and appraisals, finalized closing, and packed boxes. We changed addresses, closed out or moved accounts, ordered a truck and two trailers, and coordinated the arrival of family to help. We dug up our 50th Anniversary rosebush and put it in an antique coal scuttle, where it stayed until spring 2009.

Matt and Jenni came with their kids, including Jonathan William who we met for the first time. Kent and Karen came with their girls. Bill and Janice were there, and Kathy and Becky stopped by.

We attended Clintwood Bible Church on Sunday and Bill preached the morning message. The Cox-Rice-Rainey chorus sang for special music with Janice accompanying. It was a nostalgic time.

As we drove our caravan of vehicles out of Skeetrock we waved to the new owners on their way to their new home.

When we arrived at our new homesite, we realized God had been doing some remarkable things. Paul and Marcia had a surprise for us. Our double-wide was sitting in place. It wasn't completely hooked up but we could put our furniture inside—no need to store it.

Carlstroms had rooms ready for all of us and we spent time getting to know Jonathan and enjoying our kids and grandkids.

NORTH CAROLINA
UNRAVELING THE STICHES

We stayed with Paul and Marcia until our home was ready for occupancy. As soon as it was stable enough for me to go inside, I unpacked boxes and tried to stay out of Paul's way. He did all the connections, saving us a lot of money. He also arranged for whatever he couldn't do. We could not have done it without him.

Bill attempted putting shelves in a kitchen closet but had difficulty figuring out what to do. It was then I realized how much he had declined. I'm sure he did also. He finished the shelves but Paul took on the rest of the projects. Paul asked him what he wanted to do or how he wanted it done, showing loving sensitivity to Bill's situation.

As soon as the air conditioning was working we moved into our home. We *olderly*, as Kensey used to call us, missed the cool mountain nights.

Dr. M didn't personally know an oncologist in our new area BUT he suggested an oncologist in Asheville. He didn't have Dr. M's bedside manner and I found him abrupt. He ordered a K-raz test to see if additional chemo was feasible.

Rather than deal with city traffic we decided to see an oncologist who had office hours in Marion, just twenty minutes from home. Bill felt comfortable with him. The cancer had multiplied and grown in both liver and lungs since the last chemo. We knew chemo wouldn't eliminate the cancer but might prolong Bill's life by a few months.

Though Dr. M was no longer Bill's oncologist he was willing to give us his opinion. He even called us on his car phone one evening while he was driving home from the Cancer Center. He had his radiologist's report on the most recent tests. He knew Bill for six years and believed Bill wasn't ready to throw in the towel, but he agreed the K-raz test would show what could be done.

In September, we received the results from the K-raz test. Bill was not a candidate for the last chemo drug available for his type of cancer. Up until then there was always something that could be done. Now …

We tried some herbal supplements that might enhance Bill's quality of life. A doctor with Equip used artemesia tea and her tumors shrank. However, she used it right away and not after six and a half years of chemo. Graviola and pawpaw show promise in some cases. Pawpaw was used in studies at Purdue. Both oncologists said to go ahead and try them, they couldn't hurt him. We were at least doing something.

When cancer first arrived in our lives there were folks who suggested radical changes in diet that might be helpful. It's easy to find conflicting information on how and why this may happen. I believe the way we eat today is vastly different than it was years ago, and it's not better for us. A change in diet might have made a difference but when I suggested it to Bill he said he wasn't interested. He was mostly an amiable man but when you started to mess with his food you were going too far.

We were now on the final leg of our journey. In retrospect, I know I didn't fully comprehend what that meant. However, we continually chose to trust God and focus on the positives, not wasting precious time in despair. We had peace knowing God was in control.

"I will put my trust in Him."
(Hebrews 2:13)

LIFE CONTINUES

So, we went home, pulled the curtains, and waited for the end. No, we did not! Paul and Marcia asked if we'd like to go to the beach with them in October. They had a time-share and there was room for us. We said, yes! We were right off the beach and Bill enjoyed sitting in a gazebo overlooking the ocean.

We visited the Wright Brothers Museum and lighthouses. Bill walked everywhere we went. We went on a dolphin watch and saw lots of dolphins, quaint harbors and boats.

In October, Bill brought a message from Habbakuk in our new

church home. He also taught Sunday School dressed as Tertius.

Paul gathered materials for our back deck and planned to build it Thanksgiving week when Matt and Kent were there to help.

The second week in November Bill was fair and looked forward to our kids visiting. He dozed a lot.

Our niece, Suzie, wrote, "I will continue to pray that however this progresses it is allowed to be a gentle journey." Bill's comment, "Beautiful!" Her sister Shelley sent emails giving helpful tips on hospice care from her nursing experience.

By the third week he was weaker but the arrival of kids and grandkids cheered him. Our home was dedicated to the Lord on Thanksgiving Eve with Pastor Paul Adelgren officiating. We had a houseful of family and friends.

"As for me and my house, we will serve the Lord."
(Joshua 24:15)

Thanksgiving Day found us cooking, building, baking, and eating! We had all of Bill's favorites. We cooked a large turkey breast and Carlstroms brought a deep-fried turkey. Marcia wanted to leave some turkey but I told her we had plenty. After they went home I realized we didn't have *any* turkey. I will never live that down with my family. We also had a surprise visitor, Eva Blair, a good friend from Virginia.

Bill was hospitalized December 1, Matt's birthday, with a blood clot in his lung. Matt planned to leave that weekend but remained until Bill came home. His hospital care was disappointing. He couldn't breathe lying down so he stayed in a chair which was not like the Geri chair at Holston Valley Hospital and he developed a bedsore.

When Bill was released, Matt brought us home. He asked if they should stay but we told him we'd be fine. Not a wise decision. Though hospital care was poor, our Home Healthcare nurses were great. Kristi, our RN, secured a foam pad that helped to relieve pressure on the bedsore and it began to heal.

Ralph and Linda Magill visited on their way home from vacation. Bill and Ralph had a special relationship and their visit was meaningful to both of us.

Bill recuperated slowly from his hospital stay. On Monday, December 8th his pajama leg was wet. We thought we'd spilled water but found his leg was weeping. We tried elevating his legs but that didn't help. He also developed a yeast infection.

Eating and drinking were increasingly difficult. I crushed his medication and put it in applesauce. He drank a little by sipping through a straw. His nurse and physical therapist came on Thursday morning and he asked that the aide not come in the afternoon to bathe him. He was worn out and ached all over. Kristi said his swollen abdomen was normal with a malfunctioning liver.

We received notes of encouragement. Janice wrote to reassure me. She cared for her father at home during his last days and knew I was probably second guessing my caregiving skills.

Kent sent an email, "If I find myself in the same boat (as Bill is now) I'm going to want to have a Louise taking care of me, too!" He included a verse:

"You will not have to fight this battle. Take up your positions;
stand firm and see the deliverance the LORD will give you, O Judah
and Jerusalem. Do not be afraid; do not be discouraged.
Go out to face them tomorrow, and the LORD will be with you."
(II Chronicles 20:17)

Bill asked Kristi to give him some idea of how much time he had left. She said she usually didn't share that with patients but would make an exception due to our faith. Bill told her he hoped to make it to Christmas, or even better his 80th birthday. She said he might be here for Christmas but probably not his birthday. He seemed to process that. I don't think I did.

I tried to get Bill out on the back deck as often as possible. He enjoyed looking out over the fields and woods.

On Sunday, the fourteenth, Clintwood Bible Church had a special time of prayer for us during their morning service. On Monday, there was mottling on his legs. By Tuesday we were under hospice care. We went with the facility recommended by Home Healthcare and the oncologist. They had a visiting doctor, our hospice in Marion didn't have one. I could have used closer help.

The doctor ordered morphine drops, which I administered. Bill seemed agitated so I called the hospice nurse and she told me to cut back on the dosage. Since then I've read that when first started opiate medicines can suppress breathing in people who haven't used them before. Now I believe this was why he was agitated. He had a long-time fear of smothering.

He wasn't eating or drinking much but felt the urge to use the toilet. We had pillows to raise his legs and blankets to keep him warm so it was complicated getting him from the chair to the commode even though it was next to his chair. Late Wednesday night he fell to the floor with his leg turned under him and I couldn't get him up. I called Paul and Marcia and they lifted him back into his chair.

I talked with the hospice nurse who suggested he be taken to the hospice house to be evaluated and then come home. Did she believe that? I know he didn't want to leave the house and I didn't want him to have to leave.

The next morning, hospice sent an ambulance to pick him up. I had mixed feelings about his going. Maybe they could stabilize him so he was more comfortable.

Our nephew, Mark, and his girlfriend were to arrive that evening. They were both EMTs. They planned to be with us for a few days and could have helped but that just didn't click with me.

Bill was in good spirits when the ambulance crew arrived. He joked with them and I told him not to flirt with the pretty girls. Paul and I followed the ambulance. We arrived about 11 am on Thursday, December 18. The hospice house was a lovely new facility. We had a suite with a pull-out couch, a kitchenette, private bathroom, and an outside patio area. Bill was settled in a recliner, I sat next to him in a straight chair.

In the afternoon, a technician arrived with a CPAP machine. He told me it would help Bill breath. He seemed to be doing fine with the nasal cannula but maybe this would be better. I watched while he fitted the mask over his face. Bill was immediately distressed. The technician kept explaining how it should be done to a young nurse with him. Bill's eyes showed his fear of smothering. I finally asked the technician to forget the mask. He did so reluctantly.

We sat with my arm around him, his head resting against me. By then it was late afternoon and the room darkened. I couldn't reach a light. I felt alone and afraid. Could I have reached a call button?

341

Suddenly Bill's eyes opened wider and he focused on the ceiling. Was this what happened in the hospital room years before? His expression was like it was in the ambulance when he had trouble breathing, but I didn't think of that at the time. He could also have experienced internal trauma, perhaps with his liver.

Paul and Marcia came as soon as she got home from work. Bill interacted some with them. They offered to stay but a heavy fog was closing in and I knew Marcia had to leave for work early in the morning. Mark and Kim arrived. Paul prayed with us and they left for home.

I must have looked tired because Kim opened the sofa bed and suggested I lie down. I didn't want to leave Bill's side but I also didn't fully realize he was dying. When Mark came over and took my place I knew he was in good hands. Kim showed me the bed she'd prepared.

As I looked toward Bill, I heard Mark say, "It's okay, Uncle Bill, we'll take care of Aunt Pat." Within moments, he was gone. He left us at 10:10 pm — just eleven hours after we arrived.

Mark and Kim put a mattress on the floor and laid Bill on it. He didn't look like the man we all knew. I'm glad that picture has faded and my memories now are of when he was still with us.

Kim sang *The Old Rugged Cross*. I cried, but there was relief that he was now without pain and he no longer had cancer. The body that lay on the mattress was simply the shell he lived in here on earth, just as he said in his prayer letter about *Solomon Peas.*

Though Bill was no longer with us, we hadn't *lost* him. We knew where he was. He was beginning his new assignment in Heaven!

"Sir, William Franklin Cox III reporting for duty, Sir!"

<O><

"Should we wait for the mortician to arrive?" I asked.

"Not necessary," Mark replied.

We thanked the nurse at the reception desk and stepped out into the parking lot; it was shrouded in fog. We walked to Mark's car and started home.

"Are you sure it's okay we just left him lying there?"

"Yes, Aunt Pat, it's okay."

"I know it's not really him—he's with the Lord."

… but that body was what I could see, what I knew … this is the fourth person I've been with when they left for Heaven … it doesn't get easier … the others were important to me but this time it was the other half of me!

Our headlights barely pierced the thick fog encasing us. Finally, I recognized the familiar lights of Marion shimmering through the mist.

"I see where we are. I know my way from here," I said confidently.

"I'll turn off the GPS," Mark replied.

We were soon past the colorful blur of the Wal-Mart plaza and on a country road. I peered through the windshield watching for landmarks. Where were we?

"We turn right at the end of the red fences, but I can't see them."

Mark chuckled, "Are you sure you know your way home?"

I laughed nervously. I had no idea where we were!

"Wait, this looks familiar but we shouldn't be here. We should have turned before this. I'm sorry, Mark, it all looks so different with the fog."

After several adjustments we were finally on the right road. I breathed a sigh of relief when we saw the mailboxes at the end of Shea Drive. Thanks to Paul's foresight, the light on our front porch was a welcome sight. I unlocked the front door and turned on the living room lights while Mark and Kim brought their bags into the house. I gave them a quick tour and showed them where they would sleep.

Kim was concerned, "Will you be able to sleep, Aunt Pat?"

"Honey, I could sleep standing in a corner."

After an exchange of good night hugs, I changed into nightwear, snuggled under the covers, and was sound asleep. I didn't even visit the loo during the night. It's likely I was dehydrated.

JOY COMES IN THE MORNING

The sun was streaming in the window when I awoke to the smell of coffee. To my delight, Kim had taken over the kitchen. Though Biblical angels are very different than humans, I believe God sometimes assigns angelic duties to humans. He did that with

Mark and Kim. Though we knew about Kim, we'd not met her before they arrived at Hospice House. It seemed she might be the one for Mark. She was a seasoned believer and a pastor's daughter. Mark was a babe in Christ. Kim was instrumental in introducing him to the Savior.

As I sipped my coffee I wondered what the day would bring. This was the beginning of a new life. Who was I? Two had become one and now I was the remaining half. Did that make me less than one? Maybe one-half? What now?

Karen and Matt were en route from Pennsylvania to North Carolina with their families. Kathy and Becky had been notified and were awaiting information. When the Rices and MMR Coxes arrived, the Carlstroms came to our rescue with extra beds. Before long we were doing what we do well, enjoying each other though we were missing an important family member. We seem to generate a lot of energy when we're together and I tend to thrive on the chaos, as Jenni so aptly calls it.

We decided on three memorial services. Did we know anyone who had three memorial services? No. It was right to have a service at CMA in Marion. We were members, they prayed for us for years and went through the final weeks with us. We'd recently moved from our long-time home in Virginia so it seemed right to have a service there. Finally, most of our family and oldest friends were in New Jersey and Bill's final resting place was to be in the Hardingville Church cemetery. His memorials were unique, like him.

Kim continued as queen of the kitchen. She was family and fit in seamlessly. She held her own in our hodge-podge of emotion, banter, and overall craziness. She could give it out and she could take it! What's not to love!

This brings me to an uncommon occurrence that brought excitement and joy. Mark and Kim were considering marriage but their relationship seemed to be at a stalemate. One evening the young ones were playing in the back room and the rest of us were scattered about the house.

"Mark, why aren't you and Kim married?" My question took him by surprise. Truly, I surprised myself. I only remember snippets of the conversation but I do know Mark said, "I don't have an engagement ring." Not considering that a good excuse, I invited him to my bedroom and shut the door. I showed him two gold rings with small diamonds that were my Nana's. I offered him his choice. When he chose the lesser one, I suggested the better one. This was a start. They could find something else later.

We went back to the living room and Mark asked Kim to join us. Jenni remembers that they wondered if they should leave but Mark told them to stay. He wanted them to hear what he had to say. He then proceeded to ask Kim to marry him. They recently celebrated their eighth wedding anniversary. God did it again!

If Bill had been there, he might have given me a look when I questioned Mark, but he'd be pleased with the outcome.

<O><

There was sadness as we went through the grieving process, not for Bill but for us. We had moments of sheer joy, even comic relief, as we shared memories of our years together. Bill would have approved.

I gave the kids anything of Bill's they might use. Karen took the sweater she used to borrow and forget to give back to him when she was in college. Kensey recently came into my sitting room to show me the sweater she was wearing from *the Poppop collection*. He would love that! I still wear his sweat pants and Kent frequently wears one of his sweaters when he's preaching.

Our principle oncologist sent me an email when he heard of Bill's Homegoing:

> *"I just heard about Bill's passing from this temporary physical realm into His eternal permanent spiritual one yesterday. He truly was a man of God, and his life was a living testimony to the reality of his Lord. I admired his courage and both of your acceptance of God's will throughout my association with him. I will miss him and count it a privilege to have gotten to know you both.*
>
> *My prayer is that you will sense the Lord's presence daily and draw strength from His love, comfort and peace.*
>
> *With Christian love, David Miller."*

Each memorial service was different. Pastor Paul Adelgren led the service at Marion CMA. Bill's military service was honored by Navy personnel. His ashes were in a flag-draped box and the flag was folded and presented while a bugler played taps. After the service, we prepared to leave the next day for Clintwood where Becky and Kathy joined us.

In Clintwood, Pastor Mike Yates led the service. He remarked that Bill was a warrior to the end. Several related how Bill had impacted their lives. Bob Phipps said that one thing he remembered about Bill was that he was "no respecter of persons." He was right! Bill didn't kowtow to folks who were rich or powerful, he accepted people on their own merits.

The Apostle Peter said it well in Acts 10:34, (KJV):
"...Of a truth I perceive that God is no respecter of persons"

Leaving Clintwood, we pressed on to New Jersey. Kathy and Becky offered to go with us but I encouraged them to go home since their trip to and from Florida was already long for them and their vehicle. The Rices drove home through the night. Since the Coxes planned to stop in a motel I went with them; I needed sleep. Eight of us piled into one motel room.

Jenni went out to the car to get diapers while we were bedding down. She was laughing when she came back into the room. "I just apologized to Dad for him having to be in such a jumbled mess in the back of the Suburban." Thank You, God, for laughter!

We were close to being late for the memorial service in Hardingville because of torrential rain and heavy traffic on the Baltimore beltway. Pastor Franklin greeted us and Matt led the service. Kim sang *The Old Rugged Cross.* Our old church home provided a delicious meal for family and friends, giving time for fellowship.

My brother prepared a place for Bill's ashes at the edge of my parents' plot and Matt buried them after the service. Several months later I delivered the headstone provided by the Veterans Administration and my brother installed it. There was only room for Bill's name and dates. When I join Bill, a metal plate might fit on the stone.

After Christmas with the Rices and a wedding and New Years at MMR, Jenni and the kids took me home. They helped me settle in but an approaching storm front hurried their departure.

Attending church for the first time wasn't as difficult as I thought it might be but communion Sundays were emotional for months. I attended a grief and grieving class with MMR discipleship students. I began to wonder if something was wrong with me. I missed Bill but wasn't grief-stricken. I learned that grieving before death may put you farther along the path after the fact. Bill was leaving us for years and I missed him even when we were together during the final weeks.

I was alone but seldom lonely. I talked to Bill even knowing he couldn't hear me and wrote to him several times. Sometimes I wrote to God and sometimes I journaled. There were times I wrestled with a myriad of 'what ifs.' I believe they are now put to rest; they rarely rear their ugly heads.

I enjoyed having more closet space, and then felt guilty! I would gladly share space again. It took a while not to buy foods I normally bought for him. I still notice what he liked, I just don't buy it. I also notice clothing with him in mind. Old habits depart slowly.

What did God want me to do now that it was just me? That's when I began this book in earnest. I'd already written some about us and our ancestors but I started to focus on what I should write as a heritage for our grandchildren.

I am a creationist. I believe God is eternal—past, present and future and He created everything that was, is or ever will be. I don't believe people and animals have evolved but I do believe a book can evolve. My book began as a few pages about my early life—then included Bill because we were, and are, one—then added our ancestors—then because God has been, and is, a major part of our lives, I desired to honor and glorify Him.

I found this quote from Charles Haddon Spurgeon:
"May we live here like strangers and make the world not a house,
but an inn, in which we sup and lodge,
expecting to be on our journey tomorrow."

On Valentine's Day, 2009, Richard and Carol Lee invited me out for a gourmet dinner at Bruce's Fabulous Foods. We were the only three-some, the rest were couples. The dinner was delicious and the fellowship sweet. I was thankful for their thoughtfulness. They both lost spouses so knew holidays can be difficult.

MY ADVENTURES BEGIN
DOUBLE TO SINGLE

Early in 2009, we replanted our 50th anniversary rosebush in a raised bed. It survived spending the winter in an antique coal scuttle and I hoped it would fare better than in Virginia. I loved growing camellias and crape myrtle for the first time.

Paul and Marcia asked if I would I like to accompany them on a bus trip out west. Anticipation grew as our September departure drew near. The trip started near Miracle Mountain Ranch so we spent the night with family and boarded the bus early in the morning. The first day we traveled through Ohio and Indiana, and stayed the night in Illinois. We soon added Wisconsin, Minnesota, North and South Dakota, Montana, Wyoming and Iowa to our ports of call.

When I originally told Matt about the trip, he said, "Be sure to sample the local cuisine." I was surprised to discover I like a bit of heat in my victuals! Bill and I always avoided spicy foods. We weren't exposed to them growing up and he liked to stay with what he knew. *(Sorry, Honey, you missed out on some great food!)*

The tour director and bus driver were great. They played gospel music on Sundays as well as country/western from back in my day. Traveling through acres of prairie I silently sang along, *"Oh, give me land, lots of land under starry skies above. Don't fence me in."*

Ranchlands stretched to the horizon. I expected to see herds of cattle but the stock was scattered over the dry grassland. Horses also were sparse. At one point, we saw cowboys next to a holding pen. They were driving four-wheelers and pickup trucks. The ranch homes were humble dwellings. Trees were few and grew next to houses or along irrigation ditches. Wind farms with their huge turbines on metal stilts reminded me of regiments of extraterrestrials.

The terrain constantly changed as we drove west. After the farmland and plains, we enjoyed mountains, streams and waterfalls. Then we were again in prairie or wilderness. Rocks were abundant, tempting a recovering rock hound like me! The only thing that restrained me was lack of room in my suitcase and not wanting to strain my friendship with Paul who often carried it.

The height of the Rocky Mountains puzzled me at first. They were beautiful but shouldn't they be higher? Indeed, they were higher than they appeared. Our vantage point was already several thousand feet above sea level.

We traveled through the Theodore Roosevelt National Park and saw prairie dog towns and badlands. I'm sure some of those rocks and trails are the ones I saw in old westerns!

The Range Riders Museum in Montana had an abundance of mounted animals and birds on display. Bill would have enjoyed them as well as the antique weapons, tools, wagons and farm equipment.

I'd love to go back to Jamestown, North Dakota. We visited a Frontier Village with a variety of exhibits. One was the Louis L'Amour Writer's Shack. He's one of my favorite authors. Another favorite was The National Buffalo Museum. The bison herd was way across a pasture. We could see White Cloud, an albino cow, in the distance. We heeded the sign on the fence:

"Do not cross this field unless you can do it in 9.9 seconds. The bull can do it in 10!"

Grant-Kohrs Ranch National Park in Montana is a working ranch with a legacy begun during the time of the open-range. We toured the home, visited the blacksmith shop, and were treated to cowboy coffee over an outdoor fire.

In Yellowstone National Park we walked paths around geysers, hot springs and thermal holes while we waited for Old Faithful to perform. It was worth the wait. At the visitor center, elk lounged around the entrance with signs warning us not to bother them. We also saw an abundance of bison and antelope.

In Cody, Wyoming we visited The Buffalo Bill Cody museum that included the Plains Indian Museum, western art museum, firearms museum, and documents & history museum. We could have spent a lot more time there and barely scratched the surface of the Rogers and Clark Museum.

One night we stayed at the Mineral Palace in Deadwood, South Dakota. We enjoyed the Boot Hill open-air bus tour and saw the graves of Wild Bill Hickok and Calamity Jane. We also saw a shoot-out during a historic street show.

There was gambling everywhere. In Deadwood, we heard the proceeds go toward historic preservation. I found a rubber ducky in our bathroom, all decked out in a western hat and neckerchief. He was to be used at the gaming tables. I elected not to risk my money, or the duck, so he now lives in Jonathan's and my bathroom.

We had old timey photos taken. Paul and Marcia dressed as pioneers. I decided on a flouncy dress with a big hat. I declined pulling up my skirt to show a little leg, partly because I had on jeans, partly due to the innuendo. I was disappointed the photo with the six-gun didn't turn out but I like my final choice. I look like a matronly madam.

Devil's Tower National Park was interesting. It's regarded as sacred by over twenty Indian tribes and there are many legends connected to it. We were cautioned not to disturb the little prayer bundles and cloths hanging in the bushes and trees since they are sacred to the native Americans. I prayed for those who placed them there, hoping they meet the one true God.

I wondered why we were stopping at a drugstore. Wall Drug is a rustic western mall. They have five-cent coffee and free ice water. You can buy anything from a Jackalope hunting permit to a chunk of fool's gold. Not only are there shops but also exhibits. We saw mechanical creations of all kinds, like a life-size T-Rex head that roars and cowboys who sing Tumbling Tumbleweeds.

Their roadside billboards advertising five-cent coffee and free ice water reminded me of the Burma-Shave signs from my childhood. A nice touch is that military veterans and honeymooners receive free doughnuts and coffee!

The Corn Palace was another stop I wondered about but it was more interesting than expected. The building is decorated with corn, other grains, and native grasses. The decorating begins in late August and is completed by October first.

We were disappointed that the shuttle bus at Glacier National Park wasn't operating so we weren't able to get a closer look at the glaciers. However, I'm thankful God provided the opportunity to see so much of our beautiful country.

The first anniversary of Bill's Home-going was three months after our trip. I wrote in my journal:

"God continues to fill the hole in my life left by
Bill when he got away from us."

I believe I like that term better than *he left us* or *we lost him*.

I learned a lot those first months following Bill's Homegoing. I was pleasantly surprised I didn't mind being alone. I had lots of projects to keep me busy. However, with Bill gone our ministry together was finished and I wondered what I should be doing. Pastor Paul prompted me to come alongside several widows and soon I was reaching out to them, and several other women.

Virgie was a close neighbor. She was ten years my senior and had been widowed for fifteen years. Her husband had been a pastor. We began shopping and having lunch together. At first, we took turns driving. Later, I was the driver. She had a great sense of humor and we enjoyed our time together!

One day I mentioned I needed to go to the church and practice the hymns for Sunday. She said I could use her piano. Our church was a half hour away, and she was happy to have company.

After several visits I asked, "Virgie, why don't you play something for me?"

"No, I'll just listen to you play."

I practiced and she listened until I finally convinced her to play. She didn't even bother with the hymnal—she didn't need it! If you were to rate her playing on a scale from one to ten, she was a ten. If you were to rate mine, I wonder where adequate would be on the scale?

She died a short time before I moved away. She was a dear friend and I look forward to seeing her when I go Home.

Bill and I met Reese Hurley at the Marion CMA Church several years before we moved to North Carolina. He and Bill were close in age and enjoyed talking together. We were impressed with his mission trips to countries around the world. Neither Bill nor I believed we should retire from God's work and Reese's example encouraged me to volunteer at Miracle Mountain Ranch.

My first full summer at the ranch was in 2010. I stayed in a little apartment in the back of town hall. Though there was still snow on the ground, going to work was easy. I walked through the gymnasium to the office. The next few summers I stayed in a little trailer in the ranch RV park. I enjoyed being near family but it was nice having my own space. My closest neighbors were young men in the discipleship program. One summer my nephew Jordan Rainey was my neighbor. Dave Cooper, long-time volunteer at the ranch, was also a neighbor, as were couples who traveled with the ministries of MAPPERS and Sowers.

The first couple of summers I worked full time and it was gratifying to know I could still do that. I now work part time. Over the years my tasks have varied, ranging from answering phone and proofreading to putting data into the computer and filing. Proofreading is my favorite but answering the phone sometimes offers opportunities to encourage or pray with callers. I also do a variety of projects, including sewing and mending.

The past few years I've been paired with summer camp counsellors as a mentor/prayer partner. It's a joy getting to know these young women, and a privilege to hear their concerns and pray for them.

This year I began doing a daily prayer walk through the camp, praying for the ranch in general, staff families, summer staff and volunteers, and those who come for camp and retreats. I pray for safety, that the equipment works, the horses are sound and obedient, and most of all for positive spiritual change in lives.

One perk of volunteering is being around diverse age groups. Many years ago, I asked my grandmother how it felt to be old. She answered, "I still feel like seventeen inside!" I believe it helps energize that young person inside when my friends aren't limited to people my own age.

Do I feel seventeen inside? No, and I have no desire to be a teen again. Each age has positives and negatives. A more youthful body would be nice but that would change everything else and I'd just as soon stay as I am. I am content being eighty-four.

The first weekend in August 2013, the Rices were enjoying a visit with the us at the ranch. Late Friday evening I left the gathering to go to my little trailer. I sometimes tell folks I turn into a pumpkin at ten p.m. I put my cell phone on the bedside stand, turned out the light and snuggled down to sleep. Saturday was going to be a full day. Karen and family were leaving in the morning and the rest of us were going to the summer staff outing.

Around six a.m. I roused to visit the loo and noticed the light on my cell phone. I had turned off the sound so I didn't know my family had been calling me since three a.m. Three barns were on fire and the fire departments were filling their water tankers from the lake behind my trailer. I hadn't noticed the lights since there were no windows on that side of my bedroom, and obviously I had not heard all the commotion. I returned their call and Karen said she would meet me at Town Hall.

By the time I saw the damage the fires were contained, though timbers and hay were still smoldering. That continued for several days. No people were harmed and no horses were injured. Most of the small animals housed in the Critter Corral were lost, along with 6000 bales of hay, tack, feed and ranch equipment.

The fire was an act of arson. The state police and fire marshal had a confession from a young man by Saturday evening. He was clearly repentant and Matt, representing the ranch, forgave him but he still faced charges.

The quick response by ranch personnel and Spring Creek Volunteer Fire Department, along with several other fire departments, lessened what might have been a greater tragedy.

Bales of hay began arriving that very day. By the middle of August cleanup was underway. Donations of hay, money and labor poured in. God prompted His people to shower an abundance of grace.

Matt told reporters, "Although this is a terrific loss, with the Lord's help, prayer, and lots of volunteers we will rebuild." And rebuild they did!

"I will sing of the mercies of the Lord forever: with my mouth
will I make known thy faithfulness to all generations.
Blessed be the Lord for evermore. Amen, and Amen."
(Psalm 89:1,52)

PENNSYLVANIA
SORTING THE SCRAPS

Living in North Carolina was good and I was fine living on my own. However, I knew I wasn't always going to be able to drive eleven hours to visit my children and couldn't expect them to do it either. Marcia and I often discussed wanting to be closer to family. The distance to their family was even greater than to mine.

I wanted to make a move while I could make the decision rationally instead of waiting until it was essential so I talked with my kids about options and put my name on a waiting list for a retirement apartment. The application was to be renewed annually, but one summer it was misplaced when my mail was forwarded. Both families suggested I consider living with them, they would share me. After prayer and careful consideration, I thought the plan might work.

Matt, Jenni, and Paul helped get my home ready to sell and I began downsizing again, this time more radically. Both families began planning rooms for me. I'm not sure how many loads of stuff I gave away. Most of it I don't miss but there are a few things ...

I advertised my home in our local Penny-saver. Several people came to see it. One couple wanted to rent-to-buy which was not a viable option. Finally, I contacted a realtor recommended by a friend. He appeared to be a good choice and it was under contract quickly.

On July 7, 2014, I officially moved from North Carolina to Pennsylvania. Some of my belongings went to Matt's, some went to Karen's. I lived in a little trailer at the ranch that summer and moved into the Rice's in the fall. The next summer when I went to the ranch, I lived in the Cooper's basement apartment until the finishing touches were put on my room at the Cox's. I guess Bill wasn't the only one who did things differently!

The move has been a positive one though integrating into two different households can be challenging. Both families have made me feel at home and my accommodations meet my needs. I spend roughly a half year with each family. Since they live about five hours apart, the driving time is half what it used to be.

We again replanted our 50th Anniversary rosebush, this time in Pennsylvania soil beneath my sitting room window at Karen's. It is undoubtedly a northern rosebush. It is flourishing and loves its new digs.

Not only did I move during the summer of 2014, but on May 22, Garrett Cooper asked Hannah to be his wife. On that day Bill and I would have celebrated our 60th wedding anniversary.

I alternate Christmas with each family. That is already beginning to change as grandchildren grow and become new family units. At the ranch, I look forward to going on the hunt for the perfect tree, meeting old friends at the MMR Community Christmas party, going caroling and delivering Christmas cookies. On Christmas morning, the Coxes open the special chest containing slips of paper telling of their gifts to Jesus. The gifts may range from caring for a neighbor's dog to doing someone's chores.

When I'm at the Rices I enjoy hearing QuintEssentially Brass perform in church—my Sunday School teacher plays the tuba. Though Bill liked brass, I wasn't a fan until I heard this ensemble. I also enjoy the orchestra and choir. Early in the month is the Gingerbread House Competition. I've sometimes helped judge the entries. It's a fun time. Last Christmas Kent and Karen made several appearances as Mr. and Mrs. Santa Claus. Kent wore the same costume I made for my dad years ago.

Even within families, households differ. I live in two worlds. There are adjustments to be made, which is true of any relationship and we all need to adapt to different situations.

Here's a section of my prayer list, written long before I moved in with my kids:

I pray that I will be a help not a hindrance,
a balm not an irritant, be useful and useable,
be an encourager not an enabler,
and be a peacemaker not a pot-stirrer.

One of the most difficult things is knowing when to speak and when to keep quiet. Increasingly I find keeping quiet is the best choice but it isn't always easy to do!

"When words are many, sin is not absent,
but he who holds his tongue is wise."
(Proverbs 10:19)
"Set a guard over my mouth, O LORD;
keep watch over the door of my lips."
(Psalm 141:3)

I'm thankful for my family and their willingness to share their lives with me. I thoroughly enjoy being with them but know they need time for themselves, as do I. Finding the right balance is ongoing, hopefully always improving. We don't know what the future will bring but we know the One who does!

MISSION TRIPS
DOMINICAN REPUBLIC

In a conversation with friends at the ranch I casually mentioned, "I've never been on an overseas mission trip."

Carmie responded, "Why don't you go with me to the Dominican Republic in January?"

Taken by surprise I replied, "If I go, would there be something I could do? I'm not just looking for a trip."

Carmie assured me I could be useful so we agreed to pray about it. There was one problem, I hoped to go to Texas in January to join in a family outing. Maybe I could do both? Not so, the dates conflicted. I had to decide between the two.

As I left the dining hall I saw a paper on the floor near the waste can. I reached down to pick it up and noticed writing on it, *The Next Step Missions.* I tossed it into the waste can. Walking to the office, I began to wonder about those words. I retraced my steps. The paper was in plain view. Though somewhat skeptical, I plucked it out and put it in my pocket.

I later shared my find with Matt and learned he had written the note during a lunch meeting. We agreed I shouldn't attach too much significance to it, but I did wonder.

In recent years, I've learned a lot about myself. One major realization was that God wasn't my top priority. I put Bill and my family before Him. Would I be doing that if I chose family over missions? I pondered and prayed, and decided I could go to Texas another time. I signed up for the mission trip.

This was my first time out of country which required a passport. Moving from one state to another evidently puts up red flags. I needed additional documentation to prove my citizenship. I scanned documents, newspaper clippings and photographs. My passport finally arrived.

Kent drove me across the state to Pittsburgh airport, an act of love since I needed to be there at 4 a.m. Our group wore orange t-shirts with Meeting God in Missions in bold letters. When I arrived, there wasn't one orange t-shirt in sight. I clumsily pulled my wheeled suitcases toward the busiest area and there they were.

My first glimpse of the terminal at Punta Cana International airport confirmed we were on a tropical island. The huge vaulted roof was thatched! When driving in the Dominican the order of the day is, "He who honks first goes first!" I always felt safe with the MGM drivers and was glad I wasn't driving.

The locals often ride motorcycles, sometimes with 3 or 4 people on board. We saw a man riding with a propane gas tank in his lap while a woman rode sidesaddle on the back of the cycle holding a small child and bags of groceries.

We were instructed to use hand sanitizer frequently and never eat anything that wasn't prepackaged or produced at the compound. We refilled our water bottles from large containers and used that water for everything but showering. We had indoor toilets but only flushed when necessary. The instructions were "water yellow, let it mellow; water brown, flush it down." We never flushed toilet tissue. The first night I wasn't fully awake and dropped tissue into the toilet. There was a plunger nearby, so I scooped it out, saying to myself, "I'll never do that again." I did do it again. There was no plunger but I did NOT flush the paper.

Our meals were prepared by Dominican women and were delicious, especially the fresh fruit. I drank my coffee black—it was good coffee. The only milk was the box-on-the-shelf variety. By the end of the week I craved a cold glass of fresh milk.

All meals were served buffet style. As we went through the line for our first breakfast I selected scrambled eggs and topped them with a dipper of gravy. It wasn't until I was eating I realized it wasn't gravy. It was oatmeal! Though not what I expected, it was very good. Their oatmeal is more liquid and loaded with sugar and spices. On later mornings I ate it from a bowl.

Each day we had a worship service in the Upper Room where we could watch the sun rise. Then we went to villages with dentistry and optical clinics, Bible stories and games for the children, and prayer.

When we reached the village, we gathered for prayer. Some of the villagers joined us and there were always children. I volunteered with the prayer team in the optical clinic. We asked clients if they had a personal relationship with Jesus. If they did, we asked how we could pray for them. Most asked us to pray for the spiritual condition of family members, or sometimes for improvement of health but no one spoke of lack of food or money. If they weren't believers, we shared the gospel with them.

Speaking through an interpreter is a challenge. Though I was a novice, the interpreters were pros. Some were fluent in Creole and French, as well as English and Spanish.

On Sunday I attended a mountain church in the morning and a cowboy church in the evening. There were no cowboys, not even a hitching post. The dirt roads to the churches were rutted and washed out. We rode in cattle trucks because the school bus couldn't make it. They insisted I sit in the front with the driver because of my age. I only felt slightly guilty.

In the cowboy church, one song I knew was *When the Saints Go Marching In.* When those saints went to marching, they marched—all around the inside of the church and then into the yard surrounding the church. Everyone had flashlights so the march was well lit. Since the ground was uneven, I decided it was prudent to stay inside and sing along.

One of our American pastors brought the message. Speaking through an interpreter made it a little long but no one seemed to care. Here in the states, people often watch the clock instead of heeding the message. At the end of the service three young women indicated a desire to have a personal relationship with Christ. These were neither Dominican nor Haitian, they were part of our group! The founder of MGM told us that the mission trips are more for the Americans than the people they come to serve.

We visited a village where Matt worked the previous year and witnessed the dedication of their church and pastor. Over the week we worshipped in three different churches and were blessed by the people's enthusiasm and love for the Lord.

The trip back to the USA was uneventful but we arrived in Atlanta right after a bomb scare and the sniffer dogs were still at work. I was surprised that one was a beagle!

Possibly the most important aspect of the trip was that all our lives were changed.

"Strive to enter through the narrow gate,
for many, I say to you,
will seek to enter and will not be able."
(Luke 13:24)

When I came home from the Dominican I planned to return but I knew groups from MMR went to Mexico. Should I change my destination? Jenni suggested I seek financial and prayer support. I wasn't enthused with the idea until she reminded me, "If you don't ask, you may be denying someone else a blessing." I sent out letters and all but the $50 deposit was provided. I had a ministry team with prayer support.

MEXICO

It was a cold, frosty Sunday morning in March when we boarded the bus in front of MMR's Town Hall. Was I shivering from excitement, or was it the frigid morning air? Probably both! When we were aboard, some snuggled under blankets to sleep. I watched recognizable landmarks become unfamiliar ones.

Some of my companions were old friends but I also met new ones. Megan, a student in the School of Discipleship, was my seatmate and I learned of her heart for missions. I shared rooms with Allison and Nikki who quickly and quietly helped everyone, and especially me.

Before we crossed the border, we unloaded baggage and equipment onto the ground in a church parking lot. Then it was loaded into three vans licensed in Mexico. Would it all fit? It did, though some was lashed on top.

Our men drove the vans, following Pipo's truck. Pipo works with the mission in Babicora. He guided us and facilitated our encounters with military checkpoints. Even when our leaders were questioned by men with big guns, I never felt endangered.

Mission groups are welcome—they help people.

We traveled vast expanses of flat land with mountains rising abruptly around the rim. We were at elevations of 5000 to 6000 feet, even on flat land. The landscape was more brown than green. The roads were reasonably maintained, except in the back country where the word 'road' was a stretch. The towns had brightly painted buildings with walls and wrought iron fences. Some walls were topped with sharp objects or curls of barbed wire.

There were impressive speed bumps when approaching a village so speed wasn't an option. Some villages were ghost towns with empty stores and houses. Cartels who dominate the area had decimated them and residents didn't return. Most restrooms were okay. Some even provided toilet tissue but we had our own. Flushing tissue was discouraged everywhere.

Our group was involved with a variety of work projects during a two-day visit to Rio Chico, the mission base for the Pima Indian village of Babicora. While there, Jen Brenner and I prepared materials for the Day Camps and Women's Meetings at the village of Babicora. Crafts were correlated with the Bible lessons.

The next leg of the trip was over rough, steep, rocky, dusty roads replete with switchbacks. Sometimes we could barely travel ten miles per hour. The area might best be described as mountainous desert. I've never seen so many rocks, ranging in size from pebbles to boulders. They were used to build low walls on hills to prevent erosion and the fields were divided with rock walls enclosing relatively rock free range. Signs signified entrances to ranches but we saw few dwellings. We drove over metal cattle guards and saw holding pens but few cattle.

There were little shrines along the side of the road, often to the Virgin of Guadalupe. Some were in front yards, others along lonely stretches of road. Some were well maintained, others neglected.

On Saturday evening we arrived in Babicora, elevation 7,000 feet. Our women slept in the church and our men slept in the dining area. The church was like our churches except for wall hangings with Bible verses en Español. .

The village was bleak. The earth was brown. The grass was tan. The buildings were beige adobe, except for those that were painted. It reminded me of a landscape in neutral shades waiting for a splash of color. When the people come out of their homes, the color arrives. They smile, they laugh, they live! It would be easy to be depressed by the drabness of their surroundings, but most seem to rise above that.

Some homes have solar panels. The church has indoor plumbing but there were outhouses throughout the village. Chickens, cows and horses wander at will, but not in abundance. Running through the village is a shallow stream which becomes a river when it rains.

Spring rains also bring contamination to the village's water source and the entire village has diarrhea! Our men researched their water situation and last fall they drove new wells giving them a safe supply of water. The project is ongoing.

On Sunday we had an English service at ten and attended their Spanish service at three. The Catholic church just down the road has mass at two and some villagers attend both services.

The Women's Meetings and children's Day Camps went well. On the last day, tables were set up and gifts from the states were laid out. There were dresses for little girls, quilts and afghans, baby blankets, crocheted hats and headbands—many handmade. There were also games, books and puzzles.

Before we left, some of the village women brought lovely handmade crafts to sell. We again traveled over rough roads, this time to the CMA Bible Institute in Juárez. Then, back over the border and we were on American soil.

Along with ministry we enjoyed side trips. My favorite was a surprise visit to the Grand Canyon. I'd like to return some day and spend more time. I have no desire to hike or ride to the bottom. I'll be content to see it from the rim, not too close to the edge.

Another surprise! I hoped to see my Texas grandgirl Hannah briefly but she took me to her home in Electra to spend the night. I then traveled home with her husband's parents, the Coopers.

The trip was a wonderful adventure but wasn't without a few vehicle incidents. We ran out of gas at Carlsbad Caverns. Then on our way to Ransom Wind Ranch in Oklahoma the left front tire blew. We were merging from one highway to another when we heard a loud POP! Mark Brenner muscled the bus to a stop on the right berm. The bus could have turned over into the ditch on the left. Time out to praise God!

It's good to have mechanics on board. Mark Carpenter found a tire dealer and we were on our way again. But, a short distance down the road we smelled burning rubber. The right front tire was affected by the previous incident so another tire had to be replaced. Back on the road, we again thanked God. We were blessed with excellent drivers, Ben Freeman made the third.

One more incident was with the Cooper's vehicle. We were going through Indianapolis when Dan noticed the battery wasn't charging. Was it coincidence that we were near Dan's brother's home? They provided excellent hospitality for the night and Dan replaced the alternator in the morning.

It was good to be home. It would be great to visit Babicora again but a missionary friend from Brazil invited me to visit her.

Maria said, "Come for the month of July! It's our winter and the weather is wonderful."

I replied hesitantly, "Well, maybe—for a couple of weeks." It's intriguing!

Here's the deal. God is in control, and I'm good with that. I'm looking forward to whatever He has for me. Is it a mission trip to Brazil? Not this year, but someday. Does He want me to stay put? Should I concentrate on being his missionary right where I am? I'm not sure—but I'm waiting for His direction.

"Trust in the Lord with all your heart,
and lean not on your own understanding;
In all your ways acknowledge Him,
And He shall direct your paths."
(Proverbs 3:5-6)

SCRAPS
BITS AND PIECES OF ALL KINDS

Quilting projects use scraps but they also may leave us with scraps. Some go into the wastebasket. Some go into the scrap basket for future use. What shall I do with the leftover scraps? I've used life scraps of all materials, shapes and sizes to make this crazy quilt. I'm going to use those bits and pieces that just didn't seem to fit and piece them into this chapter. There will be even less rhyme or reason, and certainly no continuity. I think they are important enough to be included, so I don't want to toss them away.

Thoughts on Adventure

Several years ago, I began to title my prayer letters *Adventures.* Life is an adventure and we should enjoy all its twists and turns. Some adventures happen at home, some at school or work. Some adventures take place when we travel. I believe attitude plays a role, so I always expect an adventure!

Praying can be an adventure. We may pray for friends and family or for people we've never met. Even if I don't return to the Dominican Republic or Mexico, or go to Brazil, I am praying for people there. Our lives (quilts) are woven together by the threads of prayer.

"The Lord is far from the wicked,
But He hears the prayer of the righteous."
(Proverbs 15:29)

Thoughts on living alone

After Bill died, I was sometimes lonely but didn't dwell on it. I filled my life with projects, including reading, painting and writing. I didn't focus on being alone. Even so, I don't have to be alone to feel lonely. Maybe you've also found that to be true? I can be in a group of family or friends and feel lonely. Since my other-half left, I don't always feel like I fit in. Being alone isn't the same as feeling lonely. Now that I live with family, I sometimes choose to be alone. When I don't feel like being alone, I can dwell on being left out or I can be thankful for family and choose to be involved.

Travel alone is fine. Ongoing prayer, and rabbit trails, have taken the place of books-on-tape. I was concerned that changing CDs took my attention from the road. When I traveled with Bill I wanted to stop and see the local sights. Now I have little desire to see them. It's not much fun to visit them alone.

Jesus was lonely even though he had disciples and friends. He was lonely for Heaven. What did He do? He prayed! Maybe we should do that?

Thoughts on friends

I've had few close friends. My family filled that need in my life. What about confidants? Even fewer! I'm slow to share my deepest thoughts and feelings. That was sometimes governed by wisdom—sometimes by fear or lack of trust. Bill knew me best but even with him there were things I didn't share.

With some friends, we've grown apart and have little in common except our past. With others, when we see each other we just pick up where we left off. I'm thankful for all my friends, especially those who have been a part of my adventures.

"Friends for a season, friends for a reason, friends for a lifetime."

Thoughts on intelligence

Intelligence is a good thing, but without common sense and godly wisdom it is nothing! Every day I ask God for wisdom and discernment.

"If any of you lack wisdom let him ask of God,
who gives to all liberally and without reproach,
and it will be given to him."
(James 1:5)

Thoughts on living

Our lives touch those closest to us but also others with whom we come in contact. What we do has a ripple effect and the ripples spread over a larger area than we could ever imagine. My prayer is that my ripples will honor and glorify God. That people may see Christ in my attitude, actions, and reactions.

"Do not be deceived, God is not mocked;
for whatever a man sows, that he will also reap."
(Galatians 6:7)

Thoughts on prayer

Major changes in my life happened when I began to read the Bible and pray regularly. Though I knew I should do it before, if I had really wanted to I would have found a way!

I suspect many Christians, even those in ministry, spend too little time reading God's Word, or even talking with Him. If our children seldom talked with us, how would we feel?

Two of my daily prayer concerns are: I want to know God better and I want to love Him more. He loves me but do I love Him? If I love Him I should want to spend time with Him. When Bill and I were dating I eagerly looked forward to being with him. Do I feel that way about God?

I've used several reading systems. Whatever works for you is the one for you. For several years I've been studying and reading a Bible which I then give to one of my grandchildren. I underline, make comments and write personal notes as I read.

Time with the Lord must be a priority. For years it was low on my priority list, and often bumped off.

Martin Luther said, "I have so much to do today that I'm going to need to spend three hours in prayer in order to be able to get it all done."

No, I don't spend that much time in prayer but I do pray before I read my Bible. I find praying more difficult than reading. I have a personal prayer list. I've heard it said that a list limits your prayers but I need a list to keep focused. Why didn't I commit to this earlier in my life?

"Vee Get Too Soon Oldt, und Too Late Schmardt!"
(PA Dutch Proverb)

"My days are swifter than a weaver's shuttle,
and they all come to an end with a sigh..."
(Job 7:6)

Thoughts on a friend

If you read the acknowledgements at the beginning of the book you saw the name Barbara. We met via email through Janice Rainey but never met face-to-face. She asked to be on my mailing list and was the first person to say she wanted to buy my first book, before a book was even begun. I especially valued her encouragement because she didn't know me — just my writing.

She is no longer with us and sad to say I'm not sure where she is. She was raised in a nominally Jewish home, and didn't attend synagogue. Her mother taught her to have nothing to do with Jesus or the New Testament, though even she didn't practice Judaism.

God used Janice in her life, as well as a granddaughter who is a believer. She read my prayer letters and they often contained the Gospel. I hope she may have accepted God's gift of salvation before it was too late.

I'm sorry she can't critique this book.

TRIMMING THE THREADS
QUILTING COTTON

My crazy quilt is about finished. The original purpose was to share my growing up years with my grandchildren. That grew to include much more and ultimately to honor and glorify God. I trust I have accomplished those goals.

The first time I shared the darker side of my past was with immediate family and very close friends. My purpose was to help young women choose a godly path rather than the one I traveled. Now it's out there for all the world to see. I've chosen not to be anxious about that and pray God will use what I've shared to bring some to salvation or a deeper relationship with Him.

I shared my testimony early on. We have already established I was a sinner, and I am still a work in progress. Since I have broken one of the commandments, I have broken them all! God's Word says it very clearly:

> *"For whoever shall keep the whole law,*
> *and yet stumble in one point,*
> *he is guilty of all."*
> James 2:10

Are you wondering if another version of the Bible is less convicting? They all say the same thing. However, not only am I guilty because of James 2:10 but I have committed some of these crimes!

I was a thief. I'm not proud of the fact but here are two examples:

#1. I worked in an office years ago, and I took home more than one roll of scotch tape around the Christmas holidays. Others did the same thing but that didn't make it right. I shared this with someone who told me I was overreacting. I don't agree. There are no small sins. We may categorize sins, even become adept at rationalizing them, but sin is sin and holy is holy. There is no neutral position, hence no justification.

#2. Now, for something that hits where it hurts—money! God's money! I'm speaking now to fellow Christians; non-believers won't relate, nor do they need to. The Bible teaches we should tithe. In the Old Testament, they were to tithe not only on their income but on their crops and possessions. The New Testament teaches not just the generally accepted 10% but above and beyond. Everything I have belongs to Him. When I don't give back, I am withholding what is rightfully His. That is stealing!

For several years after we gave our lives to Christ we didn't tithe. We thought we couldn't afford to. We began to half-tithe, hoping someday we would be able to give a full tithe. Sometime in the 1960s I was balancing the checkbook and realized we had been tithing for several weeks. Instead of putting our check in the offering plate every other week, we had been putting it in every week. We hadn't starved, our bills were paid and we were tithing. We kept on doing it! We have never been rich by the world's standards but God has blessed us.

I said two examples but I'm going to throw in a third for no extra charge. Time! We all have the same amount of time—24 hours a day. What I do with that time is pretty much up to me. Of course, there are constraints due to work and other responsibilities but we all have some discretionary time to do with as we wish.

How much time do we devote to God? Should it be a tithe? Maybe. Are we getting to know Him by reading the Bible? Do we talk with Him regularly? We won't count, "Help me Lord!" while careening into a ditch. How often do we just quietly listen to Him? Are we robbing God of time?

It's also possible to rob God of time when we don't whole-heartedly do whatever He has given us to do. That's not just in ministry but in the secular workplace as well. If you have a job you should be thankful for it, even if it's not the one you desire. Why would God give you something better if you're not doing your best at the job you already have?

When I pray each morning, I ask God to help me be a better steward of resources—money, stuff, and time. Time is probably the most difficult of the three.

Okay, I've written a couple pages and haven't gotten beyond thievery. Next is lying. Am I talking about little white lies or big black lies? It doesn't matter, they're all the same. A lie is a lie no matter what name we assign to it. Specific instances probably aren't needed for lying. I believe I can speak for most of us by saying we all have lied. We have lied to protect ourselves or someone else, we have exaggerated the truth or have avoided telling the whole truth. It all comes under the heading of lying.

Abraham was good at lying. He told Pharaoh that his wife, Sarai, was his sister, to save his neck. He was found out and chastised. Later he did the same thing with Abimelech, and this was after his life-changing encounter with God. This time he explains how he avoided the whole truth. Sarah was his sister because they had the same father but different mothers. He still wasn't totally off the hook.

I'm personally not as disturbed with Abraham's lying as I am with the fact that in both cases these men took Sarah to their houses. She was to become one of their women. Oh, Abraham, what a dastardly thing to do.

Lastly, I have murdered. Yes, I've run over a rabbit and hit more than one bird with my car but that isn't the kind of murder I'm talking about. If you've read the book this far you may remember the little girl who lived across the street from us in Narberth. I hated her and hate is tantamount to murder. I never thought about killing her, but it's scary to look back into my young mind. At just about any age we are capable of much more than we would like to believe. Matthew 15:18-19 speaks of our hearts and what comes out of them. I'm arbitrarily going with the New American Standard Bible on this one:

> *"But the things that proceed out of the mouth*
> *come from the heart, and those defile the man.*
> *For out of the heart come evil thoughts..."*

Both evil and good begin within us, in our hearts or minds. What we do doesn't just happen, we have purposed it, or at least laid the groundwork. This is true of my sins and it's also true of yours. I need to keep my thoughts under control. For Jeremiah 17:9 I like good ole King James:

"The heart is deceitful above all things,
and desperately wicked:
who can know it?"

Some versions say the heart is sick. No, it's not sick, it's wicked. You can take a pill for sick. There's no pill for wicked. Redemption through Jesus is the only cure and He provided it when He shed His blood on the cross, and came back to life. I hope your heart has been cleansed by the blood of Jesus. If not, why not ask Him to forgive your sins and allow Him to be Lord of your life? Sadly, even after we're saved we sin, but He provides for that also!

"If we confess our sins,
He is faithful and just to forgive us our sins
and to cleanse us from all unrighteousness."
(I John 1:9)

The messes I make while sewing can usually be fixed by ripping out stitches. I can't fix the messes in my life so easily. I am so thankful that God took all the pieces of my life, including my messes, and put them together to make a one-of-a-kind treasure. Some of my quilt pieces are plain, some are lovely. He even used the torn and dirty pieces after He washed and mended them. Then He pieced them together with His grace and mercy. But He didn't stop there, He embellished them with His love and blessings. The design is all His, but I had to be willing to let Him have the pieces. I gave me to Him.

I wish that was a one-time deal but every day I need to give myself back to Him because I often want my own way. He is still working on my quilt! He never gives up!

I intended to fold up my quilt and put it away at the end of this book but I can't do that! This quilt is my life story and it's not finished. When the last piece is added, God will be the one to fold it up and put it away.

Until then, I'm thankful He never gave up on me. He won't give up on you either! That's just how He is!

FAMILY TREE BRANCHES
RAINEY
James Rainey + Mary? (Northern Ireland)
    William John Rainey
William John Rainey + Unknown (N.I.)
    Robert Rainey (1837)
Alexander McDowell (1815) + Annie McCaughey (1814) (N. I.)
    Margaret McDowell (1838)
Robert Rainey + Margaret McDowell (N.I.)
    Charters Rainey (1876) (USA)
WEBSTER
John Webster (1807) + Mary Ann Haw (?) (1804) (England)
    William Pardoe Webster (1844)
Robert C Sheldon (1810) + Unknown (Eng.)
    Arabella Sarah Sheldon (1842)
William Pardoe Webster + Arabella Sheldon (1842) (Eng.)
    Charlotte Webster (1878) (Eng.)
RAINEY—WEBSTER
Charters Rainey + Charlotte Webster
    William John Rainey (1905)
REICHNER
George Reichner (1805) + Ann Bethia Smith (1807)
    Lewis Reichner (1846)
WILHELM
Nicholas B Wilhelm (1820) + Catherine E Walvarine (1823)
    Anna Eliza Wilhelm (1846)
REICHNER—WILHELM
Lewis Reichner + Anna Eliza Wilhelm
    Samuel Vautier Reichner (1880)
GODEFROY (changed from LaTour)
Emile LaTour + Ella Louise Godreau
    Edward Lewis (LaTour) Godefroy (1862)
BILLINGS
William Warren Billings + Eleanor Louise. Delatache
    Ida Louise Billings (1864)
GODEFROY—BILLINGS
Edward Lewis Godefroy + Ida Louise Billings
    Ella Louise Godefroy (1881)
REICHNER—GODEFROY
Samuel Vautier Reichner + Ella Louise Godefroy
    Gertrude Louise Reichner (1911)

RAINEY—REICHNER

William John Rainey Sr. + Gertrude Louise Reichner
    Patricia Louise Rainey (1933)
    William John Rainey Jr. (1939)

RAINEY—COX

Patricia Louise Rainey + William Franklin Cox III
    William Franklin Cox IV (1955) + Kathy Lynn Baker (1955)
        Rebecca Coetta (1982)
    Karen Louise Cox (1965) + Kent Phillip Rice (1963)
        Morgan Louise (1995)
        Kensey Jane (1999)
    Matthew Duval Cox (1968) + Jennifer Myers (1974)
        Hannah Lynn Cox (1995) + Garrett Daniel Cooper (1993)
        Megan Elizabeth (1996)
        Lydia Nicole (1999)
        Emily Grace (2003)
        Jonathan William (2008)

William John Rainey Jr. + Janice Ware (1939)
    Jeffrey Michael Rainey (1962) + Linda Carol Cassaday (1963)
        Leah Rainey () + Barak Havens ()
        Jordan ()
        Jeremy (1997)
    Brian Andrew Rainey (1966) + Sharon Bostwick (1963)
        Christopher Adam (1995)
        Matthew David (1998)

COX—PARKER

Cheyney Cox (1820) + Anna Speakman (1825) Eng.
    William Franklin Cox (1853)
John Parker (1835) Eng. + Anna M (1829)
    Clara Elmira Parker (1857)
William Franklin Cox + Clara Elmira Parker
    Harry Parker Cox Sr. (1877)

MORROW—LONG

James Edward Morrow (1832) (Ireland) + Elizabeth Ann. Marshall (1835)
    James Edward Morrow (1856)
Kersey Long (1821) + Elizabeth Frederick (1823)
    Annie F Long (1859)
James Edward Morrow + Annie F Long
    Ella R Morrow (1882)

COX—MORROW

Harry Parker Cox Sr + Ella R Morrow
    William Franklin Cox II (1906)

ZIEGLER—SITTER

Frederick Sitter + Leona Mooy
    Franziska L Sitter (Bavaria) (1863)
George J Ziegler (Bavaria) (1859) + Franziska L Sitter (1863)
    Catherine Ziegler (1883)
    John G. Ziegler (1888) + Pearl Hendricks McNeill (1893)
Catherine Ziegler + Unknown
    Frances Georgianna Duval (1906)
    (Catherine married Claude Ormonde Duval in 1911)
William Franklin Cox II (1906) + Frances Georgianna Duval
    William Franklin Cox III (1929)
    Barbara Kay Cox (1938)
Michel Andre Remy (France) (1937) + Barbara Kay Cox
    Michelle Andrea (1959)
    Suzanne Renee (1962)
    Mark Andre (1968)
    Steven Michael (1971)
Michelle Andrea Remy + Robert Sorter Phillips (1955)
    Katie Elizabeth (1984)
    Megan Elise (1987)
        Adriana Grace (2008)
    Sara Louise (1986) + Albert Henry Stiteler III
        Taylor Remy Stiteler (2009)
        Albert Harry Stiteler (2011)
Suzanne Renee Remy + Walter Larcombe (1950)
    Christopher (1985)
        Chase (2009)
    Gregory (1988)
Mark Andrew Remy + Kimberly Michelle Roane (1972)
    Amber Lynn Mae Roane (1993)
    Nichole Marie Remy (1994)
    Aaron Eugene Kaderli (1995)
    Andrew Michael Remy (1995)
    Jake Maguire Remy (1999)
Steven Michael Remy + Cécile Francoise Agnes Bastien-Remy (France) (1972)
    Ilana Gabrielle Remy (France) (2005)
    Céleste Marie Remy (Switzerland) (2007)

45304190R00216

Made in the USA
Middletown, DE
15 May 2019